BOOKS AND THEIR MAKERS
DURING THE MIDDLE AGES

BOOKS AND THEIR MAKERS DURING THE MIDDLE AGES

BOOKS AND THEIR MAKERS DURING THE MIDDLE AGES

A STUDY OF THE CONDITIONS OF THE PRODUCTION AND
DISTRIBUTION OF LITERATURE FROM THE FALL OF
THE ROMAN EMPIRE TO THE CLOSE OF
THE SEVENTEENTH CENTURY

BY

GEO. HAVEN PUTNAM, A.M.

AUTHOR OF "AUTHORS AND THEIR PUBLIC IN ANCIENT TIMES"
"THE QUESTION OF COPYRIGHT," ETC.

VOLUME I.
476–1600

New York
HILLARY HOUSE PUBLISHERS LTD.

26119

This is an unaltered and unabridged reprint
of the last (1896-1897) edition

Reprinted 1962 by
Hillary House Publishers Ltd

PRINTED IN THE U.S.A. BY
NOBLE OFFSET PRINTERS, INC.

TO
THE MEMORY OF MY WIFE
WHO SERVED ME FOR YEARS BOTH AS EYESIGHT
AND AS WRITING-ARM
AND BY WHOSE HAND THE FOLLOWING PAGES
WERE IN LARGE PART TRANSCRIBED
THIS WORK IS DEDICATED

PREFACE.

IN a previous volume I undertook to describe, or rather
to indicate, the methods of the production and distribution of the earlier literature of the world and to sketch out
the relations which existed between the author and his
public during the ages known, rather vaguely, as classic,
that is, in the periods of literary activity in Greece and
ancient Rome. The materials for such a record were at
best but fragmentary, and it was doubtless the case that,
in a first attempt of the kind, I failed to get before me
not a few of the references which are scattered through
the works of classic writers, and which in any fairly complete presentation of the subject ought to have been
utilised.

Imperfect as my study was, I felt, however, that I was
justified in basing upon it certain general conclusions. It
seems evident that in Greece, even during the period of
the highest literary development, there did not exist anything that could be described as a system for the production and distribution of books. The number of copies of
any work of Greek literature available for the use of the
general public must at any time have been exceedingly
limited, and it would probably be safe to say that, before
the development of Alexandria as a centre of book-production, no such thing as a reading public existed. The
few manuscripts that had been produced, and that possessed any measure of authenticity, were contained in
royal archives or in such a State collection as that of

Athens, or in the studies of the small group of scholarly
teachers whose fame was sometimes in part due to the
fact that they were owners of books.

The contemporary writers, including the authors of
works treasured as masterpieces through all later ages,
were not only content to do their work without any
thought of material compensation, but appear to have
been strangely oblivious of what would seem to us to be
the ordinary practical measures for the preservation and
circulation of their productions. The only reward for
which they could look was fame with their own generation, and even for this it would seem that some effective
distribution of their compositions was essential. The
thought of preserving their work for the appreciation of
future generations seems to have weighed with them but
little. The ambition or ideal of the author appears to
have been satisfied when his composition received in his
own immediate community the honour of dramatic presentation or of public recitation. If his fellow citizens had
accorded the approbation of the laurel crown, the approval
of the outer world or of future generations was a matter
of trifling importance. The fact that, notwithstanding this
lack of ambition or incentive on the part of the authors,
the non-existence of a reading public, and the consequent
absence of any adequate machinery for the production
and distribution of books, the knowledge of the " laurel-
crowned " works, both of the earlier poets and of contemporary writers, should have been so widely diffused
throughout the Greek community, is evidence that the
public interest in dramatic performances and in the reci-
tations of public reciters ("rhapsodists") made, for an
active-minded people like the Greeks, a very effective
substitute for the literary enlightenment given to later
generations by means of the written or the printed word.

A systematised method of book-production we find first
in Alexandria, where it had been developed, if not origi-

nally instituted, by the intelligent and all-powerful interest
of the Ptolemaic kings, but there appears to be no evidence that, even in Alexandria, which for the greater part
of two centuries was the great book-producing mart of the
world, was there any practice of compensation for authors.
It is to be borne in mind, however, in this connection,
that, with hardly an exception, the manuscripts produced
in Alexandria were copies of books accepted as classics,
the works of writers long since dead. For the editors of
what might be called the Alexandrian editions of Greek
classics, compensation was provided in the form of *honoraria* from the treasury of the Museum library or of salaried
positions in the Museum Academy.

In Rome, during the Augustan period, we find record
of a well organised body of publishers utilising connections with Athens, with Asia Minor, and with Alexandria,
for the purpose of importing Greek manuscripts and of
collecting trained Greek scribes, and carrying on an active
trade in the distribution of books not only with the
neighbouring cities of Italy, of Spain, and of Gaul, but with
such far off corners of the empire as the Roman towns in
Britain. There are not a few references in the literature
of this period, and particularly in the productions of
society writers like Martial and Horace, to the relations
of authors with their publishers and to the business interests retained by authors in the sale of their books. This
Augustan age presents, in fact, the first example in the
history of publishing, of a body of literature, produced by
contemporary writers, being manifolded and distributed
under an effective publishing and bookselling machinery,
so as to reach an extensive and widely separated reading
public. When the Roman gentleman in his villa near
Massilia (in Gaul), Colonia (on the Rhine), or Eboracum
(in far off Britain), is able to order through the imperial
post copies of the latest ode of Horace or satire of Martial, we have the beginnings of an effective publishing

organisation. It is at this time also that we first find
record of the names of noteworthy publishers, the book-
makers in Athens and in Alexandria having left their
names unrecorded. It is the period of Atticus, of Try-
phon, and of the Sosii. Concerning the matter of the
arrangements with the authors, or the extent of any compensation secured by them, the information is at best but
scanty and often confusing. It seems evident, however,
that, apart from the aid afforded by imperial favour, by the
interest of some provincial ruler of literary tendencies, or
by the bounty of a wealthy private patron like Mæcenas,
the rewards of literary producers were both scanty and
precarious.

With the downfall of the Roman Empire, the organised
book-trade of Rome and of the great cities of the Roman
provinces came to an end. This trade had of necessity
been dependent upon an effective system of communication and of transportation, a system which required for
its maintenance the well built and thoroughly guarded
roads of the empire; while it also called for the existence of a wealthy and cultivated leisure class, a class
which during the periods of civil war and of barbaric
invasions rapidly disappeared. Long before the reign of
the last of the Roman emperors, original literary production had in great part ceased and the trade in the books
of an earlier period had been materially curtailed; and by
476, when Augustulus was driven out by the triumphant
Odovacar, the literary activities of the capital were very
nearly at a close.

In the following study I have taken up the account of
the production of books in Europe from the time of the
downfall of the Empire of the West. I have endeavoured
to show by what means, after the disappearance of the
civilisation of the Roman State, were preserved the fragments of classic literature that have remained for the use
of modern readers, and to what agencies were due the

maintenance, throughout the confusion and social dis-
organisation of the early Middle Ages, of any intellectual
interest or literary activities.

I find such agencies supplied in the first place by the
scribes of the Roman Church, the organisation of which
had replaced as a central civilising influence the power of
the lost Roman Empire. The *scriptoria* of the monasteries rendered the service formerly given by the copyists
of the book-shops or of the country houses, while their
armaria, or book-chests, had to fill the place of the
destroyed or scattered libraries of the Roman cities or
the Roman villas. The work of the scribes was now
directed not by an Augustus, a Mæcenas, or an Atticus,
but by a Cassiodorus, a Benedict, or a Gregory, and the
incentive to literary labour was no longer the laurel crown
of the circus, the favours of a patron, or the *honoraria* of
the publishers, but the glory of God and the service of
the Church. Upon these agencies depended the existence of literature during the seven long centuries between
the fall of the Western Empire and the beginning of the
work of the universities, and, in fact, for many years after
the foundation of the universities of Bologna and of Paris,
the book-production of the monasteries continued to be
of material importance in connection with the preservation
of literature.

In a study of the organisation of the earliest book-trade
of Bologna and Paris and of the method under which the
text-books for the universities were produced and supplied, I have attempted to indicate the part played by
the universities in the history of literary production. In
a later chapter I have presented sketches of one or two of
the more noteworthy of the manuscript dealers, who
carried on, for a couple of centuries prior to the invention
of printing, the business of supplying books to the
increasing circles of readers outside of the universities.

In 1450 comes the invention of printing, which in

revolutionising the methods of distributing intellectual
productions, exercised such a complex and far-reaching
influence on the thought and on the history of mankind.
I have described with some detail the careers of certain
of the earlier printer-publishers of Europe, and have been
interested in noting how important and distinctive were
the services rendered by these publishers to scholarship
and to literature.

The concluding chapter sketches the growth of the
conception of the idea of property in literature, and the
gradual development and extension throughout the States
of Europe of the system of privileges which formed the
precedent and the foundations for the modern system of
the law of literature and of interstate copyright legislation. I have taken pleasure in pointing out that the
responsibility for securing this preliminary recognition of
property in literary productions and of the property rights
of literary producers rested with the printer-publishers,
and that the shaping of the beginnings of a copyright
system for Europe is due to their efforts. It was they
also who bore the chief burden of the contest, which
extended over several centuries, for the freedom of the
press from the burdensome censorship of Church and
State, a censorship which in certain communities appeared
likely for a time to throttle literary production altogether.
I can but think that the historians of literature and the
students of the social and political conditions on which
literary production is so largely dependent, have failed to
do full justice to men like Aldus, the Estiennes, Froben,
Koberger, and Plantin, who fought so sturdily against the
pretensions of pope, bishop, or monarch to stand between
the printing-press and the people and to decide what
should and what should not be printed.

I have thought it worth while, in giving the business
history of these old-time publishers, to present the lists of
their more characteristic publications,—lists which seem

to me to possess pertinence and value as giving an impression of the nature and the range of the literary interests of the time and of the particular community in which the publisher was working, while they are also, of course, indicative of the personal characteristics of the publisher himself. When we find Aldus in Venice devoting his presses almost exclusively to classical literature, and in the classics, so largely to Greek; while in Basel and Nuremberg the early printers are producing the works of the Church Fathers, in Paris the first Estienne (in the face of the fierce opposition of the theologians) is multiplying editions of the Scriptures, and in London, Caxton and his immediate successors, disregarding both the literature of the old world and the writings of the Church, are presenting to the English public a long series of romances and *fabliaux*,—we may understand that we have to do not with a series of accidental publishing selections, but with the results of a definite purpose and policy on the part of capable and observing men, a policy which gives an indication of the nature and interests of their several communities, while it characterises also the aims and the individual ideals of the publishers themselves. Some of these earlier publishers were willing simply to produce the books for which the people about them were asking, while others, with a higher ambition and a larger feeling of responsibility, proposed themselves to educate a book-reading and a book-buying public, and thus to create the demand for the higher literature which their presses were prepared to supply.

These earlier printer-publishers took upon themselves, in fact, the responsibility which had previously rested with the universities, and, back of the universities, with the monasteries, of selecting the literature that was to be utilised by the community and through which the intellectual life of the generation was to be in large part shaped and directed. They thus took their place in the series of

literary agencies by means of which the world's literature
had been selected, preserved, and rendered available for
mankind, a chain which included such diverse and widely
separated links as the Ptolemies of Alexandria, the
princely patrons of Rome, Cassiodorus, S. Benedict and
his monasteries, the schools of Charlemagne and Alcuin,
the universities of Bologna and Paris, and, finally, the
printer-publishers who utilised the great discovery of
Gutenberg.

The fact that, during both the manuscript period and
the first two centuries of printing, the writings of Cicero
were reproduced far more largely than those of any other
of the Roman writers, is interesting as indicating a distinct literary preference on the part of successive generations both of producers and of readers. The pre-eminence
of Aristotle in the lists of the mediæval issues of the
Greek classics has, I judge, a different significance. Aristotle stood for a school of philosophy, the teachings of
which had in the main been accepted by the Church, and
copies of his writings were required for the use of students. The continued demand for the works of Cicero
depended upon no such adventitious aid, and can, therefore, fairly be credited to their perennial value as literature.

My readers will bear in mind that I have not undertaken
any such impossible task as a history of literary production, or even a record of all the factors which controlled
literary production. I have attempted simply to present
a study of certain conditions in the history of the manifolding and distribution of books by which the production
and effectiveness of literature was very largely influenced
and determined, and under which the conception of such
a thing as literary property gradually developed. The
recognition of a just requirement or of an existing injustice must, of course, always precede the framing of legislation to meet the requirement or to remedy the injustice,

and the conception of literary property and a recognition of the inherent rights (and of the existing wrongs) of literary producers had to be arrived at before copyright legislation could be secured.

I have specified as the limit of the present treatise the close of the seventeenth century, although I have found it convenient in certain chapters to make reference to events of a somewhat later date. It has been my purpose, however, to present a study of the conditions of literary production in Europe prior to copyright law, and the copyright legislation of Europe may be said to begin with the English statute of 1710, known as the Act of Queen Anne.

I trust that in the near future some competent authority may find himself interested in preparing a history of copyright law, and I shall be well pleased if the present volumes may be accepted by the historian of copyright and by the students of the subject as forming a suitable general introduction to such a history.

CONTENTS.

Contents

BIBLIOGRAPHY.

WORKS CITED OR REFERRED TO AS AUTHORITIES.

Abelard and the Origin and Early History of Universities. By GABRIEL COMPAYRÉ. New York, 1893.

Actes Concernants le Pouvoir, etc., *de l' Université de Paris.* Paris, 1698.

ADAMS, G. B. *Civilization during the Middle Ages.* New York, 1894.

ADRIAN, J. V. *Catalogus Codd. MSS. Biblioth. Acad. Gissensis.* 4 vols., 1840.

Alcuini Opera. Edited by FROBEN. Basel, 1514.

AL-MAKKARI, AHMED IBN MOHAMMED. *History of the Mohammedan Dynasties in Spain.* Trans. by PASCUAL DE GAYANGOS. 2 vols., 4to. London, 1843.

AMPÈRE, J. J. *Histoire Littéraire de la France avant Charlemagne.* 2 vols. Paris, 1868.

—— *Histoire Littéraire de la France sous Charlemagne.* 2 vols. Paris, 1870.

ANSELMUS (S.) *Opuscula.* Edited by HAAS. Tübingen, 1863.

—— *Opera Omnia.* Edited by MIGNE. Paris, 1852.

Athenæ Oxoniensis. Compiled by WOOD, with Continuation by BLISS. 4 vols. Oxford, 1813–1820.

d'AUBIGNÉ, J. H. MERLE. See under "D."

BACON, ROGER. *Opera Inedita.* Edited by BREWER, J. S., in the Rolls Series. London, 1860.

BARACH, C. S. *Handschriften zu Donaueschingen.* Vienna, 1862.

BARSTCH, ADAM. *Le Peintre Graveur.* 21 vols. 8°. Vienna, 1803, 1821.

BASTARD, AUG. (Cte.). *La Librairie de Jean de France, duc de Berri.* Paris, 1834.

BAYLE, PETER. *Historical and Critical Dictionary* (English Version). 5 vols. London.

BECKMANN, J. *Beyträge zur Geschichte der Erfindungen.* Leipzig, 1786.

xvii

BEDE, (VENERABLE). *Historia Ecclesiastica Gentis Anglorum.* Edited by
    G. H. MOBERLEY. Oxford, 1869.
——— *Ecclesiastical Histy. of England.* Trans. by GILES. Lond., 1847.

BENTHAM, JAMES. *The Cathedral Church of Ely.* Cambridge, 1771.

Bibliothèque de l' École de Chartres. Cinquième Série.

BLADES, WM. *The Biography and Typography of William Caxton, Eng-
    land's First Printer.* London, 1877.

BLUME, FR. ANTON. *Iter Italicum.* Berlin, 1824.

BOSSUET. *Œuvres.* 32 vols. Paris, 1828.

BROWN, HORATIO F. *The Venetian Printing Press. An Historical
    Study.* London and New York, 1891.

BULÆUS, *Historia Universitatis Parisiensis ab anno 800.* 6 vols.
    Paris, 1665–1673.

BURCKHARDT, JACOB. *Die Cultur der Renaissance.* Berlin, 1889.

Casaubon, Isaac. Life, 1559–1614. By MARK PATTISON. 2d edition.
    Oxford, 1892.

Cassiodori Opera. Edited by GARET. 2 vols., fol. Rouen, 1679.

Cassiodorus, Das Leben von. FRANZ, J. Berlin, 1877.

Cassiodorus, Letters of. Trans., with an Introduction, by THOMAS HODG-
    KIN. London, 1884.

CASTELLANI, CARLO. *La Stampa in Venezia dalla sua Orig. alla Aldo
    Manuzio.* Venice, 1889.

Catalogue Général des Manuscrits des Bibliothèques Publiques. Paris, 1849.

Chartularium Universitatis Parisiensis. Paris, 1889.

CHASSANT. *Dictionnaire des Abréviations Latines et Françaises Usitées
    dans les Manuscrits.* Paris, 1864.

CHEVILLIER, ANDRÉ. *L'Origine de l'Imprimerie de Paris.* Paris, 1694.

CHRISTINE DE PISAN. *Les Écrits Politiques de.* Paris, 1838.

Chroniken, Die, der Deutschen Städte. 5 vols. Berlin, 1789–1792.

Chronique Métrique de Godefroy de Paris. 8 vols. Paris, 1827.

CLARK, J. W. *Libraries in the Mediæval and Renaissance Periods.*
    Oxford, 1894.

Columbæ, S. Vita Adamnani. Edited from Dr. REEVES's text, with an
    Introduction, Notes, and Glossary. By J. T. FOWLER. Oxford, 1894.

COMPAYRÉ, GABRIEL. *Abelard and the Origin and Early History of
    Universities.* New York, 1893.

COPINGER, W. A. *The Law of Copyright in Works of Literature and
    Art.* London, 1870.

COXE. *The College of Merton, Oxford.*
——— *New College, Oxford.*

CRÉVIER, J. B. L.　*Histoire de l' Université de Paris.*　8 vols.　Paris, 1761.

CURWEN, HENRY.　*A History of Booksellers, the Old and the New.*　London, 1873.

D'ACHÉRY, LUCAS.　*Vetera Analecta* (cum disquisitionibus J. MABILLON).　Paris, 1723.

———— *Spicilegium, sive Collectio Veterum Scriptorum,* etc.　3 vols.　Paris, 1823.

D'AUBIGNÉ, J. H. MERLE.　*Letter to an English Clergyman, Printed in the Record (newspaper) Dec. 12, 1844, in Reply to Strictures of Maitland.*

———— *History of the Reformation in the Sixteenth Century.*　5 vols.　London, 1866.

DE LA CAILLE.　*Histoire de l'Imprimerie.*　Paris, 1689.

DELALAIN, PAUL.　*Étude sur la Librairie Parisienne du XIIIᵉ au XVᵉ Siècle.*　Paris, 1891.

DELALANDE, E.　*Étude sur la Propriété Littéraire et Artistique.*　Paris, 1879.

DELISLE, L.　*Cartulaire de Normandie* (Mémoire des Antiquaires de Normandie).　Rouen, 1852.

———— *Recherches sur l'Ancienne Bibliothèque de Corbie* (Mémoire de l'Institut).　4 vols.　Paris, 1854.

DELPRAT, G. H. M.　*Verhandlung over de Broederschop van G. Groote.*　Amsterdam, 1853.

———— *Die Brüderschaft des gemeinsames Lebens.*　Leipzig, 1840.

DENIFLE et CHATELAIN.　*Chartularium Universitatis Parisiensis.*　Vols. I, II, III.　Paris, 1889, 1891.

DENIFLE, PÈRE.　*Die Entstehung der Universitäten des Mittelalters bis 1400.*　Vol. I.　Berlin, 1885.

DENK, V. M. OTTO.　*Geschichte des Gallo. Frankischen Unterrichts und Bildungswesens von den ältesten Zeiten bis auf Karl den Grossen.*　Mayence, 1892.

DE RANCÉ.　*Traité de la Saincteté et des Devoirs de la Vie Monastique.*　Paris, 1682.

DIBDIN, T. F.　*Typographical Antiquities ; or, The History of Printing in Great Britain.*　4 vols.　London, 1810-1819.

———— *Bibliograph. Antiquas,* and *A Picturesque Tour in France and Germany.*　3 vols.　London, 1829.

———— *The Library Companion ; or, The Young Man's Guide and the Old Man's Comfort in the Choice of a Library.*　2d edition.　London, 1825.

DIDOT, AMBR. FIRMIN.　*Histoire de la Typographie.*　Paris, 1882.

———— *Alde Manuce et l'Hellenisme à Venise.*　Paris, 1875.

DIGBY, SIR KENELM H. *Mores Catholici ; or, Ages of Faith.* 3 vols.
London, 1848.

DRUMMOND, ROBERT B. *Erasmus : His Life and Character.* 2 vols.
London, 1873.

DU BREUIL, JACQ. *Le Théâtre des Antiquités de Paris.* 6 vols., 4to.
Paris, 1612.

DUGDALE, SIR WM. *Monasticum Anglicanum.* 8 vols. London, 1849.

DÜMMLER, E. *Anselm der Peripatetiker.* Berlin, 1880.
—— *St. Gall. Denkmäler in den Mittheilungen d. Züricher Antiq.
Gesch.* 12 vols.

DÜMMLER, F. *Forschungen zür deutschen Geschichte.* 6 vols.

DURER, A. *Geschichte seines Lebens*, M. Thausing. Nuremberg, 1828.

EBERT, H. *Zur Handschriftenkunde.* Leipzig, 1825.

EKKEHARDUS. *Jun. de Cassib. Mon. St. Galli ap. Gold. Scr. Rer. Alem.*
2 vols. St. Gall.

ELLIS, GEORGE (*Editor*). *Specimens of Early English Poetry.* 3 vols.
London, 1790.

ELZEVIER, LES. *Histoire et Annales Typographiques.* Alphonse Willems.
Brussels, 1880.

ENGELHARDT. *Herrad von Landsberg und ihr Werk.* Stuttgart, 1818.

ERASMUS. *Opera.* London, 1703.

ESTIENNE, HENRI. *La Foire de Frankfort, Traduit en Français, avec le
Texte Latin.* Paris, 1875.

EVELYN, JOHN. *Memoirs.* Edited by BRAY. 4 vols. London, 1879.

FOSBROKE, J. D. *British Monachisn ; Manners and Customs of Monks
and Nuns.* London, 1843.

FOURNIER, MARCEL *Les Statuts et Priviléges des Universités Françaises.*
Paris, 1891.

FRANKLIN, ALFRED. *La Sorbonne, ses Origines, sa Bibliothèque, etc.*
2d edition. Paris, 1875.
—— *Les Anciennes Bibliothèques de Paris.* Paris, 1867.

FRIEDRICH, TH. P. *Kirchen-Geschichte Deutschlands.* 2 vols.
Halle, 1793.

FROMMANN (Editor). *Aufsätze des Buchhandels im 16ten Jahrhundert.*
Jena, 1876.

FROUDE, J. A. *Life and Letters of Erasmus.* American edition.
New York, 1894.

GÉRAUD, H. *Paris sous Philippe-le-Bel.* Paris, 1837.

GERSON, JOHANN. *Christliche Kindererziehung* (in Schultze's *Berühmte
Lehrer des Mittelalten*). Gütersloh, 1880.
—— *De Laude Scriptorum (Opera).* 2 vols. Paris, 1706.

Geschichte der Offentl. Bibliothek zu Bamberg. Nuremberg, 1832.

Geschichte der Präger Univers. Bibliothek. 8 vols. Prague, 1851.

Gesta Abb. Fontanell. (in *Monumenta Germaniæ Historica*).

GIESEBRECHT, W. *De Litterarum Studiis apud Italos primis Medii Ævi Sæculis.* Berlin, 1845.

GOLDSMIDT, EDMUND. *The Aldine Press at Venice. Privately Printed.* Edinburgh, 1877.

GÖRRES, JOSEPH VON. *Histor. Polit. Blätter.* 6 vols. Munich, 1859.

GOTTLIEB, THEODOR. *Über Mittelalterliche Bibliotheken.* Leipzig, 1890.

GÖTZE, LUDWIG. *Geschichte der Buchdrücker-Kunst in Magdeburg.* Magdeburg, 1879.

Grammatici Latini. Edited by KEIL, H. 8 vols. Leipzig, 1855–1880. (For Cassiodorus.)

GREGORY I. (the Great). *Opera.* (In *Library of the Fathers*.) 4 vols. Oxford, 1854.

GREIN. *Bibliothek der Angel-Sächsischen Poesie.* Edited by WÜLKER. Cassel, 1883.

GRESWELL, E. *A View of the Early Parisian Greek Press, Including the Lives of the Stephani, and Notices of Other Contemporary Greek Printers in Paris.* 2 vols. Oxford, 1833.

GRESWELL, WM. P. *Annals of Parisian Typography. Notices and Illustrations of the Most Remarkable Productions of the Gothic Press in Paris.* London, 1818.

GRIMM, JACOB. *Kleine Schriften.* 5 vols. Berlin, 1878–1880.

GUÉRARD. *Cartulaire de l'Église de Nôtre-Dame de Paris.* Paris.
—— *Cartulaire de St. Père-de Chartres.*

GUIGNES, DE, G. *La Typographie Orientale et Grecque de l'Imprimerie Royale.* Paris, 1787.

HAGEN, G. *Anecdota Helvet.* Leipzig, 1810.
—— *Litterär. Grundriss zür Geschichte der Deutschen Poesie.* Berlin, 1812.

HALLAM, HY. *Introduction to the Literature of Europe in the Fifteenth, Sixteenth, and Seventeenth Centuries.* 4 vols. New York, 1886.

HARDY, SIR THOS. *Descriptive Catalogue of Materials Relating to the History of Great Britain and Ireland.* Rolls Series. 3 vols. London, 1862, 1871.

HARTSHORNE, C. H. *The Book Rarities of the University of Cambridge.* London, 1829.

HASE, OSCAR. *Die Koberger, Eine Darstellung des Buchhändlerischen geschäftsbetriebes in der Zeit des überganges vom Mittelalter zür Neuzeit.* Leipzig, 1885.

HERZOG, J. J.   *Das Leben Johann Oekolampads.*   Basel, 1843.

Histoire Littéraire de la France, par des Religieux Bénédictins de la Congrégation de St. Maur.   12 vols.   Paris, 1733–1763.

——— Continuation.   7 vols.   Paris, 1814, 1838.

HODGKIN, THOMAS.   *Italy and Her Invaders.*   4 vols.   Oxford, 1880–85.

——— *The Letters of Cassiodorus.*   Translated, with an Introduction. London, 1886.

HOFFMANN, P. F. L.   *Altdeutsche Handschriften.*   Leipzig, 1862.

HROSWITHA OF GANDERSHEIM.   *Théâtre de.*   3 vols.   Paris, 1857.

HUBER, V. A.   *The English Universities.*   London, 1840.

HUMPHREYS, H. NOEL.   *History of the Art of Printing.*   London, 1868.

HÜTTEN, ULRICH VON.   *Leben, von Strauss.*   Bonn, 1878.

JUSSERAND, J. J.   *The English Novel in the Time of Shakespeare.* London and New York, 1890.

——— *English Wayfaring Life in the Middle Ages.*   4th edition. London and New York, 1892.

——— *A Literary History of the English People.*   3 vols.   London, Paris, and New York, 1895–1896.

KAPP, F.   *Geschichte des Deutschen Buchhandels bis in das 17te Jahrhundert.*   Leipzig, 1886.

KELLER, A. VON.   *Altdeutsche Handschriften.*   Leipzig, 1872.

KIRCHHOFF, ALBRECHT.   *Geschichte des Deutschen Buchhandels im 17ten Jahrhundert.*   Berlin, 1849.

——— *Die Handschriftenhändler des Mittelalters.*   2d edition.   Leipzig, 1853.

KLOSTERMANN, R.   *Das Geistige Eigenthum an Schriften, Kunstwerken und Erfindungen.*   Berlin, 1871.

KNIGHT, CHARLES.   *The Old Printer and the Modern Press.*   London, 1854.

KOHLER, I.   *Das Autorrecht.*   Jena, 1880.

KÖPKE, F. C.   *Otton. Studien.*   2 vols.   Leipzig, 1829.

KOTZEBUE, AUGUST V.   *Denkschrift über den Büchernachdruck.*   Leipzig, 1814.

LABOULAYE, ÉDOUARD.   *Études sur la Propriété Littéraire en France et en Angleterre.*   Paris, 1858.

LACROIX, PAUL.   *Science and Literature in the Middle Ages.*   London, 1886.

LALANNE, LUDOVIC.   *Curiosités Bibliographiques.*   2d edition. Paris, 1852.

LAURIE, S. S.   *The Rise and Early Constitution of Universities, with a Survey of Mediæval Education.*   New York, 1887.

LEUTER. *Hist. Wessofont.* 2 vols. Bamberg, 1837.

LINDE, A. VAN DER. *Gutenberg, Geschichte u. Erdichtung nach der Quellen ausgewiesen.* Stuttgart, 1878.

LORCK, C. B. *Hand-buch der Geschichte der Buchdrücker-Kunst.* Leipzig, 1882.

LOUISY, M. P. *Le Livre, et les Arts qui s'y rattachent, depuis les origines jusqu'à la fin du XVIIIᵉ Siècle.* Paris, 1886.

LUDEN, H. *Vom freien Geistes-Verkehr.* Leipzig, 1814.

Luther, Life. By JULIUS KÖSTLIN. Translated from the German. New York, 1893.

LYON-CAEN, CH., and DELALAIN, PAUL. *Lois Françaises et Étrangères sur la Propriété Littéraire et Artistique.* 2 vols. Paris, 1889.

MABILLON, JEAN. *Réflexions sur la Réponse de M. l'Abbé de la Trappe.* 2 vols. Paris, 1689.

—— *Acta Sanctorum Ordinis S. Benedicti.* 9 vols. Paris, 1668–1673.

—— *Annales Ordinis S. Benedicti.* 6 vols. Paris, 1703, 1759.

—— *De Re Diplomatica.* 6 vols. Paris, 1681.

Same, with supplement. 2 vols. Naples, 1789.

—— *Iter Burgundicum.* Paris, 1684.

—— *Iter Germanicum.* Paris, 1685.

—— *Iter Italicum.* Paris, 1687–1689.

—— *Traité des Études Monastiques.* 2 vols. Paris, 1753.

—— *Vetera Analecta.* (See D'Achéry.)

MADAN, FALCONER. *The Early Oxford Press. A Bibliography of Printing and Publishing at Oxford, 1468–1640.* Oxford, 1895.

MADDEN, J. P. A. *Lettres d'un Bibliographe.* 5 vols. Paris, 1878.

MAITLAND, S. R. *The Dark Ages, a Series of Essays intended to illustrate the state of religion and literature in the ninth, tenth, eleventh, and twelfth centuries.* London, 1845.

MAITTAIRE, MICHEL. *Annales Typographici ab Artis Inventæ Origine ad Annum 1557.* 9 vols. Paris, 1719–1741.

—— *Historia Typographorum Aliquot Parisiensium Vitas et Libros Complectens.* 2 vols. London, 1717.

MARSHAM. Προπύλαιον (in *Monast. Anglican*).

MARTENE, EDMOND. *De Antiquis Ecclesiæ Ritibus.* 4 vols. Antwerp, 1736–1738.

—— *De Antiquis Monachorum Ritibus.* 2 vols. London, 1690.

—— *Thesaurus Novus Anecdotorum.* 5 vols. Paris, 1717.

—— *Voyage Littératre de Deux Bénédictins de la Congrégation de St. Maur.* 1st and 2d Series. Paris, 1717, 1724.

MASSMANN. *Die Goth. Urkunden von Neapel und Arezzo.* Vienna, 1838.

MATHESIUS. *Memoirs of the Life and Death of Martin Luther.* 1566.

MALDEN. *On the Origin of the Universities.* London, 1835.

MEINERS. *Geschichte der Enstehung u. Entwickelung der hohen Schulen.* Göttingen, 1802, 1805.

MERLET. *Catalogue des Livres de l'Abbaye de St. Père-de-Chartres au XIᵉ Siècle.*

MICHAUD, ABBÉ. *Guillaume de Champeaux et les Écoles de Paris au XIIᵉ Siècle.* Paris, 1867.

MILNER, JOSEPH. *History of the Church of Christ.* London, 1875.

MILTON, JOHN. *Areopagitica. A Speech for the Liberty of Unlicensed Printing.* Edited by T. H. WHITE. London, 1819.

MITTARELLI, J. B. *Annales Camaldulenses Ordinis S. Benedicti.* 9 vols. Venice, 1755–1773.

MONE, FR. J. *Im Anzeige der deutschen Vorzeit.* 6 vols. Carlsruhe, 1846.
——— *Zeitschrift fur Gesch. des Oberrheins.*

MONTALEMBERT, THE COUNT DE. *The Monks of the West from St. Benedict to St. Bernard.* 8 vols. Edinburgh, 1861–1879.

Monumenta Germaniæ Historica. Edited by PERTZ. 6 vols. Hanover, 1826–1841.

Monumenta Germaniæ Historica. Edited by WILHELM MEYER. 10 vols. Leipzig, 1888–1894.

MORIER, SIR JAMES. *A Journey through Persia, etc.* 2 vols. London, 1812.

MOSHEIM, J. L. *Institutes of Ecclesiastical History.* Trans. by MURDOCK and SOAMES. Edited by STUBBS. London, 1863.

MUCCIOLO, J. M. *Catalogus Codd. MSS. Malatest. Cæsan. Bibliotheca.* Cæsanæ, 1780.

MULLINGER, J. BASS. *The Schools of Charles the Great and the Restoration of Education in the Ninth Century.* London, 1877.

MURATORI. *Antiquitates Italicæ Medii Ævi.* 6 vols. Mediolani, 1738–1742.

NAUDÉ, G. *Additions à l'Histoire de Lowys XI. par Comines.* Édit. par FRESNOY. 4 vols. Paris.

NEWMAN, CARDINAL. *Historical Sketches.* 3 vols. London, 1889.

O'CURRY, EUGENE. *Lectures on the MSS. Materials of the Ancient History of Ireland.* Dublin, 1874.

OESTERLY, H. *Wegweiser durch die Literatur der Urkunden-Sammlungen.* 2 vols. Berlin, 1885–1886.

OTLEY, W. Y. *An Enquiry Concerning the Invention of Printing.* London, 1837.

OZANAM. *La Civilisation Chrétienne chez les Francs.* 2 vols. Paris, 1866.

PATTISON, MARK. *Isaac Casaubon, 1559–1614.* Oxford, 1892.

PAULSEN, FRIEDRICH. *The German Universities, their Character and Historical Development.* Trans. by E. D. PERRY. New York and London, 1895.

PEIGNOT, G. *Manual du Bibliophile.* Paris, 1805.

PERRENS, F. T. *The History of Florence from the Domination of the Medici to the Fall of the Republic, 1434–1531.* Trans. by H. LYNCH. 2 vols. London, 1892.

PERTZ, GEO. HEIN. (*Editor*). *Archiv d. Gesellschaft für ältere Deutsche Geschichts-Kunde.* Berlin, 1846.

PETIT-RADEL. *Recherches sur les Bibliothèques Anciennes.* Paris, 1819.

PEZ, BERNARDUS. *Thesaurus Anecdotorum Novissimus.* 5 vols. Leipzig, 1721–1729.

———— Same, vol. iv. *Codex Diplomatico-historico-epistolaris.*

———— *Thes. Diss. Isagog.* (See vol. ii. of the *Thesaurus Anecdotorum.*)

Plantin, Christophe, Imprimeur Anversois. By MAX ROOSES. Antwerp, 1883.

PLATER, THOM. *Selbst-Biographie.* Basel, 1836.

POGGII, FLORENTINI. *Opera.* Florence, 1513.

Priviléges de l' Université de Poitiers. Poitiers, 1726.

PÜTTER, J. S. *Beyträge zum Teutschen Staats u. Fürsten-Rechte.* Göttingen, 1777.

RAHN, H. *Geschichte der Bildenden Künste in der Schweiz.* 2 vols. Leipzig, 1832.

RASHDALL, HASTINGS. *The Universities of Europe in the Middle Ages.* 2 vols. Oxford, 1895.

Recueil des Priviléges de l' Université de Paris. Paris, 1822.

REIFFERSCHEID, A. *Westfälische Volkslieder in Wort u. Weise.* Heilbronn, 1879.

RENOUARD, A. C. *Traité des Droits d'Auteurs dans la Littérature, les Sciences et les Beaux-Arts.* 2 vols. Paris, 1838.

Rheinisches Museum für Philologie. Neue Folge. Band 49. Frankfort, 1894.

ROBERTSON, ALEX. *Fra Paolo Sarpi.* London, 1895.

ROBERTSON, WM. *View of Europe during the Middle Ages.* (Introduction to his *History of Charles V.*)

———— *History of Charles V.* Edited by W. H. PRESCOTT, Boston, 1880.

ROCKINGER, L. VON. *Zum Bairischen Schriftswesen.* 2 vols.
Vienna, 1892.
—— *Die Untersuchung der Handschriften des Schwabenspiegels.*
Vienna, 1890.

ROMBERG, ÉDOUARD. *Études sur la Propriété Artistique et Littéraire.*
Brussels, 1892.

ROOSES, MAX. *Christophe Plantin, Imprimeur Anversois.*
Antwerp, 1883.

RUINART. *Iter Litterarium in Alsatiam et Lotharingiam.* Paris, 1697.

SAVIGNY, F. C. *Geschichte des Römischen Rechtes im Mittelalter.* 2 vols.
Leipzig, 1877.

SCHMIDT, C. *Geschichte der Ältesten Bibliothek in Strasburg.* Strasburg,
1881.
—— *Geschichte der ersten Buchdrücker zur Strassburg.* Strasburg,
1882.

SCHUCK, J. *Aldus Manutius u. Seine Zeitgenossen in Italien u. Deutschland.* Berlin, 1862.

SCHÜRMANN, AUG. *Die Rechtsverhältnisse der Autoren und Verleger.*
Halle, 1889.

Schwabenspiegel. Munich, 1874.

SCOTT, MARY A. *Elizabethan Translations from the Italian.* Baltimore,
1895.

SCRUTTON, T. E. *The Laws of Copyright.* London, 1883.

Social England. A Record of the Progress of the People. Edited by H. D.
TRAILL. 6 vols. London and New York, 1894–1896.

STENZEL, TH. *Geschichte der Frankischen Kaiser.* 2 vols. Leipzig, 1885.

SWEET, HENRY. *King Alfred's Version of Gregory's Pastoral Care.*
Early English Text Society. London, 1871–1872.

SYMONDS, J. A. *The Renaissance in Italy.* 7 vols. London, 1875–1886.

THOMASSY. *Les Écrits Politiques de Christine de Pisan.* Paris, 1838.

THUROT. *De l'Organisation de l'Enseignement dans l'Université de Paris
au Moyen Age.* Paris, 1850.

TIMPERLEY, C. H. *A Dictionary of Printers and Printing, with the
Progress of Literature Ancient and Modern.* London, 1839.

TIRABOSCHI, GIROLAMO. *Storia della Litteratura Italiana.* 16 vols.
Milan, 1822–1826.

TRITHEMIUS, J. *Annalium Hirsangensium.* 2 vols. St. Gall, 1690.

ULPHILAS. *Vet. et Nov, Test. Fragmenta.* Edited by GABELENTZ and
LOBE. 2 vols. Leipzig, 1843–1860.

Urkundenbuch für die Geschichte des Niederrheins. 6 vols. Cologne,
1852–1856.

VALÉRY. *Correspondance de Mabillon et de Montfaucon.* Paris.

VALLA, LORENZO. *Opera.* Basel, 1543.

VIGFUSSON and POWELL (*Editors*). *Corpus Poeticum Boreale. The Poetry of the old Northern Tongue from the Earliest to the Thirteenth Century.* 2 vols. Oxford, 1883.

VIRIVILLE, VALLET DE, *Histoire de l'Instruction Publique en Europe.* Paris, 1849.

VITALIS, ORDERICUS. *Coenobii Uticensis Monachi, Historiæ Ecclesiasticæ.* 2 vols. Paris, 1840.

VITET. *De la Presse au Seizième Siècle.*

Voyage Littéraire de deux Religieux Bénédictins (E. MARTENE et D. DURAND). 2 vols. Paris, 1717-1724.

WARTON, THOMAS. *History of English Poetry* (1774-1781). Edited by HAZLITT. 4 vols. 1871.

WATTENBACH, W. *Das Schriftwesen im Mittelalter.* Leipzig, 1875.

WEIDMANN, FR. *Geschichte der Stifts-Bibliothek.* Vienna, 1841.
—— *Geschichte der Bibliothek von St. Gallen.* St. Gall, 1842.

WEST, A. F. *Alcuin and the Rise of the Christian Schools.* New York, 1892.

WESTWOOD, J. O. *Facsimiles of Miniatures and Ornaments of Anglo-Saxon and Irish MSS.* London, 1868.

WETTER, J. *Geschichte der Erfindung der Buchdrückerkunst.* Mayence, 1836.

WILDER, DANIEL W. *The Life of Shakespeare, Compiled from the Best Sources, without Comment.* Boston, 1893.

WILKEN, R. F. *Geschichte der Heidelberg. Bücher-Sammlungen.* Heidelberg, 1817.

WILLEMS, ALPHONSE. *Les Elzevier, Histoire et Annales Typographiques.* Brussels, 1880.

WINTER, V. A. *Die Cistercianer.* Munich, 1815.

WIRTH, HERM. *Archives für die Geschichte der Stadt Heidelberg.* 4 vols. Heidelberg.

WOOD, A. *Athenæ,* etc. (See *Athenæ.*)

WRIGHT, THOMAS. *A Selection of Latin Stories from MSS. of the Thirteenth and Fourteenth Centuries.* Percy Society. London, 1842.

ZASIUS. *Epistolæ ad viros ætatis suæ doctissimos.* Ulm, 1774.

Zeitschrift für Deutsches Alterthum.

Zeitschrift für Geschichte des Oberrheins.

ZIEGELBAUER, H. *Observationes Literariæ S. Benedicti.* 4 vols. Leipzig, 1784.

PART I.

BOOKS IN MANUSCRIPT.

PART I.

BOOKS IN MANUSCRIPT.

INTRODUCTORY.

IN the year 410, Rome was captured and sacked by Alaric the Visigoth. At this time, S. Jerome, in his cell at Bethlehem, was labouring at his *Commentaries on Ezekiel*, while it was the downfall of the imperial city which incited S. Augustine to begin the composition of his greatest work, *The City of God :* "the greatest city of the world has fallen in ruin, but the City of God abideth forever." The treatise required for its completion twenty-two books. "The influence of France and of the printing-press," remarks Hodgkin, "have combined to make impossible the production of another *De Civitate Dei*. The multiplicity of authors compels the controversialist who would now obtain a hearing, to speak promptly and concisely. The examples of Pascal and of Voltaire teach him that he must speak with point and vivacity." [1] S. Augustine was probably the most voluminous writer of the earlier Christian centuries. He was the author of no less than 232 books, in addition to many tractates or homilies and innumerable epistles.[2] His literary work was con-

---

[1] *Italy and Her Invaders*, ii., 246.
[2] Victor Vitensis, cited by Hodgkin, ii., 247.

3

tinued even during the siege of Hippo by the Vandals, and he died in Hippo (in 431), in his seventy-sixth year, while the siege was still in progress.

In regard to the lack of historical records of the time, I will again quote Hodgkin, who, in his monumental work on *Italy and Her Invaders*, has himself done so much to make good the deficiency: " It is perhaps not surprising that in Italy itself there should have been during the fifth century an utter absence of the instinct which leads men to record for the benefit of posterity events which are going on around them. When history was making itself at such breathless speed and in such terrible fashion, the leisure, the inclination, the presence of mind necessary for writing history might well be wanting. He who would under happier auspices have filled up the interval between the bath and the tennis court by reclining on the couch in the winter portico of his villa and there languidly dictating to his slave the true story of the abdication of Avitus, or the death of Anthemius, was himself now a slave keeping sheep in the wilderness under a Numidian sun or shrinking under the blows of one of the rough soldiers of Gaiseric."

Hodgkin finds it more difficult to understand " why the learned and leisurely provincial of Greece, whose country for nearly a century and a half (395–539) escaped the horrors of hostile invasion, and who had to inspire them the grandest literary traditions in the world, should have left unwritten the story of the downfall of Rome."

" The fact seems to be," he goes on to say, " that at this time all that was left of literary instinct and historiographic power in the world had concentrated itself on theological (we cannot call it religious) controversy, and what tons of worthless material the ecclesiastical historians and controversialists of the time have left us! . . . Blind, most of them, to the meaning of the mighty drama which was being enacted on the stage of the world . . .

they have left us scarcely a hint as to the inner history of the vast revolution which settled the Teuton in the lands of the Latin. . . . One man alone gives us that detailed information concerning the thoughts, characters, persons of the actors in the great drama which can make the dry bones of the chronologer live. This is Caius Sollius Apollinaris Sidonius, man of letters, imperial functionary, country gentleman, and bishop, who, notwithstanding much manifest weakness of character and a sort of epigrammatic dulness of style, is still the most interesting literary figure of the fifth century."[1]

Sidonius was born at Lyons, A.D. 430. His father, grandfather, and great-grandfather had all served as Prætorian Prefects in Gaul, in which province his own long life was passed. In 472, Sidonius became Bishop of Arverni, and from that time, as he rather naïvely tells us, he gave up (as unbecoming ecclesiastical responsibilities) the writing of compositions "based on pagan models." In 475, the year before the last of the western emperors, Augustulus, was driven from Rome by Odovacar,[2] the Herulian, the Visigoth king, Euric, became master of Auvergne. Sidonius was at first banished, but in 479 was restored to his diocese, and continued his work there as bishop and as writer until his death, ten years later. At the time of the death of Sidonius, Cassiodorus, who was, during the succeeding eighty years, to have part in so much of the eventful history of Italy, was ten years old. There are some points of similarity in the careers of the two men. Both were of noble family and both began their active work as officials, one of the Empire, the other of the Gothic kingdom of Italy, while both also became ecclesiastics. Each saw his country taken possession of by a foreign invader, and for the purpose of serving his countrymen, (with which purpose may very possibly have

[1] *Italy*, ii., 297, 298.
[2] For this form of the name I am following the authority of Hodgkin.

been combined some motives of personal ambition,) each was able and willing to make himself useful to the new ruler and thus to retain official position and influence; and finally, both had literary facility and ambition, and, holding in regard the works of the great classic writers, endeavoured to model upon these works the style of their own voluminous compositions. The political work of Cassiodorus was of course, however, much the more noteworthy and important, as Sidonius could hardly claim to be considered a statesman.

In their work as authors, the compositions of Sidonius are, as I judge from the description, to be ranked higher in literary quality than those of the later writer, and to have been more successful also in following the style of classic models. The style of Cassiodorus is described as both verbose and grandiloquent. In his ecclesiastical, or rather his monastic work, taken up after half a century of active political life, it was the fortune of Cassiodorus, as will be described later, to excercise an influence which continued for centuries, and which was possibly more far-reaching than was exerted by the career of any abbot or bishop in the later history of the Church.

The careers of both Sidonius and Cassiodorus have a special interest because the two men held rather an exceptional position between the life of the old empire which they survived and that of the new Europe of the Middle Ages, the beginning of which they lived to see.

Of the writings of Sidonius, Hodgkin speaks as follows: " A careful perusal of the three volumes of the Letters and Poems of Sidonius (written between the years 455 and 490) reveals to us the fact that in Gaul the air still teems with intellectual life, that authors were still writing, amanuenses transcribing, friends complimenting or criticising, and all the cares and pleasures of literature filling the minds of large classes of men just as when no empires were sinking and no strange nationalities suddenly arising around them. . . . A long list of forgotten philosophers did exist in that age, and their works, produced in lavish abundance, seem to have had no lack of eager students."

As an example of the literary interests of a country gentleman in Gaul, Hodgkin quotes a letter of Sidonius, written about 469: " Here too [*i. e.* in a country house in Gaul] were books in plenty; you might fancy you were looking at the breast-high book-shelves (*plantei*) of the grammarians, or the wedge-shaped cases (*cunei*) of the Athenæum, or the well-filled cupboards (*armaria*) of the booksellers. I observed, however, that if one found a manuscript beside the chair of one of the ladies of the house, it was sure to be on a religious subject, while those which lay by the seats of the fathers of the family were full of the loftiest strains of Latin eloquence. In making this distinction, I do not forget that there are some writings of equal literary excellence in both branches, that Augustine may be paired off against Varro, and Prudentius against Horace. Among these books, the works of Origen, the Adamantine, were frequently perused by readers holding our faith. I cannot understand why some of our arch-divines should stigmatise him as a dangerous and heterodox author."

In summing up the work of Sidonius, Hodgkin points out the noteworthy opportunities for making a literary reputation which were missed by him. " He might have been the Herodotus of mediæval Europe. He could have given authentic pictures of the laws and customs of the Goths, Franks, and Burgundians . . . a full portraiture of the great apostle of the Germanic races, Ulfilas, and the secret causes of his and their devotion to the Arian form of Christianity ; and he could have recorded the Gothic equivalents of the mythological tales in the Scandinavian Edda and the story of the old Runes and

[1] *Italy*, ii., 319.

their relation to the Mœso-Gothic alphabet. All these details and a hundred more, full of interest to science, to art, to literature, Sidonius might have preserved for us had his mind been as open as was that of Herodotus to the manifold impressions made by picturesque and strange nationalities."

It was doubtless fortunate for the literary reputation of Sidonius that his father-in-law, Avitus, came to be emperor. The reign of Avitus was short, but he had time to give to his brilliant son-in-law a position as Court poet or poet-laureate, while it was probably due to the imperial influence that the Senate decreed the erection (during the lifetime of the poet) of the brass statue of Sidonius, which was placed between the two libraries of Trajan. These libraries, containing the one Greek and the other Latin authors, stood between the column of Trajan and the Basilica Ulpia. Sidonius describes his statue as follows:

> *Cum meis poni statuam perennem*
> *Nerva Trajanus titulis videret,*
> *Inter auctores utriusque fixam Bibliothecæ.*
>
> (Sidonius, *Ex.*, ix., 16.)

> *Nil vatum prodest adjectum laudibus illud*
> *Ulpia quod rutilat porticus ære meo.*
>
> (Sidonius, *Carm.*, viii., 7, 8.) [1]

(Since Nerva Trajanus decreed the erection of a permanent statue, which is inscribed with the records of my honours, and is placed between the authors of the two libraries.

The fact that the entrance to the Ulpian Library is aglow with the bronze of my statue, can add nothing to the laurels of other poets.)

---

[1] Cited by Hodgkin, iv., 119, 120.

In the opinion of Hodgkin, the books in these two collections in the Bibliotheca Ulpia may very well have been of more importance to later generations than those of the library of Alexandria. The books from Trajan's libraries were, according to Vopiscus, transported in all or in part to the Baths of Diocletian. Hodgkin understands that, between 300 and 450, they were restored to their original home.[1]

In the year 537 A.D., the rule of the Goths in Italy, which had been established by Theodoric in 493, was practically brought to a close by the victories of Belisarius, the general of the Eastern Empire, and, thirty years later, the destruction of the Gothic State was completed by the invasion of the Lombards. With the Lombards in possession of Northern Italy, and the Vandals, in a series of campaigns against the armies from Constantinople, overrunning the southern portions of the peninsula, the social organisation of the country must have been almost destroyed, and the civilisation which had survived from the old Empire, while never entirely disappearing, was doubtless in large part submerged. A certain continuity of Roman rule and of Roman intellectual influence was, however, preserved through the growing power of the Church, which was already claiming the inheritance of the Empire, and which, as early as 590, under the lead of Pope Gregory the Great, succeeded in making good its claims to ecclesiastical supremacy throughout the larger part of Europe. In its control of the consciences of rulers, the Church frequently, in fact, secured a domination that was by no means limited to things spiritual.

The history of books in manuscript and of the production and distribution of literature in Europe from the beginning of the work of S. Benedict to the time when the printing-press of Gutenberg revolutionised the methods of book-making, a period covering about nine

[1] *Vita Probi*, ii., cited by Hodgkin.

centuries, may be divided into three stages. During the first, the responsibility for the preservation of the old-time literature and for keeping alive some continuity of intellectual life, rested solely with the monasteries, and the work of multiplying and of distributing such books as had survived was carried on by the monks, and by them only. During the second stage, the older universities, the organisation of which had gradually been developed from schools (themselves chiefly of monastic origin), became centres of intellectual activity and shared with the monasteries the work of producing books. The books emanating from the university scribes were, however, for the most part restricted to a few special classes, classes which had, as a rule, not been produced in the monasteries, and, as will be noted in a later chapter, the university booksellers (*stationarii* or *librarii*) were in the earlier periods not permitted to engage in any general distribution of books. With the third stage of manuscript literature, book-producing and bookselling machinery came into existence in the towns, and the knowledge of reading being no longer confined to the *cleric* or the *magister*, books were prepared for the use of the larger circles of the community, and to meet the requirements of such circles were, to an extent increasing with each generation, written in the tongue of the people.

The first period begins with the foundation by S. Benedict, in 529, of the monastery of Monte Cassino, and by Cassiodorus, in 531, of that of Vivaria or Viviers, and continues until the last decade of the twelfth century, when we find the earliest record of an organised book-business in the universities of Bologna and Paris. The beginning of literary work in the universities, to which I refer as indicating a second stage, did not, however, bring to an end, and, in fact, for a time hardly lessened, the production of books in the monasteries.

The third stage of book-production in Europe may be

said to begin with the first years of the fifteenth century, when the manuscript trade of Venice and Florence became important, when the book-men or publishers of Paris, outside of the university, had developed a business in the collecting, manifolding, and selling of manuscripts, and when manuscripts first find place in the schedules of the goods sold at the fairs of Frankfort and Nordlingen. The costliness of the skilled labour required for the production of manuscripts, and the many obstacles and difficulties in the way of their distribution, caused the development of the book-trade to proceed but slowly. It was the case, nevertheless, and particularly in Germany, that a very considerable demand for literature of certain classes had been developed among the people before the close of the manuscript period, a demand which was being met with texts produced in constantly increasing quantities and at steadily lessening cost. When the printing-press arrived it found, therefore, already in existence a wide-spread literary interest and a popular demand for books, a demand which, with the immediate cheapening of books, was, of course, enormously increased. The production of books in manuscript came to a close, not with the invention of the printing-press in 1450, but with the time when printing had become generally introduced, about twenty-five years later.

It was in the monasteries that were preserved such fragments of the classic literature as had escaped the general devastation of Italy; and it was to the labours of the monks of the West, and particularly to the labours of the monks of S. Benedict, that was due the preservation for the Middle Ages and for succeeding generations of the remembrance and the influence of the literature of classic times. For a period of more than six centuries, the safety of the literary heritage of Europe, one may say of the world, depended upon the scribes of a few dozen scattered monasteries.

The Order of S. Benedict was instituted in 529, and the monastery of Monte Cassino, near Naples, founded by him in the same year, exercised for centuries an influence of distinctive importance upon the literary interests of the Church, of Italy, and of the world. This monastery (which still exists) is not far from Subiaco, the spot chosen by S. Benedict for his first retreat. It was in the monastery of Subiaco (founded many years afterwards) that was done, nearly a thousand years later, the first printing in Italy. The Rule of S. Benedict, comprising the regulations for the government of his Order, contained a specific instruction that a certain number of hours in each day were to be devoted to labour in the *scriptorium*. The monks who were not yet competent to work as scribes were to be instructed by the others. Scribe work was to be accepted in place of an equal number of hours given to manual labour out-of-doors, while the skilled scribes, whose work was of special importance as instructors or in the *scriptorium*, were to be freed from a certain portion of their devotional exercises or observances. The monasteries of the Benedictines were for centuries more numerous, more wealthy, and more influential than those of any other Order, and this provision of a Rule which directed the actions, controlled the daily lives, and inspired the purposes of thousands of earnest workers among the monks of successive generations, must have exercised a most noteworthy influence on the history of literary production in Europe. It is not too much to say that it was S. Benedict who provided the "copy" which a thousand years later was to supply the presses of Gutenberg, Aldus, Froben, and Stephanus.

I have not been able to find in the narratives of the life of S. Benedict any record showing the origin of his interest in literature, an interest which was certainly exceptional for an ecclesiastic of the sixth century. It seems very probable, however, that Benedict's association

with Cassiodorus had not a little to do with the literary
impetus given to the work of the Benedictines. Cassiodorus, who, as Chancellor of King Theodoric, had taken
an active part in the government of the Gothic kingdom,
passed the last thirty years of his life first as a monk and
later as abbot in the monastery of Vivaria, or Viviers, in
Calabria, which he had himself founded in 531. Cassiodorus is generally classed by the Church chronicles as a
Benedictine, and his monastery is referred to by Montalembert as the second of the Benedictine foundations.
Hodgkin points out, however, that the Rule adopted by
the monks of Viviers, or prescribed for them by its founder, was not that of S. Benedict, but was drawn from the
writings of Cassian, the founder of western monachism,
who had died a century before.[1] The two Rules were,
however, fully in accord with each other in spirit, while
for the idea of using the convent as a place of literary toil
and theological training, Benedict was indebted to Cassiodorus. "At a very early date in the history of their
Order," says Hodgkin, "the Benedictines, influenced
probably by the example of the monastery of Vivaria,
commenced that long series of services to the cause of
literature which they have never wholly intermitted.
Instead of accepting the . . . formula from which some
scholars have contended that Cassiodorus was a Benedictine, we should perhaps be rather justified in maintaining
that Benedict, or at least his immediate followers, were
Cassiodorians."[2]

It was the fortune of Cassiodorus to serve as a connecting link between the world of classic Rome and that of
the Middle Ages. He saw the direction and control
of the community pass from the monarchs and the
leaders of armies to the Church and to the monas-

---

[1] *The Letters of Cassiodorus.* Translated with an Introduction by Thomas
Hodgkin, London, 1884, p. 57.
[2] *Letters of Cassiodorus,* p. 59.

teries, and he was himself an active agent in helping to bring about such transfer. Born in 479, only three years after the overthrow of the last of the Emperors of the West, he grew up under the rule of Odovacar, the Herulian. While still a youth, he had seen the Herulian kingdom destroyed by Theodoric, and he had lived to mourn over the ruins of the realm founded by the Goth, which he had himself helped to govern. He saw his beloved Italy taken possession of by the armies of Narses and Belisarius from the east, and a little later overrun by the undisciplined hordes of the Lombards from the north. The first great schism between the Eastern and the Western Churches began during his boyhood and terminated before, as Abbot of Vivaria, it became necessary for him to take a decided part on the one side or the other. A Greek by ancestry, a Roman by training, the experience of Cassiodorus included work and achievements as statesman, orator, scholar, author, and ecclesiastic. He had witnessed the extinction of the Roman Senate, of which both his father and himself had been members; the practical abolition of the Consulate, an honour to which he had also attained; and the close of the schools of philosophy in Athens, with the doctrines of which he almost alone in his generation of Italians, was familiar. He had done much to maintain in the Court and throughout the kingdom of Theodoric, such standard of scholarly interests and of literary appreciation as was practicable with the resources available; and, in like manner, he brought with him to his monastery a scholarly enthusiasm for classic literature, of which literature he may not unnaturally have felt himself to be almost the sole surviving representative. It is difficult to over-estimate the extent of the service rendered by Cassiodorus to literature and to later generations in initiating the training of monks as scribes, and in putting into their hands for their first work in the *scriptorium* the masterpieces of classic literature. He belonged both to the world of ancient Rome, which he had outlived, and to that of the Middle Ages, the thought and work of which he helped to shape. With the close of the official career of Cassiodorus as Secretary of State for the Gothic kingdom of Italy, the history of ancient Europe may, for the purpose of my narrrative, be considered to end. With the consecration of Cassiodorus, as Abbot of the monastery of Vivaria, (which took place about 550, when he was seventy years of age), and the instituting by him of the first European *scriptorium*, I may begin the record of the production of books during the Middle Ages.

CHAPTER I.

THE MAKING OF BOOKS IN THE MONASTERIES.

I HAVE used for the heading of the chapter the term "the making of books" rather than "literary work," because the service rendered by the earlier monastic scribes (a service of essential importance for the intellectual life of the world) consisted chiefly, as has been indicated not in the production of original literature, but in the reproduction and preservation of the literature that had been inherited from earlier writers,—writers whose works had been accepted as classics. While it was the case that in this literary labour it was the Benedictines who for centuries rendered the most important service, the first of the European monasteries in which such labour was carried on as a part of the prescribed routine or rule of the monastic life was that of Vivaria or Viviers, founded by Cassiodorus, which was never formally associated with the Benedictine Order, and which had, in fact, adopted, in place of the Benedictine Rule, a rule founded on the teachings of Cassian, who had died early in the fifth century. The work done, under the instructions of Cassiodorus, by the scribes of Viviers, served as an incentive and an example for Monte Cassino, the monastery founded by S. Benedict, while the *scriptorium* instituted in Monte Cassino was accepted as a model by the long series of later Benedictine monasteries which during the succeeding seven centuries became centres of literary activity.

After the destruction of the Gothic kingdom of Italy,

it was with these monasteries that rested the intellectual future of Europe.   Mankind was, for the time at least, to be directed and influenced, not so much by royal chancellors or prætorian guards, as by the monks preaching from their cells and by the monastic scribes distributing the world's literature from the *scriptorium*.

Cassiodorus and S. Benedict.—In the literary history of Europe, the part played by Cassiodorus was so important and the service rendered by him was so distinctive, that it seems pertinent for the purposes of this story to present in some detail the record of his life and work. As is indicated by the name by which he is known in history, Cassiodorus was of Greek lineage, his family belonging to the Greek city of Scyllacium in Southern Italy. His full name was Magnus Aurelius Cassiodorus Senator. His ancestors had, for several generations, held under the successive rulers of Italy positions of trust and honour, and the family ranked with the patricians. The father of the author and abbot, usually referred to as Cassiodorus the third, was finance minister under Odovacar, and when the Herulian King had been overcome and slain by Theodoric, the minister was skilful enough to make himself necessary to the Gothic conqueror, from whom he received various important posts, and by whom he was finally appointed Prætorian Prefect. The Cassiodorus with whom this study is concerned, known as Cassiodorus the fourth, was born about 479, or three years after the Gothic conquest.[1] He began his official career as early as twenty, and it was while holding, at this age, the position of Consilarius, that he brought himself to the favourable attention of Theodoric by means of an eloquent panegyric spoken in praise of that monarch.

Theodoric appointed him Quæstor, an office which made him the mouth-piece of the sovereign. To the

[1] Cassiodorus, *Letters*, 8.

Quæstor belonged the duty of conducting the official correspondence of the Court, of receiving ambassadors, and of replying in fitting harangues to their addresses, so that he was at once foreign secretary and Court orator. He also had the responsibility of giving a final revision to all the laws which received the signature of the King, and of seeing that these were properly worded and did not conflict with previous enactments.[1]   Theodoric, who had received what little education he possessed from Greek instructors in Constantinople, was said never to have mastered Latin, and he doubtless found the services of his eloquent and scholarly minister very convenient.

It was the contention of Theodoric that his kingdom represented the natural continuation of the Roman Empire, and that he was himself the legitimate successor of the emperors.   He took as his official designation not *Rex Italiæ*, but *Gothorum et Romanorum Rex*.   This contention was fully upheld by the Quæstor, who felt himself to be the representative at once of the official authority of the new kingdom and of the literary prestige of the old Empire, and who did what was in his power to preserve in Ravenna the classical traditions of old Rome and to make the Court the centre of literary influence and activity.   Theodoric and his Goths had accepted the creed of the Arians, but the influence of his minister, who was a Christian of the Athanasian or Trinitarian faith, was sufficient to preserve a spirit of toleration throughout the kingdom.   It is to Cassiodorus that is due what was probably the first official utterance of toleration that Europe had known, an utterance that in later European history was to be so largely set at nought : *Religionem imperare non possumus, quia nemo cogitur ut credat invitus.*[2]   [We must not enforce (acceptance of) a creed, since no one can think or can believe against his will.]   It is not one of the least of the services of Cassiodorus that

[1] Cassiodorus, *Letters*, 14.   [2] *Variæ*, ii., 17.

he should at this early date, when the bitterness of controversy was active in the Church, have been able to set a standard of wise and Christian toleration. His action had a good effect later in his own monastery and in the monasteries whose work was modelled on that of Viviers. It was only in monastic centres like Viviers and Monte Cassino, where Christian influence and educational work were held to be of more importance than theological issues, that literary activity became possible, and it was only in such monasteries that labour was expended in preserving the writings of " pagan " (that is, of classic) authors.

In 514, Cassiodorus became Consul, a title which, while no longer standing for any authority, was still held to be one of the highest honours, and in 515 he received the title of patrician. In 519, he published, under the title of *Chronicon*, an abstract of history from the deluge to the year 519. Hodgkin points out that in his record of events of the fifth century, a very large measure of favourable, or rather of partial attention is given to the annals of the Goths. Shortly after the publication of the *Chronicon*, Cassiodorus began work on his *History of the Goths*, which was finally completed in twelve books, and the chief purpose of which was to vindicate the claims of the Goths to rank among the historic nations of antiquity, by bringing them into connection with Greece and Rome, and by making the origin of Gothic history Roman. This history of Cassiodorus is known only by tradition, not a single copy of it having been preserved. The system of scribe-work in the monasteries, to which we owe nearly all of the old-world literature that has come down to us, did not prove adequate to preserve the greatest work of its founder. A treatise on the origin of the Goths by a later writer named Jordæus, concerning whom little is known, is avowedly based upon the history of Cassiodorus, and is the principal source of information concerning the character of this history.

At the time of the death of Theodoric, Cassiodorus was holding the important place of Master of the Offices, a post which combined many of the duties that would to-day be discharged by a Home Secretary, a Secretary of War, and a Postmaster-General. Under the regency of Queen Amalasuentha, Cassiodorus received his final official honour in his appointment as Prætorian Prefect. In the collection of letters published under the title of *Variæ*, Cassiodorus gives accounts of the work done by him in these various official stations, and these letters present vivid and interesting pictures of the methods of the administration of the kingdom, and also throw light upon many of its relations with foreign powers.

Cassiodorus continued to do service as minister for the successors of Amalasuentha, Athalaric, Theodadad, and Witigis, and retired from official responsibility only a few months before the capture of Ravenna by Belisarius, in 540, brought the Ostrogothic monarchy to an end. At the time of the entry of the Greek army, Cassiodorus, now a veteran of sixty years, was in retirement in his monastery in Bruttii (the modern Calabria). It was doubt-less because of the absence of Cassiodorus from the capital, that no mention is made of him in the narrative of the campaign written by Procopius the historian, who, as secretary to Belisarius, entered Rome with the latter after the victories over Witigis.

Cassiodorus must have possessed very exceptional adaptability of character, not to say elasticity of conscience, to be able, during a period extending over nearly half a century, to retain the favour of so many of the successive rulers of Italy and apparently to make his services necessary to each one of them. It is certain, however, that Italy benefited largely by the fact that through the various contests and changes of monarchs, it had been possible to preserve a certain continuity of executive policy and of administrative methods. The further fact that the " per-

petual " or at least the continuing minister was at once a
Greek and a Roman, and not only a statesman but a
scholar, and that he had succeeded in preserving through
all the devastations of civil wars and of foreign invasions
a great collection of classic books and a persistent (even
though restricted) interest in classic literature, exercised
an enormous influence upon the culture of Europe for
centuries to come. The career of Cassiodorus had, as we
have seen, been varied and honourable. It was, however,
his exceptional fortune to be able to render the most important and the most distinctive service of his life after
his life's work had apparently been completed.

Shortly after his withdrawal to Bruttii, and when, as
said, he was already more than sixty years old, he retired
to his monastery, Vivaria, and during the thirty-six years
of activity that remained for him, he not only completed
a number of important literary productions of his own,
but he organised the literary work of the monastery *scriptorium*, which served as a model for that of Monte Cassino, and, through Monte Cassino, for the long series of
Benedictine monasteries that came into existence throughout Europe. It was the hand of Cassiodorus which gave
the literary impetus to the Benedictine Order, and it was
from his magnificent collection of manuscripts, rescued
from the ruins of the libraries of Italy, that was supplied
material for the pens of thousands of monastic scribes.

After his retirement to Bruttii, Cassiodorus founded a
second monastery, known as Mons Castellius, the work of
which was planned for a more austere class of hermits
than those who had associated themselves together at
Vivaria. Of both monasteries he retained the practical
control, and, according to Trithemius (whose opinion is
accepted by Montalembert) of Vivaria he became abbot.[1]

---

[1] *Hic post aliquot conversionis suæ annos abbas electus est, et monasterio
multo tempore utiliter præfuit.*—Quoted by Migne, *Patrologia*, lxix., 498.

(He was elected abbot here several years after his conversion, and for a
long time he ruled the monastery wisely.)

Hodgkin, while himself citing the extract from Trithemius, thinks it possible that Cassiodorus never formally became abbot, but says that the direction and supervision of the work of the two monasteries rested in any case in his hands.[1]

His treatise on the Nature of the Soul (*De Anima*) was probably completed just before he began his monastic life, and was itself an evidence of the change in the direction of his thoughts and of his ideals.   Cassiodorus had now done with politics.   As Hodgkin points out, the dream of his life had been to build up an independent Italian State, strong with the strength of the Goths, and wise with the wisdom of the Romans.   It is evident that he also felt himself charged with a special responsibility in preserving for later generations the literature and the learning of the classic world.   With the destruction of the Gothic kingdom, that dream had been scattered to the winds.   The only institutions which retained a continuity of organisation were those belonging to the Church, and it was through the Church that must be preserved for later generations the thought and the scholarship of antiquity.   It was with a full understanding of this change in the nature of his responsibilities, that Cassiodorus decided to consecrate his old age to religious labours and to a work even more important than any of his political achievements : the preservation, by the pens of monastic copyists, of the Christian Scriptures, of the writings of the early Fathers, and of the great works of classical antiquity.

Some years before his retirement from Ravenna, Cassiodorus had endeavoured to induce Pope Agapetus (535–536) to found a school of theology and Christian literature at Rome, modelled on the plan of the schools of Alexandria and Nisibis.   The confusion consequent on the invasion of Italy by Belisarius had prevented the fulfilment

[1] *Letters of Cassiodorus*, 54.

of this scheme. The aged statesman was now, however, planning to accomplish, by means of his two monasteries, a similar educational work.

Hodgkin summarises the aims of earlier monasticism, (aims which were most fully carried out in the monasteries of the East and of Africa,) as follows: In the earlier days of monasticism, men like the hermits of the Thebaïd had thought of little else but mortifying the flesh by vigils and fastings, and withdrew from all human voices in order to enjoy an ecstatic communion with their Maker. The life in common of monks like those of Nitria and Lerinum had chastened some of the extravagances of these lonely enthusiasts, while still keeping in view their main purpose. S. Jerome, in his cell at Bethlehem, had shown what great results might be obtained for the Church of all ages from the patient literary toil of one religious recluse. And finally, S. Benedict, in that Rule of his, which was for centuries to be the code of monastic Christendom, had sanctified work as one of the most effectual preservatives of the bodily and spiritual health of the ascetic.

" It was the glory of Cassiodorus," says Hodgkin,[1] " that he first and pre-eminently insisted on the expediency of including intellectual labour in the sphere of monastic duties. . . . This thought [may we not say this divinely suggested thought?] in the mind of Cassiodorus was one of infinite importance to the human race. Here, on the one hand, were the vast armies of monks, whom both the unsettled state of the times and the religious ideas of the age were driving irresistibly into the cloister; and who, when immured there with only theology to occupy their minds, became, as the great cities of the East knew only too well, preachers of discord and mad fanaticism. Here, on the other hand, were the accumulated stores of two thousand years of literature, sacred and profane, the writings of Hebrew prophets, Greek philosophers, Latin rhetoricians,

[1] *Italy*, iv., 391.

perishing for want of men with leisure to transcribe them. The luxurious Roman noble with his slave amanuenses multiplying copies of his favourite authors for his own and his friends' libraries, was an almost extinct existence. With every movement of barbarian troops over Italy, whether those barbarians called themselves the men of Witigis or of Justinian, some towns were being sacked, some precious manuscripts were perishing from the world. Cassiodorus perceived that the boundless, the often wearisome leisure of the convent might be profitably spent in arresting this work of denudation, in preserving for future ages the intellectual treasure which must otherwise inevitably have perished. That this was one of the great services rendered by the monasteries to the human race, the most superficial student has learned, but not all who have learned it know that the monks' first decided impulse in this direction was derived from Cassiodorus."

The German biographer of Cassiodorus, Franz, uses similar language :

Das Verdienst, zuerst die Pflege der Wissenschaften in den Bereich der aufgeben des Klosterlichen Lebens aufgenommen zu haben, kann man mit vollem Rechte für Cassiodorus in anspruch nehmen.[1]

In the account given by Cassiodorus of the *scriptorium* of his monastery, he describes, with an enthusiasm which ought to have been contagious, the noble work done there by the *antiquarius*[2] : " He may fill his mind with the Scriptures while copying the sayings of the Lord ; with his fingers he gives life to men and arms against the wiles of the devil. As the *antiquarius* copies the words of Christ, so many wounds does he inflict upon Satan. What he writes in his cell will be scattered far and wide over distant provinces. Man multiplies the words of Heaven, and, if I may dare so to speak, the three fingers

[1] Franz, *Cassiodorus*, p. 42.
[2] *De Institutione Div. Litt.* xxx.   *Letters,* 57.

of his right hand are made to express the utterances of the Holy Trinity. The fast travelling reed writes down the holy words and thus avenges the malice of the Wicked One, who caused a reed to be used to smite the head of the Saviour." The passage here quoted refers only to the work of the copyists of the Christian Scriptures. There are other references, however, in the same work to indicate that the activity of the *scriptorium* was not confined to these, but was also employed on secular literature.[1]

The devotion and application of the monks produced in the course of years a class of scribes whose work in the transcribing and illuminating of manuscripts far surpassed in perfection and beauty the productions of the copyists of classic Rome. In the monasteries north of the Alps the work of the scribes was, for the earlier centuries, devoted principally to the production of copies of missals and other books of devotion and of portions of the Scriptures. In Italy, however, where classical culture never entirely disappeared, attention continued to be given to the transcription of the Latin texts of which any manuscripts had been preserved, and it was these transcripts of the monks of Cassiodorus and S. Benedict that gave the " copy " for the first editions of Cicero, Virgil, and the other classic writers, produced by the earliest printers of Germany and Italy.

Cassiodorus took pains to emphasise the importance of binding the sacred codices in covers worthy of the beauty of their contents, following the example of the householder in the parable, who provided wedding garments

[1] In chapter xv., after cautioning his copyists against rash corrections of apparent faults in the Sacred MSS., he says : *Ubicunque paragrammata in disertis hominibus* [Hodgkin interprets this term as referring to classical authors] *reperta fuerunt, intrepidus vitiosa recorrigat.* (Wherever mistakes in syntax are found in classical authors, he fearlessly corrects them.) The larger part of chapter xxviii. is devoted to an argument against *respuere sæcularium literarum studia* (rejecting the study of secular literature).

for all who came to the supper of his son. One pattern volume had been prepared containing samples of various sorts of covers, from which the scribe might choose that which pleased him best. The abbot had also provided, to help the nightly toil of the *scriptorium*, mechanical lamps of some ingenious construction which appears to have made them self-trimming and to have insured a continuously sufficient supply of oil. The labour of the scribes was regulated on bright days by sun-dials, and on cloudy days and during the hours of the night by water-clocks.

In order to set an example of literary diligence to his monks, and to be able to sympathise with the difficulties of scribe work, Cassiodorus himself transcribed (probably from the translation of Jerome) the Psalter, the Prophets, and the Epistles. In addition to his labours as a transcriber, Cassiodorus did a large amount of work as an original author and as a compiler. According to the judgment of Migne, Franz, and Hodgkin, the importance of his original writings varied very considerably, and is by no means to be estimated in proportion to their bulk. One of the most considerable of these was his great commentary on the Psalms, in the text of which he was able to discover refutations of all the heresies that had thus far racked the Church, together with the rudiments of all the sciences which had become known to the world. This was followed by a commentary on the Epistles and by a history of the Church, the latter having been undertaken in co-operation with his friend Epiphanius. This history, known as the *Historia Tripartita*, is said to have had a larger circulation than any other of the author's works. A fourth work, which gives more of the personality of the writer, was an educational treatise entitled, *Institutiones Divinarum et Humanarum Lectionum*. In the first part of this treatise, which bore the title of *De Institutione Divinarum Lit-*

terarum, the author gives an account of the organisation of his *scriptorium*. In the second division of the treatise, entitled *De Artibus ac Disciplinis Liberalium Litterarum*, the author states his view of the relative importance of the four liberal arts, Grammar, Rhetoric, Logic, and Mathematics, the last named of which he divides into the four " disciplines" of Arithmetic, Geometry, Music, and Astronomy. Geometry and Astronomy occupy together one page, Arithmetic and Music each two pages, Grammar two pages, Rhetoric six pages, while to Logic are devoted eighteen pages. The final production of his industrious life was a treatise called *De Orthographia*, which was completed when its author was ninety-three years old, and which was planned expressly to further the work of the monastic scribes in collecting and correcting the codices of ancient books.

The death of Cassiodorus occurred in 575, in the ninety-sixth year of his age. An inheritor of the traditions of imperial Rome, Cassiodorus had been able, in a career extending over nearly a century, to be of signal service to his country under a series of foreign rulers. He had succeeded, through his personal influence with these rulers, in maintaining for Italy an organisation based on Roman precedents, and in preserving for the society of the capital an interest in the preservation and cultivation of classic literature. When the political institutions of Italy had been shattered and the very existence of civilisation was imperilled, he had transferred his services to the Church, recognising, with the adaptability which was the special characteristic of the man, that with the Church now rested the hopes of any continuity of organised society, of intellectual interest, of civilisation itself. He brought to the Church the advantage of exceptional executive ability and of long official experience, and he also brought a large measure of scholarship and an earnest zeal for literary and educational interests. It

is not too much to say that the continuity of the thought
and civilisation of the ancient world with that of the Middle Ages was due, more than to any other one man, to the
life and labours of Cassiodorus.

S. Benedict.—The *Life of S. Benedict*, written by Pope
Gregory I. (who was born in 543, the year of the death of
the saint), was for centuries one of the most popular books
circulated in Europe.   The full title is : *Vita et Miracula
Venerabilis Benedicti conditoris, vel Abbatis Monasterii;
quod appellatur arcis Provinciæ Campaniæ.*   " The Life and
Miracles of the Venerable Benedict, Founder and Abbot
of the Monastery which is called (of) the Citadel of the
Province of Campania."   This biography was, later, translated by Pope Zacharias from the original Latin into
Greek.

The great achievement of Benedict was the one literary
product of his life, the *Regula*.   It comprises seventy-
three short chapters, probably not designed by the author
for use beyond the bounds of the communities under his
own immediate supervision.   It proved to be the thing
for which the world of religious and thoughtful men was
then longing, a complete code of monastic duty.   By a
strange parallelism, almost in the very year in which the
great Emperor Justinian was codifying the results of seven
centuries of Roman secular legislation for the benefit of
the judges and the statesmen of the new Europe, Benedict,
on his lonely mountain top, was composing his code for
the regulation of the daily life of the great civilisers of
Europe for seven centuries to come.

*The Rule of S. Benedict, Chap. 48.   Concerning Daily
Manual Labour.*—" Idleness is the enemy of the soul :
hence brethren ought at certain seasons to occupy themselves with manual labour, and again at certain hours
with holy reading.   Between Easter and the calends of
October let them apply themselves to reading from the
fourth hour until the sixth hour. . . . From the calends

of October to the beginning of Lent, let them apply themselves to reading until the second hour. During Lent,
let them apply themselves to reading from morning until
the end of the third hour, and in these days of Lent, let
them receive a book apiece from the library and read it
straight through. These books are to be given out at the
beginning of Lent." [1]

This simple regulation, uttered by one the power and
extent of whose far-reaching influence have rarely been
equalled among men, gave an impulse to study that grew
with the growth of the Order, and that secured a continuity of intellectual light and life through the dark ages,
the results of which have endured to modern times.
"Wherever a Benedictine house arose, or a monastery of
any one of the Orders, which were but offshoots from the
Benedictine tree, books were multiplied and a library
came into existence, small indeed at first, but increasing
year by year, till the wealthier houses had gathered together collections of books that would do credit to a
modern university." [2]

It was, of course, the case that the injunction to read,
an injunction given at a time when books were very few
and monks were becoming many, carried with it an instruction for writing until copies of the books prescribed
should have been produced in sufficient numbers to meet
the requirements of the readers. The *armaria* could be
filled only through steady and persistent work in the
scriptoria, and, as we shall see later, such scribe-work was
accepted not only as a part of the "manual labour" prescribed in the Rule, but not infrequently (in the case of
the skilled scribes) in lieu of some portion of the routine of
religious observance. Benedict would not have his monks
limit themselves to spiritual labour, to the action of the
soul upon itself. He made external labour, manual or
literary, a strict obligation of his Rule. The routine of

[1] From the version by Clark.   [2] Clark, 15.

the monastic day was to include seven hours for manual labour, two hours for reading.[1]   In later years, the Benedictine monasteries became centres of instruction, supplying the place, as far as was practicable, of the educational system of the departed empire.   As Order after Order was founded, there came to be a steady development of interest in books and an ever increasing care for their safe-keeping.   S. Benedict had contented himself with general directions for study ; the Cluniacs prescribed the selection of a special officer to take charge of the books, with an annual audit of them and the assignment to each brother of a single volume.

" The followers of the Saint continued in their patient labour, praying, digging, and transcribing.   The *scriptoria* of the Benedictine monastery will multiply copies not only of missals and theological treatises, but of the poems and histories of antiquity.   Whatever may have been the religious value or the religious dangers of the monastic life, the historian at least is bound to express his gratitude to these men, without whose life-long toil the great deeds and thoughts of Greece and Rome might have been as completely lost to us as the wars of the buried Lake-dwellers or the thoughts of the Palæolithic man.   To take an illustration from S. Benedict's own beloved Subiaco, the work of his disciples has been like one of the great aqueducts of the valley of the Arno—sometimes carried underground for centuries through the obscurity of unremembered existence, sometimes emerging to the daylight and borne high upon the arcade of noble lives, but equally through all its course, bearing the precious stream of ancient thought from the far off hills of time into the humming and crowded cities of modern civilisation." [2]

The Earlier Monkish Scribes.—The literary work begun under the direction of Cassiodorus in the *scrip-*

[1] Montalembert, ii., 45.   [2] Hodgkin, *Italy*, iv., 497, 498.

torium of Viviers, and enjoined by S. Benedict upon his monks at Monte Cassino, was, as said, carried on by successive generations of monastic scribes during a number of centuries. In fact, until the organisation of the older universities, in the latter part of the twelfth and the beginning of the thirteenth century, the production and the reproduction of literature was practically confined to the monasteries. " The monasteries," says Maitland, in his erudite and vivacious work, *The Dark Ages*, " were, in those days of misrule and turbulence, beyond all price not only as places where (it may be imperfectly, but better than elsewhere) God was worshipped, . . . but as central points whence agriculture was to spread over bleak hills and barren downs and marshy plains, and deal its bread to millions perishing with hunger and its pestilential train ; as repositories of the learning which then was, and as well-springs for the learning which was to be ; as nurseries of art and science, giving to invention the stimulus, the means, and the reward ; and attracting to themselves every head that could devise and every hand that could execute ; as the nucleus of the city which in after days of pride should crown its palaces and bulwarks with the towering cross of its cathedral."[1] It was fortunate for the literary future of Europe that the Benedictine Order, which had charged itself with literary responsibilities, should have secured almost from the outset so considerable a development and should for centuries have remained the greatest and most influential of all the monastic orders. At the beginning of the ninth century, Charlemagne ordered an inquiry to be made (as into a matter requiring careful research) as to whether there were any monks who professed any other rule than the Rule of S. Benedict ; from which it would appear that such monks were considered as rare and noteworthy exceptions.

[1] *The Dark Ages*, London, 1845, Preface.

While the two monasteries of Cassiodorus in Calabria and the Benedictine foundation of Monte Cassino near Naples, were entitled to first reference on the ground of the exceptional influence exercised by them upon the literary development of the monks, they were by no means the earliest of the western monastic foundations. This honour belongs, according to Denk,[1] to the monastery of Ligugé, near Poitiers (Monasterium Locociagense), founded in 360 A.D. by Bishop Martin of Tours. The second in point of date, that of Marmoutier, near Tours, was instituted by the same bishop a year or two later. Gaul proved to be favourable ground for the spread of monastic tenets and influence, and by the year 400 its foundations included over two thousand monks.

In 405, S. Honoratus, later Bishop of Arles, founded a monastery on the island of Lerin, on the south coast of France, which became a most important centre of learning and the mother of many monasteries.[2] In the educational work carried on at Lerin, full consideration was given to classic authors, such as Cicero, Virgil, and Xenophon, as well as to the writings of the Fathers, and the scribes were kept busied in the production of copies.

There must have been a certain amount of literary activity also in the monasteries of the East and of Africa some time before any of the monastic foundations in Europe had come into existence. The numerous writings of the Fathers secured a wide circulation among the faithful, a circulation which could have been possible only through the existence of efficient staffs of skilled scribes and in connection with some system of distribution between widely separated churches. Teachers like Origen in Cæsarea, in the third century, and S. Jerome in Bethlehem and S. Augustine in Hippo, in the fifth century, put

---

[1] *Gesch. des Gallo—Frankischen Unterrichts und Bildungs-wesens von den ältesten Zeiten bis auf Karl den Grossen*, Mainz, 1892, p. 37.

[2] Montalembert, *The Monks of the West*, i., 225.

forth long series of writings, religious, philosophical, and
polemical, with apparently an assured confidence that
these would reach wide circles of contemporary readers,
and that they would be preserved also for generations to
come. The sacking of Rome by Alaric (in 410) is used
by S. Augustine as a text or occasion for the publication
of his beautiful conception of "The City of God" in
much the same manner as a preacher of later times might
have based a homily on the burning of Moscow or the
fall of Paris. The preacher of Hippo speaks as if he were
addressing, not the small circle of his African diocese, but
mankind at large. And he was, of course, justified in his
faith, for the *De Civitate Dei* was the book which, next to
the Scriptures, was most surely to be found in every
monastery in Europe, while when the work of the *scripto-*
rium was replaced by the printing-press, it became one of
the most frequently printed books in Europe. It appears
from a reference by S. Augustine, that nuns as well as
monks were included among the African scribes. In
speaking of a nun named Melania, who, early in the fifth
century, founded a convent at Tagaste, near Carthage, he
says that she had "gained her living by transcribing
manuscripts," and mentions that she wrote swiftly, beautifully, and correctly,—*scribebat et celeriter et pulchre, citra*
errorem.[1]

The scribe-work in the monasteries of Africa and of the
East was, therefore, sufficiently effective to preserve large
portions of the writings of the Fathers and of other early
Christian teachers, and it is, in fact, to the libraries of
these Eastern monasteries that is chiefly due the preservation of the long series of Greek texts which found
their way into Europe after the Renaissance. I have, however, been able to find no record of the system pursued in
the *scriptoria* and *armaria* of the Greek monasteries, and
the narrative in the present chapter is, therefore, confined

[1] *Epistle*, 225. Cited by Montalembert.

to a sketch of the literary undertakings of the monks of the West.

The earliest known example of the work of a European monk dates from the year 517. The manuscript is in the Capitular library in Verona, and has been reproduced in fac-simile by Ottley. The script is that known as half uncial.[1] At the time this manuscript was being written, Theodoric the Goth was ruling in Italy, with Cassiodorus as his minister, and the monastery at Viviers was still to be founded.

S. Gregory the Great, who became Pope in 590, exercised an important influence over the intellectual interests of his age. Gregory had been charged with having destroyed the ancient monuments of Rome, with having burned the Palatine library, including the writings of Cicero and Livy, with having expelled the mathematicians from Rome, and with having reprimanded Bishop Didier of Vienna (in Gaul) for teaching grammar to children. Montalembert contends that these charges are all slanders and that the Pope was not only an unequalled scholar, but that he fully appreciated the importance for the intellectual development of the Church, of a knowledge of the classics. Gregory is quoted as saying, in substance: "The devils know well that the knowledge of profane literature helps us to understand sacred literature. In dissuading us from this study, they act as the Philistines did when they interdicted the Israelites from making swords and lances, and obliged that nation to come to them for the sharpening of their axes and plough-shares."[2] Gregory was himself the author of a considerable series of writings, and, while his Latin was not that of Cicero, he contributed (according to Ozanam) as much as did S. Augustine to form the new Latin, what might be called the Christian Latin, which was destined to become

[1] Denk, 127.
[2] Liv. v. *Primum Regum*, ch. xxx., Sec. 30. Montalembert, i., p. 144.

the language of the pulpit and the school, and which forms the more immediate foundation of an important group of the languages of modern Europe.

His works include the *Sacramentary*, which determined the language and the form of the Liturgy, a series of *Dialogues*, and a *Pastoral*, in which were collected a series of discourses planned to regulate the vocation, life, and doctrines of the pastors. Of this book, Ozanam says that it gave form and life to the entire hierarchical body. Then came a series of commentaries on the Scriptures, followed by no less than thirty-five books called *Moralia*, which were commentaries on the Book of Job. His last important production was a series of *Epistles*, comprised in thirteen volumes. He may possibly have been the most voluminous author since classic times, and his books had the special advantage of reaching circles of readers who were waiting for them, and of being distributed through the already extended machinery of the Church.

Another important ecclesiastical author of the same generation was Isidore, Bishop of Seville. The Spanish Liturgy compiled by him and known as the Mozarabic, survived the ruin of the Visigothic Church and was thought by the great Cardinal Ximenes worthy of resuscitation. Isidore also wrote a history of the Goths and a translation of the philosophy of Aristotle. He may be considered as the first scholar to introduce to Europe of the Middle Ages the teachings of Greek philosophy. His greatest undertaking was, however, in the form of an encyclopædia, treating, under the heading of the Seven Liberal Arts, of all the learning that was within his reach. It was entitled *Twenty Books of Etymologies*, or *The Origin of Things*, and included in its volumes a number of classical fragments which, without the care of its editor, would probably have perished forever.

Isidore is the first Christian who arranged and edited for Christians the literature of antiquity. He died in 636,

but the incentive that he had given to learning and to
literature survived him in a numerous group of disciples.[1]
Among Isidore's pupils was King Sisebut, whose interest
in scholarship caused him to endow liberally a number of
the Spanish monasteries.

**The Ecclesiastical Schools and the Clerics as
Scribes.**—The so-called secular clergy were, during the
earlier Middle Ages, employed very largely in connection
with the business of the government, being in fact in
many regions the only class of the population possessing
the education necessary for the preparation of documents
and the preservation of records.   In Italy, towards the
close of the thirteenth century, there came into existence
the class of *notaries* who took charge of a good many business details which in Germany and France were cared for
by the clergy.   Under the Merovingian kings, there were
government officials and judiciary officials who were laymen.   During the rule of the Carlovingians, however, the
writing work of the chapel and of the government offices
was consolidated, falling into the hands of the clerics, or
secular clergy.   For a number of centuries, outside of
Italy, it was very exceptional for any documents or for
any correspondence to be written by other than the
clergy.   Every citizen of importance was obliged to have
his special *clericus, clerc,* or *pfaff,* who took care of his
correspondence and accounts.   A post of this kind was
in fact the surest means for an ambitious priest to secure
in the first place, a footing in the world, and later, ecclesiastical positions and income.   The secretary or chancellor
of the king, was almost always, as a matter of routine,
sooner or later rewarded with a bishopric.

Charlemagne took from among the poor boys in the
court school, one, who was described as *optimus dictator
et scriptor,* and having trained him as chaplain and secretary, provided for him later a bishopric.[2]

---

[1] Ozanam, *La Civilisation Chrétienne chez les Francs,* c. 9.
[2] Koepke, *Otton. Studien,* ii., p. 387.

The use of the word *dictator* is to be noted as indicating the mediæval employment of the term in connection with writing. *Dictare* seems, from an early date, to have been used in the first place to indicate instruction in the art of writing, while later it is employed constantly to specify the direct work of the writer or composer, in the sense in which one would say to-day that he had indited a letter. With the same general sense, the term *dictamen* is used for the thing indited or for a composition. Hroswitha, the nun of Gandersheim (whose poems later had the honour of forming the material for one of the first books printed in South Germany), used the term *dictare* continually for activity in authorship. Wattenbach quotes from the *Legenda Aurea* of S. Ambrose the words *libros quos dictabat propria manu scribebat* (he wrote out with his own hand the books that he composed).

As long as any portions of the Roman Empire held together and the classic culture still preserved its influence, a considerable class of men secured their support through work as scribes. In Italy this class seems never entirely to have disappeared. Some small circles of the people retained, even after the land had been many times overrun by invaders, some interest in the classics, and were prepared to pay for more or less trustworthy manuscript copies of these. In Italy also there appears to have been a much larger use of writing in connection with trade and commerce than obtained throughout the rest of Europe until a much later time. While in Germany and France such scholarship as remained was restricted almost entirely to the ecclesiastics and to the monastery centres, in Italy the Church, during the earlier period, took a smaller interest in scholarship. There came into existence, however, a group of literary laymen, who were in a measure a continuation of or a succession to the old Latin grammarians, and who maintained some of their interest in classic culture and preserved, however imperfectly, some remnants of classic knowledge.

Wattenbach quotes the words of Gerbert,[1] *Nosti Quot Scriptores in Urbibus aut in Agris Italiæ Passim Habeantur* (you know how many writers there are here and there throughout the cities and fields of Italy).

The schools established under the rule of the Lombards helped to preserve the art of writing and to widen the range of its experts. By the time, therefore, of the establishment of the earlier Italian universities, an organised class of scribes was already in existence whose skill could be utilised for university work, and, as will be shown more specifically in a later chapter, the universities took these scribes under their jurisdiction and extended over them the protection of university privilege.[2]

In France, after the time of Charlemagne, it was the case, as we have seen, that those who had any educational or literary ambitions were almost necessarily obliged to become ecclesiastics, as it was only in monasteries and in the training schools attached to the monasteries, that the necessary education could be secured. As one result of this, the number of ecclesiastics increased much more rapidly than the number of places in which they could be occupied or of foundations upon which they could be supported. Priests for whom no priestly work was found became, therefore, what might be called lay-clerics, and were employed in connection with the work of the courts, or of magistrates, or as scribes and secretaries.

In this manner there came into the hands of these lay-clerics, not only the management of correspondence, personal, official, and diplomatic, but a very large proportion of the direction of the affairs with which such correspondence had to do. As far, therefore, as the clerical personality represented ecclesiastical purposes and aims, the influence of ecclesiasticism must have been very

[1] Ep. 130.
[2] Wattenbach, *Das Schriftwesen im Mittelalter*, p. 396.

much greater during the age in which the art of writing was confined to the Church than at any earlier or any later period of the world's history. Such influence was, however, probably less in fact than in appearance, as it seems to have been the case that a very large proportion of such clerics were priests in name only, and that their interests, purposes, and ambitions were outside of the Church, and were not necessarily even in sympathy with the development of the control of the Church over the affairs of the world.

Wattenbach is of opinion that the scribes of this period secured a larger return for their work than came to any other class of labourers or officials. Among many other examples, he gives a quotation from Dümmler concerning a Lombard cleric of Rotland, named Anselm, who, in 1050, prided himself upon the number of books he had written, and said: *Multos oportet libros scriberes, ut inde precium sumeres, quo a tuis lenonibus te redimeres.*[1] (You ought to write many books in order to obtain money with which to buy yourself off from those having claims upon you.)

Notker wrote in 1020 to the Bishop of Sitten, who wanted to obtain some books: *Si vultis ea, sumtibus enim indigent, mittite plures pergamenas et scribentibus præmia et suscipietis eorum exempla.*[2] (If you want these books, you must send more parchment and also moneys, for the scribes are in need. You will then receive your copies.)

In the twelfth century, the monks of Tegernsee, under the Abbot Rupert, were working on the production of the books for the library of some noble lady.[3] The Brother Liaupold, in Mallerstorf, spoke of having "earned much money through his pen." This happened in the last quarter of the twelfth century. The lines quoted by

---

[1] Dümmler, *Anselm der Peripatetiker*, 32.
[2] Grimm, J., *Kleine Schriften*, v., 190.
[3] *Pez, Thes.*, vi., 2.

Wattenbach were found upon a manuscript bearing Liaupold's name.[1]

For the libraries of their own monasteries, the monks
worked without direct pay, and it was only later, as the
ambition of the librarians increased or as the business of
distributing copies of manuscripts became more important,
that the monasteries found it worth while to employ,
either in place of or in addition to their own monks,
scribes from outside.   In Salzburg, Pastor Peter Gril-
linger paid, in 1435, to the scribes of the neighbouring
monasteries three hundred gulden for the production of a
Bible (probably an illuminated copy), and presented this
to the library of the Cathedral.[2]

In the accounts of the monastery at Aldersbach, Rockinger finds entries, in 1304, of payments for *scriptores
librorum.*

The well-known manuscript of Henri Bohic was written
in 1374 by a monk of Corbie, who, according to the cash
record of his monastery, received for his work, in addition
to the parchment and other materials, the sum of thirty-
six solidos.   For the monastery at St. Gall, Mathias Burer,
of Lindau, who was chaplain in Meminger, and who died
in 1485, wrote twenty-four volumes.

In 1470, the same Burer gave to the monastery, in exchange for a benefice, his entire library.   The record does
not specify how many volumes the library comprised.   In
1350, a certain Constantine was arrested in Erfurt as a
heretic.   Special efforts were made to save him from
death or banishment on the ground that he was a skilled
scribe.   The record does not appear to show whether or
not this plea was successful.

Conrad de Mure speaks of women working as scribes
during the latter part of the thirteenth century.   It is
probable that these women were nuns, but it is not so

[1] *Das Schriftwesen*, p. 399.
[2] *Barstch, im anz. d. Germ. Mus.*, v. 293.

specified. In the *Histoire de l'Imprimerie*[1] reference is
made to a woman who appears to have acted as an independent scribe—that is to say, not to have been attached
to the university or to the guild of booksellers.

On the tax list of Paris, in 1292, are recorded twenty-four
escrivains.[2] It is probable that the actual number was
much greater, as the scribes who were ecclesiastics were
exempt from taxation, and their names, therefore, would
not have appeared upon the list.

In 1460, a certain Ducret, *clerc à Dijon*, received from
the Duke for his work as scribe, a groschen for each sheet,
which is referred to as the *prix accoustumé.*[3]

In 1401, Peter of Bacharach, described as a citizen of
Mainz, wrote out for the Court at Eltville (Elfeld) a *Schwabenspiegel.* This is to be noted because it is an example of
scribe work being done by one who was not a cleric.
Burkard Zink tells us that in 1420, being in Augsburg, he
took unto himself a wife. She had nothing and he had
nothing, but she earned money with her spinning-wheel
and he with his pen. In the first week he wrote *vier
sextern des grossen papiers, karta regal*, and the ecclesiastics for whom the work was being done were so well
pleased with it that they gave him for two sexterns four
groschen. His week's work brought him sixteen groschen,
or forty cents.[4] Clara Hatzlern, a citizen of Augsburg, is
recorded as having written for money between the years
1452 and 1476. A copy of a *Schwabenspiegel* transcribed
by her was contained in the collection at Lambach.[5]

The examples named indicate what was, in any case,
probably the only class of scribe work done outside of the
monasteries and outside of the universities or before the

---

[1] Paris, 1852, page 54.
[2] Geraud, *Paris sous Philippe-le-Bel*, 1837, p. 506.
[3] Lalanne, *Curiosités Bibl.*, p. 318.
[4] *Die Chroniken der Deutschen Stadte*, v., 129.
[5] Barack, *Handschriften zu Donaueschingen*, p. 564.

university period, by the few laymen who were able to write. Their labour was devoted exclusively to the production of books in the tongue of the people ; if work in Latin were required, it was still necessary (at least until the institution in the thirteenth century of university scribes) to apply to the monasteries. With the development of literature in Italy, during the following century, there came many complaints concerning the lack of educated scribes competent to manifold the works. These complaints, as well as to the lack of writers as concerning the ignorance and carelessness shown in their work, continued as late as the time of the Humanists, and are repeated by Petrarch and Boccaccio.

Terms Used for Scribe-Work.—With the Greeks, the term γραμματεύς denoted frequently a "magistrate." The term ταχυγράφοι corresponded as nearly as might be with our "stenographer." For this the Romans used the form *notarius*. The scribes whose work was devoted to books were called, under the later empire, *bibliographoi* or καλλιγράφοι. The name καλλιγράφος was applied to the Emperor, Theodosius II. Montfaucon gives a list of the names of the Greek scribes who were known to him.[1] The oldest dates from 759, and the next in order from 890 A.D. The oldest Plato manuscript in the Bodleian library was written in 896 for the Diaconus Arethas of Patras. Arethas was, later, Archbishop of Cæsarea, and had also had written for him a Euclid, and in 914 a group of theological works. His scribes were the *calligraph* John, a cleric named Stephen, and a *notarius* whose name is not given.[2]

The terms *librarius*, *scriptor*, and *antiquarius* were also used for scribes making copies of books, while *notarius* was more likely to denote a clerk whose work was limited to the preparation of documents. Alcuin speaks of employing *notarii*.

[1] Wattenbach, 351.   [2] Wattenbach, 351.

In the inscription in a manuscript by Engelberg of the twelfth century, we find the lines: *Hic Augustini liber est atque Frowini ; alter dictavit, alter scribendo notavit.*[1] This indicates that Augustine was the author, while Frowin served as scribe. A manuscript of the sixth century, contained in the Chapter-House library in Verona, bears the signature *Antiquarius Eulalius.* A manuscript of Orosius, written in the seventh century, is inscribed : *Confectus codex in statione Viliaric Antiquarii.* (A codex completed in the writing-stall of Viliaric the scribe.) This scribe was probably a Goth, as among the signatures in a Ravenna document, containing the list of the clerics of the Gothic Church, occurs the name *Viljaric bokareis.*[2] Otto von Freising says of his *notarius*, Ragewin : *Qui hanc historiam ex ore nostro subnotavit* (who wrote down this story from my lips) ; and Gunther, in 1212, complains of a headache which he had brought upon himself *ut verba inventa notario vix possim exprimere*, that is in the attempt to shape the words that he was dictating to his clerks. It was in Italy that the *notarii* first became of sufficient importance to organise themselves into a profession and to undertake the training, for other work, of young scribes, and it was from Italy that the scribes were gradually distributed throughout Europe. Their most important employment for some time in Italy was in connection with the work of the Church, and particularly in the preparation and manifolding of the documents sent out from Rome. The special script that was adopted for the work of the Papal office was known as *scripta notaria.*[3]

According to Wattenbach, the use of papyrus for the documents of the Church, and even for the Papal Bulls, extended as late as the tenth century. Sickel speaks of a

---

[1] Rahn, *Gesch. der Bildenden Künste in der Schweiz*, i., 34.

[2] Massmann, *Die Goth. Urkunden von Neapel und Arezzo*, Wien, 1838, 402.

[3] Wattenbach, 90.

Bull of Benedict VIII., of 1022, as the latest known to him which is written on papyrus.

The term *chartularii*, or *cartularii*, was applied to clerics originally trained for the work of the Church, but who occasionally devoted themselves also to the manifolding of books.   In the memoir of Arnest, who was the first Archbishop of Prague, it was related that he always kept three *cartularii* at work in the transcribing of books.   In the twelfth century, Ordericus speaks of the monks who write books both as *antiquarii* and as *librarii*.[1]   Richard de Bury uses the term in describing the renewal of old manuscripts, and restricts it to scribes who possessed scholarly and critical knowledge.   Petrarch makes a similar application.[2]   The term *dictare* was, during the Middle Ages, usually employed to describe the author's work in composing, or in composing and writing with his own hand, and bears but seldom the meaning of " dictate."   The proper rendering would be more nearly our word " indite."

The term used during the earlier Middle Ages to denote the Scriptures was not *Biblia*, but *Bibliotheca*.   According to Maitland, the latter term has its origin with S. Jerome, who, in offering to lend books to his correspondent Florentius, writes: . . . *et quoniam largiente Domino, multis sacræ bibliothecæ codicibus abundamus*, etc.[3] (And since by the grace of God, we possess a great many codices of the sacred writings.)

In nearly every instance in which reference is made to the complete collection of the Scriptures, the term used is *Bibliotheca integra*, or *Bibliotheca tota*.   It was evidently the case that for centuries after the acceptance of the Canon, the several divisions or books of which the Bible consists were still frequently considered in the light of separate and independent works, and were transcribed and circulated separately.

---

[1] Wattenbach, 357.
[2] *De Remediis Utriusque Fortunæ*, lib. i., dial. 43.
[3] Ep. vi., *Ad Flor.*, i., 19.

S. Columba, the Apostle to Caledonia.—One of the earliest of the monks of the North of Europe whose life was associated with scholarship and intellectual influence, was S. Columba, the Apostle to Caledonia, whose life covered the term between the years 521 and 597. Columba belongs to the list of Irish saints, although the larger portion of his life's work was done in Scotland. Before he had reached the age of twenty-five, he had presided over the foundation of no less than twenty-seven monasteries in Ireland, the oldest of which were Darrow and Derry; the latter, having long been the seat of a great Catholic bishopric, became, under its modern name of Londonderry, the bulwark of the Protestant contest against the efforts of the last of the Stuart kings.

The texts have been preserved of a number of songs ascribed to Columba, and, whether or not these verses were really the work of the monk, the tradition that he was the first of the Irish poets doubtless has foundation. In the time of Columba, the Irish monasteries already possessed texts in greater quantity than could be found in the monasteries of Scotland or England, but even in Ireland manuscripts were rare and costly, and were preserved with jealous care in the monastic libraries. Not only was very great value put upon these volumes, but they were even supposed to possess the emotions and the passions of living beings. Columba was himself a collector of manuscripts, and his biography by O'Donnell attributes to him the laborious feat of having transcribed with his own hand three hundred copies of the Psalter. According to one of the stories, Columba journeyed to Ossory in the south-west to visit a holy and very learned recluse, a doctor of laws and philosophy, named Longarad. Columba asked leave to examine the doctor's books, and when the old man refused, the monk burst out in an imprecation: "May thy books no longer do thee any good, neither to them who come after thee, since thou

takest occasion by them to show thine inhospitality."
The curse was heard, and after Longarad died, his books
became unintelligible. An author of the ninth century
says that the books still existed, but that no man could
read them.[1]

Another story speaks of Columba's undertaking, while
visiting his ancient master Finnian, to make a clandestine
and hurried copy of the abbot's Psalter. He shut himself up at night in the church where the Psalter was
deposited, and the light needed for his nocturnal work
radiated from his left hand while he wrote with the right.
A curious wanderer, passing the church, was attracted by
the singular light, and looked in through the keyhole, and
while his face was pressed against the door his eye was
suddenly torn out by a crane which was roosting in the
church. The wanderer went with his story to the abbot,
and Finnian, indignant at what he considered to be a
theft, claimed from Columba the copy which the monk
had prepared, contending that a copy made without permission ought to belong to the owner of the original, on
the ground that the transcript is the offspring of the
original work. As far as I have been able to ascertain,
this is the first instance which occurs in the history of
European literature of a contention for copyright.
Columba refused to give up his manuscript, and the
question was referred to King Diarmid, or Dermott, in
the palace at Tara. The King's judgment was given in a
rustic phrase which has passed into a proverb in Ireland:
"To every cow her calf [*le gach boin a boinin*], and conse-
quently to every book its copy."[2]

Columba protested loudly, and threatened the King
with vengeance. He retired to his own province chanting
the song of trust, the text of which has been preserved
and which is sacred as one of the most authentic relics of

[1] *Festilogium of Angus the Culdee.*   Quoted by O'Curry.
[2] Montalembert, iii., 122.

the ancient Irish tongue. He succeeded in arousing
against the King the great and powerful clans of his relatives and friends, and after a fierce struggle the King was
overcome and was obliged to take refuge at Tara.

The manuscript which had been the object of this
strange conflict of copyright, a conflict which developed
into a civil war, was afterwards venerated as a kind of national military and religious palladium. Under the name
of *Cathac*, or "the fighter," the Latin Psalter said to have
been transcribed by Columba was enshrined in the base of a
portable altar as the national relic of the O'Donnell clan.
It was preserved for 1300 years in the O'Donnell family,
and as late as 1867, belonged to a baronet of that name,
who placed it on exhibition in the Museum of the Royal
Irish Academy. O'Curry prints a fac-simile of a fragment
of the manuscript, which he believes to be in the hand-
writing of S. Columba, and O'Curry and Reeves are in
accord in the opinion that the famous copy of the Gospels
known as the "Book of Kells" is also the work of the
poet monk.[1]

After the successful issue of his contest with Finnian,
S. Columba journeyed through Gaul, making a kind of
expiatory pilgrimage for the purpose of atoning for the
bloodshed of which he had been the cause. He remained
in Gaul long enough to found the monasteries of Anagray,
Luxeuil, and Fontaine. Having for some reason been
banished from Gaul, he went to Italy, where he founded,
near Milan, the monastery of Bobbio. He returned to
Ireland, but finding himself still oppressed with a sense
of blood-guiltiness, he finally took up his abode in the
desolate little island of Iona, on the coast of Scotland.
Other refugees were attracted to the island by the fame
of the saint, and there finally came into existence on
the barren rocks a great monastery which for centuries
exercised throughout Britain and North Europe a wide-

[1] Montalembert, iii., 127.

spread influence in behalf of higher Christianity and of intellectual life.

From Iona and its associated monasteries of Ireland and Scotland came scholarly teachers to France and Germany whose influence was important in giving a new direction to the work of later generations of monks. Among the Continental monasteries in which was developed through such influence a higher range of scholarly activity, were Luxeuil (in the Vosges Mountains), Corbie (on the Somme), Bobbio (in Lombardy), and St. Gall (in Switzerland). Wattenbach says that, notwithstanding their scholarly knowledge, these Scotch monks were wild and careless in their orthography. As an example of the barbarity of style and of form, he quotes a manuscript of the date of 750 (written during the rule of Pepin).

A number of years later, when, through the monks of Iona and under the general direction of S. Columba, a number of monasteries had been founded throughout Scotland, Columba had occasion to plead before the Parliament of Drumceitt in behalf of the Bards, who might be called the authors of their time, and with whom the poet monk had a keen personal sympathy. The Bards of Ireland and Britain were at once the poets, the genealogists, the historians, and the musicians of their countries, and their position and their influence constituted a very characteristic feature of Celtic life in the centuries between 500 and 800.

The Irish nation, always enamoured of its traditions, its fabulous antiquity, and its local glories, regarded with ardent sympathy the men who could clothe in a poetic dress all the law and the superstitions of the past, and who could give literary form and force to the passions and the interests of the present. The Bards were divided into three orders: The *Fileas*, who sang of religion and war; the *Brehons*, whose name is associated with the ancient laws of the country which they versified and

recited; and the *Seanachies*, who enshrined in verse the
national history and antiquities, and, above all, the gene-
alogies and the prerogatives of the ancient families who
were regarded as especially representative of the national
and warlike passions of the Irish people.[1]

The great influence and power enjoyed by the Bards
had naturally produced not a few abuses, and at the time
of the Parliament of Drumceitt their popularity had
suffered and a violent opposition had been raised against
them. They were charged with insolence and with greed,
and they were particularly censured for having made a
traffic and a trade of their poetry, a charge which recalls
some of the criticisms of classic times.

The enmities raised against them had gathered so much
force that King Aedh found himself compelled to propose
to the Assembly of Drumceitt the abolition of the Order
and the abandonment, or, as one authority suggests, the
massacre of the Bards. It would appear as if Ireland had
been suffering from an excess of poetic utterances and
felt that some revolutionary methods were required in
order to restore to the land quiet and peace. Montalembert is of opinion that the clergy did not take any
part in the prosecution of a class which they might, not
unnaturally, have regarded as their rivals. The Bards
had, however, for the most part kept in friendly relations
with the bishops, monks, and saints, and each monastery,
like each prince and lord, possessed a Bard (who in later
years became an annalist) whose chief office it was to sing
the glory and record the history of the community.

Nevertheless, the Bards were certainly, as a body, a
residuum of the paganism that had been so recently
supplanted, and it is probable that the Church, if not join-
ing in the onslaught upon their body, was not prepared
to take any active part in their defence. It seems as if
the decision of the Assembly, under the influence of King

[1] Montalembert, iii., 193.

Aedh, would certainly have been adverse to the poets. It was Columba, the poet monk, who saved them. He, who was born a poet and who, to the last day of his life, remained a poet, interceded for the Bards with such eloquence and earnestness that his plea had to be listened to. He claimed that the general exile of the poets would be the death of a venerated antiquity and of a literature which was a part of the country's life. "The bright corn must not be burned," he said, "because of the weeds that mingled with it." [1]   Influenced by his impassioned plea, the Assembly yielded at length, under the condition that the number of Bards should be henceforth limited and that the Order should be placed under certain rules to be framed by Columba himself. Thus poetry was to continue to exist, but it was not to be allowed to oppress the community with its redundance.

It is doubtless the case that one reason for the exceptional fame of Columba and the large amount of legendary detail that has been preserved of his achievements, was this great service that he had rendered to the poets of his time. They showed their gratitude by exalting his glory in numberless songs and recitals, and it is chiefly from these that has been made up the narrative of the saint's life. Another result of this intervention on the part of the monk for the protection of the poets was a still closer association between the Church and the literary spirit of the age. All antagonism between the religious ideal and the influence of the poetry of the Bards seems from this time to have disappeared. The songs of the Bards were no longer in any measure devoted to the cause of paganism, but music and poetry became closely identified with the ideals of the Church and with the work of the monasteries. The Church had preserved the poets, and poetry became the faithful handmaid of the Church.

[1] Adamnani, *Vita S. Columbæ*, edit. J. T. Forster, Introduction.

Nuns as Scribes.—One of the oldest rules relating to convents, that of S. Cæsarius of Arles, instituted in the fifth century and brought a hundred years later to Poitiers by S. Radegonde, required that all the sisters should be able to read and that they should devote two hours a day to study—*Omnes bonæ litteras discant*, etc.[1]

While the educational work in the convent schools was for the most part not carried on beyond what might be called elementary classes, there were not a few examples of abbesses whose scholastic attainments would rival those of the abbots. Montalembert speaks of convents founded, under the auspices of S. Jerome, by S. Paula and her daughter, and is not prepared to admit that in any essential detail the history of S. Paula is legendary. He reminds us that Hebrew and Greek were the daily study of these two admirable women, who advised S. Jerome in all his difficulties and cheered him under all discouragements.[2] Montalembert is probably on firmer ground when he speaks of the scholarly attainments of S. Aura, the friend of S. Eloi, and of the nun Bertile, whose learned lectures on Holy Scripture drew to Chelles in the sixth century a large concourse of auditors of both sexes. S. Radegonde, known by her profound studies of the three Fathers, S. Gregory, S. Basle, and S. Athanasius, is commemorated by Fortunatus, as is also Gertrude, Abbess of Nivelle, who sent messengers to Rome and to Ireland to buy books.[3] I do not find a record of the date of these book-buying expeditions of the abbess.

In Germany, the list of the learned nuns includes S. Lioba, who was said to be so eager for knowledge that she never left her books except for divine service. She was a pupil of S. Boniface, and to her was due the framing of the system of instruction instituted after the mission of S. Boniface in North Germany.

[1] Montalembert, vi., 167.   [2] Montalembert, vi., 169.
[3] *Fortunat. Oper.*, lib. viii., c. i.

Hroswitha, the illustrious nun of Gandersheim (who died
in 997), has been referred to more than once. Hroswitha's
dramatic poetry has been preserved for nearly eight
centuries, and has had the honour of being reprinted as
late as 1857. Her writings included a history in verse of
Otho the Great, and the lives of several saints. Her
most important works, however, were sacred dramas composed by her to be acted by the nuns of the convent. M.
Magin points out that these dramas show an intimate
acquaintance with the authors of classic antiquity.[1] Curiously enough, there was, nearly a century earlier, another
Hroswitha in Gandersheim, who was the daughter of the
Duke of Saxony, and who became the fourth abbess of
the convent. She composed a much esteemed treatise on
logic.[2]

Cecilia, daughter of William the Conqueror, who was
Abbess of Kucaen, won fame for her school in grammar,
philosophy, and in poetry. Herrad of Landsberg, who
governed forty-six noble nuns at Mont St. Odile in Alsace,
composed, under the name of *Hortus Delictarum*, a sort
of cosmology, which is recorded as the first attempt at a
scientific encyclopædia, and which is noted for the breadth
of its ideas on painting, philosophy, mythology, and history. This was issued shortly after the death of William
the Conqueror.[3] To the Abbess of Eichstadt, who died
about 1120, Germany is indebted for the preservation of
the *Heldenbuch*, a treasury of heroic stories.[4]

The principal and most constant occupation of the
learned Benedictine nuns was the transcription of manuscripts. It is difficult to estimate too highly the extent of
the services rendered by these feminine hands to learning
and to history throughout the Middle Ages. They brought

[1] *Théâtre de Hroswitha*, Paris, 1857.
[2] *Hist. Litt. de France*, ix., 130.
[3] Engelhart, *Herrad von Landsberg und ihr Werk*, Stuttgart, 1818.
[4] Görres, *Histor. Polit. Blätter*, xviii., 482.

to the work a dexterity, an elegance of attainment, and an assiduity which the monks themselves could not attain, and some of the most beautiful specimens of caligraphy which have been preserved from the Middle Ages are the work of the nuns. The devotion of nuns as scribes began indeed with the early ages of Christian times. Eusebius speaks of young maidens whom the learned men of his time employed as copyists.[1] In the fifth century, S. Melania the younger distinguished herself by the beauty and exactness of her transcripts.[2] In the sixth century, the nuns of the convent at Arles, incited by the example of the Abbess of St. Césaire, acquired a no less brilliant reputation. In the seventh century, S. Gertrude, who was learned in the Holy Scriptures, sent to Rome to ask not only for works of the highest Christian poetry, but also for teachers capable of instructing her nuns to comprehend certain allegories.[3] In the eighth century, S. Boniface begged the abbess to write out for him in golden letters the Epistle of S. Peter. Cæsarius of Arles gave instructions that in the convents which had been founded by him and the supervision of which rested with his sister, the "Virgins of Christ" should give their time between their prayers and psalms to the reading and to the writing of holy works.[4] In the eighth century the nuns of Maseyk, in Holland, busied themselves in a similar fashion, not only in writing, but particularly in illuminating (*etiam scribendo atque pingendo*), in which they became proficients.[5]

In the ninth century, the Benedictine nuns of Eck on the Meuse, and especially the two abbesses Harlinde and Renilde, attained great celebrity by their caligraphic

[1] Père Cahier, c. i., 215.
[2] Mabillon, *Traité*, etc., 39.
[3] Montalembert, iv., 174.
[4] *Vita Cæsarii*, i., 33, 375.
[5] *Vita Harlindis et Reinilæ* (written between 850 and 880), p. 5.

work and by the beauty of the illuminated designs used in
their manuscripts.[1] In the time of S. Gregory VII., a nun
at Wessobrunn, in Bavaria, named Diemude, undertook
to transcribe a series of important works, the mere enum-
eration of which would startle modern readers. These
works formed, as we read in the saint's epitaph, a whole
library, which she offered as a tribute to S. Peter. The
production of this library still left time for Diemude to
carry on with Herluca, a nun of the neighbouring
convent of Eppach, a correspondence remarkable as
well for its grace of expression as for its spiritual
insight.[2] A list of her transcripts is given in the section
on the *scriptorium*.

Among other convent scribes is recorded the name of
the nun Gita, in Schwarzenthau, who made transcripts,
about 1175, of the writings of her abbot, Irimbert. In
Mallesdorf, at about the same time, a nun of Scottish
parents, named Leukardis, who understood Greek, Latin,
and German, was active in the *scriptorium*, and her work
excited so much admiration that the monk Laiupold,
himself a famous scribe, instituted in her memory an
anniversarium.[3]

Brother Idung sent his dialogues concerning the monks
of Clugni and the Cistercians to the nuns of Niedermünster, near Regensburg, *ut legibiliter scribatur et diligenter
emendetur ab aliquibus sororibus.*[4] In the same century
(the twelfth) the names of Gertrude, Sibilia, and other
nuns appear on the transcript of the codex written for the
Domini Monasterienses, which codex came into the library
of Arnstein in exchange for a copy of the *Pastorals* of
Gregory. Johann Gerson, writing in 1423, refers with
cordial approbation to some beautiful copies prepared by
the nuns, of the works of Origen.[5] In St. Gall, where the

---

[1] Montalembert, iv., 375.   [3] Leuter, *Hist. Wessofont.*, i., 166.
[2] Rockinger, ii., 7.   [4] Rockinger, ii., 13.
            [5] *De Laude Scriptorum*, ii., 697.   Paris, 1708.

literary activity of the monks has already been referred to, the nuns in the convent of S. Catharine were, in the thirteenth and in the first half of the fourteenth centuries, also engaged in preparing transcripts of holy books.

Monkish Chroniclers.—In addition to the services rendered by the monks in the preservation of classic literature, and in addition also to the great amount of work required of them in the routine of their monastery for the preparation of books of devotion and instruction, a most valuable task was performed by many of the monastic scribes in the production of the records or annals of their times. The work of the literary monks included the functions not only of scribes, but of librarians, collectors, teachers, and historians. The records that have come down to us of several centuries of mediæval European history are due almost exclusively to the labours of the monastic chroniclers. Even those who did not compose books which can properly be described as historical, have left in their *cartularies* documents by the help of which the archæologists can to-day solve the most important problems relating to the social, civil, domestic, and agricultural life of their ancestors. The *cartularies*, says M. C. Giraud, were the most curious monuments of the history of the time.[1]

Without the monks, says Marsham (a Protestant writer), we should have been as ignorant of our history as children.[2] England, converted by her monks, has special reason to be proud of the historians furnished by her abbeys.[3] One chronicler, Gildas, has painted with fiery touches the miseries of Great Britain after the departure of the Romans. To another, the Venerable Bede, author of the ecclesiastical history of Britain, we owe the detailed account of the Catholic Renaissance under the

---

[1] *Recherches sur la Bretagne*, 579.
[2] Marsham, Προπύλαιον, in *Monast. Anglican.*, i.
[3] *De Excidio Britannorum*, London, 1586.

Saxons. Bede's chronicle extends to the year 731. Its author died four years later. Among later monkish chroniclers may be mentioned Ingulphus, Abbot of Croyland, whose history extends to 1091 ; Vitalis, a monk of Shrewsbury, whose chronicle reached to 1141, and many others. The chronicle of Vitalis gives an animated picture of the struggle between the Saxons and the Normans, and of the vicissitudes during this period of the Church of England. Later monastic historians were: William of Malmesbury (*circa* 1095–1143), Geoffrey of Monmouth (*circa* 1090–1154), Henry of Huntingdon (*circa* 1120–1180), Roger of Wendover (*circa* 1169–1237), Matthew Paris (*circa* 1185–1259), and Ralph Higden (*circa* 1280–1370). Further reference to the work of these English chroniclers is made in the chapter on Books in England during the Manuscript Period. This series of monkish chronicles presents, says Montalembert, an inexhaustible amount of information as to the manners, laws, and ideas of the times, and unites with the important information of history the personal attractiveness of biography.[1]

Among the chroniclers of France are to be noted S. Gregory of Tours ; S. Abbon, of St. Germain des Prés, who wrote the history of the wars of King Eudes and an account of the sieges of Paris by the Normans ; Frodoard, who died in 968, and who wrote the annals of the tenth century ; Richer, whose history covers the period between 880 and 995 ; Helgaud, who wrote the life of King Robert ; Aimoin, a monk of Fleury, who died in 1008, and who wrote a very curious life of S. Abbon and a record of the miracles at Fleury of S. Bénoît ; Chabanais, a monk of St. Cybar in Angoulême, who died in 1028, and whose record reaches to 1025. It has been republished by Pertz in the fourth volume of the *Scriptores*. Raoul Glaber, a monk of St. Germain d'Auxerre, wrote a history of his own time in five books, which covers the period from the

[1] Mont., iv., 204.

accession of Hugh Capet to 1046. Hugh, Abbot of Fla-
vigny, wrote with considerable detail the history of the
eleventh century. These various monkish chronicles have
served as a basis for the first national and popular monuments of French history. The famous chronicles of S.
Denys, which were written very early in Latin, were translated into French in the beginning of the thirteenth
century. They contain the essence of the historic and
poetic traditions of old France.

The mediæval history of Italy is in like manner dependent almost entirely upon the records of the literary
monks. The great collection of Muratori is based upon
the monkish chronicles, especially of those of Volturna,
Novalese, Farfa, Casa Aurio, and of Monte Cassino. From
the latter abbey, there sprang a series of distinguished
historians: Johannes Diaconus, the biographer of S.
Gregory the Great, who wrote during the reign of Charlemagne; Paulus Diaconus, the friend of Charlemagne;
Leo, Bishop of Ostia, first author of the famous chronicle
of Monte Cassino, and Peter Diaconus, who continued its
chronicle. Another monk of Monte Cassino recounts the
wonderful story of the conquest gained by the Norman
chivalry in the two Sicilies, a story reproduced and completed by the Sicilian monk Malaterra.

The list of the learned historians in the German monasteries is also an important one. The German collections
of *scriptories*, such as those of Eckard, Pez, Leibnitz, and
others, present an enormous mass of monastic chronicles.
Among the earlier chroniclers were to be noted Eginard,
Theganus, and Rodolphus of Fulda, who preserved the
records of the dynasty of the Carlovingians. One of the
earlier historians of Charlemagne was a monk of St. Gall,
while the chronicles of that abbey, carried on by a long
series of its writers, have left a most valuable and picturesque representation of successive epochs of its history.
Regino, Abbot of Prüm, wrote a history of the ninth

century.   Wittikind, a monk of Corvey, wrote the chronicles of the reign of Henry I., and of Otho the Great. Ditmar, who was at first a monk of Magdeburg and later Bishop of Mersebourg, has left a detailed chronicle, extending from 920 to 1018, of the emperors of the House of Saxony.   Among the eleventh-century writers, is Hermannus Contractus, son of the Count of Woegen, who was brought up at St. Gall but was later attached to Reichenau.   The history of the great struggle between the Church and the Empire was written by Lambert, a monk of Hersfeld, and continued by Berthold of Reichenau, Bernold of St. Blaise, and by Ekkhard, Abbot of Aurach.[1]   The first historian of Poland was a French monk named Martin, while another monk of Polish origin, named Nestor, who died in 1116, composed the earliest annals of Russia (then newly converted to Christianity) which were known to Europe.   Among the monkish historians of the eleventh century, the most noteworthy were William of Malmesbury, Gilbert of Nogent, Abbot Suger, and Odo of Deuil.

The persistent labour given by these monkish chroniclers to works, the interest and importance of which were largely outside the routine of their home monasteries and had in many cases no direct connection with religious observances, indicates that they were looking to a larger circle of readers than could be secured within the walls of their own homes.   While the evidences concerning the arrangements for the circulation of these chronicles are at best but scanty, the inference is fairly to be drawn that through the interchange of books between the libraries of the monasteries, by means of the services of travelling monks, and in connection with the educational work of the majority of the monasteries, there came to be, as early as the ninth century, a very general circulation of the long series of chronicles among the scholarly readers of

[1] Mabillon, *Annal. Bened.*, book lxxii., ch. xlvi.

Europe. Even the literary style in which the majority of
the chronicles were written gives evidence that the writers
were addressing themselves, not to one locality or to restricted circles of readers, but to the world as they knew
it, and that they also had an assured confidence in the
preservation of their work for the service and information
of future generations. The historian Stenzel (himself a
Protestant) points out that these monkish historians wrote
under certain exceptional advantages which secured for
their work a larger amount of impartiality and of accuracy
of statement than could safely be depended upon with, for
instance, what might be called Court chronicles, that is to
say, histories which were the work of writers attached to
the Courts. The monks, said Stenzel, in daring to speak
the truth of those in power, had neither family nor property to endanger, and their writings, prepared under the
eye of their monastic superiors and under the sovereign
protection of the Church, escaped at once the coercion or
the influence of contemporary rulers and the dangers of
flattery for immediate popular appreciation.[1] In the same
strain, Montalembert contends that the literary monks
worked neither for gain nor for fame, but simply for the
glory of God. They wrote amidst the peace and freedom
of the cloister in all the candour and sincerity of their
minds. Their only ambition was to be faithful interpre-
ters of the teaching which God gives to men in history by
reminding them of the ruin of the proud, the exaltation
of the humble, and the terrible certainty of eternal judgment. He goes on to say that if princes and nobles never
wearied of founding, endowing, and enriching monasteries, neither did the monks grow weary of chronicling
the services and the exploits of their benefactors, in order
to transmit these to posterity. Thus did they pay to the
Catholic chivalry a just debt of gratitude.[2]

This pious opinion of Montalembert is a little naïve

[1] *Gesch. der Frank. Kaiser*, ii., 15, 16.   [2] Mont., vi., 213.

in its expression when taken in connection with his
previous conclusion that the records of the monks could
be trusted implicitly for candour, sincerity, and impartiality.   It is difficult·to avoid the impression that in record-
ing the deeds of the noble leaders of their time, the monks
would naturally have given at least a full measure of attention and praise to those nobles who had been the greatest
benefactors to their Order or to the particular monastery
of the writer.   The converse may also not unnaturally be
assumed.   If a monarch, prince, or noble leader should be
neglectful of the claims of the monastery within his realm,
if there might be ground to suspect the soundness of his
faith to the Catholic Church, or doubt in regard to the
adequacy of his liberality to his ecclesiastical subjects, it
is probable that his exploits in war or in other directions
were minimised or unrecorded.   It is safe to assume also
that after the Reformation, the Protestant side of the long
series of complicated contests could hardly have been presented by the monkish chroniclers with perfect impartiality.   Bearing in mind, however, how many personal influences may have operated to impair the accuracy and the
impartiality of these chroniclers, they are certainly entitled
to a full measure of appreciation for the inestimable service rendered by them in the long ages in which, outside
of the monasteries, there were no historians.   It seems
also to have been the case that with many of the monks
who devoted the larger portion of their lives to literary
work, their ambition and ideals as authors overshadowed
any petty monkish zeal for their Order or their monastery, and that it was their aim to present the events of
their times simply as faithful historians.

An example of this high standard of work is presented
by Ordericus Vitalis, who, as an English monk in a Norman abbey,[1] was able to say: "I will describe the revolu-
tions of England and of Normandie without flattery to

[1] Mont., vi., 215.

any, for I expect my reward neither from the victors nor the vanquished." [1]

The Work of the Scriptorium.—The words employed at the consecration of the *scriptorium* are evidence of the spirit in which the devout scholars approached their work: *Benedicere digneris, Domine, hoc scriptorium famulorum tuorum, ut quidquid scriptum fuerit, sensu capiant, opere perficiant.* (Vouchsafe, O Lord, to bless this workroom of Thy servants, that all which they write therein may be comprehended by their intelligence and realised in their works.) [2]

Louis IX. took the ground that it was better to transcribe books than to purchase the originals, because in this way the mass of books available for the community was increased. Louis was, however, speaking only of religious literature; he could not believe that the world would be benefited by any distribution of the works of profane writers. Ziegelbauer is in accord with Montalembert and others in giving to the Benedictines of Iceland the credit for the collections made of the Eddas and for the preservation of the principal traditions of the Scandinavian mythology. He also confirms the conclusion arrived at by the Catholic historians generally, that the literary monuments of Greece and Rome which escaped the devastation of the barbarians were saved by the monks and by them alone. He cites, as a few examples from the long list of classics that were thus preserved, five books of the *Annals* of Tacitus, found at Corbie; the treatise of Lactantius on the *Death of Persecutors*, preserved at Moissac; the *Aularia* of Plautus, and the *Commentaries* of Servius on Virgil, preserved in Fleury; the *Republic* of Cicero, found in the library of Fleury in the tenth century, etc. [3]

---

[1] Vitalis, book iii., chap. xv.   [2] D'Achéry, in *Not. Oper. Guibert Novig.*
[3] Ziegelbauer, ii., 520.

In confirmation of the statement that the classics were by no means neglected by the earlier monastery collectors, Montalembert cites Alcuin, who enumerated among the books in his library at York the works of Aristotle, Cicero, Pliny, Virgil, Statius, Lucan, and Trogus Pompeïus. A further reference to this library will be found in the chapter on the Monastery Schools. In Alcuin's correspondence with Charlemagne, he quotes Ovid, Horace, Terence, and Cicero, and acknowledges that in his youth he had been more moved by the tears of Dido than by the Psalms of David.[1] Loup de Ferrières speaks of having borrowed from his friends the treatise *De Oratore* of Cicero, a *Commentary on Terence*, the works of Quintilian, Sallust, and Suetonius. He says further that he was occupying himself in correcting the text of the oration of Cicero against Verres, and that of Macrobius.[2] Abbot Didier of Monte Cassino, who later became Pope, succeeding Gregory VII., had transcripts made by his monks of the works of Horace and Seneca, of several treatises of Cicero, and of the *Fasti* of Ovid.[3] S. Anselm, Abbot of Bec in the time of Gregory VII., recommends to his pupils the careful study of Virgil and of other profane writers, "omitting the licentious passages." *Exceptis his in quibus aliqua turpitudo sonat.*[4] It is not clear what method the abbot proposed to have pursued in regard to the selection of the passages to be eliminated. It is hardly probable that at this time there had been prepared, either for the use of the monks or of any other readers, anything in the form of expurgated editions. S. Peter Damian seems to have expressed the true mind of an important group at least of the churchmen of his time, when he referred to the study of pagan writers. He says: "To study poets and philosophers for the purpose of rendering the wit more keen and better fitted to penetrate

[1] Mont., vi., 185.
[2] Mont., vi., 186.
[3] Giesebrecht, *De Litter. Studiis apud Italos*, 52.
[4] *Epist.*, i., 55.

the mysteries of the Divine Word, is to spoil the Egypt-
ians of their treasures in order to build a tabernacle for
God.'"

Montalembert is of opinion, from his study of monastic
history in France, that, at least during the eleventh and
twelfth centuries, classic writers were probably more
generally known and more generally appreciated than at
the present day.   He points out that the very fact of
the existence of various ordinances and instructions
intended to repress any intemperate devotion to the pagan
writers is sufficient evidence of the extent of the interest
in or passion for pagan literature.   He cites among other
rulers of the Church who issued protests or cautions
against pagan literature, S. Basil, S. Jerome, S. Gregory,
S. Radbert, S. Peter Damian, Lanfranc, etc., etc.'   In the
Customs of Clugni, there is a curious passage prescribing
the different signs that were to be used in asking for
books during the hours of silence, which indicates at once
the frequency of these pagan studies, and also the grade
of esteem in which they ought to be held by the faithful
monk.   The general rule, when asking for any book, was
to extend the hand, making motions similar to those of
turning over the leaves.   In order, however, to indicate a
pagan work, a monk was directed to scratch his ear as a
dog does, because, says the regulation, unbelievers may
well be compared to that animal.'

As before indicated, the work of transcribing manuscripts was held under the monastic rules to be a full
equivalent of manual labour in the fields.   The Rule of S.
Ferreol, written in the sixth century, says that, " He who
does not turn up the earth with the plough ought to write
the parchment with his fingers." '   It is quite possible

---

[1] *Petri Dam. Opusc.*, c. ix., p. 635.
[2] Mont., vi., 188.
[3] Martene, *De Antiq. Monach. Ritibus*, book iv., c. xviii., p. 289.
[4] Mont., vi., 191.

that for men of the Middle Ages, who had little fondness
for a sedentary life, work in the *scriptorium* may have
been a more exacting task than work that could be
carried on out-of-doors.   There were no fires in the cells
of the monks, and in many portions of Europe the cold
during certain months of the year must, in the long hours
of the day and night, have been severe.   Montalembert
quotes a monk of St. Gall who, on a corner of one of the
beautiful manuscripts prepared in that abbey, has left
the words: " He who does not know how to write
imagines it to be no labour, but although these fingers
only hold the pen, the whole body grows weary."   It
became, therefore, natural enough to use this kind of
labour as a penitential exercise.[1]   Othlo, a monk of
Tegernsee, who was born in 1013, has left an enumera-
tion of the work of his pen which makes it difficult to
understand how years enough had been found for such
labour.   The list includes nineteen missals, written and
illuminated with his own hand, the production of which,
he tells us, nearly cost him his eyesight.[2]

Dietrich or Theodoric, the first Abbot of St. Evroul
(1050–1057), who was himself a skilled scribe (*Ipse manu
propria scribendo volumina plura*), and who desired to in-
cite his monks to earnest work as writers, related to them
the story of a worldly and sinful Brother, who, notwithstanding his frivolities, was a zealous scribe, and who had,
in industrious moments, written out an enormous folio
volume containing religious instruction.   When he died,
the devil claimed his soul.   The angels, however, brought
before the throne of judgment the great book, and for each
letter therein written, pardon was given for one sin, and
behold, when the count was completed, there was one letter
over ; and, says Dietrich naïvely, it was a very big book.
Thereupon, judgment was given that the soul of the monk

[1] Mont., vi., 194.
[2] Mabillon, *Analect.*, book iv., p. 448.

should be permitted again to enter his body, in order that he might go through a period of penance on earth.[1]

In the monastery of Wedinghausen, near Arnsberg in Westphalia, there was a skilled and zealous scribe named Richard, an Englishman, who spent many years in adding to the library of the institution. Twenty years after his death, when the rest of his body had crumbled into dust, the right hand, with which this holy work had been accomplished, was found intact, and has since been preserved under the altar as a holy relic.[2]

There has been more or less discussion as to whether in the *scriptoria*, it was the practice for monks to write at dictation. Knittel[3] takes the ground that the larger portion of the work was done so slowly, and probably with such a different degree of rapidity on the part of the different scribes, that it would have been as impracticable for it to have been prepared under dictation as it would be to do copper engraving under dictation. Ebert,[4] confirming Knittel's conclusions, points out that when works were needed in haste, it was probably arranged to divide up the sheets to be copied among a number of scribes. He finds evidence of this arrangement of the work in a number of manuscripts, the different portions of which, put together under one cover, are evidently the work of different hands. Wattenbach specifies manuscripts in which not only are the different pages in different script, but the divisions have been written with varying arrangements of space; in some cases the space, which had been left for an interpolated chapter having evidently been wrongly measured, so that the script of such interpolated chapter had to be crowded together instead of having the

---

[1] Ordericus Vitalis, cited by Mabillon, A. S. ix., 137.

[2] *Cæsar. Heisterb.*, xii., 47. W. Schmidt. *Im Anz. des Germ. Mus. Iq.*, 328–366.

[3] *Ulphilæ Fragm.*, 380.

[4] *Zur Handschriftenkunde*, 138–140.

same spacing as that of the body of the work. Sickel
presents examples of the letters of Alcuin which are
evidently the work of a number of scribes. Each began
his work with a new letter, and where, at the end of the
divisions, leaves remained free, other letters were later
written in. In the later Middle Ages, however, there is
evidence of writing at dictation, and this practice began
to obtain more generally as the results of the work of the
scribes came to have commercial value. When the work
of preparing manuscripts was transferred from the monasteries to the universities, dictation became the rule, and
individual copying the exception. West finds evidence
that as early as the time of Alcuin, the monks trained
by him or in his schools, wrote from dictation. " In
the intervals between the hours of prayer and the observance of the round of cloister life, come hours for
the copying of books under the presiding direction of
Alcuin. The young monks file into the *scriptorium* and
one of them is given the precious parchment volume containing a work of Bede or Isidore or Augustine, or else
some portion of the Latin Scriptures, or even a heathen
author. He reads slowly and clearly at a measured rate
while all the others, seated at their desks, take down his
words; thus perhaps a score of copies are made at once.
Alcuin's observant eye watches each in turn and his correcting hand points out the mistakes in orthography and
punctuation. The master of Charles the Great, in that
true humility that is the charm of his whole behaviour, ·
makes himself the writing-master of his monks, stooping
to the drudgery of faithfully and gently correcting many
puerile mistakes, and all for the love of studies and for
the love of Christ. Under such guidance and deeply impressed by the fact that in the copying of a few books
they were saving learning and knowledge from perishing,
and thereby offering a service most acceptable to God,
the copying in the *scriptorium* went on in sobriety from

day to day. Thus were produced those improved copies
of books which mark the beginning of a new age in the
conserving and transmission of learning. Alcuin's anxiety
in this regard was not undue, for the few monasteries
where books could be accurately transcribed were as necessary for publication in that time as are the great publishing houses to-day." [1]

Among the monasteries which, as early as the time of
Charlemagne, developed special literary activity, was that
of S. Wandrille, where the Abbot Gerwold (786–806) instituted one of the earlier schools of the empire. A priest
named Harduin took charge of this school. He was said
to be *in hac arte non mediocriter doctus.* It was further
stated that, *plurima ecclesiæ nostræ proprio sudore con-
scripta reliquit volumina, id est volumen quatuor evangelio-
rum Romana litera scriptum.* [2] (He had left for one church
many books written by the sweat of his brow, that is to
say, a volume of the four Evangelists written in the
"Roman letter.") This expression, *litera Romana*, occurs
frequently in the monastery chronicles and appears to
indicate the uncial script. The *scriptorium* of St. Gall, in
which was done some of the most elaborate or important
of the earlier literary work of the monks, is frequently
referred to in the chronicles of the monasteries. Another
important *scriptorium* was that in the monastery of
Tournai, which, under the rule of the Abbot Odo, won
for itself great fame, so that its manuscripts were sought
by the Fathers of the Church far and wide, for the purpose
of correcting by them copies with less scholarly authority. [3]

The work of the scribes was not always voluntary;
there is evidence that it was not unfrequently imposed as
a penance. In a codex from Lorch [4] occur after the words,

---

[1] *Alcuin and the Rise of the Christian Schools*, 73.
[2] *Gesta Abb. Fontanell.*, iii., 16. *Mon. Germ.*, xi., 292.
[3] *Mon. Germ.*, ii., 95.
[4] Laurisheim, in Hesse-Darmstadt.

Jacob scripsit, written in by another hand, the lines:
*Quandam partem hujus libri non spontanea voluntate, sed
coactus, compedibus constrictus sicut oportet vagum atque
fugitivum vincire.*[1] (Jacob wrote . . . a certain portion
of this book not of his own free will but under compulsion,
bound by fetters, just as a runaway and fugitive has to be
bound.)

The aid of the students in the monastery schools was
not unfrequently called in. Fromund of Tegernsee wrote
under a codex: *Cœpi hunc libellum, sed pueri nostri quos
docui, meo juvamine prescripserunt.*[2] (I began this book,
but the students whom I taught, finished transcribing it
with my help.)

The monk who was placed in charge of the *armarium*
was called the *armarius*, and upon him fell the responsibility of providing the writing materials, of dividing the
work, and probably also of preserving silence while the
work was going on, and of reprimanding the writers of
careless or inaccurate script. In some monasteries the
armarius must also have been the librarian, and, in fact,
as much of the work done in the writing-room was for the
filling up of the gaps in the library, it would be natural
enough for the librarian to have the planning of it. It
was also the librarian, who, being in correspondence with
the custodians of the libraries of other monasteries, was
best able to judge what work would prove of service in
securing new books in exchange for duplicates of those in
his own monastery. Upon the *librarius* or *armarius*, or
both, fell the responsibility of securing the loans of the
codices of which copies were to be made. On such loans
it was usually necessary to give security in the shape of
pledges either of other manuscripts or of property apart
from manuscripts.

The scribes were absolved from certain of the routine
of the monastery work. They were called into the fields

[1] Reifferscheid, lvi., 451.   [2] Maitland, 371.

or gardens only at the time of harvest, or in case of special need. They had also the privilege of visiting the kitchen, in order to polish their writing tablets, to melt their wax, and to dry their parchment.[1]

The custom of reading at meals, while a part of the usual monastic routine, was by no means confined to the monasteries. References to the use of books at the tables of the more scholarly noblemen are found as early as the time of Charlemagne. Eginhart records that Charlemagne himself while at supper was accustomed to listen to histories and the deeds of ancient kings. He delighted also in the books of S. Augustine and especially in the *Civitate Dei.*[2]

In England, after the Norman conquest, there was for a time a cessation of literary work in the Saxon monasteries. The Norman ecclesiastics, however, in taking possession of certain of the older monasteries and instituting also new monasteries of their own, carried on the production of manuscripts with no less zeal. One of the most important centres of literary activity in England was the monastery of St. Albans, where the Abbot Paul secured, about the year 1100, funds for instituting a *scriptorium,* and induced some wealthy friends to present some valuable codices for the first work of the scribes. As the monks at that time in St. Albans were not themselves skilled in writing, Paul brought scribes from a distance, and, through the liberality of his friends, secured funds by which they were paid daily wages, and were able to work undisturbed. It would appear from this description that some at least among these scribes were not themselves monks.

In the thirteenth century, Matthew Paris compiled his chronicles, the writing in which appears to have been, for the greater part at least, done by his own hand, but at this time, in a large proportion of the literary work car-

---

[1] Winter, *Die Cisterc.,* ii., 145.   [2] Cited by Maitland, 341.

ried on in the English monasteries, the transcribing was
done by paid scribes. This, however, was much less the
case in the Continental monasteries. In Corbie, towards
the latter half of the century, there is a record of zealous
writing on the part of a certain Brother Nevelo. Nevelo
tells us that he had a penance to work off for a grave sin,
and that he was allowed to do this by work in the *scriptorium*.[1] During this century, the monasteries of the
Carthusians were particularly active in their literary
work, but this work was limited almost entirely to
theological and religious undertakings. An exception
is presented in the chronicles of the Frisian monk Emo.
While Emo was still a school-boy, he gave the hours
which his companions employed in play, to mastering
penmanship and the art of illuminating. Later, he was,
with his brother Addo, a student in the schools in Paris,
Orleans, and Oxford, and while in these schools, in addition to their work as students, they gave long hours of
labour, extending sometimes through the entire night, to
the transcribing of chronicles and to the preparation of
copies of the so-called heathen literature.

Emo was the first abbot of the monastery in Witte-
wierum (1204–1237), and it is recorded that the abbot,
while his brothers were sleeping, devoted his nights to the
writing and illuminating of the choir books. In this
monastery, Emo succeeded in bringing together in the
armarium librorum an important collection of manuscripts,
and he took pains himself to give instructions to the
monks in their work as scribes.

The quaint monastic record entitled the *Customs of
Clugni* was written by Ulrich, a monk of Clugni, some
time between the years 1077 and 1093, at the request or
under the instructions of William, Abbot of Hirschau.
This was the Abbot William extolled by Trithemius as
having restored the Order of S. Benedict, which had

[1] Delisle, *Recherches sur l'Ancienne Bibliothèque de Corbie*, xxiv., 288.

almost fallen into ruin in Germany.   Trithemius speaks of
his having founded eight monasteries and restored more
than one hundred, and says that next to the reformation
wrought by the foundation and influence of Clugni, the
work done by Abbot William was the most important
recorded in the annals of his Order.

William trained twelve of his monks to be excellent
writers, and to these was committed the office of transcribing the Holy Scriptures and the treatises of the
Fathers.   Besides these, there were in the *scriptorium* of
Hirschau a large number of lesser scribes, who wrought
with equal diligence in the transcription of other books.
In charge of the *scriptorium* was placed a monk " well
versed in all kinds of knowledge," whose business it was
to assign the task for each scribe and to correct the mistakes of those who wrote negligently.   William was Abbot
of Hirschau for twenty-two years, and during this time his
monks wrote a great many volumes, a large proportion of
which were distributed to supply the wants of other and
more needy monasteries.

There was often difficulty, particularly in the less
wealthy monasteries, in securing the parchment required
for their work.   It is evident from such account-books as
have been preserved, that throughout the whole of Europe,
but particularly in the north of the Continent and in
England, parchment continued to be a very costly com-
modity until quite late in the thirteenth century.   It was
not unnatural that, as a result of this difficulty, the monastic scribes should, when pressed for material, have occasionally utilised some old manuscript by cleaning off the
surface, for the purpose of making a transcript of the
Scriptures, of some saintly legend, or of any other religious work the writing of which came within the range
of their daily duty.

There has been much mourning on the part of the
scholars over the supposed value of precious classics which

may thus have been destroyed, or of which but scanty
fragments have been preserved in the lower stratum of the
palimpsest.   Robertson is particularly severe upon the
ignorant clumsiness of the monks in thus destroying, for
the sake of futile legends, so much of the great literature
of the world.   Among other authors, Robertson quotes in
this connection Montfaucon as saying that the greater
part of the manuscripts on parchment which he had seen
(those of an ancient date excepted), are written on parchment from which some former treatise had been erased.
Maitland, who is of opinion that the destruction of ancient
literature brought about by the monks has been much
overestimated, points out that Robertson has not quoted
Montfaucon correctly, the statement of the latter being
expressly limited to manuscripts written since the "twelfth
century."   It is Maitland's belief that a large proportion
of the palimpsests or doubly written manuscripts which
bear date during the twelfth, thirteenth, or fourteenth
centuries, represent, as far as they are monastic at all, not
monastery writings placed upon classic texts, but monastery work replacing earlier works of the monastery *scriptoria*.   Partial confirmation of this view is the fact that so
large an interest was taken by monks in all parts of
Europe in the preservation and transcribing of such
classical works as came into their hands.   In fact, as
previously pointed out, the preservation of any fragments
whatsoever of classical literature is due to the intelligent
care of the monks.   To the world outside of the monastery, the old-time manuscripts were, with hardly an
exception, little more than dirty parchments.

It seems probable that a great part of such scraping of
old manuscripts as was done was not due to the requirements of the legends or missals, but was perpetrated in
order to carry on the worldly business of secular men.
An indication of the considerable use of parchment for
business purposes, and of instances of what we should

to-day call its abuse, is the fact that, as late as the fourteenth and fifteenth centuries, notaries were forbidden to
practise until they had taken an oath to use none but new
parchment.[1]

The belief that the transcribing of good books was in
itself a protection against the wiles of the evil one, naturally added to the feeling of regard in which the writer
held his work, a feeling under the influence of which it
became not unusual to add at the close of the manuscript
an anathema against any person who should destroy or
deface it. A manuscript of St. Gall contains the following:

> *Auferat hunc librum nullus hinc omne per ævum*
> *Cum Gallo partem quisquis habere cupit.*[2]

[Let no one through all ages who wishes to have any part
with Gallus (the Saint or the Abbey) injure (or destroy) this
book.]

In a Sacramentary of the ninth century given to St.
Bénoît-sur-Loire, the donor, having sent the volume as a
present from across seas, devotes to destruction like to
that which came upon Judas, Ananias, and Caiaphas any
person who should remove the book from the monastery.[3]
In a manuscript of S. Augustine, now in the Bodleian
Library is written: " This book belongs to S. Mary of
Robert's Bridge; whosoever shall steal it or sell it, or in
any way alienate it from this house, or mutilate it, let him
be anathema maranatha. Amen." A later owner had
found himself sufficiently troubled by this imprecation to
write beneath: "I, John, Bishop of Exeter, know not
where the aforesaid house is, nor did I steal this book,
but acquired it in a lawful way."[4]

In an exhortation to his monks, delivered in 1486, by
John of Trittenheim (or Trithemius), Abbot of Sponheim,

---

[1] Maitland, 40.
[2] *Canis. Ant. Lect.* ii., 230, cited by Maitland.
[3] Martene, *Voy. Lit.*, 67.
[4] Wanley, *Cat. Lib. Sept.*, p. 152.

the abbot, after rebuking the monks for their sloth and neg-
ligence, goes on to say : " I have diminished your labours
out of the monastery, lest by working badly you should
only add to your sins; and have enjoined on you the
manual labour of writing and binding books. . . .
There is, in my opinion, no labour more becoming a
monk than the writing of ecclesiastical books, and preparing what is needful for others who write them, for this
holy labour will generally admit of being interrupted by
prayer and of watching for the food of the soul no less
than of the body.   Need also urges us to labour diligently
in writing books if we desire to have at hand the means
of usefully employing ourselves in spiritual studies.   For
you will recall that all the library of this monastery, which
formerly was so fine and complete, had been dissipated,
sold, and made away with by the disorderly monks before
us, so that when I came here, I found but fourteen volumes.   It is true that the industry of the printing art,
lately, in our own day, discovered at Mentz, produces
many volumes every day; but depressed as we are by
poverty, it is impossible for us to buy them all." [1]

It was certainly the case that, after the invention of
printing, there was a time during which manuscripts came
to be undervalued, neglected, and even destroyed by
wholesale, but Maitland is of opinion that this time had
been prepared for by a long period of gradually increasing
laxity of discipline and morals in many monastic institutions.   This view is borne out by the history of the
Reformation, the popular feeling in regard to which was
undoubtedly very much furthered by the demoralisation
of the monasteries, a demoralisation which naturally
carried with it a breaking down of literary interests and
pursuits.   There had, for some time, been less multiplication, less care, and less use of books, and many a fine
collection had mouldered away.   According to Martene

[1] Martene, *Voy. Lit.*, 56.

and Mabillon, the destruction due to the heedlessness of
the monks themselves was largely a matter of the later
times, that is, of the fifteenth century and the last half of
the fourteenth century.

Maitland is of the opinion that in the later portions of
the Middle Ages the work of the monastic scribes was
more frequently carried on not in a general writing-room,
but in separate apartments or cells, which were not usually
large enough to contain more than one person. Owing to
the fact that writing was the chief and almost only in-doors
business of a monk not engaged in religious service, and because of the great quantity of work that was done and the
number of cells devoted to it, these small rooms came to be
generally referred to as *scriptoria*, even when not actually
used or particularly intended for the purpose of writing.
Thus we are told that Arnold, Abbot of Villers in Brabant,
from 1240 to 1250, when he resigned his office, occupied a
scriptorium (he called it a *scriptoriolum* or little writing
cell), where he lived as a private person in his own apartment.[1] These separate cells were usually colder and in
other ways less comfortable than the common *scriptorium*.
Lewis, a monk of Wessobrunn in Bavaria, in an inscription addressed to the reader, in a copy he had prepared
of Jerome's *Commentary on Daniel*, says: *Dum scripsit
friguit, et quod cum lumine solis scribere non potuit, perfecit
lumine noctis.*[2] (He was stiff with cold, while he wrote,
and what he could not write by the light of the sun, he
completed by the light of night.) There is evidence,
however, in some of the better equipped monasteries, of
the warming of the cells by hot air from the stove in the
calefactory. Martene mentions that when S. Bernard,
owing to the illness produced by his early austerities, was
compelled by the Bishop of Chalons to retire to a cell, he
could not be persuaded to relax the severity of his asceti-

[1] Mait., 405.
[2] Pez, *Thes. Anecd. Noviss. Diss. Isagog.* in tom. i., 20.

cism so far as to permit the introduction of any fireplace or other means of warming it. His friends, however, contrived, with pious fraud, to heat his cell without his knowledge, by introducing hot air through the stone floor under the bed.[1]

The *scriptorium* of earlier times was, however, as previously described, an apartment specially set aside as a general workroom and capable of containing many workers, and in which many persons did, in fact, work together, usually under the direction of a *librarius* or chief scribe, in a very business-like manner, in the transcription of books. Maitland quotes from a document, which is, he states, one of the very few existing specimens of French Visigothic manuscripts in the uncial character, and which dates from the eighth century, the following form of consecration or benediction, entitled (in monastic Latin) *Orationem in scriptorio :* " Vouchsafe, O Lord, to bless this *scriptorium* of Thy servants and all that work therein : that whatsoever sacred writings shall be here read or written by them, they may receive with understanding and may bring the same to good effect."[2] (see also page 61).

In the more carefully constructed monasteries, the *scriptorium* was placed to adjoin the calefactory, which simplified the problem of the introduction of hot air.

A further evidence, if such were needed, that the larger literary undertakings were carried on in a *scriptorium* common room and not in separate cells, is given by the regulation of the general Chapter of the Cistercian Order in 1134, which directs that the same silence should be maintained in the *scriptorium* as in the cloister : *In omnibus scriptoriis ubicunque ex consuetudine monachi scribunt, silentium teneatur sicut in claustro.*[3]

Odo, who in 1093 became Abbot of S. Martin at Tour-

[1] *Voy. Lit.*, 99.
[2] *Nouv. Traité de Diplom.*, iii., 190, cited by Mait., 407.
[3] *Ap. Nomast. Cisterc.*, cap. lxxxvii. 272.

nai, writes that he confided the management of the outside work of the monastery to Ralph, the prior. This left the abbot free to devote himself to reading and to supervising the work in his *scriptorium*. Odo exulted in the number of writers whom the Lord had given to him. "If you had gone into the cloister during the working hours, you would have seen a dozen scribes writing, in perfect silence, at tables constructed for the purpose." Odo caused to be transcribed all of Jerome's *Commentaries on the Prophets*, all the works of S. Gregory, and all the works that he could find of S. Augustine, S. Ambrose, Bishop Isidore, the Venerable Bede, and Anselm, then Abbot of Bec and afterwards Archbishop of Canterbury. Odo's successor, Heriman, who gives this account, says with pride that such a library as Odo brought together in S. Martin could hardly be paralleled in any monastery in the country, and that other monasteries were begging for texts from S. Martin's with which to collate and correct their own copies.[1]

Maitland mentions that certain of the manuscripts written in Odo's *scriptorium*, including the fourth volume of the *Gregorialis* of Alulfus, were (in 1845) in the library of Dr. Todd, of Trinity College, Dublin.[2]

In estimating the extent of book production of the manuscript period, we may very easily place too large a comparative weight on the productive power of the Press. Maitland points out that although the power of multiplication of literary productions was, of course, during the Dark Ages infinitely below that which now exists, and while the entire book production of the two periods may not be compared, yet as regards those books which were considered as the standard works in sacred literature and in the approved secular literature, the difference was not so extreme as may easily be supposed. He enquires, to

---

[1] *Herimanni Narratio Rest. Abb. S. Martini Torn.*, 79 ; *Ap. Dach. Spicileg.*, ii., 913.   [2] Mait., 414.

emphasise his point, what proportion the copies of Augustine's *City of God* and of Gregory's *Morals, printed* between the years 1700 and 1800, bear to those *written* between the years 1100 and 1200.[1]

I think, with Maitland, that, according to the evidence on record, for books such as those given above as typical examples, the written production during the century selected would probably have exceeded the number of copies of the same books turned out by the printing-presses during the eighteenth century. We must recall to ourselves that for a term of six or seven centuries, writing was a business, and was also a religious duty ; an occupation taken up by choice and pursued with a degree of zeal, persistence, and enthusiasm for which in the present day there is no parallel.

Mabillon speaks of a volume by Othlonus, a monk of S. Emmeram's at Ratisbon, who was born about the year 1013. In this book, which is entitled *De ipsius tentationibus, varia fortuna, et scriptis*, the monk gives an account of his literary labours and of the circumstances which led to his writing the various works bearing his name.

" For the same reason, I think proper to add an account of the great knowledge and capacity for writing which was given me by the Lord in my childhood. When as yet a little child, I was sent to school and quickly learned my letters, and I began, long before the usual time of learning and without any order from the master, to learn the art of writing. Undertaking this in a furtive and unusual manner, and without any teacher, I got a habit of holding my pen wrongly, nor were any of my teachers afterwards able to correct me on that point; for I had become too much accustomed to it to be able to change. Those who saw my earlier work unanimously decided that I should never write well. After a short time the facility came to me, and while I was in the monastery of Tegern-

[1] Mait., 416.

see (in Bavaria) I wrote many books. . . . Being sent
to Franconia while I was yet a boy, I worked so hard at
writing that before I returned I had nearly lost my
sight. . . . After I became a monk in the monastery
of S. Emmeram, I was appointed the schoolmaster. The
duties of this office so fully occupied my time, that I
was able to do the transcribing in which I was interested
only by night and on holidays. . . . I was, however,
able, in addition to writing the books which I had myself
composed, and the copies of which I gave away for the
edification of those who asked for them, to prepare
nineteen missals (ten for the abbots and monks in our
own monastery, four for the brethren at Fulda, and five
for those in other places), three books of the Gospels,
and two with the Epistles and Gospels, which are
called *Lectionaries ;* besides which, I wrote four service-
books for matins. I wrote in addition a good many
books for the brethren at Fulda, for the monks at Hirsch-
feld and at Amerbach, for the Abbot of Lorsch, for certain friends at Passau, and for other friends in Bohemia,
for the monastery of Tegernsee, for the monastery of
Pryel, for the monastery of Obermünster and for that of
Niedermünster, and for my sister's son. Moreover, to
many others I gave or sent, at different times, sermons,
proverbs, and edifying writings. . . . Afterwards, old
age's infirmity of various kinds hindered me." [1]

If there were many hundred scribes of the diligence of
Othlonus, the mass of literature produced in the *scriptorium* may very easily have rivalled the later output of the
printing-presses. The labours of Othlonus were, if the
records are to be trusted, eclipsed by those of the nun
Diemude or Diemudis of the monastery of Wessobrunn.
An anonymous monk of this monastery, writing in the
year 1513, says :

" Diemudis was formerly a most devout nun of this our

[1] Mabillon, *Anal.*, iv., 448.

monastery of Wessobrunn. [Pez states that Diemudis lived in the time of Gregory VII., who became Pope in 1073. She was, therefore, though probably somewhat younger, a contemporary of the monk Othlonus of Ratisbon.] For our monastery was formerly double or divided into two parts; that is to say, of monks and nuns. The place of the monks was where it now is; but that of the nuns, where the parish church now stands. This virgin was most skilful in the art of writing: for though she is not known to have composed any work, yet she wrote with her own hand many volumes in a most beautiful and legible character, both for divine service and for the public library of the monastery. Of these books she has left a list in a certain *plenarius*.[1] The titles are as follows:

" A *Missal, with the Gradual and Sequences.* Another *Missal, with the Gradual and Sequences*, given to the Bishop of Trèves. Another *Missal, with the Epistles, Gospels, Graduals, and Sequences.* Another *Missal, with the Epistles and Gospels for the year, the Gradual and Sequences, and the entire service for baptism.* A *Missal, with Epistles and Gospels.* A *Book of Offices.* Another *Book of Offices, with the baptismal service* (given to the Bishop of Augsburg). A *Book, with the Gospels and Lessons.* A *Book, with the Gospels.* A *Book, with the Epistles.* A *Bible*, in two volumes, given for the estate in Pisinberch. A *Bible*, in three volumes. S. Gregory *ad regaredum.* S. *Gregory on Ezekiel.* *Sermons and Homilies of certain ancient Doctors*, three volumes. *Origen on the Old Testament.* *Origen on the Canticles.* *Augustine on the Psalms*, three volumes. *Augustine on the Gospels and on the First Epistle of S. John*, two volumes. Augustine, *Epistles*, to the number of lxxv. Augustine, *Treatises.* S. *Jerome's Epistles*, to the number of clxiv. *The Tripartite History of Cassiodorus. The Ecclesiastical History of Eusebius.*

[1] A Missal, containing, in addition to its usual contents, the Epistles and Gospels.

S. Augustine, *Fifty Sermons. The Life of S. Silvester. Jerome against Vigilantius.* Jerome, *De Consolatione Mortuorum. The Life of S. Blasius. The Life of John the Almoner, Patriarch of Alexandria early in the seventh century. Paschasius on the Body and Blood of Christ. The Conflict of Lanfranc with Berengarius. The Martyrdom of S. Dionysius. The Life of S. Adrian.* S. Jerome, *De Hebraicis Quæstionibus.* S. Augustine, *Confessions. Canons. Glossa per A. B. C. Composita* (*i.e.*, a Gloss alphabetically arranged).

" These are the volumes written with her own hand by the aforesaid handmaid of God, Diemudis, to the praise of God and of the holy Apostles Peter and Paul, the patrons of the monastery." [1]

The same writer says that Diemudis (whom he calls *exaratrix diligentissima*) carried on a correspondence by very sweet letters (*epistolæ suaves valde*) with Herluca, who was for thirty-six years a nun at Eppach, and that the letters were in his time (1513), that is four and a half centuries later, extant in the monastery of Bernried.

The Influence of the Scriptorium. — Hildebrand, who, under the name Gregory VII., became Pope in 1073, appears to have made large use of the literary facilities of the monasteries to bring effectively before the public the doctrinal teachings which seemed to him essential for the wholesome development of the strength of the Church in its great contest with the imperial power and for the proper rule of the world. The histories of the time speak of monks travelling throughout the Empire circulating writings in favour of the Church, by means of which writings schism could be withstood and the zeal of good Catholics aroused.[2]

Certain of the monasteries, in connection with their

---

[1] Pez, *Thes. Anec. Noviss. Diss. Isagog.* in tom. i., p. 20.
[2] Mont. vi., p. 445.

6

literary activity in behalf of the Pope, came into special
disfavour with the Emperor.   Among them was Hirschau,
the importance of whose literary work has been previously
referred to.   This monastery fell under the displeasure of
the Emperor Frederick IV., but the monks, says their
own annalist, sustained by their prayers, braved the
sword of the tyrant and despised the menaces of offended
princes.[1]   Abbot William of Hirschau had for twenty-two
years been the soul of monastic regeneration in Germany.
He was one of the great scholars of his time and had
done not a little to further the literary pre-eminence of
his monastery, and he became one of the most valiant
defenders of the popes during this contest.   Among other
ecclesiastical writers whose pens were active in the defence
of the papal decrees and in assailing the utterances of the
schismatics, and whose work, by means of the distributing
machinery which had already been organised between
the monasteries, secured for the time a large circulation,
were Bernard, at one time master of the schools of Constance, but later a monk at Hirschau ; Bernold, a monk of
St. Blaise ; Adelbert, a monk of Constance ; and Gebhard,
another monk of Hirschau.[2]

Gregory was possibly the first pope who made effective
and extended use of the writings of devout authors for
the purpose of influencing public opinion.   If we may
judge by the results of his long series of contests with the
imperial power in Germany, the selection of these literary
weapons was one proof of his sagacity.   In this contest,
the *scriptoria* of the monasteries proved more powerful
than the armies of the emperors ; as, five hundred years
later, the printing-presses of the Protestants proved more
effective than the Bulls of the Papacy.

The most important, in connection with its influence
and consequences, of the discoveries made by scholars
concerning the fraudulent character of historic documents,

[1] Trithemius, 235, 268.   [2] Trithemius, 266.

occurred as late as the beginning of the fifteenth century. It was about 1440 when Laurentius Valla, at that time acting as secretary for King Alphonso of Naples, wrote his report upon the famous *Donation* of Constantine, the document upon which the Roman Church had for nearly a thousand years based its claims to be the direct representative in Western Europe of the old imperial authority. Valla brought down upon his head much ecclesiastical denunciation. The evidences produced by him of the fact that the document had been fabricated a century or more after the death of Constantine could not be gotten rid of, and, although for a number of years the Church continued to maintain the sacred character of the *Donation*, and has, in fact, never formally admitted that it was fraudulent, it was impossible, after the beginning of the sixteenth century, even for the ecclesiastics themselves to base any further claims for the authority of the Church upon this discredited parchment.

Of almost equal importance was the discovery of the fabrication of the pseudo Isidoric *Decretals*. The *Decretals* had been concocted early in the ninth century by certain priests in the West Frankish Church, and had been eagerly accepted by Pope Nicholas I., who retained in the archives of the Vatican the so-called originals. The conclusion that the *Decretals* had been fraudulently imposed upon the Church was not finally accepted until the beginning of the fourteenth century. It was with the humanistic movement of the Renaissance that historical criticism had its birth, and a very important portion of the work of such criticism consisted in the analysis of the lack of foundation of a large number of fabulous legends upon which many of the claims of the Church had been based.

There were evidently waves of literary interest and activity in the different monasteries, between which waves the art of writing fell more or less into disuse and the libraries were neglected. In the monastery at Murbach, for instance, in which, in the beginning of the century, important work had been done, it is recorded that in 1291 no monks were found who were able to write, and the same was said in 1297 of the more famous monastery of St. Gall.[1] On the other hand, the newly organised Orders of travelling or mendicant monks took an active interest in preparing and in distributing manuscript copies of works of doctrine at about the time when, in the older and richer Orders, literary earnestness was succumbing to laziness and luxury. With these mendicant monks, began also to come into circulation a larger proportion of original writings, transcribed and corrected, and probably to some extent sold by the authors themselves. Richard de Bury makes bitter references in his *Philobiblon* (chapters v. and vi.) to the general antagonism of the Church towards literature, but speaks with appreciation of the educational services rendered by the mendicant monks. Writing was done also by the monks of the Minorite Order, but their rules and their methods of life called for such close economy that the manuscripts left by them are distinguished by the meagreness and inadequacy of the material and the closely crowded script, which, in order further to save space, contains many abbreviations.

Roger Bacon is said to have come into perplexity because, when he wished to send his treatises to Pope Clement IV., he could find no one among the Brothers of his Order who was able to assist him in transcribing the same, while scribes outside of the Order to whom he attempted to entrust the work gave him untrustworthy and slovenly copies.[2]

With the beginning of the fourteenth century, it is possible to note a scholarly influence exercised upon certain of the monasteries by the universities. The most enter-

[1] Neugart, *Cod. Dipl. Alem.*, ii., 334-338.
[2] *Oper. Inedita*, ed. Brewer, ii., p. 13.

prising of the monks made opportunities for themselves
to pass some years of their novitiate in one or more of
the universities, or later secured leave of absence from the
monasteries for the purpose of visiting the universities.
It also happened that from the monasteries where literary
work had already been successfully carried on, monks
were occasionally called to the universities in order to
further the literary undertakings of the theological faculties. Finally, the abbots, and other high officials of the
monasteries, were, after the beginning of the fourteenth
century, more frequently appointed from among the
ecclesiastics who had had a university training.

The library in Heidelberg, the university of which
dates from 1386, received from the monastery at Salem a
large number of beautiful manuscripts, and finally, an
illuminated breviary was completed in 1494 by the Cistercian Amandus, who, after the destruction of his monastery
in Strasburg, had found refuge in Salem, where in 1529
he became abbot. There is evidence that, at this time,
both in Salem and in other monasteries in which the business of manifolding and of selling or exchanging manuscripts became important, a large proportion of the work
of illustrating or illuminating was done by paid artists.

After the reform movement which began with the
Council of Basel, there came into existence, in connection
with the renewal of theological discussions, a fresh literary
activity in many of the monasteries. In the monastery at
Camp, in 1440, the library was renewed and very much
extended, and here were written by Guillaume de Reno,
scriptor egregius nulli illo tempore in arte sua secundus,
the *Catholicon*, books of the Mass, and other devotional
works. Abbot Heinrich von Calcar provided Guillaume
for eighteen years with a yearly supply of parchment,
valued at seventeen florins, and of other writing material.

In Michelsberg, Abbot Ulrich III. (1475–1483) and his
successor Andreas restored the long-time deserted library,

and by work by the scribes of the monastery and through the exchange of works for the productions of other monasteries, secured an important collection of manuscripts. In 1492, Andreas, abbot of the monastery of Bergen, near Magdeburg, renewed the *scriptorium*, which, later, became active in the production of copies of works connected with this earlier reformation.

Adolph von Hoeck, who died in 1516, Prior of Scheda in Westphalia, was a skilled scribe as well as a zealous reformer.   In Monsee, a certain Brother, Jacob of Breslau, who died in 1480, was said to have written so many volumes that six horses could with difficulty bear the burden of them.[1]   In the monastery at Tegernsee, already referred to, there was, under Abbot Conrad V. (1461–1492), an active business in the manifolding and distribution of writings.   The same was the case in Blaubeuern, where, as early as 1475, a printing-press was put into operation, but the preparation of manuscripts continued until the end of the century.   Among the works issued from Blaubeuern in manuscript form after the beginning of printing, were the *Chronicles of Monte Cassino*, by Andreas Ysingrin, completed in 1477, and the *Life of the Holy Wilhelm of Hirschau*, by Brother Silvester, completed in 1492.[2]

This year of 1492 appears to have been one of exceptional intellectual as well as physical activity.   It records not merely the completion of a number of important works marking the close of the manuscript period of literary production, but the publication, as will be noted in a later chapter, of a long series of the more important of the earlier printed books in Mayence, Basel, Venice, Milan, and Paris.

In Belgium, through the first half of the fifteenth century, while many of the monasteries had fallen into a condition of luxurious inactivity, work was still carried on

[1] Pez, *Thes.*, *Diss.*, i., p. 4.   [2] *Mon. Germ. SS.*, xiii., 557.

in the Laurentium monastery of Liége by Johann of
Stavelot, and by other zealous scribes, and in several other
of the Benedictine monasteries of the Low Countries the
scriptoria were kept busied. Towards the end of the
fifteenth century, and for some years after the beginning
of the work of the German printers, the production of
manuscripts in Germany continued actively in the monastery of S. Peter at Erfurt, and in the monasteries of S.
Ulrich and Afra in Augsburg, the work of which has been
recorded with full precision and detail in the famous catalogue of Wilhelm Wittwer.

In 1472, in this latter monastery, Abbot Melchior
founded the first printing-office at Augsburg in order to
give to the monks continued employment, and in order
also to be able to enlarge the library by producing copies
of books for exchange. It was a long time, however, before the work of the printing-press came to be sufficiently
understood to bring to a stop the labours of the scribes in
manifolding manuscripts for sale and for exchange. The
writings of the nun Helena of Hroswitha, the *Chronicle of
Urspergense,* and other works continued to be prepared in
manuscript form after printed editions were in the market.
The same was the case with the great choir books, which
continued during nearly half the century to be very largely
prepared by hand in the *scriptoria.* This persistence of
the old methods was partly due to habit and to the difficulty of communication with the centres in which the
printing-presses were already at work, but was very largely,
of course, the result of the fact that in the monasteries was
always available a large amount of labour, and that the use
of this labour for the preparation of sacred books had come
to form part of the religious routine of the institution.

With the development of the system of common
schools, the educational work which had previously been
carried on in the convents was very largely given up, thus
throwing upon the hands of the monks a still greater pro-

portion of leisure time.   In 1492, Johann of Trittenheim, Abbot of Sponheim, wrote to the Abbot Gerlach of Deutz a letter, *De Laude Scriptorum*, in which he earnestly invokes the scribes (he was addressing the scribes of the monasteries) by no means to permit themselves to be deterred from their holy occupation by the invasion of the printing-presses.   Such admonitions might continue the work of the monks in certain of the *scriptoria*, but were, of course, futile in the attempt to preserve for any length of time the business of circulating manuscript copies in competition with the comparatively inexpensive, and often beautiful, productions of the printers.

An important part in the work of the preparation and distribution of manuscripts was taken by the so-called "Brothers of common life" (*clerici de vita communi*), who later, also occupied themselves with the new invention of printing.   They cannot properly be classed with the scribes of the monasteries, for they made their work a trade and a means of revenue.   This practice obtained, to be sure, also with certain of the monasteries, but it must be considered as exceptional with them.   The Brothers differed also from the writers in the university towns and elsewhere, who prepared manuscripts for renting out to students and readers, partly because of the special conditions of their Brotherhood, under which the earnings of individual Brothers all went into a common treasury, but chiefly because they made their work as scribes a means of religious and moral instruction.   The earnings secured from the sale of manuscripts were also largely devoted to the missionary work of the Brotherhood.   The chief authority for the history of the Brotherhood is the work of Delprat, published in Amsterdam in 1856.

The Brotherhood house in Deventer, Holland, founded by Gerhard Groote in 1383, became an important workshop for the production and distribution of manuscripts. Delprat states that the receipts from these sales were

for a time the main support of the Brotherhood house.
In 1389, a copy of the Bible which had been written out
by Brother Jan von Enkhuizen was sold for five hundred
gulden in gold.[1] In Liége, the Brothers were known as
Broeders van de Penne, because they carried quill pens in
their caps. Groote seems himself to have taken a general
supervision of this business of the production of books,
selecting the books to be manifolded, verifying the transcripts, and arranging for the sale of the copies which were
passed as approved. Florentius Radewijus had the general charge of the manuscripts (filling the rôle which
to-day would be known as that of stock clerk) and of
preparing the parchment for the scribes and writing in
the inscriptions of the finished manuscripts. Later, with
the development of the Order and the extension of its
book business, each Brotherhood house had its *librarius*,
or manager of the manufacturing and publishing department; its *rubricator*, who added the initial letters or
illuminated letters in the more expensive manuscripts;
its *ligator*, who had charge of the binding, etc.

It was a distinctive feature of the works prepared by
the Brothers that they were very largely written in the
language of the land instead of in Latin, which elsewhere
was, as we have seen, the exclusive language for literature.
It was, in fact, one of the charges made by the ecclesiastics against the Order that they put into common language
doctrinal instruction which ordinary readers, without direct
guidance of the Church, were not competent to understand, and which tended, therefore, to work mischief. In
1398, the Brothers took counsel on the point whether it
were permissible to distribute among the people religious
writings in Low German, and they appear to have secured the authorisation required. They laid great stress
upon the precision of their script, and they were, as a rule,
opposed to needless expenditure for ornamentation of

[1] Delprat, p. 324.

text or of covers. Under the influence of Groote, the work of preparing manuscripts of good books was taken up by the monks and the nuns of Windesheim, but, according to Busch, the books produced in Windesheim were but rarely sold. In some cases these seem to have been distributed gratis, while in others they were given in exchange for other books required for the library of the monastery or convent.[1]

Wattenbach says that the Brothers in the Home at Hildesheim were called upon for an exceptional amount of labour in preparing books of the Mass and other devotional works in connection with the reform movement in the monasteries of lower Saxony, which was active in the middle of the fifteenth century. In the year 1450 (the year in which Gutenberg perfected his printing-press) it is recorded that the Hildesheim Brothers earned from the sale of their manuscripts no less than a thousand gulden.[2] In connection with their interest in the production and distribution of cheap literature, the Brothers did not fail to make very prompt and intelligent utilisation of the new invention of printing, and among the earlier printing-offices established in Germany and in the Low Countries were those organised by the Brothers at Deventer, Zwoll, Gouda, Bois-le-duc, Brussels, Louvain, Marienthal, Rostock, etc.

The Literary Monks of England.—In accepting the influence of literary ideals, the Anglo-Saxon monks were much slower and less imaginative than the quicker and more idealistic Celts. The quickening of the intellectual development of the monasteries in England was finally brought about through the influence of Celtic missionaries coming directly from Ireland or from the Irish monasteries of the Scottish region, such as Iona and its associates.

Before the literary work of the English monasteries

[1] Johann Busch, *Chron. Wind.*, ii., 35, 409.
[2] *Libn. SS. Brunswick*, ii., 855.

began, there was already in existence a considerable body
of literature, which was the expression of the pre-christian
conceptions and ideals of the Anglo-Saxons and their
Scandinavian kinsmen.   Certain of the most famous of
the literary creations of the Anglo-Saxons were probably
produced subsequent to the time of the acceptance by the
people of Christianity, but these productions continued to
represent the imagination and the methods of thought of
the pagan ancestry, and to utilise as their themes the old-
time legends.   These Saxon compositions were almost
exclusively in the form of poems, epics, and ballads devoted to accounts of the achievements of heroes (more or
less legendary) in their wars with each other, and in their
adventures with the gods and with the powers of magic
and evil. In these early epics, devoted chiefly to strife,
women bear but a small part, and the element of love
enters hardly at all.

While it is doubtless the case that the Saxon epics, like
the Greek poems of the Homeric period and the compositions of the Celtic bards, were preserved for a number of
generations in the memories of the reciters, there are
references indicating that the writing of the texts on the
parchment began at a comparatively early date after the
occupation of England.   This would imply the existence
of some trained scribes before work was begun in the
scriptoria of the Saxon monasteries.   Such lay scribes
must, however, have been very few indeed, and the task
of handing down for posterity the old legendary ballads
must have depended chiefly upon the *scops*, which was the
name given to the poets or bards attached to the court of
a prince or chieftain.   It is, however, not until the acceptance of Christianity by the Saxons that there comes to be
any abiding interest in letters.   As Jusserand puts it:
"These same Anglo-Saxons, whose literature at the time
of their invasion consisted of the songs mentioned by
Tacitus, *carmina antiqua*, which they trusted to memory

alone, who compiled no books, and who for written monuments had Runic inscriptions graven on utensils or on commemorative stones, now have in their turn monks who compose chronicles and kings who know Latin. Libraries are formed in the monasteries; schools are attached to them; manuscripts are thus copied and illuminated in beautiful caligraphy and in splendid colours. The volutes and knots with which the worshippers of Woden ornamented their *fibulæ*, their arms, the prows of their ships, are reproduced in purple and azure, the initials of the Gospels. The use made of them is different, the taste remains the same."

It is undoubtedly the case that the preservation of such fragments of Anglo-Saxon literature as have come down to us, and probably of most of the Scandinavian compositions which were transmitted through the Saxons, was due to the monastery scribes whose copies were in part transcribed from the earlier parchments and in part were taken down from the recitals made in the monasteries by the bards or minstrels. The service was in fact similar to that previously rendered by the Irish monks to Celtic literature, and by the scribes of Gaul and Italy to the writings of classic times.

The identity or kinship of much of the heroic poetry of the Anglo-Saxons with that of the Scandinavians is pointed out by Grein in his *Anglo-Saxon Library*, and by Vigfusson and York-Powell in their *Corpus Poeticum Boreale*. The greatest of the old English epics, *Beowulf*, sometimes called "the Iliad of the Saxons," was put into written form some time in the eighth century and, like all similar epics, was doubtless the result of the weaving together of a series of ballads of varied dates and origins. The text of the poem has been preserved almost complete in a manuscript, now placed in the Cottonian collection in the British Museum, which dates from the latter part of the tenth century

It will be understood that, as a matter of convenience in a brief reference of this kind, I am using the term Saxon and Anglo-Saxon in no strict ethnological sense, but simply to designate the Teutonic element of the people of England, an element whose influence is usually considered to have begun with the landing of Hengist and Horsa in 451.

The first of the Anglo-Saxon monks to be ranked as a poet appears to have been the cowherd Cædmon, a vassal of the Abbess Hilda and a monk of Whitby. Cædmon's songs were sung about 670. He is reported to have put into verse the whole of Genesis and Exodus, and, later, the life of Christ and the Acts of the Apostles, but his work was not limited to the paraphrasing of the Scriptures. A thousand years before the time of *Paradise Lost*, the Northumbrian monk sang before the Abbess Hilda the *Revolt of Satan*. Fragments of this poem, discovered by Archbishop Usher, and printed for the first time in 1655, have been preserved, and have since that date been frequently published.[1] Cædmon died in 680, and Milton in 1674. The Abbess Hilda, who was herself a princess of royal family, appears to have had a large interest in furthering the study of literature, not only in the nunnery founded by her, but in a neighbouring monastery which came largely under her influence. In both nunnery and monastery, schools for the children of the district were instituted, which schools were probably the earliest of their class in that portion of Britain.

The Northumbrian poet Cynewulf, whose work was done between the years 760 and 800, may be referred to as a connecting link between the group of national or popular bards and the literary workers of the Church. His earlier years were passed as a wandering minstrel, but later in life he passed through some religious experience and entered a monastery, devoting himself thereafter to

[1] Turner's *History of the Anglo-Saxons,* iv., c. 3.

religious poetry. His conversion was doubtless the means of preserving (through the *scriptorium* of his monastery) such of his compositions as have remained, and thus of making a place for his name among the authors of England.

Among the earlier Saxon monks whose educational work was important are to be included S. Wilfred (634–709) and S. Cuthbert (637–687). Wilfred introduced into England the Rule of the Benedictines, and exercised a most important influence in instituting Benedictine monasteries and in bringing these monasteries into relations with the Church of Rome. His life was a stormy one, but notwithstanding the various contentions with the several monarchs who at that time divided between them the territory of England, and in spite of several periods of banishment, he found time to carry on a great work in furthering the intellectual life of his Benedictine monks. It was largely due to him that the Benedictine monasteries accepted almost from the first the responsibility of conducting the schools of the land. These schools achieved so great repute that Anglo-Saxons of high rank were eager to confide their children to Wilfred to be brought up in one of his monastic establishments. At the close of their school training they were to choose between the service of God and that of the King. Wilfred is also to be credited with the establishing within the English monasteries of a course of musical instruction, the teachers of which had largely been trained in the great school of Gregorian music at Canterbury.

Another of the Saxon abbots whose name remains associated with the intellectual life of the monasteries was Benedict Biscop. Montalembert speaks of Biscop as representing science and art in the Church, as Wilfred had stood for the organising of the English Church as a public body, and Cuthbert for the renewal and development of its life. The monasteries of Wearmouth and of Yarrow,

founded by Biscop, were endowed with great libraries and
became the centres of an active literary life. Biscop made
no less than six journeys to Rome in the interest of his
monastery work, and, in the seventh century, a journey
to Rome from Britain was not an easy experience. His
fourth expedition, begun in the year 671, was undertaken
partly in the interests of literature and for the purpose of
securing books for the education of his monks. He
obtained in the Papal capital a rich cargo of books, some
of which he had purchased while others were given to
him. In Vienne, the ancient capital of Gaul, he secured
a further collection. The monastery of Wearmouth,
founded in 673, had the benefit of a large portion of the
books brought from Italy by the abbot. It was his desire
that each monastery for which he was responsible should
possess a library, which seemed to him indispensable for
the instruction, discipline, and the good organisation of
the community. Biscop's fifth journey was made partly
for the purpose of securing pictures, coloured images, and
artistic decorations for the chapel of the monastery, but
the sixth pilgrimage, made in 685, was again devoted
almost entirely to the collection of books.

For the details of the work of Biscop in the organisation of his monasteries and in the supervision of the work
in their *scriptoria*, and concerning his various architectural
and artistic undertakings, we are largely indebted to the
historian Beda, or Bede. Bede was a pupil of Biscop in
the monastery of Yarrow, and it was in this monastery
that were written the famous *Chronicles*. It was the time
of comparative peace in the island which preceded the
first Danish invasion. The fame of the scholar who produced these chronicles was destined to eclipse that of
nearly all the Saxon saints and kings, who were in fact
known to posterity principally through the pen of the
Venerable Bede. It is to Biscop, however, that should be
credited the literary surroundings under which Bede was

educated, and it is probable that without the stimulating
influence of the books secured by the abbot in his wearisome journeys to Southern Europe, the monk would
hardly have had the capacity or the incentive to complete
his work.

Coelfried, who later became Abbot of Yarrow, and who,
after the death of Biscop, was in charge also of the monastery of Wearmouth, continued the interest of his predecessor in the libraries and in the work done by the scribes
in the *scriptoria*.   Among the books brought from Rome
by Biscop was a curious work on cosmography, which
King Alfred was very anxious to possess.   Abbot Coelfried finally consented to let the King have the book in
exchange for land sufficient to support eight families.
Coelfried had had made in the *scriptorium* of Wearmouth
two complete copies of the Bible according to the version
of S. Jerome, the text of which had been brought from
Rome.   These copies were placed, one in the church of
Wearmouth and one in that of Yarrow, and were open
for the use not only of the monks, but of any others who
might desire to consult them and who might be able to
read the script.   Montalembert refers to this instance as
a refutation of " the stupid calumny " which represents
the Church as having in former times interdicted to her
children the knowledge of the sacred Scriptures.[1]

When Aldhelm, who became Bishop of Sherborn in the
year 705, went to Canterbury to be consecrated by his old
friend and companion Berthwold (*pariter literis studu-
erant, pariterque viam religionis triverant*—together they
had studied literature and together they had followed the
path of religion), the Archbishop kept him there many
days, taking counsel with him about the affairs of his
diocese.   Hearing of the arrival during this time of ships
at Dover, he went there to inspect their unloading and
to see if they had brought anything in his way (*si quid*

---

[1] Montalembert, iv., 464.

forte commodum ecclesiastico usui attulissent nautæ qui e Gallico sinu in Angliam provecti librorum copiam apportassent—to see whether the ships which had arrived from the French coast had brought, with the books which formed a part of their cargoes, any volumes of value for the work of the Church). Among many other books he saw one containing the whole of the Old and New Testaments, which book he bought, and which, according to William of Malmesbury, who in the twelfth century wrote the life of Aldhelm, was at that time still preserved at Sherborn.[1]

The great Bible given by King Offa, in 780, to the church at Worcester is described in the chronicle of Malmesbury as *Magnam Bibliam*.[2] As before indicated, however, the common name of this time for a collection of the Scriptures was not *Biblia* but *Bibliotheca*. In a return of their property which the monks of St. Riquier at Centule made in the year 831, by order of Louis the Débonnaire, we find, among a considerable quantity of books: *Bibliotheca integra ubi continentur libri lxxii., in uno volumine* (a complete Bible, in which seventy-two books are comprised in one volume), and also *Bibliotheca dispersa in voluminibus xiv.*[3] (a Bible divided into fourteen volumes).

Fleury says of Olbert, Abbot of Gembloux: *Étant abbé, il amassa à Gembloux plus de cent volumes d'auteurs ecclésiastiques, et cinquante d'auteurs profanes, ce qui passoit pour une grande Bibliothèque.*[4] Warton, using Fleury for his authority, speaks of the "incredible labour and immense expense" which Olbert had given to the formation of this library. There is, however, no authority in the quotation from Fleury for such a description of the exceptional nature of the labour and of the outlay. On the contrary, Fleury goes on to say that Olbert, who had been

---

[1] *Ang. Sac.*, ii., 21. [3] *Chron. Centul. ap. Dach. Sp.*, ii., 311.
[2] *Ibid.*, i., 470. [4] Liv. lviii., chap. lii., p. 424.

sent to reform and restore the monastery, which was in a
state of great poverty and disorder, had put the monks to
work at writing, in order to keep them from being idle.
He himself set an example of industry as a scribe by writing out, with his own hand, the whole of the Old and the
New Testament, a work which was completed in the year
1040.[1] Maitland calculates that a scribe must be both
expert and industrious to perform in less than ten months
the task of transcribing all the books of the Old and the
New Testament. He estimates, further, that at the rate
at which the law stationers of London paid their writers
in his time (1845), such a transcript would cost, for the
writing only, between sixty and seventy pounds.[2]

The sterling service rendered by King Alfred to the literary interests of England was important in more ways than
one, and while his work does not strictly belong to the
record of the English monasteries, it may properly enough
be associated with the literary history of the English
Church; for the King had been adopted as a spiritual son
by Pope Leo IV., and in organising and supervising the work
of the Church, he took upon himself a large measure of
the responsibilities which later were discharged by the
Primate. Alfred ruled over the West Saxons from 871 to
901. His reign was a stormy one, and during a number
of years it seemed doubtful whether the existence of the
little Saxon Kingdom could be maintained against the
assaults of the Danes. There came finally, however, a
period of peace when Alfred, with Winchester as his
capital, was able to give attention to the organisation of
education in his kingdom.

During the long years of invasion and of civil war, the
literary interests and culture that had come to the
Saxons through the Romans had been in great part swept
away. The collections of books had been burned and
could not be replaced because the clerics had forgotten

[1] Mab., A. S., vii., 36.   [2] Maitland, 202.

their Latin. Alfred complained that at the time of his accession in Winchester he could not find south of the Thames a single Englishman able to translate a letter from Latin into English. "When I considered all this, I remembered also how I saw, before it had all been ravaged and burned, how the churches throughout the whole of England stood filled with treasures and books, and there was also a great multitude of God's servants, but they had very little knowledge of the books; they could not understand any of them because they were not written in their own language." Alfred can find but one explanation for the omission of the "good and wise men who were formerly all over England" to leave translations of these books. "They did not think that men could ever be so careless and that learning could so soon decay." The King recalls, however, that there are still left many who "can read English writing." "I began therefore among the many and manifold troubles of this Kingdom, to translate into English the book which is called in Latin *Pastoralis* and in English *Shepherd's Book* (*Hirdeboc*), sometimes word for word and sometimes according to the sense, as I had learned it from Plegmund, my Archbishop, and Asser, my Bishop, and Grimbold my Mass-priest, and John my Mass-priest."[1] It will be noted in these references of King Alfred, that the collections of books, the loss of which he laments, had been contained in the churches. It was also to the ecclesiastics that he was turning for help in the work of rendering into English the instruction for his people to be found in the few Latin volumes that had been preserved.

Jusserand says that Asser was to Alfred what Alcuin had been to Charlemagne, and that he helped the King, by means of the production of translations and by founding schools, to preserve and to spread learning. King Alfred

[1] Sweet, H. King Alfred's version of Gregory's *Pastoral Care*. Early English Text Society. Lond., 1871-1872.

was, however, not content with using his royal authority and influence for the instituting of schools, but himself gave to work as a translator personal time and labour which must have been spared with difficulty from his duties as a ruler and as a military commander. He chooses for his translations books likely to fill up the greatest gaps in the minds of his countrymen, " some books that are most needful for all men to know " : the *Book of Orosius,* which is to serve as a hand-book of universal history ; the *Chronicles of Bede,* that will instruct them concerning the history of their own ancestors ; the *Pastoral Rule of S. Gregory,* which will make clear to churchmen their ecclesiastical duties ; and the *Consolation of Philosophy of Boëthius,* recommended as a guide for the lives of both ecclesiastics and laymen. These royal translations are at once placed in the *scriptoria* of the monasteries and in the writing-rooms of the monastery schools for manifolding, and secure through these channels an immediate and important educational influence.

It is also under the instructions of Alfred that the old national chronicles, written in the Anglo-Saxon tongue, are copied, corrected, and continued. Of these chronicles, seven, more or less complete and differing from each other to some extent, have been preserved. The history of the world presents possibly no other instance of a monarch who devoted himself so steadfastly, with his own personal labour, to the educational and spiritual development of his people.

In the latter portion of the tenth century, S. Dunstan, Archbishop of Canterbury under King Edgar, takes up the task of instructing the clergy and people. Under his influence, new monasteries are endowed, a further series of monastery schools is instituted, and special attention is given in the *scriptoria* and in the writing-rooms of the schools to the production of copies of translations of pious works. The special literary feature of the work done in

Dunstan's school was the attention given to the production of collections of sermons in the vulgar tongue. A number of these collections has been preserved, an example of which, known as the *Blickling Homilies* (from Blickling Hall, Norfolk, where the MS. was found) was compiled before 971. The series also included homilies by Ælfric, who was Abbot of Eynsham in 1005, and sermons of Wulfstan, who was Bishop of York in 1002.

The canons of Ælfric were written between the years 950 and 1000. The authorities do not appear to be clear whether these canons were the work of the Archbishop or of a grammarian of the same name, while, according to one theory, the Archbishop and the grammarian were the same person. The canons were addressed to Wulfin, Bishop of Sherborn, and they were written in such a form that the Bishop might communicate them to his clergy as a kind of episcopal charge. The twenty-first canon orders: " Every priest also, before he is ordained, must have the arms belonging to his spiritual work; that is, the holy books, namely, the *Psalter*, the *Book of Epistles*, the *Book of Gospels*, the *Missal*, the *Book of Hymns*, the *Manual*, the *Calendar* (*Compotus*), the *Passional*, the *Penitential*, the *Lectionary*. These books a priest requires and cannot do without, if he would properly fulfil his office and desires to teach the law to the people belonging to him. And let him carefully see that they are well written." [1]

The library of the English monastery or priory was under the care of the chantor, who could neither sell, pawn, nor lend books without an equivalent pledge; he might, however, with respect to neighbouring churches or to persons of consideration, relax somewhat the strictness of this rule. In the case of a new foundation, the King sometimes sent letters-patent to the different abbeys requesting them to give copies of theological and religious books in their own collections. In certain instances, the

[1] Maitland, 29.

King himself provided such transcripts for the new foundation. In the catalogue of the abbatial libraries of
England, prepared by Leland, record is found of only the
following classics : Cicero and Aristotle (these two appear
in nearly all the catalogues), Terence, Euclid, Quintus
Curtius, Sidonius Apollinaris, Julius Frontinus, Apuleius,
and Seneca.[1] It is difficult from such a list to arrive at the
basis or standard of selection.

Thomas Duffus Hardy gives some interesting information concerning the later literary and historical work done
in the monasteries of Britain,[2] and for a portion of the
following notes concerning this work I am chiefly indebted to him. The Abbey of St. Albans was founded
towards the close of the eighth century, but it was not
until the latter part of the eleventh century, or nearly
three hundred years later, that the *scriptorium* was instituted. The organisation of the *scriptorium* was due to
Paul, the fourteenth abbot, who presided over the monastery from 1077 to 1093, and who had the assistance in this
work of the Bishop Lanfranc. Paul was by birth a Norman, and was esteemed a man of learning as well as of
piety. After the *scriptorium* had been opened, the abbot
placed in it eight *Psalters*, a *Book of Collects*, a *Book of
Epistles*, a book containing the Gospels for the year, two
Gospels bound in gold and silver and ornamented with
gems, and twenty-eight other notable volumes. In addition to these, there was a number of ordinals, costumals,
missals, troparies, collectories, and other books for the use
of the monks in their devotions. This summary of the
first contents of the library is taken by Hardy from the
Gesta Abbatum, a chronicle of St. Albans.

The literary interests of Paul were, it appears, continued
by a large proportion at least of his successors, and many

---

[1] *Collect.*, iii., 7, 17.
[2] Descriptive catalogue of materials relating to the *History of Great Britain and Ireland*, vol. iii., preface

of these made important contributions to the library. Geoffrey, the sixteenth abbot, gave to the *scriptorium* a missal bound in gold, and another missal in two volumes, both incomparably illuminated in gold and written in an open and legible script. He also gave a precious illuminated psalter, a book containing the benediction and sacraments, a book of exorcism, and a collectory. (The description is taken from the *Gesta*.)

Ralph, the seventeenth abbot, was said to have become a lover of books after having heard Wodo of Italy expound the Scriptures. He collected with diligence a large number of valuable manuscripts. Robert de Gorham, who was called the reformer of the liberty of the Church of St. Albans, after becoming prior, gave many books to the *scriptorium*, more than could be mentioned by the author of the *Gesta*. Simon, who became abbot in 1166, caused to be created the office of historiographer. Simon had been educated in the abbey, and did not a little to add to its fame as a centre of literature. He repaired and enlarged the *scriptorium*, and he kept two or three scribes constantly employed in it. The previous literary abbots had for the most part brought from without the books added to the collection, but it was under Simon that the abbey became a place of literary production as well as of literary reproduction. He had an ordinance enacted to the effect that every abbot must support out of his personal funds one adequate scribe. Simon presented to the abbey a considerable group of books that he had himself been collecting before his appointment as abbot, together with a very beautiful copy of the Old and New Testaments.

The next literary abbot was John de Cell, who had been educated in the schools of Paris, and who was profoundly learned in grammar, poetry, and physics. On being elected abbot, he gave over the management of the temporal affairs of the abbey to his prior, Reymond,

and devoted himself to religious duties and to study.
Reymond himself was a zealous collector, and it was
through him that was secured for the library, among
many other books, a copy of the *Historica Scholastica cum
Allegoriis,* of Peter Comester. The exertions of these
scholarly abbots and priors won for St. Albans a special
distinction among the monasteries of Britain, and naturally led to the compilation of the historic annals which
gave to the abbey a continued literary fame. Hardy is
of opinion that these historic annals date from the administration of Simon, between the years 1166 and 1183.

Richard of Wendover, who succeeded Walter as historiographer, compiled, between the years 1230 and 1236,
the *Flores Historiarum,* one of the most important of the
earlier chronicles of England. Hardy points out that it
could have been possible to complete so great a work
within the term of six years, only on the assumption that
Richard found available much material collected by Walter, and it is also probable that other compilations were
utilised by Richard for the work bearing his name. It is
to be borne in mind that the monastic chronicles were but
seldom the production of a single hand, as was the case
with the chronicles of Malmesbury and of Beda. The
greater number of such chronicles grew up from period to
period, fresh material being added in succeeding generations, while in every monastic house in which there were
transcribers, fresh local information was interpolated until
the tributary streams had grown more important than the
original current. In this manner, the monastic annals
were at one time a transcript, at another time an abridg-
ment, and at another an original work. " With the
chronicler, plagiarism was no crime and no degradation.
He epitomised or curtailed or adapted the words of his
predecessors in the same path with or without alteration
(and usually without acknowledgment), whichever best
suited his purpose or that of his monastery. He did not

work for himself but at the command of others, and thus it was that a monastery chronicle grew, like a monastery house, at different times, and by the labour of different hands."

Of the heads that planned such chronicles or of the hands that executed them, or of the exact proportion contributed by the several writers, no satisfactory record has been preserved. The individual is lost in the community.

In the earlier divisions of Wendover's chronicle, covering the centuries from 231 down to about 1000, Wendover certainly relied, says Hardy, upon some previous compilation. About the year 1014, that narrative, down to the death of Stephen, showed a marked change in style, giving evidence that after this period some other authority had been adopted, while there was also a larger introduction of legendary matter. From the accession of Henry II., in 1235, when the *Flores Historiarum* ends, Wendover may be said to assume the character of an original author. On the death of Richard, the work of historiographer was taken up by Matthew Paris. His *Lives of the Two Offas* and his famous *Chronicles* were produced between the years 1236 and 1259.

In certain of the more literary of the English monasteries, the divine offices were moderated in order to allow time for study, and, under the regulations of some foundations, "lettered" persons were entitled to special exemption from the performance of certain daily services, and from church duty. [1]

At a visitation of the treasury of St. Pauls, made in the year 1295, by Ralph de Baudoke, the Dean (afterwards Bishop of London), there were found twelve copies of the Gospels adorned, some with silver, and others with pearls and gems, and a thirteenth, the case (*capsa*) containing which was decorated not merely with gilding but with

[1] Wilkins, *Monast.*, ii., 708.

relics.[1] The treasury also contained a number of other divisions of the Scriptures, together with a *Commentary* of Thomas Aquinas. Maitland says that the use of relics as a decoration was an unusual feature. He goes on to point out that the practice of using for manuscripts a decorated case, caused the case, not infrequently, to be more valuable than the manuscript itself, so that it would be mentioned among the treasures of the church, when the book contained in it was not sufficiently important to be even specified.

The binding of the books which were in general use in the English monasteries for reference was usually in parchment or in plain leather. The use of jewels, gold, or silver for the covers, or for the *capsæ*, was, with rare exceptions, limited to the special copies retained in the church treasury. William of Malmesbury in the account which he gives of the chapel made at Glastonbury by King Ina, mentions that twenty pounds and sixty marks of gold were used in the preparation of the *Coöpertoria Librorum Evangelii*.[2]

The Earlier Monastery Schools.—At the time when neither local nor national governments had assumed any responsibilities in connection with elementary education, and when the municipalities were too ignorant, and in many cases too poor, to make provision for the education of the children, the monks took up the task as a part of the regular routine of their duty. The Rule of S. Benedict had in fact made express provision for the education of pupils.

An exception to the general statement concerning the neglect of the rulers to make provision for education should, however, be made in the case of Charlemagne, whose reign covered the period 790 to 830. It was the aim of Charlemagne to correct or at least to lessen the provincial differences and local barbarities of style, ex-

---

[1] Dugd., *Monast.*, iii., 309.   [2] *Ap. Gale. ser.*, xiv., 311.

pression, orthography, etc., in the rendering of Latin, and it was with this end in view that he planned out his great scheme of an imperial series of schools, through which should be established an imperial or academic standard of style and expression. This appears to have been the first attempt since the time of the Academy of Alexandria to secure a scholarly uniformity of the standard throughout the civilised world, and the school at Tours may be considered as a precursor of the French Academy of modern times. For such a scheme the Emperor was dependent upon the monks, as it was only in the monasteries that could be found the scholarship that was required for the work. He entrusted to Alcuin, a scholarly English Benedictine, the task of organising the imperial schools. The first schools instituted by Alcuin in Aachen and Tours, and later in Milan, were placed in charge of Benedictine monks, and formed the models for a long series of monastic schools during the succeeding centuries. Alcuin had been trained in the cathedral schools founded in York by Egbert, and Egbert had been brought up by Benedict Biscop in the monastery of Yarrow, where he had for friend and fellow pupil the chronicler Bede. The results of the toilsome journeys taken by Biscop to collect books for his beloved monasteries of Wearmouth and Yarrow[1] were far-reaching. The training secured by Alcuin as a scribe and as a student of the Scriptures, the classics, and the " seven liberal arts " was more immediately due to his master Ælbert, who afterward succeeded Egbert as archbishop.

The script which was accepted as the standard for the imperial schools, and which, transmitted through successive Benedictine *scriptoria*, served seven centuries later as a model for the first type-founders of Italy and France, can be traced directly to the school at York.

Alcuin commemorated his school and its master in a

[1] See p. 95.

descriptive poem *On the Saints of the Church at York*, which is quoted in full by West.[1] In 780, Alcuin succeeded Ælbert as master of the school, and later, was placed in charge of the cathedral library, which was at the time one of the most important collections in Christendom. In one of his poems he gives a kind of metrical summary of the chief contents of this library. The lines are worth quoting because of the information presented as to the authors at that time to be looked for in a really great monastic library. The list includes a distinctive though very restricted group of Latin writers, but, as West points out, the works " by glorious Greece transferred to Rome " form but a meagre group. The catalogue omits Isidore, although previous references make clear that the writings of the great Spanish bishop were important works of reference in York as in all the British schools. It is West's opinion that the *Aristotle* and other Greek authors referred to were probably present only in Latin versions. These manuscripts in the York library were undoubtedly for the most part transcripts of the parchments collected for Wearmouth and Yarrow by Biscop.

The Library of York Cathedral.

There shalt thou find the volumes that contain
All of the ancient Fathers who remain ;
There all the Latin writers make their home
With those that glorious Greece transferred to Rome,
The Hebrews draw from their celestial stream,
And Africa is bright with learning's beam.

Here shines what Jerome, Ambrose, Hilary thought,
Or Athanasius and Augustine wrought.
Orosius, Leo, Gregory the Great,
Near Basil and Fulgentius coruscate.

Alcuin, 31.

Grave Cassiodorus and John Chrysostom
Next Master Bede and learned Aldhelm come,
While Victorinus and Boëthius stand
With Pliny and Pompeius close at hand.

Wise Aristotle looks on Tully near,
Sedulius and Juvencus next appear.
Then come Albinus, Clement, Prosper too,
Paulinus and Arator.   Next we view
Lactantius, Fortunatus.   Ranged in line
Virgilius Maro, Statius, Lucan, shine.

Donatus, Priscian, Phobus, Phocas, start
The roll of masters in grammatic art.
Entychius, Servius, Pompey, each extend
The list.   Comminian brings it to an end.

There shalt thou find, O reader, many more
Famed for their style, the masters of old lore,
Whose many volumes singly to rehearse
Were far too tedious for our present verse.[1]

Alcuin's work on the Continent began in 782, when, resigning his place as master of the cathedral school in York, he took charge of the imperial or palace school at Tours.   His work in the palace school included not only the organisation of classes for the younger students, but the personal charge of a class which comprised the Emperor himself, his wife Luitgard, and other members of the royal or imperial family.   Whether for the younger or for the older students, however, the instruction given had to be of a very elementary character.   The distinctive value of the work was, it is to be borne in mind, not in the extent of the instruction given to the immediate pupils, but in making clear to the Emperor and to his sons who were to succeed him, the importance of

[1] Cited by West, 34.

securing a certain uniformity of script and of educational work throughout the Empire.

It is very probable that not a few of the earlier copyists who completed in the *scriptoria* the tasks set for them by the instructors trained in Tours and in Aachen, transcribed texts the purport of which they had not mastered. It was through their work, however, that the texts themselves were preserved and were made available for later scribes and students who were competent to comprehend the spirit as well as the letter of their contents.

Mabillon is in accord with later authorities such as Compayré and West, as to the deplorable condition of learning at this time throughout the Empire ruled by Charles. Says West : " The plight of learning in Frankland at this time was deplorable. Whatever traditions had found their way from the early Gallic schools into the education of the Franks had long since been scattered and obliterated in the wild disorders which characterised the times of the Merovingian kings. . . . The copying of books had almost ceased, and all that can be found that pretends to the name of literature in this time is the dull chronicle or ignorantly conceived legend." [1]

A description such as this emphasises the importance of the work initiated by Alcuin, work the value of which the ruler of Europe was fortunately able to appreciate and ready to support. In his relation to scholarly interests in Europe and to the preservation of the literature of the past, Alcuin may fairly be considered as the successor of Cassiodorus. He was able in the eighth century to render a service hardly less distinctive than that credited to Cassiodorus three hundred years earlier. There is the further parallel that, like Cassiodorus, he possessed a very keen and intelligent interest in the form given to literary expression, and in all the details of the work given to the copyists. The instructions given in

[1] *Alcuin*, 42.

Alcuin's treatise on orthography for the work of the scribes, follow very closely in principle, and differ, in fact, but slightly in detail from, the instructions given by Cassiodorus in his own treatise on the same subject. A couplet which stands at the head of the first page reads as follows: "Let him who would publish the sayings of the ancients read me, for he who follows me not will speak without regard to law."[1] Alcuin's care in regard to the consistency of punctuation and orthography and his intelligent selection of a clearer and neater form of script than had heretofore been employed, have impressed a special character on the series of manuscripts dating from the early portion of the ninth century and written in what is termed the Caroline minuscule. In a letter written to Charles from Tours in 799, Alcuin mentions that he has copied out on some blank parchment which the King had sent him a short treatise on correct diction, with illustrations from Bede. He goes on to speak of the special value to literature of the distinctions and subdistinctions of punctuation, the knowledge of which has, he complains, almost disappeared: "But even as the glory of all learning and the ornaments of wholesome erudition begin to be seen again by reason of your noble exertions, so also it seems most fitting that the use of punctuation should also be resumed by scribes. . . . Let your authority so instruct the youths at the palace that they may be able to utter with perfect elegance whatsoever the clear eloquence of your thought may dictate, so that whatsoever may go to the parchment bearing the royal name it may display the excellence of the royal learning."[2] A very delicate hint, remarks West, for Charles to mind his commas and his colons.

Up to the time of Charlemagne there appears to have been so little facility in writing and so few scribes were available, that government records were not kept even

---

[1] Version of West, 102.   [2] *Ep.* 101, Migne; 112, Jaffé, cited by West.

at the Courts. The schools established by Alcuin at Tours, under the direction of Charlemagne, were in fact the first schools for writers which had existed in Western Europe for centuries. One of the earlier applications made of the knowledge gained in the imperial schools was for the critical analysis of certain historical documents which had heretofore been accepted as final authorities. In the earlier centuries of the Middle Ages, anything that was in writing appears to have been accepted as necessarily trustworthy and valuable, very much as in the earlier times of printing the fact that a statement was in print caused it to be accepted as something not to be contradicted. The critical faculty, combined with the scholarly knowledge necessary and properly applied, was, however, of slow growth, and centuries must still have passed before, in this work of differentiating the value of documents, the authority of scholars secured its full recognition.

After this work of Alcuin began, that is to say, after the beginning of the ninth century, it became the rule of each properly organised monastery to include, in addition to the *scriptorium*, an *armarium*, or writing-chamber, which was utilised as a class-room for instruction in writing and in Latin. In a letter of Canonicus Geoffrey, of St.-Barbe-en-Auge, dated 1170, occurs the expression, *Claustrum sine armario est quasi castrum sine armamentario*,[1] (a monastery without a writing-chamber is like a camp without a storehouse of munitions or an armory.)

The Capitular of Charlemagne, issued in the year 789, addressed itself to the correction of the ignorance and carelessness of the monks, and to the necessity of preserving a standard of correctness for the work of transcribing holy writings. It contains the phrase:

Et pueros vestros non sinite eos vel legendo vel scribendo corrumpere. Et si opus est evangelium, psalterium et mis-

[1] Wattenbach, p. 362.

sale scribere, perfectæ ætatis homines scribant cum omni diligentia.

(Do not permit your pupils, either in reading or writing, to garble the text ;—and when you are preparing copies of the gospel, the psalter, or the missal, see that the work is confided to men of mature age, who will write with due care.)

The following lines were written by Alcuin as an injunction to pious scribes :

AD MUSÆUM LIBROS SCRIBENTIUM.

Hic sedeant sacræ scribentes famina legis,
Nec non sanctorum dicta sacrata patrum.
His interserere caveant sua frivola verbis,
Frivola ne propter erret et ipsa manus,
Correctosque sibi quærant studiose libellos,
Tramite quo recto penna volantis eat.
Per cola distinguant proprios et commata sensus.
Et punctos ponant ordine quosque suo,
Ne vel falsa legat taceat vel forte repente,
Ante pios fratres lector in ecclesia.

.   .   .   .

(Quoted from the Vienna Codex, 743.   Denis, i., 313.)

Wattenbach is of opinion that these lines stood over the door of the *scriptorium* of S. Martin's Monastery.

West says that the lines were written as an injunction to the scribes of the school at Tours.   He gives the following version, which takes in certain further lines of the original than those cited by Wattenbach :

" Here let the scribes sit who copy out the words of the Divine Law, and likewise the hallowed sayings of the holy Fathers. Let them beware of interspersing their own frivolities in the words they copy, nor let a trifler's hand make mistakes through haste. Let them earnestly seek out for themselves correctly written books to transcribe, that the flying pen may speed along the right path.

8

Let them distinguish the proper sense by colons and commas, and let them set the points each one in its due place, and let not him who reads the words to them either read falsely or pause suddenly. It is a noble work to write out holy books, nor shall the scribe fail of his due reward. Writing books is better than planting vines, for he who plants a vine serves his belly, but he who writes a book serves his soul."[1]

In a manuscript which was written in S. Jacob's Monastery in Liége, occurred the following lines:

Jacob Rebeccæ dilexit simplicitatem,
Altus mens Jacobi scribendi sedulitatem.
Ille pecus pascens se divitiis cumulavit,
Iste libros scribens meritum sibi multiplicavit.
Ille Rachel typicam præ cunctis duxit amatam,
Hic habeat vitam justis super astra paratam.[2]

[(The Hebrew) Jacob loved the simplicity of Rebecca,
The lofty soul of (the monk) Jacob (loved) the work of the
    scribe.
The former accumulated riches in pasturing his flocks,
The latter increased his glory through the writing of books.
The former won his Rachel, loved beyond all others.
The latter shall have the eternal life which is prepared above
    the stars for the just.]

The most important of the works of Alcuin that can be called original were his educational writings, comprising treatises *On Grammar, On Orthography, On Rhetoric and the Virtues, On Dialectics, A Disputation with Pepin*, and a study of astronomy entitled *De Cursu et Saltu Lunæ ac Bissexto.* West mentions three other treatises which have been ascribed to him: *On the Seven Arts, A Disputation for Boys*, and the *Propositions of Alcuin.*[3] Alcuin was more fortunate than his great predecessor Cassiodorus in

[1] West, 72.　　[2] Wattenbach, 366.　　[3] *Alcuin*, 92.

respect to the preservation of his writings.   Manuscripts
of all of these remained in existence until the time came
when the complete set of works could be issued in printed
form, and the work of the old instructor could be appreciated by a generation living a thousand years after his
life had closed.   He died at Tours in 804, in his seventieth
year.   Mabillon speaks of Alcuin as "the most learned
man of his age."   Laurie is disposed to lay stress upon
the monastic limitations of his intellect, and thinks that
his principal ability was that of an administrator; West
emphasises the "pure unselfishness of his character," and
adds, with discriminating appreciation: "We must also
credit him with a certain largeness of view, in spite of his
circumscribed horizon.   He had some notion of the continuity of the intellectual life of man, of the perils that
beset the transmission of learning from age to age, and of
the disgrace which attached to those who would allow
those noble arts to perish which the wisest of men among
the ancients had discovered. . . .   Perceiving that the
precious treasure of knowledge was then hidden in a few
books, he made it his care to transmit to future ages
copies undisfigured by slips of the pen or mistakes of the
understanding.   Thus in every way that lay within his
power, he endeavoured to put the fortunes of learning for
the times that should succeed him in a position of advantage, safeguarded by an abundance of truthfully transcribed books, interpreted by teachers of his own training,
sheltered within the Church and defended by the civil
power."[1]   Professor West's appreciative summary does
full justice to the work and the ideals of Charlemagne's
great schoolmaster.   I should only add that in the special
service he was in a position to render in the preservation,
transmission, and publication of the world's literature,
Alcuin must be accorded a very high place in the series of
literary workers which, beginning with Cassiodorus, in-

[1] *Alcuin*, 122, 123.

cludes such names as Columba, Biscop, Aurispa, Gutenberg, Aldus, Estienne, and Froben.

The most noteworthy of the successors of Alcuin in the
palace school at Tours was John Scotus Erigena, who in
845 was appointed master by Charles the Bold. The
influence of the Irish monk widened the range of study and
gave to it an active-minded and speculative tendency that
brought about a wide departure from the settled conserva-
tism which had always characterised the teaching of
Alcuin. The list of books given to the scribe for copying
was increased, and now included, for instance, works of
such doubtful orthodoxy as the *Satyricon* of Martianus
Capella, a voluminous compilation constituting a kind of
cyclopædia of the seven liberal arts. Its composition
dates from about 500.[1]

In a treatise, *De Instituto Clericorum*, written in 819
(that is, during the reign of Louis I.), by Rabanus Mau-
rus, who was Abbot of Fulda and later, Archbishop
of Mayence, is cited the following regulation: " The
canons and the decrees of Pope Zosimus have decided
that a clerk proceeding to holy orders shall continue five
years among the readers . . . and after that shall
for four years serve as an acolyte or sub-deacon." (The
Zosimus referred to was Pope for but one year, 417–418.)
Rabanus had just before remarked, " *Lectores* are so called
a legendo." He goes on to say that " he who would
rightly and properly perform the duty of a reader must be
imbued with learning and conversant with books, and
must further be instructed in the meaning of words and in
the knowledge of the words themselves," etc.[2] Rabanus
follows this with a series of very practical instructions and
suggestions for effective education on the part of the
readers. These were based upon the treatise on elocu-
tion written nearly two hundred years earlier by the

[1] Mullinger, 197.
[2] Lib. i., cap. xiii., *Ap. Bib. Pat.*, tom. x., 572, cited by Maitland.

learned Bishop Isidore of Seville, and they were again copied three years after the time of Rabanus by Ibo, Bishop of Chartres, in the treatise *De Rebus Ecclesiasticis*. Maitland, to whom I am indebted for this citation, finds cause for indignant criticism of the historian Robertson for the superficial and misleading references made by the historian to the dense ignorance of the Church in the Middle Ages. Maitland suggests that if Robertson had applied for holy orders to the Archbishop of Seville in the seventh century, the Archbishop of Mayence in the ninth, or the Bishop of Chartres in the eleventh, he would have found the examination rather more of a task than he expected. West speaks of Rabanus as " Alcuin's greatest pupil," and as intellectually " a greater man than his master." [1] He wrote a long series of theological and educational treatises.

From the *Constitutions* of Reculfus, who became Bishop of Soissons in 879, it is evident that he expected the clergy to be able both to read and to write. The Bishop says: "We admonish that each one of you should be careful to have a Missal, a Lectionary, a Book of the Gospels, a Martyrology, an Antiphonary, a Psalter, and a copy of the Forty Homilies of S. Gregory, corrected and pointed by our copies which we use in the holy mother Church; and also fail not to have as many sacred and ecclesiastical books as you can get, for from these you shall receive food and condiment for your souls. . . . If, however, any one of you is not able to obtain all the books of the Old Testament, at least let him diligently take pains to transcribe for himself correctly the first book of the whole sacred history, that is, *Genesis*, by reading which he may come to understand the creation of the world." [2] The counsel was good, even although a perfectly clear understanding of the creation might after all not have been secured.

[1] *Alcuin*, 134.   [2] *Const.*, ix., 418.

By the close of the ninth century, a large proportion of
the monasteries of the Continent and of England carried
on schools which were open to the children of as large a
district as could be reached. In many cases, the elementary classes were succeeded by classes in advanced
instruction, while from these were selected favourites or
exceptionally capable pupils, who enjoyed in still higher
studies the advantage of the guidance and service of the
best scholars in the monastery. West, in summing up
the later influence of Alcuin, speaks of the stream of
learning as having flowed from York to Tours and from
Tours (through Rabanus) to Fulda, thence to Auxerre,
Ferrières, Corbies (old and new), Reichenau, St. Gall, and
Rheims, one branch of it finally reaching Paris.[1] Mabillon
speaks of the abbey schools of Fleury as containing during
the tenth and eleventh centuries as many as five thousand
scholars.

In Italy, the most important schools were those instituted at Monte Cassino, Pomposa, and Classe. Giesebrecht is, however, of opinion that the educational
work of the Italian monasteries was less important than
that carried on by the monasteries in Germany, France,
or England. In Germany, the monasteries which have
already been mentioned as centres of intellectual activity
were also those which had instituted the most important
and effective of the schools, the list including St. Gall,
Fulda, Reichenau, Hirschau, Wissembourg, Hersfeld, and
many others.

In France and Belgium, the names of the conspicuous
abbey schools include those of Marmoutier, Fontenelle,
Fleury, Corbie, Ferrières, Bec, Clugni. In England, the
most noteworthy of the abbey schools were St. Albans,
Glastonbury, Malmesbury, Croyland, and S. Peter's of
Canterbury. From the epoch of Charlemagne to that
of S. Louis, the great abbeys of Christian Europe served

[1] *Alcuin*, 164.

in fact not only as its schools but as its universities.
The more intelligent of the nobility and the kings
themselves were interested in securing for their children
the educational advantages of the monastery schools.
Among the French kings who were brought up in this
way are to be named Pepin the Little, Robert the Pious,
and Louis the Fat.   In Spain, Sancho the Great, King of
Navarre and of Castile, was a graduate of the monastery
of Leyre.

In England, we have the noteworthy example of Alfred,
who was not ashamed, after having reached mature years,
to repair his imperfect education by attending the school
established in Oxford by the Benedictines, where he is
said to have studied grammar, philosophy, rhetoric,
history, music, and versification.[1]

A large number of the convents, following the example
of the abbeys, contained schools in which were trained not
only the future novices, but also numbers of young girls
destined for the life of the Courts or of the world.

Mabillon finds occasion to correct the impression on the
part of some writers of the sixteenth century, that the
monasteries had been established solely for the purpose
of carrying on educational work.   He writes : *C'est une
illusion de certains gens qui ont écrit dans le siècle précédent
que les monastères n'avaient esté d'abord établis que pour
servir d'écoles faisantes profession d'enseigner les sciences
humaines.*

De Rancé, who wrote a *Traité de la saincteté et du devoir
de la vie monastique*, took the ground that the pursuit of
literature was inconsistent with the monastic profession,
and that the reading of the monks ought to be confined
to the Scriptures and a few books of devotion.   The
treatise was understood to be an attack upon the Benedictine monks of St. Maur, for that they were learned was a
matter of general knowledge, and the monks of La

[1] Ziegelbauer, i., 326.

Trappe, the Order with which De Rancé had associated himself, had an old-time antagonism to their scholarly neighbours. It may be considered as a good service for literature and for monastic history that the treatise of De Rancé, narrow and unimportant in itself as it was, should have been published. Nine years later, in the year 1691, was issued the reply of the Benedictines, the learned and valuable *Traité des Études Monastiques* of Dom Mabillon, which will be referred to more particularly in the following chapter.

The historians of these monastic schools have laid stress upon the limited conceptions possessed by their founders and by the instructors, of the purpose and possibilities of education, conceptions which of necessity affected not only the work done in the school-room, but the character of the literature produced in the *scriptoria*. Laurie, for instance, writes as follows: " The Christian conception of education was, unfortunately (like that of old Cato), narrow. It tended steadily to concentrate and to contract men's intellectual interests. The Christian did not think of the culture of the whole man. He could not consistently do so. His whole purpose was the salvation of the soul. . . . Salvation was to be obtained through abnegation of the world and through faith. . . . Christianity, accordingly, found itself necessarily placed in mortal antagonism to ' Humanitas ' and to Hellenism, and had to go through the troublous experiences of nearly 1400 years before the possibility of the union of reason with authority, of religion with Hellenism, could be conserved. . . . As was indeed inevitable, theological discussion more and more occupied the active intellect of the time, to the subordination, if not total neglect of humane letters and philosophy. The Latin and Greek classics were ultimately denounced. As the offspring of the pagan world, if not indeed inspired by demons, they were dangerous to the faith." [1]

[1] *Rise and Institution of Universities*, 26.

From the *Apostolic Constitutions*, ascribed to the middle of the fourth century, Mr. Bass Mullinger quotes the injunction : " Refrain from all the writings of the heathen : for what hast thou to do with strange discourses, laws, or false prophets, which, in truth, turn aside from the faith those who are weak in the understanding . . . wherefore abstain scrupulously from all strange and devilish books." [1]

It was S. Augustine who said *Indocti cœlum rapiunt* —" It is the ignorant who take the kingdom of heaven,"— and Gregory the Great who asserted that he would blush to have Holy Scripture subjected to the rules of grammar.[2] West speaks of the conceptions of grammar and of rhetoric taught by Alcuin as " crude " and " puerile," and of his theories of language as " childish."

It is, of course, a truism to point out that the educational work done by Alcuin and the other great instructors of the monastic schools is not to be judged by the standard of later ages. The students for whose training they were responsible, whether children or adults, princes or peasants, must have been, with hardly an exception, in a very elementary condition of mental development, and it was necessary for the instruction to be in like manner elementary. In this study, I am, however, not undertaking to consider the history of education in early Europe, a subject which has been so ably presented in the works of Mullinger, Laurie, Compayré, and West. I am concerned with the work of these early schoolmasters simply because to their persistent efforts was due the preservation of literature in Europe. If Alcuin and his successors had done nothing else than to secure a substantially uniform system of writing throughout the great schools in which were trained abbots and scribes for hundreds of monasteries, they would have conferred an inestimable service upon Europe. But their work did go much further. Notwithstanding the various injunctions and warnings of

[1] *Schools of Charles the Great*, 8.   [2] Cited by West, *Alcuin*, 11.

ecclesiastical leaders against "pagan" literature, it proved impracticable to prevent this literature from being preserved and manifolded in numberless *scriptoria*. The record of the opposition has been preserved in a series of edicts and injunctions. But the fact that the interest in the writings of the ancients proved strong enough to withstand all the fulminations and censures is evidenced by the long series of manuscripts of the classics produced in the monasteries during the tenth and eleventh centuries. The writers of these manuscripts were the product of the schools instituted by Charlemagne and Alcuin.

The Benedictines of the Continent.—The two writers who have given the largest attention to the record of the literary and scholarly work of the Benedictines during the seven centuries between 500 and 1200 A.D., are Mabillon and Ziegelbauer. Dom Mabillon was himself a Benedictine monk and had a full inheritance of the literary spirit and scholarly devotion which characterised the Order. He was born in Rheims in 1632, and his treatise on monastic studies, *Traité des Études Monastiques*, which has remained the chief authority on its subject, was published in Paris in 1691. Ziegelbauer's *Observationes Literariæ S. Benedicti* appeared a century later.[1]

Mabillon's work forms a magnificent monument not only to the learning, diligence, and literary skill of its writer, but to the enormous value of the services rendered, during a number of centuries, by the monks of his Order, in the preservation of literature from the ravages of barbarism and in the development of scholarship. Mabillon also makes clear the lasting importance of the original initiative given to the literary labour of the Benedictines by the Rule of their founder. An important portion of the material upon which Mabillon's treatise was based, was collected during a series of journeys made by him in company with his brother under the instructions first of

[1] Aug. Vindeloc, 4 vols., 1784.

the great minister Colbert, and later, of Le Tellier, Archbishop of Rheims, for the purpose of examining or of searching for documents relating to the royal family and of procuring books for the royal library. The first of these journeys, undertaken in the year 1682, was completed entirely within French territory and was entitled *Iter Burgundicum*. The second covered a considerable portion of South Germany and Switzerland, and is known as the *Iter Germanicum*. The third was devoted to Italy, and is described under the title of *Iter Italicum;* while the fourth investigation was made in Alsace and Lorraine, and the record is entitled *Iter Literarium in Alsatiam et Lotharingiam.*

The plan of the journeys involved a thorough ransacking of as many libraries as they could secure admission to, the libraries being, with but few exceptions, contained in the monasteries. The immediate result of these journeys was the addition to the royal library of some three thousand volumes, chiefly collected in Italy, and the later result, the publication of the records above specified, which form a most valuable presentation of the condition of the monastic collections in the seventeenth century, and which give in their lists the titles of a considerable number of valuable works which have since entirely disappeared.

A century later than S. Benedict, an unknown hermit called " the Master " prepared a Rule under which monks were required to study until they reached the age of fifty.[1] The Rule of S. Aurelian and S. Ferreol rendered this regulation universal, and that of Grimlaïcus identified the character of the hermit with that of " doctor." [2] In all countries where the Benedictine Orders flourished, literature and scholarship exercised an abiding influence. It is impossible, contends Montalembert, to name an abbey famed for the number and holiness of its monks

---

[1] Cassiod., *Inst.*, ch. xxiii.   [2] Mabillon, *Traité*, 43, 44.

which is not also noted for learning and for its school of literature. The Benedictine monks during the four or five centuries after the foundation of the Order certainly appear to have held themselves faithful to the precept of S. Jerome, " A book always in your hand or under your eyes." (*Nunquam de manu necque oculis recedat liber.*[1]) They also accepted very generally the example of Bede, who said that it had been for him always delightful either to learn, to teach, or to write.[2] Warton is authority for the statement that in the year 790 Charlemagne granted to the abbot and monks of Sithiu an unlimited right of hunting, in order that they might procure from the skins of the deer killed, gloves, girdles, and covers for their books. He goes on to say : " We may imagine that these religious were more fond of hunting than of reading. It is certain that they were obliged to hunt before they could read, and it seems probable that under these circumstances they did not manufacture many volumes." [3] Maitland, in referring to the original text of the concession, finds, however, that this has been misread by Warton. The permission to hunt, for the useful purpose specified, was given not for the monks but for the servants of the monastery.

With all the great Benedictine monasteries, it was the routine to institute first a library, then a *scriptorium* for the manifolding of books, and finally schools, open, not only to students who were preparing for the Church, but to all in the neighbourhood who had need of or desire for instruction. The copies prepared in the *scriptorium* of the texts from the library were utilised in the first place for the duplicates needed of the works in most frequent reference, but more particularly for securing by exchange copies of texts not already in the library, and, in many instances, also for adding either to the direct wealth of

---

[1] *Epist. ad Rustic.*   [2] *Epist. ad Occam.*   Quoted by Mabillon, 80.
[3] *History of Poetry*, dissert. ii.

the monastery (by exchange for lands or cattle) or to its income by making sale of the works through travelling monks or by correspondence with other monasteries.

The list of monasteries which became in this manner literary and publishing centres would include nearly all the great Benedictine foundations of both Britain and the Continent. There was probably, however, a greater activity during the period between 600 and 1200, in the matter at least of collecting and circulating books, in the monasteries of France than in those of Italy, Germany, or Britain; but more important even than Clugni, Marmoutier, or Corbie, in France, was the great Swiss abbey of St. Gall, an abbey the realm of which reached almost to the proportions of a small municipality. In the shade of its walls, there dwelt a whole nation, divided into two branches, the *familia intus*, which comprised the labourers, shepherds, and workmen of all trades, and the *familia foris*, composed of serfs, who were bound to do three days' work in each week.

Within the monastery itself, there were, in the latter half of the tenth century, no less than five hundred monks, together with a great group of students. In Germany, the most noted of what might be called the literary monasteries during the ninth and tenth centuries were those of Fulda, Reichenau, Lorsch, Hirschau, and Gandersheim. It was in the latter that the nun Hroswitha composed her famous dramas. In France, in addition to those already specified, should be mentioned Fleury, St. Remy, St. Denis, Luxeuil, S. Vincent at Toul, and Aurillac. In Belgium, S. Peter's at Ghent was, during the tenth century, the most important of the scholarly monasteries. In England, in addition to the earlier foundations, already referred to, of Wearmouth and Yarrow, St. Albans and Glastonbury became the most famous. Before the eleventh century, the literature that came into existence from contemporary writers or reproductions of the works

of classic writers outside of the monasteries must have
been very trifling indeed.   One of the most noteworthy
publications which emanated from St. Gall was the great
dictionary or *Vocabulary* bearing the name of Solo-
mon (Abbot of St. Gall and later, Bishop of Constance),
a work which was in fact a kind of literary and scientific
encyclopædia.   This manuscript, comprising in all 1070
pages, was put into print in the latter part of the fifteenth
century.[1]   The records of the famous library of the monastery have been brought together by later scholars, and
it is their testimony that the manuscripts contained in it
were among the most beautiful and accurate specimens of
caligraphy known.   These St. Gall manuscripts were also
noted for their exquisite miniatures and illuminations.
The parchment used for them was prepared by the hands
of the monks, and they also did their own binding.[2]   The
fame of Sintram, one of the most noteworthy of the copyists, was known throughout all the countries north of the
Alps ; *Omnis orbis cisalpinus Sintramni digitos miratur.*[3]
In the two schools attached to St. Gall, lectures were
given, in the latter half of the tenth century, on Cicero,
Quintilian, Horace, Terence, Juvenal, Persius, Ovid, and
Sophocles.[4]   There was even said to be among the monks
of St. Gall a society established for the study of Greek,
called the Hellenic Brothers.[5]   The Duchess Hedwig of
Suabia herself taught Greek to Abbot Burckhart II. when
he was a child, and rewarded him by the gift of a
" Horace " for his readiness in verse-making.   The Abbot
later described in verse the embarrassment caused to him
by a kiss with which the learned Duchess had favoured
him.[6]   The Duchess had, when a young woman, learned
Latin from the Ekkehart who, later, became Dean of St.
Gall (Ekkehart I.), in partnership with whom she wrote

[1] Montalembert, 147.
[2] Digby, *Mores Catholica*, x., 242.
[3] Ekk. in *Cassib.*, c. i., p. 20.
[4] Ekkehart, *Lib. Benedict.*, 345.
[5] *Ibid.*, 247.
[6] Ekkehart, in *Cassib.*, c. x.

a commentary on Virgil. A very charming account of
the tuition of this fascinating young Duchess is given in
Scheffel's famous romance called *Der Treue Ekkehart.*
Arx states that Ekkehart III. and IV. and Notker Labeo
were familiar with Homer, Plato, and Aristotle, and made
from them Greek verses.[1]

There is every evidence to indicate that there was
during the tenth century a knowledge of Greek in certain
monastery centres of South Europe, which knowledge,
two centuries later, had disappeared almost entirely, so
that the re-introduction into Italy of the writings of Greek
poets and philosophers in the thirteenth and fourteenth
centuries came as a fresh revelation. Mabillon contended
that while the monks made Holy Scripture the basis for
their theological studies, it is certain that they acquired
apart from these studies, a mass of other knowledge, and
notably all that they could gather with regard to physical
science. Thence it arose that in mediæval works the
term *scripturæ*, or even *scripturæ sacræ*, does not always
mean the Holy Scriptures, but stands for all books which
treat of Christian or ecclesiastical truths or which are
useful aids in understanding the Word of God.[2] Montalembert, commenting on this passage, goes on to say
that to the monk of the tenth century no knowledge was
unfamiliar. Philosophy in its scholastic form, grammar
and versification, music, botany, mechanics, astronomy,
geometry in its most practical application, all of these
were the objects of their research and of their writings.
The curious poem addressed by the monk Alfano to
Theodoric, son of the Count Marses and at the time a
novice at Monte Cassino, is cited in support of this view.
The poem presents a detailed account of the daily occupations in the great monastery, in which occupations
literary work holds a very large place. It also gives a

[1] Arx, i., 260.
[2] Mabillon, *Réflexions sur la Réponse de M. l'Abbé de la Trappe*, i., 199.

summary of the scholastic pursuits carried on in the monastery.[1]

A service possibly even greater than that of the pre-servation of literature and of the keeping alive of an intellectual spirit, was rendered by the monks in the great educational work carried on by them. In the Monasterium Resbacense, in Brieggan, founded by Bishop Andœnus in 634, whose first abbot, S. Ægilius, was a pupil of S. Columban's, the list of books in the *scriptorium* included Cicero, Virgil, Horace, Terence, Donatus, Priscian, and Boëthius. Of later authors, the works of Beda, Isidore, Aldhelm, the *Gesta Francorum*, etc.[2] By the time of Charles Martel and the battle of Poitiers, there had been much plundering and devastation of the monasteries and convents, the effects of which remained even after the Arabs were driven back. During the tumultuous reigns of the Pepins, many clerics returned to or took up the profession of arms, and devotion and literature were alike neglected.[3] The biographer of S. Eligius, writing in 760 (under Pepin) says : [4]

" What do we want with the so-called philosophies of Pythagoras, Socrates, Plato, and Aristotle, or with the rubbish and nonsense of such shameless poets as Homer, Virgil, and Menander? What service can be rendered to the servants of God by the writings of the heathen Sallust, Herodotus, Livy, Demosthenes, or Cicero?" Fredegar, called *Scholasticus*, wrote his chronicle in a Burgundian monastery, about 600. He complains that "the world is in its decrepitude. Intellectual activity is dead, and the ancient writers have no successors."

The man to whom the revival of the literary interests of the northern monasteries was largely due was the Archbishop Chrodegang of Metz, 742–766, Chancellor of Charles Martel, a Benedictine. He framed rules for the monas-

[1] Giesebrecht. Quoted by Montalembert, vi., 150.   [2] Denk, 260.
[3] Denk, 270.   [4] D'Achéry, *Spicill.*, ii., 77 (*Vita S. Eligii*).

teries which restored discipline and infused new life. His code was adopted throughout France, Italy, and Germany, and even in England. A certain uniformity of instruction was thus secured in the monastery schools in singing, language, and script, which persisted almost until the time of Alcuin, and the influence of which extended even beyond the monasteries.

Mabillon tells a story of Odo, Abbot of Clugni (who died about 942), who was so seduced by the love of knowledge that he was led to employ himself with the vanities of the poets, and resolved to read the works of Virgil regularly through. On the following night, however, he saw in a dream a large vase of marvellous beauty, but filled with innumerable serpents, which, springing forth, twined about him, but without doing him any injury. The holy man, waking and prudently considering the vision, took the serpents to stand for the figments of the poets, and the vase to represent Virgil's book, which was painted outwardly with worldly eloquence, but was internally defiled with the vanity of impure meaning. From thenceforward, renouncing Virgil and his pomps, and keeping the poets out of his chamber, he sought his mental nourishment solely from the sacred writings. [1]

Honorius, the reputed author of the *Gemma Animæ*, writes in 1120: "It grieves me when I consider in my mind the number of persons who, having lost their senses, are not ashamed to give their utmost labour to the investigation of the abominable figments of the poets, and the captious arguments of the philosophers, which are wont inextricably to bind the mind that is drawn away from God in the bonds of vices and to be ignorant of the Christian profession whereby the soul may come to reign everlastingly with God; as it is the height of madness to be anxious to learn the laws of an usurper and to be ignorant of the edicts of the lawful sovereign. Moreover,

[1] Mab., *Traité*, vii., 187.

how is the soul profited by the strife of Hector, or the argumentation of Plato, or the poems of Virgil, or the elegies of Ovid, who now, with their like, are gnashing their teeth in the prison of the infernal Babylon, under the cruel tyranny of Pluto." [1]

Peter the Venerable, who was Abbot of Clugni in the middle of the twelfth century, is referred to by the historian Milner as a flagrant example of the ignorance of the monastic authorities of his time. Maitland finds cause for no little indignation with the hasty and ill-founded statements of Milner, and devotes several chapters to an account of the monastery of Clugni under the rule of Peter, presenting very ample evidence of the literary activity and scholarly interests of the abbot and of his close relations with the intellectual leaders of his time, leaders who were, with hardly an exception, monks and ecclesiastics. "Who will venture to say," writes Maitland, "that Peter would have been pilloried as an ignorant and trifling writer if Milner had happened to have any personal knowledge of his history and his works and if he had read in one of the long series of Peter's Epistles the words, *Libri et maxime Augustiniani, ut nosti, apud nos auro preciosiores sunt.*" [2] (Books, and especially those of S. Augustine, are esteemed by us as more precious than gold.)

The literary journeys of Mabillon were followed by similar journeys on the part of Father Montfaucon and Edouard Martene, who were both, like Mabillon, members of the learned Benedictines of St. Maur. Mabillon's journeys covered the period of the long wars following the revocation of the Edict of Nantes (in 1685), including the campaigns between France and England in the Low Countries. It was probably due to these campaigns that his researches did not include any of the monasteries of the lower Rhine, of Flanders, or of Brabant. Martene's

[1] *Prov. Bib. Pat.*, x., 1179.   [2] Maitland, 364.

journeys continued during a term of six years, in which time he examined manuscripts in more than one hundred cathedrals and at least eight hundred abbeys. The materials collected were utilised first in the new edition of the *Gallia Christiana*, and later, in five folio volumes, comprising only matter previously unpublished, issued under the title *Thesaurus Novum Anecdotorum*. The account of the journey was printed under the title *Voyage Littéraire de Deux Religieux Benedictins*.

In 1718, Martene and Montfaucon were again sent on their literary travels, and the later collections were issued in 1724 in nine folio volumes, under the title *Veterum Scriptorum et Monumentorum Historicorum, Dogmaticorum, Moralium, Amplissima Collectio*. I specify these works of the literary Benedictines because, although by their date they do not properly belong to my narrative, they form a very important authority for what is known of the literary history of the monasteries. In some of the monasteries which had in earlier times been famous as centres of literary activity, the libraries were found by Mabillon and Martene in a grievous condition of destitution and dilapidation. At Clugni, for instance, they describe the catalogue (itself six hundred years old), written on parchment-covered boards three feet and a half long and eighteen inches wide (*grandes tablettes qu'on ferme comme un livre*), containing some thousands of titles, but of the books there remained scarcely one hundred. Martene was told that the Huguenots had carried them off to Geneva. At Novantula, of all its former riches Mabillon found but two manuscripts; and at Beaupré, of the great collection of manuscripts there remained but two or three; while many other famous libraries were in similar condition. The destruction of so large a portion of the collection of manuscripts and of the earlier printed books was due to a variety of causes. During the ninth century, the ravages of the Danes and Normans brought desolation upon a long list of the monasteries throughout Europe which, could most easily be reached from the coast. In the index to the third volume of Mabillon's annals, is given a long list of the Benedictine monasteries pillaged or destroyed by the Normans. The record begins *Normanni, monasteria et eis incensa, eversa, direpta.* In many of these visitations the loss of books must have been considerable. When, for instance, the abbey of Peterborough in Northamptonshire was burned by the Danes in the year 870, Ingulph records the destruction of a large collection of books, *sanctorum librorum ingens bibliotheca.*[1] Maitland points out that this expression probably stood for really a great library, as when Ingulph speaks of the destruction in 1091 of the collection of 700 volumes belonging to his own monastery, he does not so describe it.[2]

Serious ravages were also made in Central Europe in the tenth century by the Hungarians. Martene says that after the battle on the river Brenta, the pagans advanced to Novantula, killed many of the monks, and burned the monastery with a number of books, *codices multos concremavere.*[3] The monasteries in Italy suffered primarily from the Saracens, and those in Spain from the Moors. The losses caused by the religious wars of the later centuries were, however, according to Mabillon, much more serious than those brought about by the pagans. The Calvinists are held responsible for the destruction, among others, of St. Theodore, near Vienna, of St. Jean, Grimberg, Dilighen, of Jouaire, and, most important of all, of Fleury.[4] The ravages caused by fire were possibly greater than those produced by war, many of the collections having been kept in wooden buildings. Among the noted monasteries which suffered in this way were Gembloux, Liége, Lucelle, Loroy, St. Gall, Fulda, Lorsch, Croyland,

---

[1] Ingulph, *Ap. Gale. ser.*, v. 23.   [3] *Voy. Lit.*, 252, cited by Maitland.
[2] Maitland, 229.   [4] *Voy. Lit.*, ii., 13.

and Teano near Monte Cassino. In the burning of the latter perished, as Mabillon was informed, the original manuscript of the famous Rule of S. Benedict. Martene speaks of the Church of Romans in Dauphiny as having been ruined six times: by the Moors, by the Archbishop Sebon, twice by fire, by Guigne Dauphin in the twelfth century, and finally by the Calvinists. The library at the time of his visit still contained a few manuscripts.

In view of these various classes of perils, it may well be a matter of wonder, not that the monastic collections have so largely perished, but that so considerable a number of manuscripts has been preserved. The fact that so many mediæval manuscripts have escaped destruction by fire and flood, and have been saved from the ravages of invading pagans or of contending Christians, seems indeed to be good presumptive evidence of the enormous activity of literary production in the monastery scriptoria during the centuries between 529 and 1450, the date of the founding of Monte Cassino, and that of the invention of printing.

The Libraries of the Monasteries and Their Arrangements for the Exchange of Books.—Geoffrey, sub-prior of S. Barbe, in Normandy, is the author of a phrase which has since been frequently quoted. In a letter written in 1170 to Peter Mangot, a monk of Baugercy, in the diocese of Tours, he says: " A monastery (*claustrum*) without a library (*sine armario*) is like a castle (*castrum*) without an armory (*sine armamentario*). Our library is our armory. Thence it is that we bring forth the sentences of the Divine Law like sharp arrows to attack the enemy. Thence we take the armour of righteousness, the helmet of salvation, the shield of faith, and the sword of the spirit, which is the Word of God." [1]

Among the monasteries whose collections of books were noteworthy and whose literary exchanges were not

[1] Maitland, 200 (cited also by Wattenbach, see p. 112).

infrequently sufficiently important to be described as a
publishing or bookselling trade, may be mentioned the
following: Wearmouth and Yarrow, already referred to,
the book production in which was active as early as the
seventh century; St. Josse-sur-Mer, where, in the ninth
century, the Abbot Loup of Ferrières is reported to have
kept a depot of books, from which he carried on an
active trade with England[1]; Bobbio in Lombardy, the
literary treasures in which have been largely preserved in
the Ambrosian library; the monastery of Pomposa near
Ravenna, whose library, collected by Abbot Jerome in
1093, was said to be finer than any other of the time in
Italy; La Chiusa, whose collection rivalled that of Pomposa; Novalese, whose library, at the time of the destruction of the abbey by the Saracens in 905, is reported to
have contained no less than 6500 volumes[2]; and Monte
Cassino, which under the Abbot Didia, a friend of
Gregory VII., possessed a very rich collection. This collection was the result of the researches in Italy of the
African Constantine, who, after having passed forty years
in the East studying the scientific treatises of Egypt,
Persia, Chaldea, and India, had been driven from Carthage
by envious rivals. He came to the tomb of S. Benedict,
where he assumed the monastic habit, and he endowed
his new dwelling with the rich treasures collected in his
wanderings.[3] There are also to be mentioned Fulda,
whose library at one time surpassed all others in Germany, excepting perhaps that of St. Gall; Croyland, whose
library in the eleventh century numbered 3000 volumes;
and many others.

The work of Ziegelbauer gives in detail the old catalogue of the library of Fulda and those of a number of
other abbeys. The estimates of the relative importance
of these collections are in the main based upon Ziegel-

[1] Loup Ferrar, *Epist.*, 62.   [2] Mont., vii., 178.
[3] *Petr. Diac. Chron. Cassin L.*, iii., chap. xxxv.

bauer's statistics. There seems to be no question that these monastery libraries carried on with each other an active correspondence and exchange of books, and that this exchange business developed in not a few cases, as in that of St. Josse-sur-Mer, into what was practically a book-trade. It is the conclusion of Mabillon, as of Montalembert, that during the time in which Christian Europe was covered with active monasteries and convents in which thousands of monks and nuns were engaged in constant transcription, books could hardly have been really rare, at least as compared with the extent of the circle of scholars and readers who required them.

Cahier points out that in addition to these great monastery collections, there were libraries of greater or less importance in nearly all the cathedrals, in many of the collegiate churches, and in not a few of the castles. Mabillon is of opinion that the prices of books during the Middle Ages have been very much overestimated, and that the impression as to such prices has been largely based upon isolated and misunderstood instances.[1] Robertson speaks of the collection of Homilies bought in 1056 by Grecia, Countess of Arizon, for two hundred sheep, a measure of wheat, one of millet, one of rye, several marten skins, and four pounds of silver, but Robertson omits to mention that the volumes so purchased were exceptionally beautiful specimens of caligraphy, of painting, and of carving. Maitland points out that it would be as reasonable to quote as examples of prices in the nineteenth century the exorbitant sums paid at special sales by the bibliomaniacs of to-day. " May not some literary historian of the future," he goes on to say, " at a time when the march of intellect has got past the age of cumbersome and expansive penny magazines and is revelling in farthing cyclopædias, record as an evidence of the scarcity and costliness of books in the nineteenth cen-

[1] Mabillon, *Annal.*, book 70, chap. vi.

tury, that in the year 1812 an English nobleman gave £2260 and another £1060 for a single volume, and that the next year a Johnson's Dictionary was sold by public auction for £200. A few such facts would quite set up some future Robertson, whose readers would never dream that we could get better reading, and plenty of it, very much cheaper at that very time." [1]

It is, of course, the case that there has been such a thing as bibliomania since there have been books in the world, no less in the manuscript period than after the age of printing. " The art of printing," says Morier, " is unknown in Persia, and beautiful writing is, therefore, considered a high accomplishment. It is carefully taught in the schools, and those who excel in it are almost classed with literary men. They are employed to copy books, and some have attained to such eminence in this art, that a few lines written by one of these celebrated penmen are often sold for a considerable sum. I have known seven pounds given for four lines written by Dervish Musjeed, a celebrated penman, who has been dead for some time, and whose beautiful specimens of writing are now scarce." [2]

Robertson quotes in support of his general contention a statement of Naudé to the following effect: " In 1471, when Louis XI. borrowed from the Faculty of Medicine in Paris the works of Rasis, the Arabian physician, he not only deposited as a pledge a considerable quantity of plate, but was obliged to procure a nobleman to join with him as surety in a deed, binding himself, under a great forfeiture, to restore the volumes." [3] In the eighteenth century, however, when Selden wished to borrow a manuscript from the Bodleian Library, he was required to give

---

[1] Maitland, 67.

[2] *Travels in Persia*, ii., 582.

[3] Gabr. Naudé, *Addit. à l'Histoire de Lowys XI.*, par Comines, edit. de Fresnoy, iv., 281.

a bond for a thousand pounds. It does not, therefore, follow that the reign of George II. was a dark age in English literature.[1]

Maitland points out one very important detail, which served to give to some individual manuscript a value that might, when later referred to, appear disproportionate to the expense of the hand labour in its preparation. Under the process of the multiplication of books by printing, each copy of a given edition must of course be a facsimile of all the other copies, sharing their measure of correctness, and equally sharing their blunders. In the manuscript period, however, every copy of a work was of necessity unique, and the correctness of a particular manuscript was no pledge for the quality even of those which had been copied directly from it. " In fact, the correctness of every single copy could be ascertained only by minute and laborious collation, and by the same minuteness of method which is now requisite from an editor who revises the text of an ancient writer. . . . If a manuscript had received such a collation at the hands of trustworthy scholars, and if it had been shown to present a text of such completeness and accuracy as might safely be trusted as copy for future transcripts, such a manuscript would undoubtedly be valued at an exceptional price." [2]

Muratori speaks of books when presented to churches being offered at the altar, *pro remedio animæ suæ*,[3] and on this quotation Robertson bases a further argument concerning the high value of books. It was, however, the ordinary routine that when a person made a present of anything to a church, it was offered at the altar, and it was understood, if not always specifically expressed, that such offering was made either for his own spiritual benefit or for that of some other person. It was doubtless the case that gifts of books to a church were rare as compared with the gifts of other things, for the simple reason

[1] Maitland, 68.   [2] Maitland, 70.   [3] Muratori, iii., 836.

that nearly all the books that came into existence were produced in the churches or in the attendant monasteries.

Delisle says that the loan of books from monastery libraries was considered one of the most meritorious of all acts of mercy. Against this view there are many examples of the formal prohibition of the lending of any books outside of the walls of the monastery. Some communities placed the books of their libraries under an anathema,— that is to say, they forbade under pain of excommunication either borrowing or lending. This selfish policy was, however, formally condemned in 1212 by the Council of Paris, the Fathers of which urged more charitable sentiments on these bibliophiles: "We forbid monks to bind themselves by any oath not to lend books to the poor, seeing that such a loan is one of the chief works of mercy. We desire that the books of a community should be divided into two classes, one to remain in the house for the use of the Brothers, the other to be lent out to the poor according to the judgment of the abbot." [1]

In support of his contention concerning the general disappearance of literature during the Middle Ages, Robertson quotes the authority of Muratori to the effect that, " even monasteries of considerable note had only one missal." [2] Maitland has no difficulty in showing that the passage cited has been wrongly understood, and that the generalisation based upon it is absurd. Muratori was referring to a letter of a certain Bonus, who was for thirty years (1018–1048) Abbot of the monastery of S. Michael, in Pisa. In this letter, Bonus gives an account of the founding of the monastery, and says that when he came to Pisa he found there, not a monastery, but simply a chapel, which was in a most deplorable and destitute condition, wanting vessels, vestments, bells, and nearly all

[1] Montalembert, vi., 184.

[2] Murat., *Antiq.*, iv., 789. (Quoted by Robertson as vol. ix. The work contains but six volumes.)

the requisites for the performance of divine service, and having no service-books but a missal (*nisi unum missale*). The statement so worded is of course no evidence that there may not have been several copies of the missal. It simply shows that there were no other books (such as texts of the Epistles or Gospels) for use in the service. Bonus goes on to say, with commendable pride, that in fifteen years' time "the little hut," as he calls it, had expanded into a monastery, with suitable offices and with a considerable estate in land, the single tin cup had been exchanged for gold and silver chalices, and in place of one "missal," the monks rejoiced in the possession of a library of thirty-four volumes. It is difficult to understand how Robertson could have justified himself in basing, on a careless version of a statement concerning a missal in a single half-ruined chapel, a broad and misleading generalisation concerning the general absence of books from monasteries. The list of the library later secured by the abbot includes copies of the Gospels, the Psalms, and the Epistles, the Rule of S. Benedict, the Book of Job, the Book of Ezekiel, five Diurnals, eight *Antiphonarii*, three Nocturnals, a tractate by S. Augustine on Genesis, a book of Dialogues, a Glossary, a Pastoral, a book of Canons, a book entitled *Summum Bonum*, five Missals, a book entitled *Passionarum unum novum ubi sunt omnes passiones ecclesiasticæ* (I give the wording from the catalogue), and the *Liber Bibliotheca*. "Bibliotheca" is the term very generally applied at this period to the Bible, and often used for a collection comprising but a few books of the Bible. The catalogue shows that the good Abbot had made a very fair beginning towards a monastic library.

The letters of Gerbert, Abbot of Bobbio (who, in 998, became Pope under the name of Sylvester II.), throw some light upon the literary interests of that famous monastery and of the time. He writes (about 984) to a monk named Rainald (letter 130 of the collection): "You know with what zeal I seek for copies of books from all quarters, and you know how many scribes there are everywhere in Italy, both in the cities and in the rural districts, I entreat you then . . . that you will have transcripts made for me of M. Manilius' *De Astrologia*, Victorinus' *De Rhetorica*, and of the *Ophthalmicus* of Demosthenes. . . . Whatever you lay out I will repay you to the full, according to your accounts." In letter 123, Gerbert writes to Thietmar of Mayence for a portion of one of the works of Boëthius, his copy being defective. In letter 9, written to Abbot Giselbert, he asks for assistance in making good certain deficiencies in his manuscript of the oration of Cicero, *Pro Rege Deiotaro*. In letter 8, to the Archbishop of Rheims, he requests that prelate to borrow for him from Abbot Azo a copy of Cæsar's *Commentaries*. In return he offers the loan of eight volumes of Boëthius. In letter 7, he requests his friend Airard to attend to the correction of the manuscript of Pliny, and to preparing transcripts of two other manuscripts. In letter 44, to Egbert, Abbot of Tours, he states that he has been much occupied in collecting a library, and that he had for a long time been paying transcribers in Rome, in other parts of Italy, in Germany, and in Belgium, and in buying at great expense texts of important authors. He asks the Abbot to aid in doing similar work in France, and he gives a list (unfortunately lost) of the works for transcripts of which he is looking. He is ready to supply the parchment and to defray all the expenses of the work. In other letters he makes reference to his own writings on rhetoric, arithmetic, and spherical geometry.

These letters, for the reference to which I am indebted to Maitland,[1] assuredly give the impression that even in the dark period of the tenth century, there was no little activity in certain ecclesiastical circles and monastic cen-

[1] 55, note.

tres in the transcribing, collecting, and exchanging of books, and not merely of missals, breviaries, or monkish legends, but of literature recognised as classic.

Another letter, written a century and a half later, makes reference to the practice of exchanging books or of using them as pledges. A prior writes to an abbot in 1150: " To his Lord, the Venerable Abbot of —— wishes health and happiness. Although you desire to have the books of Tully, I know that you are a Christian and not a Ciceronian. But you go over to the camp of the enemy not as a deserter, but as a spy. I should, therefore, have sent you the books of Tully which we have, *De Re Agraria*, the Philippics, and the Epistles, but that it is not our custom that any books should be lent to any person without good pledges. Send us, therefore, the *Noctes Atticæ* of Aulus Gellius and Origen on the Canticles. The books which we have just brought from France, if you wish for any of them, I will send you." The Abbot replies at the end of a long letter : " I have sent you as pledges for your books, Origen on the Canticles, and instead of Aulus Gellius (which I could not have at this time), a book which is called *Strategematon*, which is military." [1]

The custom of securing books by chains, which prevailed with the libraries of all the earlier religious institutions, did not originate with these. Eusebius mentions that the Roman Senate in the time of Claudius ordered the treatise of Philo Judæus on the Impiety of Caligula to be chained in the library as a famous monument. There appears to have been an early appreciation on the part of certain of the monastery scholars of the importance of indexes. Fosbroke quotes among others the example of John Brome, Prior of Gorlestone, who, in the fifteenth century, put indexes to almost all the books in his library. From an examination of the catalogues of various of the ecclesiastical libraries, Fosbroke arrives at the calculation

[1] Maitland, 177.

that the proportion of the works contained under the several main sub-headings was approximately as follows: Divinity, 175; scholastic literature, 89; epistles and controversial literature, 65; history, 54; biography, 32; arts, mathematics, and astrology, 31; philosophy, 13; law, 6.[1] This classification does not give any separate heading for allegory, although this was a subject in which not a few of the earlier monkish writers largely interested themselves.

As an example of monkish allegorical literature, Fosbroke mentions a work written in 1435, under the instructions of a cloth shearer in France, whose name he does not give. The cloth cutter, being a great lover of tennis, had written a ballad upon that game. When he was old, he wished to atone for his early sins and frivolities, and he secured the services of a Dominican monk, who wrote, at his instance and expense, an allegory on the game of tennis. The wall of the tennis court stood for faith, which should always rest on a solid foundation, while in the other conditions of the game the Dominican finds the cardinal virtues, the evangelists, active and contemplative life, the old and the new law, etc.

In the thirteenth century, Omons, who might be described as the Lucretius of his day, wrote a work entitled *The Picture of the World*, from which one could gather an impression of the character of the philosophy of the early Middle Ages. In the department of metaphysics, Omons (using largely material borrowed from Thales, Anaxagoras, Epicurus, and Plato) described God as comparatively an idle being, and speaks of Him as having at the time of creating Matter also created Nature. Nature executed the will of God as an axe executes the will of the carpenter; it sometimes, however, through want or excess of matter, produces deformities.

The Liberal Arts, Omons divides under the usual sep-

[1] Fosbroke, 172.

tenary arrangement, which is adopted as early as the fifth
century by Capella. Omons makes mathematics, however,
not a mere science of numbers, but the knowledge of
everything that is produced in any regular order whatever,
while rhetoric includes judicial verdicts, decretals, laws,
etc. The term "liberal" he applied only to an art
which explicitly appertained to the mind ; and therefore,
medicine, painting, sculpture, navigation, the military art,
architecture, etc., although in their theories as intellectual
as are mathematics and astronomy, were, because applic-
able to bodily purposes, denominated trades. The term
"philosopher" means only men versed in the occult
sciences of nature, and among the later philosophers
Omons held no one so eminent as Virgil. This was not
the Bard of Mantua, but an ugly little Italian conjurer,
who, during the tenth century, had performed various
feats of legerdemain.

When Peter of Celle had borrowed two volumes of S.
Bernard's works, he wrote to him: "Make haste and quickly
copy these and send them to me; and according to my
bargain, cause a copy to be made for me, and both those
which I have sent to you, and the copies, as I have said,
send to me, and take care that I do not lose a single tittle."
Writing to the Dean of Troyes, he says: " Send me the
Epistles of the Bishop of Le Mans, for I want to copy
them " ; and, indeed, he seems to have a constant eye to
the acquisition and multiplication of books.[1]

As to this *commercium librorum*, it would be easy, says
Maitland, to multiply examples. In a letter of the Abbot
Peter to Guigo, Prior of Chartreuse, he mentions that he
had sent him the Lives of S. Nazianzen and S. Chrysostom,
and the argument of S. Ambrose against Symmachus.
That he had not sent the work of Hilary on the Psalms
because his copy contained the same defect as the Prior's.
That he did not possess *Prosper against Cassius*, but that

[1] Maitland, 441.

he had sent to Aquitaine for a copy. He begs the Prior to send the greater volume of S. Augustine, containing the letters which passed between him and S. Jerome, because a great part of their copy, while lying in one of the cells, had been eaten by a bear (*casu comedit ursus*),[1] a novel difficulty in the way of preserving literature.

Peter of Clugni, known as Peter the Venerable, became abbot of the monastery in 1122. Clugni, the *Caput Ordinis*, was at that time the most considerable of the Benedictine foundations, and might, in fact, be termed the most important monastery of its age. The correspondence of Peter and of his secretary Nicholas, who was for a time also secretary of Bernard of Clairvaux, forms an important contribution to the monastic history of the country and contain not a few references throwing light on the literary conditions of the time. Nicholas had, in addition to his business as the Abbot's amanuensis, what Mabillon calls a *librorum commercium* with various persons. It appears from his letters that he used to lend books on condition that a copy should be returned with the volume lent. Nicholas, while a diligent scribe and an active-minded scholar, was discovered later, to be a very untrustworthy person. He left Clairvaux with books, money, and gold service that did not belong to him, and also (which Abbot Bernard mentions as a special grievance) with three seals, his own, the prior's, and the abbot's. His further career was a checkered one, but does not belong to this narrative.

Abbot Peter of Clugni, writing to Master Peter of Poitiers in 1170, lays some emphasis on the inadvisability of devoting too much time to the study of the ancients. "See, now, without the study of Plato, without the disputations of the Academy, without the subtleties of Aristotle, without the teaching of philosophers, the place and the way of happiness are discovered . . . You run from

[1] Lib. i., ep. xxiv., Bib. Clun., 653.

school to school, and why are you labouring to teach and
to be taught? Why is it that you are seeking through
thousands of words and multiplied labours, what you
might, if you pleased, obtain in plain language and with
little labour? Why, vainly studious, are you reciting with
the comedians, lamenting with the tragedians, trifling
with the metricians, deceiving with the poets and deceived
with the philosophers? Why is it that you are now taking so much trouble about what is not in fact philosophy
but should rather (if I may say it without offence) be
called foolishness."

Counsels of this kind give some indication at least of
the tendency in Poitiers, and doubtless also in Clugni,
to devote to the old-time poetry and philosophy some of
the hours which, under a stricter observance, should be
reserved for the Scriptures or the Fathers. The venerable
Abbot must himself have had some fairly comprehensive
knowledge of the literature he was criticising, and the
gentle satire of the phrase " deceived with the philosophers " does not give one the impression of coming from
a clumsy-minded and ignorant monk such as Robertson
describes Peter the Venerable to have been.

A further evidence not only of comprehensive knowledge but of a liberal spirit, is afforded by the fact that
Peter gave to the West a translation (possibly the first)
of the Alkoran. This is the form used by Peter himself
for the Mohammedan scriptures. In a letter to S. Bernard,
he speaks of having had this translation prepared of a work
which had so greatly influenced the thought of the world
that it ought to be known to Europe. He says further
that the defenders of the true faith should familiarise
themselves with the contentions of the Mohammedan
heretics, in order to be able to refute these when the
necessity arose.[1]

[1] Lib. iv., ch. xvii., Bib. Clun., 843.

CHAPTER II.

SOME LIBRARIES OF THE MANUSCRIPT PERIOD.

THE following are some of the more important collections referred to in the records of the Middle Ages.

In Constantinople the Patriarch had a library in Thomaïtes which was said to be of considerable importance, and the works in it are referred to very often in the transactions of the Synods. This collection was destroyed by fire in 780, but was speedily replaced. Many of the monasteries of the Greek Church possessed libraries, and in some of these libraries were preserved the oldest manuscripts known to the world. Among the most important of these collections was that contained in the monastery of Mt. Athos, some of the treasures of which have been preserved to the present day. During the time of Basilius Macedo (867–886), much work was said to have been done by the scribes of this monastery.[1]

In Egypt it is claimed that until the conquest by the Arab, there was a good deal of literary activity in the monasteries, and in the monastery of S. Catherine of the Sinai range were preserved some specimens of the earlier manuscripts, of which the Testament discovered by Tischendorf is the most important example.

The Library of S. Giovanni in Naples, from which many valuable Greek manuscripts were secured for the Royal Library in Vienna, was not an old monastery collection, but had its origin, according to Blume, with Janus Par-

[1] Watt., 482.

rhasius.[1] The Augustin monks presented the collection in 1729 to the Emperor Charles VI., in order that they might not be disturbed in their seclusion by the visits of zealous scholars.[2]

The earliest of ecclesiastical libraries was probably that collected by Bishop Alexander, in Jerusalem, at the beginning of the third century. Fifty years later a library was founded at Cesarea by Origen, which is described 'as extensive and important.[3] Collections were also made at an early date at Hippo, at Cirta, at Constantinople, and at S. Peter's and the Lateran in Rome. All these earlier libraries were apparently connected with the churches, and in most cases places had been found for them within the church walls. Clark quotes from a narrative of the persecution of 303–304 a paragraph saying that the officers " went to the church where the Christians used to assemble, and spoiled it of chalices, lamps, etc., but when they came to the library (*bibliothecam*), the presses (*armaria*) were found empty." [4] From this reference we may conclude that the several vessels and the books were in different parts of the same building.

The library of S. Augustine was bequeathed to the church of Hippo, and the collection was preserved within the church building.

The regulations of the libraries in all the Benedictine monasteries were based upon the Rule of S. Benedict (see *ante*, p. 28). As Order after Order was founded, there came to be a steady development of feeling in regard to books, and an ever increasing care for their safe-keeping. S. Benedict had contented himself with general directions for study ; the Cluniacs prescribe the selection of a special officer to take charge of the books, with an annual audit

[1] *Iter Ital.*, iv., 3.
[2] Valery, *Correspondance de Mabillon et de Montfaucon*, i., 185.
[3] J. W. Clark *Libraries in Mediæval Periods*, 12.
[4] Clark, 13.

of the collection, and the assignment to each Brother of a single volume for his year's study. The Cistercians and Carthusians provide for the loan of books to outsiders under certain conditions, and the practice was later adopted by the Benedictines. The Augustinians prescribe the kind of press (*armarium*) in which the books are to be kept, and both they and the Premonstratensians permit their books to be lent on receipt of pledges of sufficient value. Even the Mendicant Friars, who, under the original Rule of their Order, had restrained themselves from holding possessions of any kind, found before long that books were indispensable, so that their libraries came to excel those of most other Orders. Richard de Bury, in his *Philobiblon*, says of the Mendicants : " These men are as ants, ever preparing their meat in the summer, or as ingenious bees continually fabricating cells of honey. . . . although they lately at the eleventh hour have entered the Lord's vineyard, they have added more in this brief hour to the stock of sacred books than all the other vine-dressers."

Clark points out that the word *Library* was used by the Benedictines long before any special room was assigned in the Benedictine House as a storage place for the books. He is of opinion that until the thirteenth and fourteenth centuries the books were for the most part kept in the cloisters, the only portions of the monastery buildings, except the refectory and occasionally the *califactorium* (warming-house), in which the monks were allowed to congregate. The books so stored in the cloisters were shut up in presses, which secured for them a certain amount of protection. The term applied to these presses, *armaria*, was that used by the Romans for their book-cases. The monk charged with the care of the books took his name not from the books themselves, as in later times, but from the presses which contained them, and was generally styled *armarius*.

In some of the monasteries where literary studies were pursued with special ardour, the more persistent readers and scribes were provided with small wooden compartments or studies called *carrells*. In the book called the *Rites of Durham* is given the following description of these carrells: " In the north syde of the cloister, from the corner over againste the church dour to the corner over againste the Dorter dour, was all fynely glased from the hight to the ṣole within a little of the ground into the Cloister garth, and in every window *iij* Pewes or Carrells, where every one of the old monks had his carrell, several by himselfs, that, when they had dyned, they dyd resort to that place of Cloister, and there studyed upon these books, every one in his carrell, all the after nonne, unto evensong tyme. This was there exercise every daie. . . . In every carrell was a deske to lye there books upon, and the carrell was no greater than from one stanchell of the wyndowe to another, and over againste the carrells against the church wall, did stande certain great almeries (or cupbords) of waynscott all full of bookes (with great store of ancient manuscripts to help them in their study) wherein did lye as well the old anncyent written Doctors of the Church as other prophane authors, with dyverse other holie men's wourks, so that every one did studye what Doctor pleased them best, havinge the Librarie at all tymes to goe studye in besydes there carrells." [1]

In the *Customs* of the Augustinian priory of Barnwell, written towards the end of the thirteenth century, the following passage occurs: " The press in which the books are kept ought to be lined inside with wood, that the damp of the walls may not moisten or stain the books. This press should be divided vertically as well as horizontally by sundry partitions, on which the books may be ranged so as to be separated from one another: for fear they be packed so close as to injure each other, or to delay those who want them."

[1] Quoted by Clark, 21.

The catalogue of the House of the White Canons at Titchfield in Hampshire, dated 1400, shows that the books were kept in a small room, on shelves called *columpnæ*, and set against the walls. A closet of this kind was evidently not a working place, but simply a place of storage. By the beginning of the fifteenth century, the larger monasteries had accumulated many hundred volumes, and it began to be customary to provide for the collections separate quarters, rooms constructed for the purpose. The presses in the cloisters were still utilised for books in daily reference.

In Christ Church, Canterbury, where as early as the fourteenth century, the collection comprised as many as 698 books, a library at Durham was built about 1425 by Archbishop Chichele: the library at Durham was built about the same time by Prior Wessyngton. That at Citeaux, which was placed over the *scriptorium*, dates from 1480, and that of St. Germain des Prés from 1513. The collection of the latter foundation was one of the earliest in France, and as early as the beginning of the thirteenth century, there is record of its being consulted by strangers. At the time of the French Revolution, it contained 7000 manuscripts and 4900 printed books.[1]

The Queen of Sicily, who in 1517 visited Clairvaux, one of the two great Cistercian foundations in France, describes the library as follows: " On the same side of the cloister are fourteen studies, where the monks do their reading and writing, and over these studies, one mounts by a broad spiral staircase to the new library. This library is 189 feet long by 17 feet wide. It contains 48 seats (*bancs*) and in each *banc* four shelves (*poulpitres*) furnished with books on all subjects, but chiefly theology ; the greater number of the said books are of vellum and are written by hand, richly storied and illuminated."

The phrase " written by hand," indicates that the Queen

[1] Clark, 27.

was already acquainted with books produced from type, some of which had in fact been produced in Italy as early as 1464.

Another description, written in 1723 by the author of the *Voyage Littéraire*, speaks of "the fifteen little cells, all in a row, where the Brethren formerly used to write books, for which reason they are still called the writing rooms. Over these cells is the library, the building for which is large, vaulted, well lighted, and stocked with a large number of manuscripts, fastened by chains to desks; but there are not many printed books."

The provisions of the statutes affecting the library imposed upon the colleges of Oxford and Cambridge, were evidently borrowed directly from the customs of the monasteries. The statutes of Oriel College, Oxford, dated 1329, present an example: "The common books (*libri communes*) of the House are to be brought out and inspected once a year, on the feast of the Commemoration of Souls (November 2d) in the presence of the Provost or his deputy, and of the scholars (Fellows). Each one of the scholars, in the order of seniority, may select a single book which either treats of the science to which he is devoting himself, or which he requires for his use. This he may keep until the same festival in the succeeding year, when a similar selection of books is to take place, and so on, from year to year. If there should happen to be more books than persons, those that remain are to be selected in the same manner."

A statute of Archbishop Lanfranc, for the English Benedictines, dated 1070, and based, as he tells us, on the general monastic practice of his time, gives the following regulation: "On the Monday after the first Sunday in Lent, before Brethren come into the Chapter House, the librarian [here called not *armarius* but *custos librorum*] shall have a carpet laid down and all the books got together upon it, except those which the year previous had been assigned for reading. These the Brethren are to bring with them, when they come into the Chapter House, each his book in his hand. Then the librarian shall read a statement as to the manner in which Brethren have had books during the past year. As each Brother hears his name pronounced, he is to give back the book which had been entrusted to him for reading ; and he whose conscience accuses him of not having read through the book which he had received, is to fall on his face, confess his fault, and entreat forgiveness. The librarian shall then make a fresh distribution of books, namely a different volume to each Brother for his reading."

It would appear from this reference as if Lanfranc's monks were under obligations to read through but one book each year, which was certainly a very moderate allowance. It is also to be noted that the books appear not to have been distributed according to the preferences of the readers, but to have been assigned at the will of the librarian. There must certainly have been no little difference in the character and extent of the duty imposed of reading through one book (even with so long an allowance of time) according to the particular volume which the *custos* saw fit to assign. The worthy Archbishop writes, however, as if a book were a book and one as good for edification or as fitting for penance as another.

It is evident that there were two classes of volumes, one utilised for distribution for separate reading, and the other reserved for reference and placed in a separate room (first called *armarium* and later *bibliotheca*) where they were fastened with irons chains to lecterns or reading-desks.

In the various details concerning the distribution of books, the arrangement of the lecterns for the chained books, etc., the practice in the early colleges was evidently modelled on that of the monasteries. The system of chaining, as adopted in England, would allow of the books

being readily taken down from the shelves and placed on
the lectern for reading. One end of the chain was attached to the middle of the upper edge of the right-hand
board or cover; the other to a ring which played on a bar
which set in front of the shelf on which the book stood.
The fore-edge of the books, not the back, was turned to
the front. A swivel, usually in the middle of the chain,
prevented tangling. The chains varied in length according to the distance of the shelf from the desk.[1]

In a copy of Locke's *Treatise on the Epistles*, printed in
1711, Maitland found inscribed the following " advertisement": " Since, to the great reproach of the nations and
a much greater one of our Holy Religion, the thievish
disposition of some that enter into libraries to learn there
no good, hath made it necessary to secure the innocent
books, and even the sacred volumes themselves, with
chains (which are better deserved by those ill persons who
have too much learning to be hanged and too little to be
honest), care should be taken hereafter that as additions
shall be made to this library (of which there is a hopeful
expectation), the chains should neither be longer nor
more clumsy than the use of them requires, and that the
loops whereby they are fastened to the books may be
rivetted on such a part of the cover and so smoothly as
not to gall or raze the books while these are removed from
or to their respective places." [2]

Isidore, Bishop of Seville (*c.* 560–636), possessed probably the largest collection of books at that time in Europe.
It was contained in fourteen presses or *armaria*, each of
which was ornamented with a bust and inscribed with
verses. The series of verses concludes with the following
notice addressed *ad interventorem*, a term which may be
interpreted *a talkative intruder* :

> *Non patitur quemquam coram se scriba loquentem ;*
> *Non est hic quod agas, garrule, perge foras.*

[1] Clark, 42.   [2] Maitland, 286.

(The scribe allows no one to speak in his presence; there is nothing for you to do here, chatterbox; you had better go outside)—a motto which would serve very well for a reading-room of to-day.

In Rome the Church had, from an early date, preserved a collection of manuscripts which related more particularly to church matters, but which included also some specimens of the Roman Classics. In 855, Lupus, of Ferrières, writes to Pope Benedict III., begging for the loan of certain texts from which to make transcripts. He specifies the Commentary of S. Jerome on Jeremiah, Cicero *de Oratore*, Quintilian, and Terence.[1]

In the centuries following, however, as the Roman Church sank into a condition of ignorance and strife, and Italy was continuously upset by invasions, the library in Rome and the collections which had been instituted in certain churches outside of Rome were either seriously lessened or entirely destroyed. As late, however, as 1276, a few valuable manuscripts were still to be found in the church collections. Wattenbach speaks of the collection in Verona, in the library of the Town Hall, as one of the most important of those in Italy in which old manuscripts have been preserved to the present time. Next in importance among the older collections, he mentions that of Hexham in England, which had been originally collected by Bishop Acca in the year 700, and which is referred to by Bede.[2]

With this is to be mentioned the library of York, which is first described by Alcuin.[3]

Among the earlier important library collections was that of the monastery of Vivaria, which had been founded by Cassiodorus; the writings were classified according to their contents, and were arranged in a series of *armaria*.

[1] Blume, *Iter Ital.*, i., 41.
[2] Bede, v., 20.
[3] Alcuin, *De Epp. Eborac*, v., 532. (See p. 108.)

After the beginning of the seventh century, the most noteworthy collection was that of Bobbio, a portion of which remained as late as 1618, and was taken by Paul V. for the Vatican Library. Another portion found its way to Turin.

The literary activity of the monastery of Corbie has already been mentioned, and the library there continued in existence during the entire lifetime of the monastery. After 1350 the monks appear to have themselves given up the work of writing. Étienne de Conty is recorded as one of the special benefactors of the library. He collected books for it, and he employed special scribes to add to the collection.[1]

In Germany, the monastery of Reichenau was noted as early as 821 for its excellent collection of manuscripts. The librarian Reginbert prepared in 821 an exhaustive catalogue of the collection. Not a few of the manuscripts were, as appeared by the notes in the catalogue, the work of his own hands. Of these manuscripts, which he had prepared with so great zeal and labour, there have remained but five sheets of one book, with a portion of the catalogue.

Of nearly as early a date is the first catalogue of the library of St. Gall, previously referred to; in the catalogue of this there are beneath the titles various critical notes. There is record of the loan of books to the Emperor Charles III., to Frau Rickert, and to Liutward, Bishop of Vercelli.[2]

In the monastery of Pomposa, in Lombardy, Abbot Jerome brought together in the eleventh century (in spite of certain grumblings on the part of the monks, the ground for which is not clearly explained) a great collection of manuscripts.[3] A certain Henricus Clericus, writ-

---

[1] *Recherches sur l'Ancienne Bibliothèque de Corbie*, par Léopold Delisle. *Mém. de l'Institut*, xxiv., 266–342.

[2] *Gesch. der Stifts-Bibliothek*, Weidmann, 1841 (p. 486, Watt.).

[3] Wattenbach, 486.

ing in 1093, describing this collection to a friend, says that in no church, not even in Rome, could so wonderful a group of books be found. Henricus prepared a catalogue of the library, and at the close of the catalogue he finds it necessary, as a matter of consistency, to apologise for the abbot who had ventured to include in the collection heathen books. The presence of such books, known at the time as *libri scholastici*, was, however, by no means exceptional in monastery collections, and in many of these were to be found copies of Virgil, Ovid, and particularly Cicero. While this was more frequently the case in Italy, it occurred also in Germany. An inventory made in 1233 of the monastery of Neumünster, near Wurzburg, includes in a special list the titles of a number of the Classics.

A similar separate catalogue of *libri scholastici* was made in 1297 for the collection in the cathedral library of Lübeck.

While the principal increase in the monastery libraries had been secured through the work of scribes and through exchanges, and occasionally through purchases, a considerable proportion of the books came to them through gifts or bequests. The gift that it was customary for a novice to make on entering a monastery very frequently took the form of books.

In 1055, the priest Richlof, in placing his son with the Benedictines, gave as an accompanying present a farm and some books, and his mother gave a copy of a treatise of S. Ambrose.[1]

Léon Maitre says that in Fleury, each new scholar was expected to present at least two codices. Towards the end of the eleventh century, a noble cleric, who entered as a monk the monastery at Tegernsee, brought with him so many books that, according to the account, when placed by the principal altar they covered this from top to bottom.[2]

---

[1] *Mon. Boic.*, vii., 40, cited by Wattenbach.
[2] *Chron. Teg.* in Pez, *Thes.*, iii., 3, 516.

In what was known as the Scottish Monastery, near Vienna, there was kept in the thirteenth century a record of gifts, which record includes a long list of presents of books. In the latter part of the century, the monastery appears to have degenerated, the library fell into disuse, and the presents of books ceased. In 1418 the so-called Scottish monks were driven out, and the foundation was taken possession of by Germans. From this date the record of gifts of books again began.

In 1453, the monastery received as a bequest from Dr. Johannes Polzmacher his entire library. The library came to include a considerable list of works on jurisprudence together with a series of classics, including several copies of Ovid. The latter appears to have been a special favourite in the monastic collections. The books on jurisprudence were utilised for the profit of the monastery by being loaned out to the jurisprudence Faculty of the university. They were, it appears, also occasionally loaned to the students for transcribing. In the chance of the manuscripts suffering damage while out on hire, the borrower was compelled to deposit an adequate pledge in the shape either of money or other valuable property.[1]

The monastery in Bobbio received books from wandering Irishmen, as is indicated by the following inscription:

Sancte Columba, tibi Scotto tuus incola Dungal,
Tradidit hunc librum, quo fratrum corda beentur.
Qui legis ergo, Deus pretium sit muneris ora.[2]

(Holy Columba of Scotland, thy votary Dungal has bestowed upon thee this book, whereby the hearts of the brothers may be gladdened. Do thou who readest it pray that God may be the reward of thy labour.)

[1] "Die Kongregation der Schöttenkloster," *Archäol. Zeitschrift* von Otte. und Quast., i., 55.
[2] Reifferscheid, quoted by Wattenbach, p. 489.

In the monastery of St. Père-de-Chartres the Abbot Alveus, who died in 955, presented to S. Peter a book *Pro Vita Æterna*.[1]

Dietrich Schreiber, a citizen of Halle, who, notwithstanding his name, is said not to have been a scribe, gave, in 1239, for the good of his soul, to the preaching Brothers of Leipzig, a canonistic manuscript, with the condition that either of his sons should have the privilege of redeeming the same for the sum of five marks, in case he might require it in connection with his study of the law.[2] Robert of Lille, who died in 1339, left in his will to his daughters a certain illuminated calendar, with the condition attached that after their death the calendar was to be given to the nuns of Chikessaund.[3]

It is also the case that bequests securing an annual income were occasionally given with the specific purpose of founding or endowing monastery *scriptoria* and libraries. The Abbot of St. Père-de-Chartres ordered, in 1145, that the tenants or others recognising the authority of the monastery must take up each year for the support of the library the sum of eighty-six solidos.[4]

His successor, Fulbert, instituted a new room for the collection and kept the monks themselves at work, so that in 1367 a catalogue, inscribed in four rolls, gives the titles of 201 volumes.[5]

Also in Evesham, in Worcestershire, England, a statute enacted in 1215 provides that certain tenths coming into the priory should be reserved for the purpose of buying parchment and for the increase of the library. During the following year the amount available for this purpose was five solidos, eighteen deniers.[6]

[1] Cod. 93, Schrift. v. Merlet, s. 263.

[2] Schulte, in d. *Wiener*, lxviii., 37 (Wattenbach, p. 490).

[3] *Arundel Catal.*, p. 22.

[4] Guérard, *Cartulaire de St. Père-de-Ch.*, ii., 395.

[5] Merlet, *Catal. des Livres de l'Abbaye de St. P.-de-Ch. au XIe Siècle*.

[6] Merryweather, p. 134. Dugdale, *Monast. Anglican*, ii., 24.

The account books of the monks of Ely showed that in the year 1300 they purchased five dozen sheets of parchment, four pounds of ink, eight calf-skins, four sheep-skins, five dozen sheets of vellum, and six pairs of book clasps. In the same year they paid six shillings for a *Decretal* and two shillings for a *Speculum Gregor.* In 1329, the Precentor received six shillings and seven pence with which he was instructed to go to Balsham to purchase books. In the same year, four shillings were paid for twelve iron chains (used, of course, for fastening the books safely to the reading-desks). Between 1350 and 1356, the purchases appear to have included no less than seventy dozen sheets of parchment and thirty dozen sheets of vellum.[1]

Prince Borwin, of Rostock, in 1240 presented the monastery of Dargun with a hide of land, the proceeds of which were to be used for the repairing and preservation of the books in the library.[2] Adam, treasurer of the Chapter of Rennes, in 1231, presented his library to the abbey of Penfont, with the condition that the books were never to be diverted from the abbey, and that copies were to be lent only against adequate pledges.

In 1345, a library was founded in the House of the German Brothers of Beuggen, near Rheinfelden, through the exertions of Wulfram of Nellenberg. He directed that all books left by deceased Brothers throughout Elsass were to be brought to this library, and the living Brothers were also earnestly urged to present their own books to the same collection.[3]

The great library of the monastery of Admunt was catalogued in 1380 by Brother Peter of Arbonne. The Chapter of S. Pancras, in Leyden, received in 1380,

[1] Bentham, *Church of Ely*, p. 52, and Stevenson's supplement to the same, p. 167.

[2] *Mecklenburger Urkundenbuch*, i., 501.

[3] Mone, *Zeitschr. f. Gesch. d. Oberrh.*, viii., 308.

through a bequest of Philip of Leyden, a collection of eighty manuscripts, the catalogue of which has been preserved.[1]

As before indicated, the Monastery Reform, which was instituted with the beginning of the fifteenth century, exercised a very decided influence upon the interest in books and upon the development of libraries. In Tegernsee, where the once noted library had fallen into ruins, the Abbot Casper (1426–1461) reorganised it, restored such of the old manuscripts as were still in existence, bought new codices, and put to work a number of hired scribes. His successor, Conrad V., carried on the work actively and purchased for the sum of eleven hundred pounds heller no less than 450 volumes, in addition to which he secured a number of gifts or devout presents.[2]

In Salzburg, the Archbishop Johann II. (1429–1441) caused a new library building to be erected, and collected for it many beautiful manuscripts. In the monastery of Bergen, near Magdeburg, the Abbot Bursfelder (1450–1478) organised a library, and utilised for his books an old chapel. In 1477, the Prior Martin instituted a library in Bordesholm, and Brother Liborius, who was a professor in Rostock, gave over, in 1405, to this library, for the good of his soul, his works on jurisprudence, with the provision that they were to be placed in chains and to remain forever in the reading-room. A catalogue of this collection, which was prepared in 1498, and which contains more than five hundred titles, has been preserved.[3] The library of the Benedictine monastery of St. Ulrich, near Augsburg, retained its early importance until the invention of printing, and in 1472, as before mentioned, a printing office was instituted in connection with the monastery, by the Abbot and the Chapter, in which active work was carried on. Abbot Trithemius presented to the mon-

---

[1] Watt., p. 495.   [2] Pez, *Thes.*, iii., 3, 541.
[3] Merzdorf, *Bibliothek Unterh.*, N. S., 1850, p. 7.

astery of Sponheim, in 1480, the sum of fifteen hundred ducats for the enlargement of its library.

As before stated, the Brothers of Common Life planned their collections of books expressly with reference to the service of the students in their schools, and these libraries contained, therefore, a much larger proportion of books in the vernacular than were to be found in other monasteries. In some of the Brotherhood Homes, the library was divided into the collection for the Brothers and the collection for the students. It was ordered that at least once a year all books that were not out on loan should be called in and should be inspected in the presence of the Brothers.

Public Libraries.—Of the libraries of antiquity, only a single one, and that the latest in foundation, the Imperial Library of Constantinople, continued in existence as late as the Middle Ages. This library, founded in 354 by the Emperor Constantius, was largely added to by Julian the Philosopher. Under the Emperor Basiliscus, the original library, which at that time was said to have contained no less than 120,000 volumes, was destroyed by fire. It was afterwards reinstituted by the Emperor Zeno, the prefect of the city, Julian, having given to the work his personal supervision. References are made to this library in 1276, and again early in the fourteenth century, when John Palæologus was able to present from it certain manuscripts (probably duplicates) to the well known manuscript dealer Aurispa of Venice. It is probable that the manuscripts of the imperial collection had been to some extent scattered before the fall of the city in 1453. Such manuscripts as had escaped destruction during the confusion of the siege of the city were hidden away by the scholars interested, in various monasteries and in out-of-the-way corners, from which they were brought out by degrees during the following two or three centuries.

Large quantities of these manuscripts found their way,. however, very promptly to Italy, chiefly through Venice, and, as is described in another chapter, not a few of the Greek scholars who were driven from the Byzantine territories, or who refused to live under the rule of the Turk, brought with them into Italy, as their sole valuable possessions, collections of manuscripts, more or less important, which they used either as texts for their lectures or for transcribing for sale.

The collections in the monasteries of the West, brought together in the first place simply for the requirements of the monks and restricted (at least in theory) to devotional or doctrinal books, were, in large measure at least, placed at the disposal of scholars and readers outside of the monasteries, as the interest in literature came to extend beyond the class of ecclesiastics. With this extension of the use of the libraries, there came a natural development in the range of the books collected.

Long after the monks or ecclesiastics had ceased to exercise any control over the books or to be themselves the only readers interested in their preservation and use, the most convenient space for the collection was to be found in the church buildings. Many of the collections came, in fact, to be known as cathedral libraries.

In certain cases, books or money for the purchase of books was bequeathed in trust to ecclesiastical authorities with the direct purpose of providing a library for the use of the general public. The cathedral Prior of Vercelli (in Piedmont), Jacob Carnarius, who died in 1234, left his books to the Dominicans of S. Paul. He made it, however, a condition of the bequest that under proper security of deposit or pledge, the books should be placed at the disposal of any scholars desiring their use, and particularly of instructors in the Theological Faculty of the University of Vercelli.

Petrarch's library was bequeathed in 1362 to the Church

of S. Mark in Venice, with the condition that the collection was to be for the use of the general public. The books were neglected, and for some time disappeared altogether, and it was only in 1635 that a portion of them were recovered. The famous library of S. Mark dates from 1468, when Cardinal Bessarion presented to the city eight hundred manuscripts, assigning as his reason for the gift the generous hospitality extended by Venice to the refugees from Constantinople. These books were to be for the use of any qualified citizens of the city, a pledge of double the value being deposited for any manuscript borrowed. The library of Boccaccio, who died in 1375, was bequeathed to the monks of the Holy Ghost in Florence. This library was afterwards added to by the collection of the famous theologian, Luigi Marsigli, and that of Niccolo Niccoli.[1]

To Florence, which stood at the front of the intellectual development of Italy, belongs the credit of instituting the largest and most important of the earlier public libraries of Italy. Niccolo Niccoli, one of the most energetic of the scholarly book collectors, specified in his will, made in 1430, that his manuscripts should be placed in the Camal-dulensian monastery of S. Maria, where his friend Traversari was prior, and that these manuscripts were to be available for public use. In 1437, however, the day before his death, he added a codicil to his will, under which the decision as to the abiding-place for his manuscripts was left to sixteen trustees.

He died in debt, however, and the books would have been seized by his creditors if they had not been redeemed by Cosimo de' Medici. Cosimo placed them in the Dominican monastery of S. Mark, the collection in which, in 1444, comprised four hundred Latin and Greek manuscripts. Cosimo gave much care to the further development of this collection. As has already been mentioned,

[1] Blume, *Iter Ital.*, ii., 78.

he used for the purpose the services of the great manuscript dealer, Vespasiano. After the earthquake of 1453, he caused the library building to be restored with greater magnificence than before. The care of the library was continued, after the death of Cosimo, by his son Pietro, and the collection finally became the foundation of the famous Laurentian library, which is in existence to-day.

Pietro took pains to send the Greek grammarian, Laskaris, twice to the Orient to collect further manuscripts. From his first journey, Laskaris brought back no less than two hundred works, of which eighty had not heretofore been known in Italy. On his second journey, Laskaris died.

The library suffered much during the invasion of Charles VIII., but a large proportion of the books were redeemed from the French invaders by the Dominican monks, who paid for them three thousand gulden.

Cardinal Giovanni de' Medici (later Pope Leo X.) took the collection from the monastery with him to Rome, but it was afterwards returned to Florence by Pope Clemens VII.

Clemens gave to Michel Angelo the commission to build a hall for the library, but both Pope and architect died before the work was completed, and the building took shape only finally in 1571, the plan of Michel Angelo having been carried out in substance.

The library of the Vatican passed through various vicissitudes according to the interest or the lack of interest of the successive popes, but under Pope Nicholas V. (1447–1455) it became one of the most important collections in the world for the use of scholars. In 1471, Sixtus IV. completed the library building and the rooms for the archives and added many works, and it was under this Pope that the use of the books was thrown open (under certain conditions) to the general public.

Frederick, Duke of Urbino, is reported to have spent as

much as 40,000 ducats on the ducal collection in Urbino, and Vespasiano rendered important services in the selection and development of this library. The books were, in 1657, under the papacy of Alexander VII., transferred to the Vatican.

During the fourteenth and fifteenth centuries, there was very considerable interest in literary work in Hungary and some noteworthy collections of manuscripts were there brought together. The collectors in Italy found in fact some of their richest treasures, particularly in manuscripts in Greek, in the monasteries of Hungary and of Transylvania. The cause of literature was much furthered by King Matthias Corvinus, who brought together a very valuable collection in Ofen. He kept four scribes in Florence preparing works for the Ofen library, and thirty were continually at work in Ofen itself. His wife, Beatrix, who was a daughter of King Ferdinand of Naples, and a granddaughter of Alfonso the Good, is said to have exercised no little influence upon the literary culture of the Hungarian Court. At her instance, many Italian scholars were brought to Hungary, and their aid utilised in completing the library. The *codices Budences* came to be well known in the scholarly world, and secured fame both for the beauty of their script and the richness of their adornment. Wattenbach says of these, however, that their text is very largely inaccurate, giving the impression that the transcripts had been prepared hurriedly and to order. After the death of King Matthias, a number of his books came into the possession of Emperor Maximilian, who used them for the foundation of the Court Library of Vienna. This was the only portion of the original Hungarian collection which escaped destruction at the hands of the Turks.

Among the public libraries in France is to be noted that of Louis IX., which was open for the use of scholars, but which, being limited almost entirely to devotional books, could not have been of any great scholarly service. In the middle of the thirteenth century, Richard de Furnival, chancellor of the Cathedral of Amiens, instituted a public library, and himself wrote, as a guide for the same, a work entited *Biblionomia*.

The libraries of S. Ulrich and Afra in Augsburg have already been referred to.[1]

According to Savigny, there were before the time of printing no university libraries in Italy. The *stationarii* provided both instructors and students with such books as were prescribed in the courses, and the demand for others appears not to have been great. In Paris, on the other hand, a collection of books for the use of the students was instituted as early as 1270, the first benefactor being Stephen, Archdeacon of Canterbury. Stephen gave his books to the church of Notre Dame to be loaned to poor students of theology. In 1297, Peter of Joigny, in continuation of the same work, gave a collection of books in trust to the university directly for the use of these poor students of theology. The famous College of the Sorbonne probably dates from 1253. The *librarium* of the college was instituted in 1289, and it was specified that the books were for the common use of the instructors and students. The catalogue of this collection, prepared in the following year, is still in existence and contains 1017 titles.[2]

Each *socius* of the college had a key to the library rooms and was permitted to take guests in with him. The books were all fastened to the wall or to the reading-desks by chains, so that the risk of abstraction was not a serious one. The statutes of 1321 prescribed that of every work issued, one copy in the best form must be preserved for the Sorbonne collection. This is probably the first statute of the kind having in view the preservation, in a public collection, of copies of all works produced. It is to be borne in mind, however, in the first place, that it could

[1] *Histoire Lit. de la France*, xxiii., 710–714.   [2] A. Franklin, 224.

have had reference only to books produced under the direct supervision of the college, and secondly, that there was here no question of original literary production, but merely of copies of the older works accepted as possessing doctrinal authority. The books in this library (and probably in other similar libraries) which were not protected by chains were called *libri vagantes*, and these could, under certain restrictions, be loaned out. Wattenbach is of opinion, however, that no books other than duplicates were placed in this class.

Another library of importance was contained in the College of Narbonne, which had been founded in 1316, and which was itself a continuation of an earlier foundation instituted in 1238 by the Archbishop Peter, at the time he was about to take part in the Crusade. The books were to be open for the use of students as well in Paris as of Narbonne.[1]

In the College of Plessis, the statutes of 1455 described that all books, with the exception of the Missals, must be chained, and that no unchaining should be permitted except with the authorisation of the master of all the bursars. In the College of the Scots, the loaning of books outside of the building was absolutely forbidden.

To the College of the Sorbonne belongs the credit of taking the initiative step in inviting the first printers to Paris. In 1469, the prior and the librarian made themselves responsible for finding work and support for two printers, called to Paris from Mayence. The fact that the Prior Johann Heynlin was himself a German was doubtless of influence in bringing to the college early information concerning the importance of the new art.[2] The first book which was printed in Paris was the letters of Gasparin of Bergamo, which appeared in 1470 (twenty years after the perfecting of the Gutenberg press), and bore the imprint *in ædibus Sorbonnæ*.

[1] Franklin, i., 340.　　　　　[2] Franklin, i., 257.

In England, the foundation of the Franciscans in
Oxford took, early in the thirteenth century, active part
in furthering library facilities for the clerics and the
students. They appear to have had two collections, one
called *libraria conventus*, doubtless restricted to theological and religious books, and one described as *libraria
scholarium* or *studentium*, which contained a number of
examples of the classics. It was to the Franciscans that
Bishop Grosseteste, who died in 1253, bequeathed all his
books.

The interest in literature of Richard de Bury, the friend
of Petrarch, has already been referred to. He was the
instructor of King Edward III., and exercised later, important official responsibilities. He served as a foreign
representative more than once, and was for a time chancellor of the kingdom. At the time of his death in 1345,
he was Bishop of Durham. He had a passion for the collecting of books, and with the exceptional advantages of
wealth, official station, and knowledge of distant countries,
he had advantages in this pursuit possessed by no other
Englishman of the time. It is said that the other rooms
in his house having already been crowded with books,
these were massed in his bedroom also in such quantities
that he could get to his bed only by stepping upon them.
His library was bequeathed to Durham College in Oxford,
which had been founded by himself. The college was
discontinued by Henry VIII., and the books were scattered, not even the catalogue, which Bury had himself
prepared, having been preserved. In confiding his books
to Oxford for the use of the students, Richard gives various earnest injunctions as to the proper respect in which
they should be held and the care with which they should
be handled. A reader who should handle the books with
dirty hands or while eating or drinking, could, in Bury's
opinion, be fitly punished with nothing less than banishment. The collection of Durham College was to be open

not only to the use of the members of the college itself, but of all masters and students in Oxford, but no books of which there were no duplicates were to be taken out of the building.

The earliest university library of Germany was that of the College Carolinum in Prague, instituted by Charles IV. The next in date appears to have been that of Heidelberg, where as early as 1386 the Faculty of Arts had a library for itself in addition to the general collection belonging to the university. As before stated, there was also a collection in the Castle which was open for the use of all readers, students, citizens, or strangers. The university library in Vienna dates from 1415, and that in Erfurt from 1433. The town library in Leipzig had for its origin a collection possessed by the Augustinian monks in the monastery of S. Thomas, which collection was thrown open for the use of the public in 1445. Additions to the library were to be made only under the inspection and supervision of the monastery authorities.

The most noteworthy library which had no connection with any university was instituted at Alzei (in Hesse Cassel) in 1409. Its founders were Johannes of Kirchdorf, Prebendary of the Cathedral of Worms and chaplain of King Rupert.

The books were given in order that the clerics and other scholarly people who belonged to the city of Alzei " could use the same for entertainment and instruction, and could spread among the community at large the learning contained therein." [1]

In Hamburg there was, as early as 1469, a collection comprising forty volumes of medical books, for the use more particularly of the city physician and his assistant, and also for general reference. In 1480 the burgermeister Neuermeister left a considerable legacy for the foundation of a city library. In Frankfort, the library of the

[1] J. Mone, *Im Anz. d. deutsch. Vorzeit*, vi., 255.

Carmelite monastery was taken over in 1477 for the use
of the city, in order that the " books could be made of
service for the enlightenment of the community to the
greater glory of God and of the Mother of God."

Collections by Individuals.—Among the laity (outside, at least, of Italy) it was particularly the kings who
from time to time interested themselves in collecting
books. Pepin received from Pope Paul I., at his own
urgent request, a collection of books which included
certain Greek manuscripts. The latter could, however,
hardly have been of any particular service either to the
King or to any members of his Court.[1]

The collection formed by Charlemagne has already
been referred to, and also the provision of his will, under
which, after his death, the books were to be sold and the
proceeds given to the poor. Charles the Bald, with whose
name it is not easy to associate intellectual activity, appears to have been a great collector of books. After his
death his library was, under his directions, divided between St. Denis, Compiègne, and his son.[2] It is recorded
of William the Great of Aquitaine, who died in 1030,
and who was the father of the Empress Agnes, that " he
had many books and read zealously therein."[3] Count
Baldwin of Guines, who died in 1205, brought together a
collection of books which he had translated into the Romance tongue. Louis IX. of France was interested in the
idea of bringing together a collection of devout books,
and, although he did not live to carry out his plan, the
manuscripts which were left by him served for the scholar
Vincennes of Beauvais in the preparation of his great
encyclopedia.

Louis heard, during his crusade, of some sultan who
had caused to be prepared transcripts of all the noted
works of philosophy. This example incited the zeal

---

[1] *Codex Carolinus*, Jaffé. *Bibl.*, iv., 101.
[2] Watt., p. 501.   [3] *Adem. Caban.*, iii., 54.

of Louis, who gave directions that all the "authentic, useful, and devout books" which were to be found within his realm were to be transcribed, and the transcripts placed in the Royal Library. The collection was, however, not allowed to remain complete, as in his will Louis directed that the books should be divided between the preacher monks and the Minorites of Paris, the Abbey Royaumont, and the Dominican monks of Compiègne.[1]

John, Duke of Berry, son of the Good King John, and brother of King Charles V., found opportunity, even during the troublous times which culminated with the battle of Poitiers and the imprisonment of his father, to bring together a noteworthy collection of books. It was this collection that made the beginning of the library of the Louvre, instituted by Charles V., a library for which Gilles Mallet prepared in 1373 a very complete catalogue. Barrois published in 1830, in Paris, a work devoted entirely to a description of the books collected by Prince John and his brother Charles.

David Aubert, whose translation of the *History of the Emperors* was published[2] in 1457, makes, in the preface to this history, special mention of the literary tastes of Philip, Duke of Burgundy. He says that Philip made a daily practice of having read to him ancient histories and that he kept employed a great number of skilled translators, learned historians, and capable scribes who were busied in adding to his great library. This collection of Philip appears later to have been scattered as there is no record of its preservation.

The Duke of Bedford found time, between his frequent campaigns, to interest himself in the collection of manuscripts, and more particularly of works which were beautifully illuminated. He purchased, for 1200 francs, a portion of the library of Charles V., which had been

[1] Watt., p. 502.   [2] Barrois, iv., 2.

captured, and, these books being taken to Oxford, finally found place in the Bodleian collection.

Philip of Cleves, who died in 1528 and who was connected with the Burgundy House, shared the passion of his relatives for magnificent manuscripts.

An inventory of Margaret, Duchess of Brittany, contains the descriptive titles of eleven books of devotion and four romances, " all bound in satin." [1]

The name of Anne of Brittany, the wife of King Charles VIII., and later of Louis XII., has long been famous in connection with her fondness for books of devotion and with the great collection which she succeeded in making of these. An inventory of 1498 gives the titles of 1140 books as belonging to Anne's collection. [2]

In Italy, it was not until the time of Petrarch that there came to be any general interest in the collection of books. This interest was naturally associated with the great Humanistic movement of which it may be considered as partly the cause and partly the effect. The development of literary interests in Italy during the fourteenth and fifteenth centuries will be considered in the chapter on the Renaissance.

In Germany, the collections outside of the monasteries appear to have been less important than in Burgundy and in France, the difference being probably in part due to the narrower cultivation of the German noblemen, and probably also in part to their smaller resources. In fact, the more important collections do not appear to have been in the possession of the nobility at all, but to have come into existence through the public spirit of citizens of lower degree. The library of two hundred volumes brought together as early as 1260 by Hugo Trimberg, a schoolmaster of St. Gangolf, has already been referred to.

[1] *Bibliothèque d. l'École de Chartres*, série v., iii., 45.
[2] Le Roux d. Lincy, in the *Bibl. de Lec. des Ch.*, série iii., i., 151.

Duke Ludwig of Brieg is described as having had as early as 1360 a considerable collection of books, and as having had written, in 1353, by some scribe whose name has not been preserved, the Hedwig legends.

The Electors of the Palatinate interested themselves in the formation of libraries, having possibly been influenced to some extent by their relations with their neighbours on the other side of the Rhine. Authors such as Matthias of Kemnat and Michel Behaim worked at the instance of the Electors and under pay from them. The books of Kemnat and Behaim were either originally written in German, or were promptly translated into German for the use of the Electors and of their wives. A number of books in this series are also ornamented with pictures, but, according to the descriptions, the art work in these illustrations was much inferior to that done at the same time in Burgundy.

The most important group of the Heidelberg manuscripts was collected by Ludwig III., who died in 1437.[1] His daughter Mechthild, whose first husband was the Count Ludwig of Wurtemberg, and whose second, the Archduke Albrich, retained in her widowhood in her castle at Rotenburg a collection of ninety-four volumes of the mediæval poets, whose works were written in the vernacular.[2] Ulbrich of Rappoldstein kept two scribes engaged for five years in transcribing the *Parsival*, and the cost of the work amounted to £200.

It is apparent from the preceding sketch that the development of literature and the circulation of books during the Middle Ages were considerable, notwithstanding the serious difficulties there were to contend with during the ten centuries between the fall of the Roman Empire of the West and the time of the invention of printing.

---

[1] Wilkens, *Gesch. d. Heidelb. Büchersammlungen.*
[2] Martin, Erzherzogin Mechthild, in *Der Zeitschrift für Gesch. Freiburgs.* 1871.

Under the "Peace of the World" secured by the
imperial rule, there had come to be an active literary production and a development of literary interests throughout the community which called for a wide distribution
and a general use of books. There was available for the
use of publishers a great list of accepted classics, Greek
and Latin, and there were also various epochs during
which there came into existence works by contemporary
writers of distinctive importance, many of which have
been preserved as classics for future generations.

The publishers of this period had a convenient and
inexpensive material to use for the making of books,
and they had available for book production the labour
of skilled and inexpensive scribes,—chiefly slaves. The
well established means of communication throughout the
Empire enabled the publishers of Rome and Massilia
and other literary centres to keep open connections with
cities in the farthest districts of the realm, and there
is adequate evidence of a well organised trade in the distribution of books over almost the entire civilised world,
a trade which continued active until the latter part of the
fourth century.

With the fall of the Empire of the West and with the
destruction of so much of the civilised organisation and
machinery which had been dependent upon Roman rule,
the book trade, or, at least, the trade outside of Italy,
practically disappeared. There remained, however, with
certain classes a knowledge of the classics and an interest
in their preservation, and there remained also in the monasteries the knowledge and practice of writing and the collections of the works of the early Church Fathers, the
multiplication of which, for the use of the increasing number of priests, called for continued labour on the part of
the clerical scribes.

When the work of writing came to be instituted,
particularly in the Benedictine Order, as a part of the

regular routine of the life of a properly ordered monastery, and when such work came to be accepted as a
part of the daily or weekly services rendered by the
monks, the preservation of the art of writing and the
preservation of the manuscripts, the existence of which
depended upon this continued knowledge, were assured.

For centuries after 476, such literary vitality as there
was depended practically upon these Benedictine monasteries. After the tenth century, we find a wider literary
interest throughout the community, and in certain Courts
and circles of nobility, literature began to be accepted as
fashionable, and an interest in literature to be accepted as
part of the proper outfit of a gentleman.

The second stage, therefore, in the development of the
interest in books which secured the multiplication of
enough copies of many of the older books to prevent them
from passing out of existence, was in the formation of the
collections by princes and nobles, collections which were,
as we have noted, usually under the charge of clerical
scribes.

The third and more important stage of development
came with the recognition, on the part of the newly
founded universities of Bologna, Paris, Prague, Heidelberg, and Oxford, of the fact that the work of higher
education required the use of collections of books for the
reference of instructors and for the direct use of the
students. With the instituting in the universities of a
class of scribes (*stationarii, librarii*) recognised as university officials, a recognition which carried with it certain
privileges and protection, and which went far to offset
the hampering restrictions of university and ecclesiastical
supervision, the book production of Europe took a more
assured form.

The fourth step in the extension of literary interests
was taken by the towns-people, partly at the instance of
priests who were themselves sprung from the people, and

partly under the influence of students returning from university work to their native towns ; and collections of books were made for the use of the towns-people, while libraries, originally planned only for the work of the monasteries and for the use of clerics, were thrown open to students generally. There appear to have been in the manuscript period and in the earlier ages of printing a larger number of such town libraries and a larger extent of literary interest among the citizen class in Germany than in either France or England.

In Italy, the development of literary interests and of literary production worked from an early date much more outside of church organisations than was the case either in Germany or in France.

In such centres of literary activity as Florence, Milan, Padua, Rome, and later, Venice, the production of the classics and the multiplying of the books of the Italian writers themselves was carried on at the instance and to a large extent with the money of the wealthier citizens, citizens who in many cases held no official positions whatever. The intellectual life of Italy was, however, from an early date, very largely influenced by the thought and the learning that came to it from the Greeks of Constantinople, an influence which was increasing in importance for a quarter of a century before the fall of the Greek Empire, and which, after 1453, was naturally still more extended and emphasised by the large immigration of Greek scholars flying from Turkish rule and bringing with them the literary treasures of the East. It was this invasion of Greek thought and the restoration of the knowledge of the poetry and philosophy of classic Greece, which gave the immediate impetus to the great intellectual movement known as the Renaissance.

As the Renaissance movement took hold of the imagination of Italian scholars, it found ready for its use the new invention of printing, and through the presses of

Aldus and his associates, the thought of the Old World, reshaped with the knowledge of the fifteenth century, gave a fresh inspiration to the intellectual life of Europe.

In Germany, where the Renaissance movement also influenced the intellectual life of the time, a more important impetus to the intellectual activity came with the work of the Reformation. The printing-press made the teachings of Luther and his associates available for the widest popular distribution, and the towns-people and villagers who bought from the book peddlers the tracts containing the vigorous statements of the Reformers, and who bought also the answering arguments of the defenders of the Roman Church, were not merely wrestling with a religious or theological issue, but were furthering the general education of the community and were helping to lay the foundation of the book trade of the future. From the earliest date of the printing-press, it was the case that there was in Germany a larger distribution of books, printed in the vernacular, among what one may call (for purposes of classification) the lower orders of the community, than was the case in either Italy, France, or Germany. The development of the relation between literature and the community, which came after the establishment of the new art of printing, belongs, however, to a later chapter.

12

CHAPTER III.

THE MAKING OF BOOKS IN THE EARLY UNIVERSITIES.

THE first revival of the long slumbering trade in manuscripts took place in Italy, the cradle of the universities. Although after the breaking down of the old civilisation of the Western Empire, Italy had suffered more through invasions and devastations than any other country of Europe, it had nevertheless succeeded in preserving a certain continuity of cultivation and some remnants of learning or germs of intellectual life, from which germs there came again into growth an intellectual development for Europe. For the purposes of this study, I am concerned with the history of the early universities of Europe only in connection with their relations to the production of books. I propose, therefore, to give a brief description of the organisation and the character of the book-trade that came into existence in one or two of the representative university towns, with some reference to the general influence of the first universities upon the development and the distribution of literature.

As has been indicated in the introductory chapter, it is my understanding that, with the beginning of the thirteenth century, the responsibility for the preservation and the development of the intellectual life of Europe, for the mental training of the increasing proportion of the community which was conscious of intellectual existence, and for the transmission to the existing generations of what had been preserved of the thought and learning of the past, was transferred from the monasteries and the ecclesiastical schools to the newly organised universities.

This change meant among other things that the control and direction of education no longer rested with the ecclesiastics, that the class of scholars was no longer limited to the clerics, and that there were other directions in which scholarly achievement was to be sought than those heretofore marked out by the Church. I do not mean to say that after the beginning of the thirteenth century, when the schools of Bologna and Paris had developed into universities, the Church consciously abandoned the control of education, a control which had rested in its hands for eight centuries. The representatives of the Church authority themselves took an important part in bringing into existence not a few of the universities, and in connection with the organisation of the theological Faculties and in other ways, the popes and the bishops retained for a long series of years an important and abiding influence over much of the university work. Heretical doctrines, or what Rome believed to be heretical doctrines, were taught not infrequently in university lecture-rooms, but the authority on the part of the Church to interfere with such teaching, and to secure the withdrawal of the license from the lecturer, was continually claimed and was frequently enforced. The fact remained, however, that the general direction and control of the work of higher education rested no longer with ecclesiastics but with laymen. Of the four great divisions of university instruction, Theology, Philosophy (or Art), Law, and Medicine, the first remained of necessity under the direction of the Church, while in the supervision of the second the Church undertook to exercise an influence which of necessity varied greatly from time to time according to the institution and according also to the character of the particular popes and bishops. The third and fourth Faculties were, however, entirely independent of ecclesiastical influence, and the mere fact of the existence outside of the Church of an important division of learning and of a great body of scholars must have had a powerful effect on the imagination of communities which had for so many generations been accustomed to look to the Church as the source or as the interpreter of all knowledge.

The principal authorities on the rise and the general history of the earlier universities are Denifle, Laurie, Mullinger, and Compayré. The titles of their several works, on which have in the main been based such statements or conclusions as are expressed in the following pages, are given in full in the bibliography. The details concerning the work of the university scribes and the manuscript dealers are chiefly derived from the works of Wattenbach and Kirchhoff.[1]

It is to be noted that several centuries before the institution in Christian Europe of the first of the universities, and at a time when, outside of a few monastic *scriptoria*, the interest in literature in Christian states was almost non-existent, in the countries which had accepted the faith of Mahomet a system of higher education had been effectively organised, and in connection with the intellectual activity of the universities and libraries of Bagdad, Alexandria, Cairo, and Cordova, there had been a very considerable production of literature in the departments of jurisprudence, philosophy, and science. In fact, the first knowledge that came to the Europe of the Middle Ages concerning Greek thought and Greek literature was brought to it through Arabian scholars, and it was by means of the lecturers of Cordova that the doctrines of

---

[1] The great work of Rashdall on the Universities of the Middle Ages was, unfortunately for me, published too late in 1895, to be available for use in the preparation of this chapter. It seemed proper, however, to include its title in my bibliography.

Aristotle were made known to the philosophers of Paris. The list of the scholarly writers who were associated during the eleventh and twelfth centuries with the great Arabian schools is a long one, and the books produced by them included not a few works which had an abiding influence on the thought of Europe. I have, however, no information concerning the methods employed for the manifolding and distribution of the books, and a consideration of them does not properly find place in this study. The names of Avicenna (d. 1027) and Averrhoes (d. 1198) will be recognised as representative of the class of authors referred to, the men who, by their translations of Hippocrates, Galen, Aristotle, and other Greek classics, recalled what Laurie calls the university life of the Greeks.[1]

In explaining how the universities are to be distinguished from the cathedral schools or the Benedictine schools out of which they were developed, Laurie gives the following definition of the first universities : "They were *specialised* schools, as opposed to the schools of Arts, and they were *open to all*, without restriction, as *studia publica* or *generalia*, as opposed to the more restricted ecclesiastical schools, which were under a Rule."[2]

For the older institutions, it is not practicable to fix with any precision the date of their beginning, and no year can be named in which they first exercised the functions of a university. The first university that was formally founded was that of Prague, which dates from April, 1348. Bologna, Paris, Padua, Oxford, and Cambridge were not founded but grew, that is, were developed under special influences out of pre-existing schools. The first European school which, while never developing into a university, did do specialised university work, was that of Salerno, which may be said to have initiated for Europe systematised and scientific instruction in medicine. *Fons*

---

[1] Laurie, 69.   [2] Laurie, 101.

Medicinæ was the name given to it by Petrarch. The school of Salerno has one special claim to commemoration in any general sketch of the intellectual life of Europe. Its foundation and early development were due to the famous Benedictine monastery of Monte Cassino, the monastery which had been established by S. Benedict (in 529), and the *scriptorium* in which was the creation of Cassiodorus. Salerno, which was later affiliated with the University of Naples, fills, therefore, the place of a connecting link between the educational work of the old-time Benedictine *scriptorium* and the scientific activities and intellectual life of the new university system of Europe. Indeed, through that wonderful old man, Cassiodorus, at once Greek, Roman, and Goth, statesman, author, and monk, the chain of continuity is borne directly back to the classic world of imperial Rome.

The study of letters in Monte Cassino had come to include medicine, and the writings of Galen and Hippocrates were transcribed in the *scriptorium*, and were later made the first text-books in the medical school established by the monks at Salerno. Charlemagne is said to have interested himself in the school and in 802 to have ordered certain Greek medical treatises to be translated for its use from the Arabic into Latin.[1] The man who finally developed the monks' medical school (then known as the *civitas Hippocratica*) into a great and specialised *studium publicum* was, however, Constantine, a Carthaginian Christian. His work was done between the years of 1065 and 1087, under the special favour and patronage of Robert Guiscard, who was at that time ruler of Apulia. In the time of Robert the school contained some women students, probably the earliest in Europe. There are references also at this period to several female writers on medical subjects. Salerno dates as a privileged school from 1100. The University of Naples, with which the medical college

[1] Compayré, 112.

of Salerno was later affiliated, was instituted by Frederick
II. (the "Wonder of the World") in 1224. Notwithstanding the brilliancy of the Court of Frederick and the
feverish energy of the monarch himself, the literary work
done in his university was not of abiding importance, and
it is Bologna which serves as the type of the earlier universities of Europe, and which divides with the University
of Paris the honour of having served as a general model
for later foundations.

The University of Bologna lays claim to be the oldest
in Europe. According to one tradition it was founded by
Charlemagne about 800, but the celebration in 1890 of its
thousandth anniversary indicates that its modern historians
have contented themselves with a somewhat later date.
The jurist Irnerius, who gave instruction in civil law in
Bologna between 1100 and 1135, was able to do for the
school of law a very similar work to that done by Constantine a century earlier for the school of medicine at
Salerno, and under his direction the school became a
studium publicum or *generale*. Bologna dates as a privileged *studium* from 1158, when the *Universitas* secured a
formal recognition from Frederick I. Tiraboschi speaks
of the university as having been in a flourishing condition
as early as the twelfth century, and in 1224, when the
Emperor Frederick II., in his zeal on behalf of his newly
founded university at Naples, undertook to suppress that
of Bologna, the latter is reported to have had no less than
10,000 students. Its great jurist of that time was Azo or
Azolinus. The edict was revoked in 1227, and the schools
of the university were, in fact, never closed. The University of Padua dates from about 1215, and that of
Vercelli (in Piedmont) from 1228. In 1248, Innocent IV.
established the University of Piacenza, with privileges
similar to those enjoyed by Paris and Bologna. Pisa
dates from about 1340, Florence from 1321, and Pavia
from 1362. Galeazzo Visconti secured for Pavia from

Charles IV. a charter with the privileges of Paris, Bologna, and Oxford. Notwithstanding the competition of so many rival institutions, and the special favour shown from time to time to certain of these by one prince or another (as in the case of the Emperor Frederick to Naples), Bologna not only retained its pre-eminence among the universities of Italy, but secured for itself a great reputation throughout Europe, attracting students of every nationality. In Bologna, Padua, and Pavia special attention was given to jurisprudence, while the school of Florence was noted for the liberal remuneration granted to its instructors in rhetoric and in belles-lettres. In this respect, however, Florence stood almost alone. The instructors in literature, classed as Humanists, were obliged for the most part to seek appreciation and remuneration not in the universities, but at the Courts of the cultivated princes and in the palaces of the more intellectual of the noblemen, and, fortunately for the literary life of Italy, literature had, during the fourteenth and fifteenth centuries, a popularity and acceptance among princes and nobles to an extent not known elsewhere in Europe.

While the university life of Italy dates from the close of the twelfth century, it is not until the beginning of the thirteenth century that we find any trace of regulations concerning the production and distribution of manuscripts. It appears that for a term of perhaps a quarter of a century there had been in Bologna and in the other older university towns a certain amount of interest in the production, hiring, and selling of manuscripts, a trade which had been carried on without any supervision or restriction on the part of the university authorities, and the same was the case with the work of the earlier manuscript dealers in Paris.

The term *stationarii*, which first appears in Bologna in 1259 and in Paris some years later, indicates at once a change in the method of work of these university scribes

as compared with previous writers who had been ready to
do work in one place or another as opportunity offered.
For a number of years there was, in connection with this
university work, practically no selling of books. The
special responsibility of the *stationarii* was to keep in
stock a sufficient number of authorised and verified transcripts or copies of the books ordered or recommended
in the educational courses of the university, and to rent
these to the students or to the instructors at rates which
were prescribed by university regulations. The *stationarii*
also took over the books of the students who died while
in the university, or of departing students, as in most of
the universities it was a misdemeanour to carry any books
at all out of the university town.

In Bologna, Padua, and probably other Italian universities, the Jews were forbidden to carry on any trade in
books. If, therefore, Jews coming into a town had manuscripts which they wished to dispose of, it was necessary
for them to place these manuscripts in the hands of the
stationarii, and they would make sale of them on commission. As before specified, however, the buyers of books
in a university town could purchase only the use of the
books during their sojourn in such town. On leaving the
town, it was necessary that the books should be placed
again with the *stationarii* for sale to others connected
with the university. It is probable, however, that this
regulation applied only to the special list of text-books or
reference books authorised and prescribed by the university. A certain Heinrichs of Kirchberg relates that on
leaving Padua in 1256, he had managed to bring away
with him a considerable package of books. He had accomplished this by hiding the books in a load of hay
which he took with him through the town gates without
being discovered.[1] In 1334, the university regulation was
modified so that after having secured the special permis-

---

[1] Tiraboschi, Girolamo, *Litteratura Italiana*, tom. v., lib. i., p. 4.

sion of the authorities, a student could take with him from
the university books which he had purchased.

Until the time when the manuscript traders were replaced by the dealers in printed books, the most important
function of the university dealers was not in the sale, but
in the hiring out of manuscripts, and the term *stationarius*
came from a very early date to be limited to the functionary who, under the regulations of the university, provided,
for hire, the students, and in some cases the instructors,
with the material required for their work.

In order to facilitate the manifolding and prompt distribution of the texts needed, and in order also to lessen
for the students the cost of securing these texts, the practice obtained from the beginning of dividing the manuscripts into portions, to which portions were given the
name *peciæ* or *petiæ*—or in the Italian form, *pezze*. At
first, the extent of these divisions must have been more
or less arbitrary, but later, the number of pages or sheets
to be contained in them was made a matter of specific
university regulation. According to the regulation, the
pecia was to contain sixteen columns, each with sixty-
two lines, and each line with thirty-two letters, and the
material was to be written on sheets comprising together
a form, *quaterne*.

The *pecia* served as the unit of the calculation for the
charge for the rental. The older manuscripts had been
written in a much larger *format* than that found convenient for university work, and the above specified form
was now arrived at as, on the whole, best meeting the
requirements of the students and the convenience of the
scribes.

For some years after the formal recognition by the
university statutes of the *stationarii*, the number of these
was naturally limited, a limitation which had a service for
the university authorities in facilitating the supervision
considered important, and which was, of course, of business

value for the *stationarii* themselves. A certain amount
not only of scholarly knowledge but also of capital must
have been requisite on the part of the *stationarii* in
order to bring together for manifolding authentic codices
or texts, and also to keep themselves supplied with writing materials, which during the thirteenth century continued to be costly. There is evidence that in certain
cases, particularly in Padua, a salary was paid from the
university chest to the *stationarii*, which was an admission
on the part of the university authorities that the prices
prescribed for the rent of the *peciæ* were not in themselves
adequate to secure a living income for the scribes.

The *stationarii* were occasionally known in the Italian
universities by the name of *bedelli*, or *bidelli*. The *bedelli*
were originally university officials, whose functions probably covered some such disciplinary work as that which is
to-day in the hands of the Oxford proctors. The name
suggests also the English term *beadle*, applied to the
English parish official who was charged with the duty of
keeping the peace, and I find that the lexicographers de-
rive the word *beadle* directly from the earlier term *bedel*,
the name given to the English university functionary who
had to do with matters of discipline and particularly with
the direction of public functions, processions, etc. The
name is derived from *pedum*, a stick, the allusion being probably to the baton or staff of office. The use in Italy of the
term *bidellus* for the scribes hiring out manuscripts, was
evidently due to the fact that the privileges of this business were in certain cases given to the university officials,
in addition, probably, to their other duties.

The name of *peciarii* was sometimes applied to the
officials whose duty it was to supervise the work of the
stationarii. In 1300, there is reference to six *peciarii* in
Bologna.

The earliest Italian reference to university scribes dates
from 1228, and concerns not the University of Bologna,

but the smaller institution of Vercelli in Piedmont. The Vercelli regulations order the employment of two *exemplatores*, who were to be charged with the duty of providing the texts required for the use of the instructors and students in the Faculties of jurisprudence and theology. The prices to be paid for these manuscripts were to be fixed by the rector of the university. As this is the earliest regulation of which there is record concerning bookselling in the universities, I think it worth while to cite the text itself :

Item habebit Commune Vercellarum duos exemplatores, quibus taliter providebit, quod eos scholares habere possint, qui habeant exemplantia in utroque jure et in Theologia competentia et correcta tam in textu quam in glossa ; ita quod solutio fiat a scholaribus pro exemplis secundum quod convenit, ad taxationem Rectoris.[1]

[The University of Vercelli shall also employ two *exemplatores*, for whom suitable provision shall be made, so that they may be at the service of the scholars who require manuscripts authoritative and correct both as to the text and in the commentaries, either in the department of law or in that of theology, and in return for the copies (or for the use of the copies) received from the *exemplatores*, the students shall pay a fitting price (or rental) to be fixed by the Rector of the university.]

In similar fashion, the statutes of the University of Padua of the year 1283 provide that two *stationarii* or *bidelli* should be employed, one of whom should be at the service of the Faculty of jurisprudence, and the other should serve those of arts and of medicine. The theological Faculty was not instituted in Padua until much later. The two *bidelli* drew salaries, the first of eight ducats per year, and the second of two ducats, forty sols. They were charged with the duty of keeping a supply of *peciæ* of the texts prescribed in the lists and of placing these supplies

[1] Tiraboschi, v., ii., 39.

at the disposal of the students and scholars calling for the same. In the year 1420, the statutes of the High School of Modena prescribed that the *stationarius* (there appears to have been question of but one official for the entire institution) must keep a supply of the texts of the Roman and Canonical law, the *summa notaria*, the *speculum*, the Lectures of Cinus and of Innocentius.

The *stationarius* was to charge for the rent of a *pecia* of the prescribed texts four denarii, of the *glossarii* five denarii, and of other texts six denarii. I do not find in the regulations any specification of the term covered by this rental. The city was to assure the *stationarius* of freedom from military service, and was to give him the yearly compensation of ten lire." [1]

A reference by the Italian scholar Filelfo indicates that from this university arrangement the term *bidellus* came to be applied to scribes outside of university towns. Filelfo speaks of a *librarius publicus*, "who, in the ordinary speech, is called *bidellus*."

With the increase in the larger universities, such as Bologna and Padua, of the number of students and instructors requiring literary material, the practice gradually took shape of purchasing instead of hiring the texts required, and the *stationarii* developed into *librarii*. In its original signification, the term *librarius* stood for librarian ; and as late as the fourteenth century the French word *librairie* was used for a library or a collection of books. It seems to have been only after the introduction of printing that the use of the term *librairie* finally came to be restricted in France to a collection of books held for sale, that is to say, to a book-shop.

The book-dealers, who in the earlier years of the manuscript period devoted themselves to keeping collections of manuscripts, filled, in fact, rather the rôle of librarians than of booksellers. They were ready to rent out their

[1] Savigny, i., 590.

manuscripts for a consideration, or to permit customers
to consult the texts without taking them from the shop.
The practice of making from their original stock of texts
authenticated copies for general sale, was a matter of comparatively slow development.

Bologna had become the most important school in
Europe for the study of Roman and Canonical law, and it
was in Bologna that the undertakings of the university
bookseller first became important.   The booksellers were
not only subject to the supervision of the university, but
were also brought under the regulations of the town, and
the town authorities undertook to prescribe prices as well
for the renting as for the selling of the manuscripts, and
also to prescribe penalties for the renting or selling of
incorrect or incomplete texts.

The university regulations specified that there must be
on the part of the booksellers no modification of the text
under which new readings or glosses should be inserted to
replace those accepted as authoritative, and a penalty was
attached to the selling or renting of the texts in any other
form than that in which they were prescribed by the
instructors of the Faculty to which the study belonged.
In 1289, the penalty for the contravention of this regulation, previously fixed at ten lire, was raised to one hundred
lire.[1]

A few years later, a university regulation specified that
the *stationarii peciarum* who undertook to rent out the
authoritative texts, must keep in stock sufficient supplies
of 117 specified works.   In the year 1300, there were in
the university six official *stationarii*, of whom three were
Italians and three, foreigners.   They had to be appointed
each year, but it seems probable that when their work
proved satisfactory they were re-appointed from year to
year.

The responsibility for the general supervision of the

[1] Kirchhoff, 23.

texts and for their correctness and completeness rested with the *bidellus generalis*. Any reader who should discover blemishes or omissions in the *peciæ* was under obligation to report the same to the *bidellus generalis*, and the *stationarius* who was responsible for the preparation of the defective text was fined five solidos, one half of the fine going to the university chest, one quarter to the *bidellus*, and one quarter to the informant.

The *stationarii* were ordered to post up in a conspicuous place in their shops all the regulations having to do with their trade, in order that all buyers could know what they were entitled to receive. They were not at liberty to decline to rent to university members any *peciæ* on the official list. On the other hand, if they rented out *peciæ* to students who had been expelled or who were under suspension, they were themselves liable to fine. The usual rental at this time, that is to say, the beginning of the thirteenth century, was four *denarii* for a *quaterne* (four sheets) and two *denarii* for a *pecia*. The *denarius* was the equivalent of about ten cents.

The rental for works not on the official list was somewhat higher, as these would not be called for so continuously and as the preparation of supplies of the same must, therefore, be more of a speculation. In renting manuscripts outside of Bologna (which could be done only under special permission of the university authorities and which occurred as a rule only with members of other universities) an additional two *denarii* for a *quaterne* could be demanded. Students renting the *peciæ* were obliged to deposit a pledge of sufficient value to secure the *stationarii* against loss. Between the regulations applying to the *stationarii peciarum*, and those controlling the general *stationarii*, who had authority to sell as well as to rent and whose business lay outside of the university, there were various differences. The general *stationarius* appeared to have undertaken from time to time the sale of books on commission, which to the university *station-arius* was forbidden.

One of the earlier university regulations prohibited students from purchasing manuscripts with a view of selling them again for a profit, but this, according to Savigny, fell into disuse in the course of the fourteenth century. As late as 1334, the regulations of Bologna strictly prohibited students from taking with them, on leaving the universities, any books whatsoever, without a special authorisation on the part of the heads of their respective Faculties. Regulations of this kind naturally interfered with the normal development of the book trade in a city so largely dependent upon its university as was Bologna, and formed one cause for the greater activity of the general book trade in cities like Venice, where the regulations of the commune were not supplemented by those of university authorities.

The city statutes of Bologna of 1259, prohibited the *stationarii librarii* from taking a higher commission on the sale of manuscripts than two and a half per cent. It was also specified that no sale of a work left on commission should be made without the direct knowledge of the owner. The *stationarius peciarum* belonged at the outset to the membership of the university, and, in accepting the authority of its supervision and its regulations, enjoyed also the university privileges, which included freedom from certain municipal obligations. Many of the university *stationarii* belonged, as mentioned, to the class of *bidelli*.

It was forbidden for any member of the university to promise or to engage, either directly or indirectly, to pay to the *stationarius* a higher commission or compensation than that prescribed in the regulations. The penalty for an infraction of this rule, a penalty imposed upon both the parties concerned, was a fine of five livres. The student was also under obligations to denounce to the rector any attempt on the part of the dealer to secure an additional compensation.[1] The very severity of these prohibitions gives indication of difficulty in securing enforcement of the system.

The statutes of Padua and of the other Italian universities of the manuscript trade, were similar to, and were probably in the main based upon, those of Bologna. In Padua, the earliest regulations which have been preserved bear date as late as 1465, which is one year later than the introduction into Italy of the printing-press. The regulations of 1465 prescribed the size of the *peciæ* and confirmed the rental prices to the schedule of those of Bologna. The renting of manuscripts could, however, have continued but for a short period after the issue of these regulations. In Padua, as in Bologna, the *stationarii peciarum* had to make a deposit, in entering upon their business, of four hundred lire. They had also to go through with an examination at the hands of the university authorities, and they then had to take an oath of loyalty to the university. This entitled them to their formal appointment, which needed, however, as stated, to be confirmed from year to year.

In Padua, as in Bologna, there were fixed commissions for the sale of manuscripts, and these commissions, in themselves quite moderate, were to be paid half by the buyer and half by the seller. It appears, however, that the prices were probably not fully controlled by these regulations, as there are examples of so-called "presents" being given by buyers to the sellers after the sale of manuscripts on the commission basis specified in the regulations had been duly recorded.

In Padua, as in Bologna, it was strictly forbidden for Jews to take any part in the buying and selling of manuscripts. The only way in which a Jew could secure a manuscript desired by him was through the intervention

[1] Denifle, *op. cit.*, iii., 295.

of the university authorities, who might make purchase
of the same on his behalf. The *bidellus* was the official
usually employed for the purpose. It may be assumed
that some additional commission was here required, and
that the Jews had to pay more dearly for their university
texts than the Christians.

There does not appear to be record of the loaning
of manuscripts to students for their own transcribing,
although in Paris this evidently formed an important portion of the manuscript business. In Bologna, as in Padua,
the trade in bookbinding was directly associated with that
of manuscript selling, and the *ligatori librorum* carried on
their work in the shops of the *librarii*. In Bologna, the
manuscripts were in the main devoted to the subjects of
the law and scholastic theology, while in Padua the more
important division was medicine.

The literary requirements, however, for doctors of law
as for doctors of medicine, must have been at best but
moderate. Savigny states that in the thirteenth century
the collection of books belonging to a doctor of the law
in Bologna rarely comprised more than from four to six
volumes, and the medical collections were hardly as large.
It is with the beginning of the fifteenth century that there
comes to be a larger understanding of the relations of literature to education and a material increase in the demand
in the university towns for supplies of books outside of
the texts actually in use in the lecture room.

Compayré gives the following list of the books required
in the ordinary and in the extraordinary courses of law in
Bologna, a list which was, he says, practically the same at
Montpellier: The several works of the *Corpus Juris* of
Justinian, comprising the *Codex* (which dates from 529),
the *Digestum Vetus*, the *Infortiatum*, the *Digestum Novum*. These were identical with the three parts which
the pupils of Irnerius distinguished as the *Pandects* or
Digest, the *Institutes*, the *Authenticum*. To these sources

of the Roman law were later added the *Constitutiones* of Frederick I. and Frederick II., and in Montpellier the *Usus Feudorum*, a collection of feudal laws.

The statutes of the universities fixed the time within which the reading of the prescribed books must be completed. Professors were obliged, in entering upon their duties, to take the following oath : " I swear to read and to finish reading within the time fixed by the statutes, the books or parts of books which have been assigned for my lectures." Severe penalties were inflicted on those whose courses had not been completed within the required time.[1] There ought, as a rule, to have been no difficulty in completing the task assigned, for each Faculty had, as a rule, only a single work or at most a single author assigned for its consideration. The Faculty of Arts had Aristotle, that of Civil Law the *Corpus Juris* of Justinian, that of Common Law the *Decretals* of Gratian. Compayré suggests that, according to the maxim of Seneca, *timeo hominem unius libri*, the Faculties of the Middle Ages might well have been awe-inspiring.

The list of the texts of the medical Faculties was, however, somewhat more considerable. The course in Montpellier, where medicine became still more important than law, followed in the main that of Salerno. The first place was given to Hippocrates and Galen. It is somewhat surprising that as late as 1250 the teachings of these old-time practitioners (whose work was done respectively in the fourth century B.C. and the second century A.D.) should still have remained the chief authorities in medical science. Compayré refers to them as the Aristotles of Medicine. In the program of the Faculty of Paris of 1270, however, the names of Hippocrates and Galen do not appear.

With the two Greeks were associated the original works of Constantine and his translations from Rhazes Hali-Abbas, Ysaac, Avicenna, Johannicus, and other

[1] Compayré, 231.

Arabic and Persian writers, and finally the treatise of John of St. Amand, and of Nicholas of Salerno. The *Antidotarium*, or *Book of Antidotes*, known also as the *Book of Medicaments*, was for some centuries a work of standard reference and of popular sale. The influence of the Arabs in the instructional literature of medicine seems to have been almost as controlling as that of the Greeks in philosophy and of the Romans in law.

Rabelais, who studied medicine in Montpellier between 1520 and 1530, is said to have been the first among the students who was able to read his Greek authors in the original instead of in Latin translations.[1] Rabelais found time while in college not only for Greek and medicine, but for literature. The first part of the *Pantagruel* was written before he had secured his final diploma.

By the middle of the thirteenth century, the number of the books required for use in the university courses had increased to such an extent that four catalogues were issued, one for each of the four Faculties—Law, Medicine, Theology, and Arts. The lectures and the instruction were given entirely in Latin, which was the only language that could have been understood by all of the various nationalities represented, or even by the representatives of the different Italian dialects.

In Spain, the earliest university was that of Palencia, which was founded in 1212. Salamanca, founded a few years later, soon exceeded Palencia in importance, and, particularly in connection with the work of its medical Faculty, secured for itself, before the close of the thirteenth century, a repute throughout Europe. Compayré is of opinion that the instruction given in Salamanca, not only in medicine but in science generally and in philosophy, was very largely influenced by the presence in the peninsula of Moorish scholars. " The philosophy of Averrhoes and the medicine of Avicenna exerted a manifest influence

[1] Compayré, 250.

on the development of studies at Salamanca." [1]   It seems
probable, if this belief is well founded, that the Arabian
literature, produced and manifolded in Cordova, found its
way to Salamanca, and through Salamanca to Salerno,
Bologna, and Paris.

The formal constitution of the University of Paris dates
from 1202.   Certain of its historians, however, claim for
its first work as an educational institution a much earlier
date.   Crévier, for instance, says: "The University of
Paris as a school goes back to Alcuin . . . Charlemagne was its founder." [2]   Charlemagne's practical interest in education has caused his name to be associated with
the schools of Tours, Aachen, Milan, Salerno, Bologna,
and Paris.   The most recent writer on the subject, Compayré, is of opinion that this is an exaggerated statement.
He finds evidence of an unbroken succession of Benedictine schools, such as those of Rheims, Tours, Angers,
Laon, Bec, and others, which had preserved a continuity
of educational work from the time of Charlemagne to
that of Louis VIII., and which, under such leaders as
Lanfranc (1005–1089), and S. Anselm (1033–1109), had
developed and maintained a high degree of intellectual
activity.   He considers these to have constituted the
direct succession to the schools of the palace of Charlemagne, but he fails to find in them the prototype of the
university system.   For Compayré, the actual founder
of the University of Paris was Abelard, who died sixty
years before the university secured its organisation.   It
is his contention that it was Abelard who, by his learning,
his independence of thought, his eloquence, and his mastery over the minds of men, is to be credited with the
initiation of the great movement from which was to proceed not only the University of Paris, but the long series
of universities for which Paris served as an incentive and
the type.   It was Abelard, says Compayré, who, if not

[1] Compayré, 61.   [2] Crévier, *Hist. de l' Université de Paris*, vii., 92.

first, at least with the most direct and far-reaching influence, introduced dialectics into theology and reason into
authority, breaking away from the mere passive transmission of the beliefs and timid dialectics accepted by the
schools of theology, and thus making possible the development of a true university spirit. " The method of Abelard
is the soul of scholastic philosophy,"[1] the philosophy
which, until the Renaissance, reigned supreme in the University of Paris. Abelard's method, says Père Denifle, is
presented in the book which during several centuries
served as the text for theological instruction, the *Sentences*
of Peter Lombard, and its influence is also to be noted in
that other noteworthy work which became the authority
for the schools of common law, the *Decretals* of Gratian.

Abelard may be called the first professor of superior instruction. His work was certainly begun with *éclat*, for his
classes are said to have numbered at times no less than
five thousand pupils. " First of the French philosophers
. . . he may justly be considered as the precursor of
Ramus and Descartes, in other words, of the Renaissance and of the modern spirit."[2] Apart from this more
far-reaching influence, he was able to do for the school of
Paris what the jurist Irnerius was, during nearly the same
years, accomplishing for the school of Bologna, making
possible, namely, its development into the university. It
was through the work done by Abelard that "the theological school of Paris became the seminary of Christian
Europe."[3] This influence continued through the succeeding centuries in which Paris still remained the centre of
theological instruction, a result which necessarily had later
an important effect in shaping the character of the earlier
issues of the Paris Press.

The term *University* is not a synonym of the university
of science, but simply of the university of teachers and
students who composed a group and who instituted asso-

[1] Compayré, 19.　　　[2] *Ibid*, 23.　　　[3] *Ibid*, 24.

ciation of studies. " In the language of the Civil Law,"
says Malden, " all corporations were called *Universitates*,
as forming one whole out of many individuals." [1]

The organisation of the University of Paris, while differing in certain important details from that of Bologna,
was substantially identical with the Italian institutions
in respect to the privileges conceded to instructors and
students. In successive enactments or crown edicts, the
members of the universities of Paris, Montpellier, and
Poitiers were exempted, not only from the regular national
taxes and from the town dues (*octroi*), but also from
special war taxes. In 1295, Philip the Fair decreed that
under no pretext could the goods of the members of the
universities be taken or their revenues attached. [2] The
following statute of the University of Padua represented
fairly enough the status of students in all the universities
of France and of Italy : " Students must be considered as
citizens in what concerns the advantages, but not in that
which constitutes the burdens of citizens." Under this
same principle, members of the universities were also
exempt from military service.

The authorities of the University of Paris exercised a
very direct control from the outset over all the details
of the business of making, renting, and selling books.
This authority became in Paris a matter of much more
immediate importance and abiding influence than in Bologna. In the latter, as we have seen, the business of the
book-dealers was very closely limited to the production of
the texts immediately required for the work of the class-
room. In Paris, however, in the manuscript period, two
and a half centuries before the introduction of the printing-press, the book-trade of the university had become in
great measure the book-trade of the city. During a large
part of this time, moreover, Paris shared with Florence
the position of the centre of the intellectual activities of

[1] Malden, 15.   [2] Fournier, i., 8, cited by Compayré.

Europe. The scribes and their masters who were manifolding manuscripts in the Latin quarter, were not only
supplying text-books to the students of the university,
but were preparing literature for the scholarly readers of
Paris, of France, and of Europe. The book-dealers of
Paris constituted, however, for several centuries, with a
few exceptions, a guild organised within the university.
The members of this guild, the *libraires jurés*, were members of the university, and the operations of the guild
were under the direct control of the university authorities.
This arrangement gave to the book-dealers material advantages in the possession of university privileges and in
the control of a practical monopoly of the business of
producing books. It involved, however, certain corresponding disadvantages. University control meant supervision, censorship, restriction, regulation of prices,
interference with trade facilities, and various hampering
conditions which delayed very seriously, both before and
after the introduction of printing, the development of the
business of making and of circulating books, and, as a
result of this, placed not a few obstacles in the way of the
literary and the intellectual development of the community. Chevillier says : " The book-trade of Paris owes its
origin to the university, by which, under the approval of
the king, it was organised into an association of masters.
This association was, from the outset, controlled directly
by the university, from the authorities of which it received
its statutes and regulations, and by which the master
libraires were licensed, *jurés*." [1]

" The reproduction of a work of scholarship (to which
class belonged of necessity the text-books prescribed for
the work of the university," remarks Delalain, " called for
on the part of the scribe a considerable measure of scholarly knowledge and also for a detailed and careful supervision. It was held, therefore, by the university authorities

[1] Chevillier, Preface.

that the responsibility properly belonged to them to supervise the series of operations by means of which these
university texts were prepared and were circulated. It
was essential that the completeness and the correctness of
each copy should be verified, and that these copies should
be confided to trustworthy persons for their sale or their
hire, in order that there should be no risk of inaccuracies
in the texts themselves or of any unnecessary enhance-
ment of the cost to instructors or to students of their
purchase or their hire. On this ground, the university
of Paris asserted from the beginning of its history the
right to control the book-trade of the city, a contention
which was confirmed and maintained by all the kings of
France after Philip Augustus." [1]

The "book-trade" was held to include all the dealers
and artisans who were concerned with the production and
distribution of manuscripts ; that is, the copyists and their
employers, the binders, the illuminators, the sellers of
parchment, and, later, the manufacturers of paper. While
the control of the university was exercised over the entire
book-trade, the interest of the authorities was naturally
much keener in regard to the divisions having to do with
the production of books than in the work of the booksellers. The matter of chief importance, in fact, according to the accepted theory, the sole purpose for the
existence of the book-trade, was to secure for the members of the university a sufficient supply, at a fixed and
moderate charge, of correct and complete texts of the
prescribed works; while it was also essential to protect
those members from the contamination of heretical
writings or of heretical comments on books of accepted
orthodoxy.

A regulation of December, 1316, prescribes that no
stationarius shall employ a copyist until such employee
shall have been duly sworn before the university, or before

[1] Delalain, xi.

the Rector and four *procureurs*, to execute his functions
faithfully, and, having been accepted as a trustworthy
scribe, shall have had his name inscribed on the official
register.

As a partial offset to the series of restrictions and limitations under which was carried on the work of these
early publishers, it is in order to specify certain privileges
and exemptions enjoyed by them as members of the university.   These included exemption from taxes ; exemption from service on the watch or on the city guard ; and
the privilege of jurisdiction, commonly known as *commit-
timus*.   Under this last, they were empowered in suits
or cases, civil or personal, and whether engaged as plain-
tiffs or defendants, to bring witnesses or other principals
before the *Juges Conservateurs*, functionaries charged with
the maintenance or protection of privileges.[1]

Issues concerning personal rights arising between the
members of the university were decided before the tribu-
nal or court of the Rector.   Cases affecting realty, and all
cases between the members and outsiders, were tried before the *Conservateurs des Priviléges*, an authority of necessity favourably disposed to the members of the university.
The ground assigned for this privilege was that instructors and pupils, and those engaged in aiding their work
(*i. e.* the makers of books), should not be exposed to loss
of valuable time by being called away from their work to
distant parts.[2]   An edict of Philip Augustus, in 1200,
confirmed by S. Louis in 1229, and by Philip the Fair in
1302, directed that the cases of university members be
brought before the Bishop of Paris.   The university found
disadvantages in being under the jurisdiction of the Bishop
(whose censorship later proved particularly troublesome
for the publishers), and applications were made to replace
the authority of the ecclesiastical courts with that of the

[1] *Recueil des Priviléges de Paris*, 1-9.
[2] *Cartulaire de l' Univ. de Paris*, i., 59.

royal courts. In 1334, letters-patent of Philip of Valois directed the provost of Paris, who was at that time *conservateur* of the royal privileges, to take the university under his special protection, and in 1341 the members of the university were forbidden to enter proceedings before any other authority. In 1361, under an edict of King John, the members of the university were again declared exempt from taxes and assessments of all kinds (*portes, gabelles, impositions, aides, et subsides*). The repetition from reign to reign of certain edicts and regulations such as the above does not imply that the earlier ones had been recalled, but that they had to some extent fallen into desuetude, or that attempts had been made to override them.

By letters-patent issued in 1369, Charles V. declared that all dealers in books and makers of books required for the use of " our scholars " should be exempt from all taxes, etc. The exemption included binders, illuminators, parchment-makers, etc. It appears that some abuses had crept in under this exemption, as in 1384 it was ordered that no book-dealers should be freed from taxes if they carried on for gain any other occupation.[1]

The policy of favouring the production and sale of books by freeing the publishers and dealers from taxes and other burdens was continued and even developed after the introduction of printing. The kings, impressed with the possibilities of this great discovery, recognised that it was for the interest of the realm to free books, printed or written, not only from *octroi* or city duties, but from customs or importation charges. Letters-patent of Henry II., dated 1553, read as follows : *Avons ordonné et ordonnons lesdits livres, escrits ou imprimez, reliez ou non reliez, estre et demeurer exempts desdits droits de traicte foraine, Domaine forain et haut passage.*[2] This was a more liberal policy than at that time prevailed in Italy or in England,

[1] *Recueil des Priviléges*, v., 88.   [2] *Recueil des Priviléges*.

or, in fact, than has as yet been accepted in the nineteenth
century by the United States. In order to obtain the
advantage of such exemption, the publishers had to secure
from the Rector of the university a passport or certificate
for their packages.

One of the earlier regulations of the university affecting
the book-trade was that under which the supervision of
the sale of parchment was left in the hands of the Rector.
This sale was usually authorised only at the annual Lendit
fair. The dealers, bringing their parchment, exposed this
for inspection. Before any other purchases were permitted, the Rector selected the quantity needed for
the university, for which payment was made at a price
fixed in advance. He then received from the parchment-
dealers, for the treasury of the university, or for the special fund of the book guild, a gratuity which amounted
to from two thousand to three thousand francs.

In Paris, as in Bologna, during the whole of the thirteenth century and the first portion of the fourteenth, the
principal work of the university book-dealers was not the
selling but the renting of books. The regulations concerning the division of manuscripts into chapters or *peciæ*
were, however, not carried out with the same precision in
Paris as in the Italian universities, nor was it practicable
to exercise in the larger city, or even within the confines
of the Latin Quarter, as close a supervision as in Bologna
or Padua over the rates for renting and over the stock of
copies kept by the *stationarii*. The general purpose of
the regulations was, however, the same, and the routine
of renting prices and the general rate of commission on
the books sold were, as said, matters of university regulation. With a community of students ranging in number
from ten thousand to (in the most prosperous days of the
university) as high as thirty thousand, the monopoly of
supplying text-books, whether through sale or through
renting, must have constituted an important business. It

was not until some time after the introduction of printing
that the importance and prospect of profit of publishing
done outside of the university limits, and freed from a portion of the university restrictions, came to be sufficient to
make it worth while for certain of the more enterprising
of the printers to give up the trade in text-books and their
privileges as *libraires jurés* and to establish themselves as
independent dealers.

In the University of Paris we find in use in the twelfth
century, in addition to the terms *librarii, stationarii,* and
petiarii, the term *mangones.*   The word *mango* originally
designated a merchant or dealer, but appears to have carried an implication of untrustworthiness or slipperiness.
It is satisfactory, therefore, to understand that *mangones*
very speedily went out of use as a name for dealers in
books.[1]   The *petiarii* are not mentioned in the statutes
of the university, where they appear to be replaced by
the *parcheminii.*[2]

Guérard interprets the term *stationarius* as standing
first for a scribe with a fixed location (*un écrivain séden-
taire*), as opposed to a copyist who was prepared to accept work in any place where it could be secured.   Later,
the term was understood to designate a master scribe
who directed the work of a bureau of copyists; and still
later, the *stationarius,* sometimes then called *stationarius
librorum,* possessed a complete book-making establishment, where were employed, in addition to the copyists,
the illuminators, binders, and other artisans.   At this
stage of his development, the *stationarius* has become the
equivalent of the printer-publisher of a later generation.
Guérard is inclined to limit the earlier use in Paris of the
term *librarius* to the keeper of a shop in which books
were kept for sale, but in which no book-production was
carried on.[3]   It is evident, however, that in France, as in

---

[1] Pierre de Blois, cited by Vallet de Viriville, 96.   [2] Delalain, xi.
[3] Guérard, *Cartulaire de l'Église de Notre Dame de Paris*, iii., 73.   1270.

Italy, there was no very definite or consistent use of the several terms, and that before the introduction of printing, *librarius* and *stationarius* were applied almost indifferently to dealers having to do either with the production or with the sale of books. Chassant is authority for the statement that at the time of the introduction of printing into France there were in the two cities of Paris and Orleans more than ten thousand individual scribes or copyists who gained their living with their pens.[1] It is not surprising that the first printers, whose diabolical invention took the bread away from these workers, had their lives threatened and their work interrupted.

The letters-patent of Charles V., dated November 5, 1368, specify fourteen *libraires* and eleven *écrivains* (employing *stationarii*) as at that time registered in Paris. No one was admitted to the profession of *librarius* or *stationarius* who was not a man of approved standing and character, and who had not also given evidence of an adequate and scholarly knowledge of manuscript interpretation and of the subject to which he proposed to give attention. The examination was made before the four chief publishers (*les quatre grands libraires*). Having secured the approval of the board of publishers, the applicant was obliged to secure also acceptance from the representatives of the Rector, and to submit certain guarantees for the satisfactory performance of his responsibilities. He was called upon to submit, for himself and heirs, all his property as well as his person to the control of the court of Paris as a pledge for the execution of his trust. As late as 1618, in the reign of Charles IX., the master printers (*i. e.*, printer-publishers) were obliged to hold certificates from the Rector and the university, to the effect that they were skilled in the art of printing, and that they possessed full knowledge of Latin and of Greek.

[1] Chassant, *Dict. des Abréviations Latines et Françaises Usitées dans les Manuscrits*, Paris, 1864.

The *libraires jurés* comprised two classes, the *libraires grands* (*officium magni librariatus*), and the *libraires petits* (*officium parvi librariatus*).[1] The immediate responsibility for the government of the body rested with the four chief *libraires* (*les quatre grands libraires*). It was they who fixed the prices for the sale or hire of manuscripts, and who supervised the examination of manuscripts with reference, first, as to their admission into the official list of the university texts, and, secondly, as to the completeness and accuracy of the particular parchment submitted. They also inspected the bookshops and the workrooms of the copyists, and verified from time to time the accuracy and the quality of the copies prepared from these accepted texts; they passed upon the qualifications of applicants for the position of *libraire juré;* and, finally, they exercised a general supervision over the enforcement of all the university regulations affecting the book-trade, and gave special attention to those prohibiting any interference with this trade by an outside dealer, one who was not a *libraire juré*. These four chief *libraires* were each under a bond or "caution" for the amount of 200 livres. In addition to the exemption from general taxes and guard duty conceded to all the *libraires jurés*, these four enjoyed from time to time certain special privileges. In October, 1418, by a regulation of Charles VI., the four chief *libraires* are exempted by name from certain special duties on wine, etc., which had been imposed for the purpose of securing funds *pour la recouvrance de nos Villes et Chastel de Monstreau ou Faut-Yonne*.[2] It was also necessary for him to find two responsible bondsmen for an amount of not less than 100 livres each.[3] [4] In Bologna in

---

[1] Chevillier, *op. cit.*, 347.

[2] *Recueil des Priviléges*, 1674, 89, 95.

[3] *Actes Concernants le Pouvoir*, etc., *de l' Université de Paris.*

[4] The *livre Parisis*. De Wailly, cited by Delalain, xxix.

1400 the bond was also fixed at 200 livres the equivalent of 5065 francs.[1]

The special obligations imposed upon and accepted by the *librarii* and *stationarii*, as specified in documents between the years 1250 and 1350, can be summarised as follows:

I. To accept faithfully and loyally all the regulations of the university concerning the production and the sale of books.

II. Not to make within the term of one month any agreement, real or nominal, transferring to themselves the ownership of books which had been placed in their hands for sale.

III. Not to permit the loss or disappearance of any book so consigned for the purpose later of acquiring ownership of the same.

IV. To declare conscientiously and exactly the just and proper price of each book offered for sale, and to specify such price, together with the name of the owner, in some conspicuous place in the work itself.

V. To make no disposition of a consigned book without having in the first place informed the owner or his representative of the price to be secured for the same, and to make immediate report and accounting of such price when received.

VI. To charge as commission for the service of selling such book not more than four deniers to a member of the university and not more than six deniers to an outsider. This commission was to be paid by the purchaser, who seems to have been considered the obliged party in the transaction.[2]

---

[1] Denifle, iii., 29.

[2] The *livre Parisis* was the equivalent of twenty sols or twenty-five francs. The *sol* equalled twelve deniers or one franc, or twenty cents. The *denier* was of the value of one and three-fifths cents. In considering these " equivalents," due allowance must of course be made for the very much larger purchasing power possessed by money in the fourteenth century than in the nineteenth. De Wailly, cited by Delalain, xxix., xl.

VII. To place conspicuously in the windows of their shops a price list of all works kept on sale.

The *stationarii* on their part were also held:

I. To employ no scribes for the production of manuscripts other than those who had been accepted and certified before the Rector.

II. To offer for sale or for hire no manuscripts that had not been passed upon and "taxed" by the appointed authority.

III. To refuse to no applicant who was a member of the university the loan for hire of a manuscript, even though the applicant should require the same for the purpose of producing copies.

It is evident that a regulation of this character would, in the case of an original work by a contemporary author, have operated as a denial of any author's rights. Such original work constituted, however, at this time the very rare exception, and their authors were evidently obliged to content themselves with the prestige of securing circulation. The case of a manuscript representing outlay and skilled labour on the part of the dealer, who might have had to make a toilsome journey to secure it, and who had later paid for the service of one or more editors for its collation and revision, was, of course, of much more frequent occurrence. It is difficult to understand why this class of effort and enterprise should not have been encouraged by the university authorities instead of being so largely nullified by regulations which made of such a manuscript common property. This regulation is, however, identical with that of Bologna. The penalty there for refusing to place a manuscript at the service of a member of the university was five livres.[1]

IV. To offer for rent no texts that were not complete and correct.

V. In the event of a work being brought to Paris by a stranger, to give immediate information to the authorities

[1] Denifle, iii., 280.

in order that before such work could be copied for hire or for sale it should be passed upon by the authorities as orthodox and as suitable for the use of the members of the university, and as being complete and correct in its own text.

Any *libraire* who, having been duly sworn, should be convicted of violation of these regulations, forfeited his office, and all the rights and privileges thereto appertaining ; and all members of the university, instructors or students, were strictly prohibited (under penalty of forfeiture of their own membership) from having further dealings with such a delinquent. [1]

These various regulations, while possibly required in connection with the general interests of the university, were certainly exacting and must have interfered not a little with any natural development of the book-trade. It is nevertheless the case that the makers of books and the book-dealers in Paris occupied a more independent and a more dignified position than had been accorded to their brethren in Bologna. The latter appear to have risen hardly above the grade of clerks or lower-class functionaries, while these earlier Parisian publishers secured from the outset recognition as belonging to the higher educational work of the university, work in the shaping of which they themselves took an important part.

In 1316 (the year of the accession of Philip V.) the association of *libraires jurés* (authorised or certified bookdealers) comprised but thirteen members.[2] A year earlier there had been twenty-two, and I can only assume that the war troubles had had their natural influence in depressing and breaking up the book business. In 1323, the list comprises twenty-nine names, including the widow of De Peronne. In 1368, the number had again fallen to twenty-five. In 1488, the university list gives the names

---

[1] This regulation was identical with that of Bologna.
[2] Delalain, p. xxxvi.

of twenty-four *libraires*, in addition to whom were registered two illuminators, two binders, and two *écrivains*.[1]
The *écrivains* specified were undoubtedly master scribes,
the register here quoted apparently not including the
names of the copyists employed. At this date, however,
the work of the printers had been going on in Paris for
fourteen years, and the business of those concerned with
the production of books in manuscript form must have
been very largely reduced. The work of the master scribes
continued, however, in the sixteenth century, but by the
close of the fifteenth had become limited to the production, for collectors, of manuscripts as works of art.

While the majority of *libraires jurés* were naturally
Frenchmen, there was no regulation to prevent the holding of such a post by a foreigner, and the list always, as a
matter of fact, included several foreign names. The presence in the university of large groups of foreign students
made it quite in order, and probably necessary, that they
should find among the book-dealers some who could speak
their home language and who could make clear to them
the requirements concerning the university texts. The
presence of these foreign book-dealers also facilitated the
arrangements for the exchange of manuscripts between
Paris and foreign universities. These foreign book-dealers,
while obliged in ordinary routine to take an oath of fealty
to the university, were not called upon to become citizens
of France.

The list includes from time to time the names of women
libraires, these women being usually widows of *libraires*
who had duly qualified themselves. The women must
themselves, however, in order to secure such appoint-
ments, have been able to pass the examination in Latin,
in palæography, and in the technicalities of manuscript
book-making. In respect as well to the admission of foreigners as to that of women, the Paris guild of the uni-

[1] Delalain, p. xxxvi.

versity book-dealers practised a more liberal policy than
that followed by the university authorities of Bologna
or the Stationers' Hall of London. Later, this liberal
policy was restricted, and in 1686 it was ordered that no
foreigners should be admitted to the lists of the master
libraires of the university.

The purchase of a manuscript during the fourteenth
century was attended with almost as many formalities and
precautions as are to-day considered necessary for the
transfer of a piece of real estate. The dealer making the
sale was obliged to give to the purchaser guarantees to the
effect, first, that he was himself the owner or the duly
authorised representative of the owner of the work; and,
secondly, that the text of this was complete and correct,
and as security for these guarantees he pledged his goods,
and sometimes even his person. As a single example of
a transaction illustrating this practice, I quote a contract
cited by Du Breuil. This bears date November, 1332, and
sets forth that a certain Geoffrey de Saint Léger, a duly
qualified *clerc libraire*, acknowledges and confesses that
he has sold, ceded, and transferred to the noble gentleman Messire Gérard de Montagu, *Avocat du Roi au
Parlement* (counsellor at the royal court), all right, title,
and interest in a work entitled *Speculum Historiale in consuetudines Parisienses*, contained in four volumes bound in
red leather. The consideration named is forty livres Parisian, the equivalent, according to the tables of de Wailly,
of 1013 francs. The vendor pledges as security for the
obligation under the contract all his worldly goods, together with his own person (*tous et chacun de ses biens, et
guarantie de son corps même*), and the contract is attested
before two notaries.[1]

While the university assumed the strictest kind of control and supervision over the work of the book-dealers, it
conceded, as an offset, to the association of these dealers

[1] Du Breuil, *op. cit.*, 608.

a very substantial monopoly of the trade of making and selling books. It was prohibited, under severe penalties, for a person not a *libraire juré* to do business in a bookshop or at any fixed stand ; that is to say, he could not sell as a *stationnaire*, but had to carry on his trade as a pedlar or chap-man, from a pack or a cart. The value of the manuscript that such pedlar was permitted to offer for sale was restricted to ten *sous*, the equivalent of half a franc. At the price at which manuscripts were held during the fourteenth century, this limitation restricted the trade of the peripatetic vendors to single sheets, or broadsides, containing usually a *Pater*, an *Ave*, or a *Credo*, or a brief calendar or astrological table. Successive edicts were issued from reign to reign, renewing the prohibition upon the selling of books, whether in French or Latin (excepting only of such maximum value), by any drapers, grocers, pedlars, or dealers of any kind.[1]

In all the official references of the thirteenth and fourteenth centuries to the book-dealers, the ground is taken that they formed a class apart from mechanics or from traders in ordinary merchandise. They were considered to be engaged in an intellectual pursuit, and were treated as members of a profession upon whose service the work of the university and that of the Church were largely dependent. Thus in 1649 the *Recueil* makes use of these words:

Les Marchands-Libraires, Imprimeurs et Relieurs seront toujours censés du corps de nostre bien aymée fille aisnée l'Université ; du tout séparés des arts méchaniques, et autres Corps de Mestiers ou marchandises ; et come tels, conservés en la jouissance de tours les droicts ; priviléges, franchises, libertez, préséances et prérogatives attribuées à ladite université et à eux par les Royes nos prédécesseux et par nous.[2]

---

[1] Kirchhoff, 68. Delalain (xl.) specifies a limit of 10 *sols*, 10.13 francs. This is, I think, an error.

[2] *Lettres Obtenues par des Imprimeurs et Libraires*, etc., 1649. *Recueil*, i., 3.

It was, therefore, not permitted to the *libraire* to bring discredit upon his profession by also engaging in any " sordid pursuits " (*viles occupations*), and in so doing he rendered himself liable to being deposed from his high post (*declaré déchu de son noble office*).   He could, however, unite with his work as *libraire* that of a notary, or that of a royal counsellor or practitioner in the higher court (*avocat du roi au Parlement*).

Notwithstanding the personal prestige and the substantial advantages which were thus enjoyed by the book-dealers of the university, there were from time to time instances of protest, amounting occasionally to insubordination, on the part of the *libraires*, who, as their business aims and possibilities developed, became restive under the long series of trammels and restrictions, and particularly in connection with those imposed by the ecclesiastical division of the university authorities.   The dread, however, of losing any portion of their privileges, and particularly the risk of any impairment of their monopoly of the book-trade of the university and of Paris, operated always as a sufficient consideration to prevent the insubordination from going to extremes.   Throughout the entire period of the Middle Ages the control of the university continued, therefore, practically absolute over the book-trade of Paris, the influence of the Church and the (more or less spasmodic) authority of the Crown being exercised by means of the university machinery.

This state of affairs continued for some period of years after the introduction of printing.   The university still insisted upon its responsibility for the correctness and the completeness of the texts issued from the Paris press, although it gave up of necessity the routine of examining individual copies of the printed editions.   On the other hand, the censorship control on the part of the theological Faculty over the moral character and orthodoxy of the works printed was insisted upon more strenuously

than ever as the Church began to recognise the enormous
importance of the influence upon public opinion of the
widely distributed printed volumes.   The effect of this
ecclesiastical control upon the business of printing books
is set forth with some detail in the chapter on the early
printers of Paris.   It is sufficient to say here that the
contention on the part of the university to control, as a
portion of the work of higher education, the business of
the makers and sellers of books, while sharply attacked
and materially undermined after the middle of the seventeenth century, was not formally abandoned until the
beginning of the eighteenth.   At this time the Crown
took over to itself all authority to regulate the press, an
authority which disappeared only with the revolution
of 1789.

For six centuries the book-trade of Paris and of France,
whether it consisted in the production of manuscripts for
the exclusive use of members of the university, or of
printed books for the enlightenment of the general public, had been obliged to do its work under the hampering
and burdensome regulations and restrictions of a varying
series of authorities.   The rectors of the university, the
theologians of the Sorbonne, the lawyers of the Parliament of Paris, the chancellors of the Crown, the kings
themselves, had all taken a hand, sometimes in turn, not
infrequently in conflict with each other, in the task of
"regulating" the trade in books.   The burden of the
restrictions was, in pretence at least, offset by various
privileges and exemptions, but they remained burdens
notwithstanding.   It may well be a cause of surprise that
in the face of such a long series of hampering difficulties,
difficulties more serious than those with which any publishers in the world, outside of Rome, had to contend, the
manuscript publishers and the later printer-publishers of
Paris should have been able to do so much to make Paris
a literary and a publishing centre.   As has been already

indicated, it was certainly the case that during the thirteenth and fourteenth centuries Paris shared with Florence the position of being the centre of the manuscript trade of Europe. It was also the case, as will be set forth in a later chapter, that the first printer-publishers of Paris did most noteworthy work in furthering the development of scholarly publishing and the production of scholarly books. It required, however, the revolution of 1789 to establish the principle that the business of producing and distributing books could secure its legitimate development only when freed from censorship restrictions and regulations, and that it was a business the control of which belonged properly not to the university, the Courts of Parliament, or the Crown, but to the people themselves.

Considering the scarcity and the costliness of books in the Middle Ages, it is somewhat surprising that the work of instruction rested so directly upon books, that is, depended upon the mastery of a text. Thurot says: " It is the distinctive character of instruction in the Middle Ages that the science was not taught directly and in itself, but by the explanation of books which derived their authority solely from their writers." [1] Roger Bacon formulates it : " When one knows the text, one knows all that concerns the science which is the object of the text." [2] Instead of taking a course of logic or of ethics, says Compayré, the phrase was reading a book on logic or ethics, *legere* or *audire librum.* This close adherence to the text secured, of course, an assured demand in the university towns first for the hired *pecias* and later for the purchased manuscripts.

The foundation of the College of the Sorbonne dates from 1257. It was organised by Robert de Sorbon, chaplain to Louis IX. The college was at once affiliated with the University of Paris, of which it became the

---

[1] Thurot, p. 65, cited by Compayré, 188.
[2] *Opus Major*, cited by Compayré, 188.

theological Faculty, and in the general direction of which it exercised at times a controlling influence. The college is connected with my subject on the ground of its assumption of the theological censorship of the Paris book-trade and of its frequent attempts to exercise a general censorship over all the productions of the Paris printing-press.

As we shall note later in the history of the Paris book-trade, various complications arose between the publishers and booksellers possessing a university license (the *libraires jurés*) and certain unlicensed dealers who undertook to come into competition with them. The locality occupied by these unlicensed booksellers was on the Island of the Cité, immediately by the precincts of Notre Dame. In fact it was the case with the book-trade generally north of the Alps that its business was very largely carried on in the portals of a church if not under the immediate shadow of the cathedral.

While in Italy the Church furthered but slightly the early production of books and, later, did not a little to hamper the undertakings of the publishers, it was the case in France and quite largely also in South Germany, that the publishers found themselves very largely dependent upon the scholary interests and the scholarly co-operation of the clerics, and the association of the Church with the book-trade was, for a large proportion at least of the fifteenth century, an important one.

In Paris, the booksellers licensed by the university were all in the Latin Quarter, and in the same region were to be found the sellers of parchment, the illuminators, the scribes, binders, etc., who also carried university licenses and were under university supervision. It is probable that the specification in the Tax Roll of 1292 of eight *librarii* in Paris refers only to the booksellers licensed by the university and carrying on their business in the Latin Quarter.

In Bayeux, in 1250, certain clerics were exempted from

taxation if they dealt in parchment or if they were engaged
in the copying of manuscripts, and the book-shops along
the walls of the cathedral were also exempt from taxation.
It is not clear to me in looking up this record, whether
the tax mentioned was a town tax or a general tax, or
whether it was one of the ecclesiastical levies.[1]

Roger Bacon's reference to the scribes of Paris has
already been mentioned. He could not secure from the
Brothers of his Order a transcript of his work which he
desired to present to Pope Clement, because they were
too ignorant to write the same out intelligently, while he
was afraid to confide the work to the public scribes of
France lest they might make improper use of the material.[2]
It is Wattenbach's opinion that the wrongful use of his
production dreaded by Bacon was the sale of unauthorised
copies of it by the scribes to whom the preparation of the
authorised copies should be confided.

In 1292, Wenzel, King of Bohemia, presented to the
monastery of Königsaal, 200 marks in silver for the purchase of books, and the purchases were made from the
book-sellers in Paris.   Richard de Bury extols Paris as the
great centre of the book-trade.   Of the value of the book
collections in Rome and the possibility there of securing
literary treasures, he had already spoken, but the treasures
of Paris appear to have impressed him still more keenly.
There he found occasion to open his purse freely and took
in exchange for base gold, books of inestimable value.
Joh. Gerson, in his treatise *De Laude Scriptorum* expresses the dread lest the persistent carrying away from
Florence of his books by wealthy visitors may not too
seriously diminish its literary treasures.

The Paris publishers appear to have sent out travelling
salesmen or representatives to take orders for their wares.
As early as 1480, a publisher named Guillaume Tousé,

---

[1] Delisle, *Cartulaire de Normandie, Mém. des Antiquaires de Normandie,*
1852, ii., 6, 326.   [2] *Oper. Inedita.*   Ed. Brewer, p. 13, Watt., 470.

of Paris, made complaint to the chancellor of Brittany to
the effect that he had entrusted a commission to a certain
Guillaume de l'Espine to carry books into Lower Brittany
and to make sale of the same during a period of six
months. He had taken with him books to the value of
five hundred livres and was to have a salary of ten crowns
for the six months' work. He, had, however, failed to
return or to make report of his commission. Tousé
secured a judgment against his delinquent traveller, but
the record does not show whether he ever succeeded in
getting hold of him again.[1]

In the universities of Oxford and of Cambridge, the *stationarii* began their work some years later than in Paris
or Bologna. They had the advantage, however, of freedom from the greater portion of the restrictions and special supervision which hampered the work of the scribes in
the Italian and French universities, and as a result their
business developed more promptly and more actively, and
in the course of a few years, they became the booksellers
of the university towns. It was, of course, from this university term *stationarii* that the name of stationers came
at the outset to be applied to the organised book-dealers
of Great Britain. The Guild of the British book-dealers
completed its organisation in 1403, nearly sixty years
before the introduction into England of the printing-
press.[2]

The art work put into the manuscripts produced in the
Low Countries, particularly in Belgium, was more highly
developed and was a more important part of the industry
than was the case in any other portion of the world.

---

[1] Broderie, *Bibl. de l'École de Chartres*, v., 3. 49. Watt., p. 472.

[2] The " Stationers or Text-Writers who wrote and sold all sorts of books
then in use" secured their privileges as a Guild in 1403 from the Lord
Mayor and Board of Aldermen of London.

The Company had, however, no control over printed books until it received its charter from Mary and Philip, in 1557. Curwen, 18.

In the earlier German universities, the *stationarii* also found place and found work, but this work seems to have been of less importance and the scribes appear to have secured for themselves a less definite university recognition than in Italy or in France. The explanation given by Wattenbach is that the German students, being better informed and more industrious, did for themselves a larger portion of the transcribing required and were, therefore, freed from the necessity of hiring their hefts.

The statutes of the universities of Prague and of Vienna permitted the masters and the baccalaureates to secure from the university archives, under certain pledges, the loan of the books authorised as text-books or of works of reference, for the purpose of making trustworthy copies of the same. The copyists were enjoined as follows:

Fideliter et correcte, tractim et distincte, assignando paragraphos, capitales literas, virgulas et puncta, prout sententia requirit.[1]   The practice also obtained in these universities of having texts dictated to the students by the *magisters* or the Bachelors of Arts. This was described as *librum pronuntiare*, and also as *ad pennam dare.*

In this phrase, Karoch sent word to Erfurt that *ad pennam dabit* his treatise *Arenga.*[2]

The text-books utilised in the German universities in the thirteenth and fourteenth centuries were as limited in range and in number as those of Bologna and of Padua. The instruction in the medical departments of Prague and Vienna was based in the main on the works of Hippocrates and Galen, with some of the later commentaries, principally from Arabian writers. In philosophy the chief authority was Aristotle, in mathematics Euclid, and in astronomy Ptolemy. A few works of later date were utilised, such as the *Summula* of Petrus Hispanus and the *De Sphæra Mundi* of Johannes de Sacro Bosco. Bosco is otherwise known as John Holywood or Halifax. He

[1] Kirchhoff, 115.   [2] Kirchhoff, 187.

held the chair of mathematics in the University of Paris about the middle of the thirteenth century. The use of his treatise for classes in Prague is evidence of a certain interchange between the universities of books in manuscript.

An important reason for the very large membership of the universities of the Middle Ages as compared with their successors of to-day, is to be found in the fact that they undertook to supply not only the higher education which belongs to the present university curriculum, but also the training now furnished by the *gymnasia* or High Schools, which were at that time not in existence. We find, therefore, in their membership, thousands of students who were little more than boys either in their years or in their mental development.

The universities also, on the other hand, attracted to their membership very many students of mature age, who came sometimes for special purposes, but more frequently because it was only in the university towns that circles of scholars could be found, that books were available, and that any large measure of intellectual activity was to be experienced. As Savigny puts its: " The universities were, during the Middle Ages, practically the only places where men could study or could exercise their minds with any degree of freedom." It was inevitable therefore, that, with the generations succeeding the discovery of printing, there should be a decrease in the influence and in the relative importance for the community of the universities. With the establishment of secondary schools, the training of the boys was cared for to better purpose elsewhere; and with the increasing circulation of printed books, it became possible for men to come into relations with literature in other places than in the lecture room. The universities were no longer the sole depositories of learning or the sole sources of intellectual activity. This lessening of the influence of the universities represented, or was at least coincident with, a wider development of intellectual activity and of interest in literature on the part of the masses of the people. The universities alone would never have been in a position so to direct the thought of the community as to render the masses of citizens competent to arrive at conclusions for themselves and sufficiently assured in such conclusions to be prepared to make them the basis of action. This was, of course, partly because, notwithstanding the large membership and the fact that this membership represented nearly all the classes in the community, the universities could at best come into direct relations but with a small proportion of the people. A more important cause for such lack of intellectual leadership is to be found in the fact that the standard of thought and of instruction in the universities concerned itself very little with the intellectual life or issues of the immediate time. As Biot puts it (speaking, to be sure, of a later century): " The universities were several centuries in arrears with all that concerned the sciences and the arts. Peripatetics, when all the world had renounced with Descartes the philosophy of Aristotle, they became Cartesians when the rest were Newtonians. That is the way with learned bodies which do not make discoveries."

It was the dissemination of literature through the new art of printing rather than the diffusion of education through the university lecture rooms, which brought to the masses of the people the consciousness of mental existence and of individual responsibility for arriving at sound conclusions. Prior to the printing-press, this responsibility had been left by the people with their " spiritual advisers," who were charged with the duty of doing the thinking for their flocks. It was this change in the mental status of the people which was the precursor (although at a considerable space of years) of the Reformation.

With the beginning in Germany of the movement

known as Humanism, the representatives of the new thought of the time were not to be found in the university circles, and had not received their inspiration from the lecture rooms. Says Paulsen: " The entire traditional conduct of the universities, and in particular of the instruction in arts and theology, was rejected with the utmost scorn by the new culture through its representatatives, the poets and orators, to whom form and substance alike of this teaching seemed the most outrageous barbarism, which they never wearied of denouncing. In the *Epistolæ Obscurorum Virorum*, which were issued about 1516 from the band of youthful poets gathered about Mutianus at Erfurt, the hatred and detestation felt by the Humanists for the ancient university system raised to itself a lasting monument.

Within a few years from the publication of the *Epistolæ*, the influence of the Humanists had so far extended itself as to have effected a large modification in the systems of study in all the larger universities. " The old ecclesiastical Latin was replaced by classical Latin; Roman authors, particularly the poets, were made the subject of lectures, and the old translations of Aristotelian texts were driven out by new translations on principles advocated by the Humanists. Greek was taken up in the Faculty of arts and courses in the language and literature were established in all universities." [1]

An immediate result of these changes and extensions was an active demand for printed texts. The Humanistic movement, itself in a measure the result of the printing-press, was a most important fact in providing business for the German printers during the earlier years of the sixteenth century. The strifes and contentions of the Reformation checked the development in the universities of the studies connected with the intellectual movement of the Renaissance and lessened the demand for the litera-

[1] Paulsen, 41.

ture of these studies. The active-minded were absorbed in theological controversies, and those who could not understand the questions at issue could still shout the shibboleths of the leaders. As Erasmus put it, rather bitterly, *ubi regnat Lutheranismus, ibi interitus litterarum.* The literature of the Reformation, however, itself did much to make good for the printing-presses the lessened demand for the classics, while a few years later, the organisation of the Protestant schools and universities aroused intellectual activities in new regions, and created fresh requirements for printed books. Within half a century, in fact, of the Diet of Worms, the centre of the book-absorbing population of Germany had been transferred from the Catholic states of the south to the Protestant territories of the north, and the literary preponderance of the latter has continued to increase during the succeeding generations.

CHAPTER IV.

THE BOOK-TRADE IN THE MANUSCRIPT PERIOD.

Italy.—It seems probable that the book-trade which had been introduced into Gaul from Rome still existed during the sixth century. F. J. Mone finds references to such trade in the chronicles of Cæsarius of Arles.[1] In the code of laws of the Visigoths, it is provided that copies of the volume containing the laws shall be sold at not more than six sols.[2]

Wattenbach is of opinion that not only in Rome but in other Italian centres some fragments of the classic book-trade survived the fall of the Empire and the later invasions and changes of rulers, and he finds references to book-dealers in Italy as late as the sixth century.[3] He takes the ground that, notwithstanding the destruction of buildings, library collections, and in fact of whole cities, during the various contests, first with the Barbarian invaders and later between these invaders themselves, there still remained scholarly people who retained their interest in Latin literature ; and he points out that, notwithstanding the many changes in the rulers of Italy between the year 476 and the beginning of the eleventh century, Latin never ceased to remain the official language and, as he maintains, the language of literature.

In the *Tetralogus* of Wipo are the following lines which have a bearing upon this belief in the continuation of some literary interests in Italy :

[1] *Griech. u. Lat. Messen.*, p. 155.   [2] (V., 4, 22.)   [3] p. 449.

225

Hoc servant Itali post prima crepundia cuncti,
Et sudare scholis mandatur tota juventus.
Solis Teutonicis vacuum vel turpe videtur,
Ut doceant aliquem, nisi clericus accipiatur.[1]

(From their cradle up all Italians pay heed to learning,
and their children are kept at work in the schools. It is
only among the Germans that it is held to be futile and
wrong to give instruction to one who is not to become a
cleric.)

Giesebrecht, in his treatise *De Litterarum Studiis apud
Italos*, confirms this view. He refers to a manuscript of
Orosius which was written in the seventh century and
which contains an inscription stating that this copy of the
manuscript was prepared by the scribe in the *Statione
Magistri Viliaric Antiquarii.*

This is one of the earlier examples of the use of the
term *statio*, from which is derived the term *stationarii*, indicating scribes whose work was done in a specific work-
shop or headquarters, as contrasted with writers who were
called upon to do work at the homes of their clients. As
is specified in the chapter on the universities, this term
came to be used to designate booksellers (that is to say,
producers of books) who had fixed work-shops. In the
Acts of the Council of Constantinople, the scribe who
wrote out the record of the fifth Synod is described as
*Theodorus librarius qui habuit stationem ad S. Johannem
Phocam.*[2]

In such work-shops, while the chief undertaking was
the production of books, the scribes were ready to prepare announcements and to write letters, as is even to-day
the practice of similar scribes in not a few Italian cities
and villages.

From the beginning of the seventh century, Rome was
for a considerable period practically the only book market
in the world, that is to say, the only place in which books

[1] Wipo, *Tetralogus*, v., 197 *ff.*   [2] Wattenbach, 450.

could be obtained on order and in which the machinery for their production continued to exist. In 658, S. Gertrud ordered for the newly founded monastery at Nivelle certain sacred volumes to be prepared in the city of Rome.[1] Beda reports that the Abbot Benedict of Wearmouth, in 671, secured from Rome a number of learned and sacred works, *non paucos vel placito pretio emtos vel amicorum dono largitos retulit.* (He brought back a number of books, some of which he had purchased at the prices demanded, while others he had received as gifts from his friends.) Later, the Abbot repeated his journeys, and in 678, and again in 685, brought back fresh collections. The collections secured on his last journey included even certain examples of the profane writers.[2]

A similar instance is noted in the chronicles of the monastery of St. Wandrille. The Abbot Wandregisil sent his nephew Godo to Rome in 657, and Godo brought back with him as a present from the Pope Vitalian, not only valuable relics, but many volumes of the sacred Scriptures containing both the New and the Old Testament.[3] During the time of the Abbot Austrulf (747–753) a chest was thrown up by the sea on the shore. It contained relics and also a *codicem pulcherrimum*, or beautiful manuscript, containing the four gospels, *Romana Littera Optime Scriptum.*

This term *Romana Littera* has been previously referred to as indicating a special script which had been adopted in Rome by the earlier instructors for sacred writings.

Alcuin relates of the Archbishop Ælbert of York (766–780):

> *Non semel externas peregrino tramite terras,*
> *Jam peragravit ovans, Sophiæ deductus amore,*
> *Si quid forte novi librorum seu studiorum,*

[1] *Mab. Acta. Ss.*, ii., 445, Ed. Ven.
[2] *Vita Benedicti Abb.*, c. 4, 6, 9, cited by Wattenbach, p. 450.
[3] *Chron. Fontanell.*, c. 7 ; *Mon. Germ.*, ii., 274.

Quod secum ferret, terris reperiret in illis.
Hic quoque Romuleam venit devotus ad urbem.[1]

(More than once he has travelled joyfully through re-
mote regions and by strange roads, led on by his zeal for
knowledge, and seeking to discover in foreign lands novelties in books or in studies which he could take back with
him.   And this zealous student journeyed to the city of
Romulus.)

During the Italian expeditions of the German Emperors, books were from time to time brought back to Germany.   Certain volumes referred to by Pez as having been
in the Library at Passau, in 1395, contain the inscription
isti sunt libri quos Roma detulimus.

Wattenbach finds record of an organised manuscript
business in Verona as early as 1338,[2] and of a more important trade in manuscripts being carried on in Milan at
the same time.   In the fourteenth century, Richard de
Bury speaks of buying books for his library from Rome.
The references to this early manuscript business in Italy
are, however, so fragmentary that it is difficult to determine how far the works secured were the remnants of old
libraries or collections, or how far they were the productions of scribe work-shops engaged in manifolding copies
for sale.

It seems evident, however, that while a scattered trade in
manuscripts was carried on both by the scribes in the towns
and between the monastery *scriptoria*, the facilities for
the production and manifolding of manuscript copies were
hardly adequate to meet the demand or requirements of
readers and students.   As early as 250, Origen, writing in
Cappadocia, was complaining that he found difficulty in
getting his teachings distributed.   A zealous disciple,
named Ambrosius, secured for the purpose a group of
scribes whose transcripts were afterwards submitted to

[1] *De Pontiff Eborac.*, v. 1453 ; *Alcuini Opera*, ii., 256 ; *Bibl.*, vi., 125.
[2] p. 451.

Origen for revision before being sent out through the
churches. It is further related that Origen became so
absorbed in the work of correcting these manuscripts that
he could not be called from his desk either for exercise or
for meals.[1] S. Jerome, a century later, when he was
sojourning in Bethlehem, found similar difficulty. He
had among his monks some zealous scribes, but he complained that their work was untrustworthy.[2]

Abbot Lupus of Ferrières was obliged (in the ninth
century) to apply to monks in York in order to secure the
transcribing work that he required.

In connection with this difficulty in securing books, it
became customary, when copies were loaned from libraries, to secure from the borrower a pledge or security
of equal or greater value. The correspondence of the
time gives frequent instances of the difficulty in getting
back books that had been loaned, notwithstanding the
risk of the forfeiture of the pledges. In 1020, Notker
writes from St. Gall to the Bishop of Sitten that certain
books belonging to the Bishop, for which the Bishop was
making demand, had been borrowed by the Abbot Aregia,
and that, notwithstanding many applications, he had not
succeeded in getting even a promise of their return.[3] In
Vercelli, a beautiful mass book which had been loaned by
the Abbot Erkenbald of Fulda (997–1011) to the Bishop
Henry of Wurzburg, was to have been retained for the
term of the Bishop's life. After the death of the Bishop,
reclamation was made from Fulda for the return of the
volume, but without success. During the years 1461–1463,
the Legate Marinus de Fregeno travelled through Sweden
and Norway and collected there certain manuscripts which
he claimed were those that had been taken away from
Rome at the time of its plunder by the Goths. He evidently took the ground that where books were concerned,

---

[1] *Georg. Cedrenus.*, i., 444, Ed. Bonn.   [2] Wattenbach, 452.
[3] Grimm, *Kleine Schrifter*, v., 191.

a term of one thousand years was not sufficient to constitute a " statute of limitations."

Louis IX. of France is quoted as having taken the
ground that books should be transcribed rather than borrowed, because in that way the number would be increased
and the community would be benefited. In many cases,
however, there could, of course, be no choice. The King,
for instance, desired to possess the great encyclopedia of
Vincenzo of Beauvais. He sent gold to Vincenzo, in
consideration of which a transcript of the encyclopedia
was prepared. The exact cost is not stated.[1]

In 1375, a sum equivalent to 825 francs of to-day was
paid for transcribing the commentary of Heinrich Bohic
on the Decretals of 1375. In the cost of such work was
usually included a price for the loan or use of the manuscript. A fee or rental was, in fact, always charged by
the manuscript-dealers. Up to the close of the fourteenth
century, the larger proportion of transcripts were prepared
for individual buyers and under special orders, one of the
evidences of this being the fact that upon the titles of the
manuscripts were designed or illuminated the arms or
crests of the purchasers. After the beginning of the fifteenth century, there is to be found a large number of
manuscripts in which a place has been left blank on the
title-pages for the subsequent insertion of the crest or
coat-of-arms, indicating that in these instances the manuscript had been prepared for general use instead of under
special order.[2]

As already mentioned, Charlemagne interested himself,
not only in the training of scribes, but in the collection
of books, but he does not appear to have considered it
important that the works secured by him should be retained for the use of his descendants, as he gave instructions in his will that after his death the books should be sold.

[1] *Vita S. Ludovici*, Gaufrido de Belloloco, Bouq. xx., 15.
[2] Wattenbach, 457.

One of the oldest illuminated Irish manuscripts is that of S. Ceaddæ. This was purchased, at what date is not specified, by some holy man in exchange for his best steed, and was then presented by him to the church at Llandaff. The manuscript finally made its way to Madrid and thence to Stockholm; according to the record, it had, before the purchase above mentioned, been saved out of the hands of Norman pirates.[1] It is certain that very many of the monasteries which were within reach of the incursions of the Normans were bereft by them of such books as had been collected, although it is not probable that, as a rule, the pirates had any personal interest in, or commercial appreciation for, the manuscripts that fell into their hands.

Gerbert, whose literary interests have been previously referred to, and who is described as the most zealous book collector of his time, tells us that he made purchases for his library in Italy, in South Germany, and in the Low Countries, but he does not mention whether he was purchasing from dealers or individuals. He was a native of Auvergne, and in 999 became Pope (under the name of Gregory V.). Abbot Albert of Gembloux, who died in 1048, states that he brought together, at great cost, as many as one hundred and fifty manuscripts.[2]

A certain Deopert records that he purchased for the monastery of St. Emmeran, from Vichelm, the chaplain of Count Regimpert, for a large sum of money (the price is not specified), the writings of Alcuin.[3]

Notwithstanding the very strict regulations to the contrary, it not unfrequently happened that monasteries and churches, when in special stress for money, pledged or sold their books to Jews. As the greater proportion at least of the sacred writings of the monasteries would have

[1] Westwood, *Miniatures and Ornaments*, xxii., 6.
[2] Gesta. Abb. Gemblacensium, *Mon. Germ. Ss.*, viii., 540.
[3] Wattenbach, 459.

had no personal interest for their Hebrew purchasers, it
is fair to assume that these were taken for re-sale, and
that, in fact, there came to be a certain trade in books on
the part of financiers acting in the capacity of pawn-
brokers.   In 1320, the monastery of S. Ulrich was in
need of funds, and the Abbot Marquard, of Hagel,
pawned to the mendicant monks a great collection of
valuable books, among which were certain volumes that
had been prepared as early as 1175 under the directions
of the Abbot Heinrich. The successor of Marquard, Conrad Winkler, in 1344, succeeded in getting back a portion
of the books, by the payment of 27 pounds heller, and
15 pfennigs.[1]   Instances like these give evidence that a
certain trade in manuscript books, in Northern Europe at
least, preceded by a number of years the organisation of
any systematised book-trade.

Kirchhoff speaks of usurers, dealers in old clothes, and
pedlars, carrying on the trade in the buying and selling
of books during the first half of the fifteenth century. In
Milan, a dealer in perfumery, Paolino Suordo, included in
his stock (in 1470) manuscripts for sale, and later an-
nounced himself as a dealer in printed books. Both in
England and France at this time manuscripts were dealt
in by grocers and by the mercers. The monastery of
Neuzelle, in 1409, pawned several hundred manuscripts
for 130 gulden, and the monastery at Dobrilugk, in 1420,
sold to the Prebendary of Brandenburg 1441 volumes.

In 1455, the Faculty of Arts of the University of Heidelberg bought valuable books from the estate of the
Prior of Worms. In 1402, the cathedral at Breslau rented
a number of books from Burgermeister Johann Kyner,
for which the Chapter was to pay during the lifetime
of said Kyner a yearly rental of eight marks, ten groschens.[2]

The Bishop of Speier rented to the precentor of the

---

[1] Wittwer, in Steichele's *Arch. f. Gesch. der Bisth.*, Augsburg, iii., 164.
[2] Wattenbach, p. 465.

cathedral in 1447 some separately written divisions of the Bible, which were to be held by the precentor during his lifetime only, and were then to be returned to the Bishop's heirs. The rental is not mentioned. The Chapter of the Cathedral of Basel arranged to take over certain books from the owner or donor, whose name is not given, and to pay as consideration for the use of the same, each year on the anniversary of the gift, 16 sols.[1]

Richard de Bury makes a reference to the book-trade of Europe, as it existed in the fourteenth century, as follows:

Stationariorum ac librariorum notitiam non solum intra natalis soli provinciam, sed per regnum Franciæ, Teutoniæ et Italiæ comparavimus dispersorum faciliter pecunia præ-volante, nec eos ullatenus impedivit distantia neque furor maris absterruit, nec eis æs pro expensa defecit, quin ad nos optatos libros transmitterent vel afferrent.[2]

(By means of advance payments, we have easily come into relations with the *stationarii* and *librarii* who are scattered through our native province, and also with those who are to be found in the kingdoms of France, Germany, and Italy ; and neither the great distances, nor the fury of the sea, nor lack of money for their expenses has been permitted to prevent them from bringing or sending to us the books that we desired.)

In the same work, De Bury uses the term *bibliator*, which he afterwards explained as being identical with *bibliopole*,—a seller of books.

The record of the production of books that was carried on in the earlier universities, such as Bologna and Padua, is presented in the chapter on the universities.

In connection with the very special requirements of the earlier Italian universities, and with the close control exercised by them over the scribes, it is evident that a book-

[1] Mone, in der *Zeitsch. f. Gesch. der Oberrh.*, i., 309, 310.
[2] *Philobiblon*, c. 8.

trade in the larger sense of the term could not easily come into existence. The first records of producers and dealers of books of a general character were to be found, not in the university towns, but in Milan, Florence, and particularly in Venice. In 1444, a copy of Macrobius was stolen from the scholar Filelfi, or Philelphus, which copy he recovered, as he tells us, in the shop of a public scribe in Vincenza.

Blume mentions that in Venice the *Camaldulensers* of S. Michael in Murano carried on during the earlier part of the fifteenth century an important trade in manuscripts, including with the older texts verified copies which had been prepared under their own direction.[1] The headquarters, not only for Italy but for Europe, of the trade of Greek manuscripts, was for a number of years in Venice, the close relations of Venice with Constantinople and with the East having given it an early interest in this particular class of Eastern productions.

Joh. Arretinus was busied in Florence between the years 1375 and 1417 in the sale of manuscripts, but he appears to have secured these mainly not by production in Florence, but by sending scribes to the libraries in the monasteries and elsewhere to produce the copies required.

A reference in a letter of Leonardo Bruni, written in 1416, gives indication of an organised book-trade in Florence at that time:

Priscianum quem postulas omnes tabernas librarias perscrutatus reperire nondum postui.[2] (I have hunted through all the book-shops, but have not been able to find the Priscian for which you asked.)

Bruni writes again concerning a certain Italian translation of the Bible that he had been trying to get hold of:

Jam Bibliothecas omnes et bibliopolas requisivi ut si qua veniant ad manus eligam quæque optima mihi significent. (I have already searched all the libraries and book-shops

[1] *Iter Ital.*, iv., 179.   [2] *Epp. Leon. Aret.*, Ed. Mehus., iv., 8.

in order to select from the material at hand the manuscripts which are for me the most important.)

Ambrogio Traversari wrote in 1418 in Florence:

Oro ut convenias bibliopolas civitatis et inquiri facias diligenter, an inveniamus decretales in parvo volumine.[1] (I beg you to make search in all the book-shops of the city and ascertain whether it is possible to secure in a small volume a copy of the Decretals.)

The use for book-dealers of the old classic term *bibliopola* in place of the more usual *stationarius* is to be noted.

From these references, we have a right to conclude that there were during the first quarter of the fifteenth century in Florence a number of dealers in books who handled various classes of literature.

The great publisher of the fifteenth century, Philippi Vespasianus, or Vespasiano, who was not only a producer and dealer in manuscripts, but a man possessed of a wide range of scholarship, called himself *librarius florentinus*. He held the post for a time of *bidellus* of the University of Florence. His work will be referred to more fully in a later division of this chapter.

Kirchhoff points out that the dealers of this time, among others Vespasiano himself, were sometimes termed *chartularii*, a term indicating that dealers in books were interested also in the sale of paper and probably of other writing materials. The Italian word *cartolajo* specifies a paper-dealer or perhaps more nearly a stationer in the modern signification of the term.

The influx of Greek scholars into Italy began some years before the fall of Constantinople. Some of these scholars came from towns in Asia Minor, which had fallen under the rule of the Turks before the capture of Constantinople. When the Turkish armies crossed the Bosphorus, a number of the Greeks seem to have lost hope

---

[1] *Ambrogii Epistolæ*, Ed. Mehus., p. 517.

at a comparatively early date of being able to defend
the Byzantine territory, and had betaken themselves with
such property as they could save to various places of
refuge in the south of Europe, and particularly in Italy.
As described in other chapters, many of these exiles
brought with them Greek manuscripts, and in some cases
these codices were not only important as being the first
copies of the texts brought to the knowledge of European
scholars, but were of distinctive interest and value as being
the oldest examples of such texts in existence.

The larger number of the exiles who selected Italy as
their place of refuge found homes and in many cases scholarly occupation, not in the university towns so much as in
the great commercial centres, such as Venice and Florence.
Many of these Greeks were accepted as instructors in the
families of nobles or of wealthy merchants, while others
made use of their manuscripts either through direct sale,
through making transcripts for sale, or through the loan
of the originals to the manuscript-dealers.

A little later these manuscripts served as material and
as "copy" for the editions of the Greek classics issued
by Aldus and his associates, the first thoroughly edited
and carefully printed Greek books that the world had
known. It was partly as a cause and partly as an effect
of the presence of so many scholarly Greeks, that the study
of Greek language, literature, and philosophy became
fashionable among the so-called higher circles of Italian
society during the last half of the fifteenth century.

The interest in Greek literature had, however, as
pointed out, begun nearly twenty-five years earlier. As
there came to be some knowledge of the extent of the
literary treasures of classic Greece which had been preserved in the Byzantine cities, not a few of the more enterprising dealers in manuscripts, and many also of the
wealthier and more enterprising of the scholarly noblemen
and merchants, themselves sent emissaries to search the

monasteries and cities of the East for further manuscripts which could be purchased.

One reason, apparently, for the preference given by the Greeks to Venice and Florence over Bologna and Padua was the fact that the two great universities were devoted, as we have seen, more particularly to the subjects of law, theology, and medicine, subjects in which the learning of the Greeks could be of little direct service.[1]   The philosophy and the poetry which formed the texts of the lectures given by the Greek scholars attracted many zealous and earnest students, but these students came, as stated, largely outside of the university circles.   The doctors of law and the doctors of theology were among the last of the Italian scholars to be interested in Homeric poetry or in the theories of the Greek metaphysicians.

Towards the middle of the fifteenth century and a few years before the introduction of printing, a new term came to be used for dealers in manuscripts.   The scribes had in many cases naturally associated their business interests with those of the makers of paper,—*cartolaji*, and the latter name came to be applied not only to the paper manufacturers, but to the purchasers of the paper upon which books were inscribed.   In some cases the paper-makers, or *cartolaji*, appear themselves to have organised staffs of scribes through whose labour their own raw material could be utilised, while the name of paper-maker, —*cartolajo*, came to be used to describe the entire concern.

After the introduction into Italy of printing, the association of the paper-makers with books became still more important, and not a few of the original printer-publishers were formerly paper manufacturers, and continued this branch of trade while adding to it the work of manufacturing books.   Among such paper-making publishers is

[1] The Faculty of theology in Bologna was not established until 1352, but the statement is sufficiently correct for the period here referred to.

to be noted Francesco Cartolajo, who was in business in Florence in 1507, and whose surname was, of course, derived from the trade in which his family had for some generations been engaged. Bonaccorsi turned his paper-making establishment in Florence into a printing-office and book manufactory as early as 1472, and Montali, in Parma, took the same course in 1482; Di Sasso who, in 1481, came into asssociation with the Brothers Brushi, united his printing-office with their paper factory.

Fillippo Giunta, one of the earlier publishers in Florence, calls himself *librarius et cartolajus*. It is possible that he reversed the business routine above referred to, and united a paper factory with his printing-office.

One result of the influx of Greek scholars, many of whom were themselves skilled scribes while others brought with them scribes, was the multiplying of the number of writers available for work and a corresponding reduction in the cost of such work.

The effect of this change in the business conditions was to lessen the practice of hiring manuscripts for a term of days or weeks, or of dividing manuscripts into *pecias*, and to increase the actual sale of works in manuscripts.

The university regulations, however, controlling the loaning of manuscripts and of the *pecias* appear to have been continued and renewed through the latter half of the fifteenth century, that is to say, not only after the trade in manuscripts, at popular prices, had largely developed in cities like Florence, Venice, and Milan, but even after the introduction of printing. It would almost seem as if in regard to books in manuscript, the system which had been put into shape by the university authorities had had the effect of delaying for a quarter of a century or so the introduction into Bologna and Padua of the methods of book production and book distribution which were already in vogue in other cities of Italy. I do not overlook the fact that there was in Florence also a university, but it is evident that the book-trade in that city had never been under the control of the university authorities, and that the methods of the dealers took shape rather from the general, common-sense commercial routine of the great centre of Italian trade than from the narrow scholastic theories of the professors of law or of theology.

During the twenty-five years before the art of printing, introduced into Italy in 1464, had become generally diffused, the years in which the trade in manuscripts was at its highest development, Florence succeeded Venice as the centre of this trade, both for Italy and for Europe.

The activity of the intellectual life of the city, and the fact that its citizens were cultivated and that its scholars were so largely themselves men of wealth, the convenient location of the city for trade communications with the other cities of Italy and with the great marts in the East, in the West, and in the North, and the accumulation in such libraries as those of the Medici of collections, nowhere else to be rivalled, of manuscripts, both ancient and modern, united in securing for Florence the pre-eminence for literary production and for literary interests.

Scholars, not only from the other Italian cities, but from France, Germany, and Hungary, came to Florence to consult manuscripts which in many cases could be found only in Florence, or to purchase transcripts of these manuscripts, which could be produced with greater correctness, greater beauty, and smaller expense by the *librarii* of Florence than by producers of books in any other city. After the Greek refugees began their lecture courses, there was an additional attraction for scholars from the outer world to visit the Tuscan capital.

The wealthy scholars and merchant princes of Florence, whose collections of manuscripts were given to the city during their lifetime, or who left such collections after their death to the Florentine libraries, made it, as a rule, a condition of such gifts and such bequests that the

books should be placed freely at the disposal of visitors
desiring to make transcripts of the same. Such a condition appears in the will of Bonaccorsi,[1] while a similar
condition was quoted by Poggio[2] in his funeral oration
upon Niccolo d' Niccoli, as having been the intention of
Niccolo for the books bequeathed by him to his Florentine fellow-citizens.

Foreign collectors who did not find it convenient themselves to visit Florence, such as the Duke of Burgundy,
and Matthias Corvinus of Hungary, kept employed in the
city for a number of years scribes engaged in the work of
preparing copies of these Florentine literary treasures for
the libraries of Nancy and of Buda-Pesth.

Matthias was, it seems, not content with ordering the
transcripts of the works desired by him, but employed a
scholarly editor, resident in Florence, to supervise the
work and to collate the transcripts with the originals,
and who certified to the correctness of the copies for-
warded to Buda.[3] At the death of Matthias, there appear
to have been left in Florence a number of codices ordered
by him which had not yet been paid for, and these were
taken over by the Medici.[4]

In a parchment manuscript of the Philippian orations is
inscribed a note by a previous owner, a certain Dominicus
Venetus, to the effect that he had bought the same in
Rome from a Florentine bookseller for five ducats in gold
in 1460.[5] Dominicus goes on to say that he had used
this manuscript in connection with the lectures of the
learned Brother Patrus Thomasius.

During the thirteenth century, there was a considerable
development in the art of preparing and of illuminating

[1] Blume, *Iter*, vol. ii., p. 71.
[2] Poggii Florentini, *Opera*, Argentinæ, 1513, vol. ii., 102.
[3] Schier, *De Regia Bibliothecæ Budensis*, Viennæ, 1799, vol. viii., 21.
[4] Denis, tom. i., 849.
[5] Mittarelli, p. 258.

and illustrating manuscripts. One author is quoted by Tiraboschi as saying that the work on a manuscript now required the services not of a scribe, but of an artist. For the transcribing of a missal and illuminating the same with original designs, a monk in Bologna is quoted as having received in 1260 two hundred florins gold, the equivalent of about one hundred dollars. For copying the text of the Bible, without designs, another scribe received in the same year eighty lire, about sixteen dollars.[1]

The work of the manuscript-dealers in Florence was carried on not only for the citizens and sojourners in the city itself, but for the benefit of other Italian cities in which there was no adequate machinery for the manifolding of manuscripts. Bartholomæus Facius, writing from Naples in 1448, speaks of the serious inadequacy of the scribes in that city. There were but few men engaged in the business, and these were poorly educated and badly equipped.[2] Facius was, therefore, asking a correspondent in Florence to have certain work done for him which could not be completed in Naples. Poggio writes from Rome about the same date to Niccolo in Florence to somewhat similar effect. He speaks with envy of the' larger literary facilities possessed by his Florentine friends.[3]

Next to Florence, the most important centre for the manuscript trade of North Italy was Milan. As early as the middle of the fourteenth century, there is record of no less than forty professional scribes being at work in the city. Such literary work as was required by Genoa and other Italian towns within reach of the Lombardy capital came to Milan. At the beginning of the thirteenth century, when the population of the city was about 200,000, there had been in the city but two registered copyists. More important, however, than that of either Florence or Milan,

[1] Tiraboschi, ii., 40.   [2] Mittarelli, 383.   [3] Mittarelli, 933.

was the manuscript trade of Venice, the position of which
city gave it exceptional advantages as well for the collection of codices from the East as for securing the services
of skilled scribes from Athens or from Constantinople.
One of the more noteworthy of the Venetian importers of
manuscripts was Johannes Galeotti, a Genoese by birth,
who made various journeys to Constantinople, and whose
special trade is referred to in an inscription on a manuscript dating from 1450 and containing the speeches of
Demosthenes.[1]

Reference has already been made to Aurispa, who
appears to have been the most important manuscript-
dealer of his time, not only in Venice, but possibly in the
world.   Aurispa sent various agents to Greece and to
the farther East to collect manuscripts and kept scribes
busied in his work-shop in Venice in preparing authentic
copies of these texts.   One of his travellers was Plantinerus, who was sent to the Peloponnesus in 1415, and who
succeeded in securing there some valuable codices.[2]
Plantinerus found, in executing his commissions, that he
had to come into competition with a traveller sent out by
Cosimo de' Medici on a similar errand.

Venice possessed an advantage over the other Italian
cities, not only in the collection of texts, and in its facilities for manifolding these, but in its position for securing
wide sales for the same in the cities outside of Italy, with
which it was, in connection with its active commerce, in
regular relations.   The lines of the Oxford printers, Theo.
Rood and Thomas Hunt, printed in their edition of the
Letters of Phalaris, give an indication of the relations of
the English university in the early part of the fifteenth
century with the literary marts of Southern Europe.

[1] Mucciolo, J. M., *Catalogus Codd. Mss. Malatest Cæsan.* Biblioth.
Fratr. Min. Convent, i., 95.   Cæsanæ, 1780.
[2] Petit-Radel, *Recherches sur les Bibliothèques Anciennes*, etc., Paris, 1819,
p. 155.

Celatos, Veneti, nobis transmittere libros
Cedite, nos aliis vendimus, O Veneti—[1]

(If you Venetians will send over to us the books which
have been hidden (*i.e.* difficult or rare books, or possibly
books unearthed from far off Eastern regions) we will find
sale for the same.)

There is evidence in fact of a very active book-trade
between Venice and England for many years before the
introduction into Italy of the printing-press. The work
of Aldus and of those who were associated with him in
carrying on printing and publishing undertakings in Venice
naturally very largely extended these relations with the
English scholars, but the channels for the same had
already been opened. The manuscript-dealers in Venice
fixed their place of business in the most frequented parts
of the city—the Bridge of the Rialto, and the Plaza of
S. Mark.

The trade of the Italian dealers in manuscripts was not
brought to an immediate close by the introduction of
printing. The older scholars still preferred the manuscript form for their books, and found it difficult to divest
themselves of the impression that the less costly printed
volumes were suited only for the requirements of the
vulgar herd. There are even, as Kirchhoff points out,[2]
instances of scribes preparing their manuscripts from
printed "copy," and there are examples of these manuscript copies of printed books being made with such liter-
alness as to include the imprint of the printer.

The work of Aldus (continued with scholarly enterprise
later by such men as Froben of Basel and Estienne of
Paris) in the printing of Greek texts, although begun as
early as 1495, and although exercising a very wide influence upon the distribution of Greek literature, was insufficient to supply the eager demand of the scholars, while
not many other printers were, in the early years of the

[1] Kirchhoff, p. 40.   [2] p. 41.

exercise of the art, prepared to incur the very considerable risk and expense required for the production of Greek fonts of type. The risk was, of course, by no means limited to the cost of the type; the printers of the earlier Greek books had themselves but slight familiarity with the literature of Greece, and they were obliged in many cases to confide the selection and the editing of their texts to editors to whom this literature was very largely still a novelty. The printers hardly knew what books to select and they had no adequate data upon which to base business calculations as to the extent of the demand that could be looked for for any particular book. The feeling that they were working in the dark was, therefore, a very natural one.

It was on this ground that, while printing-presses were during the century after 1450 multiplying rapidly through Europe, the printing of Greek books continued to be for a large portion of the period an exceptional class of undertakings, and work was still found for scribes who could be trusted to make accurate transcripts of Greek codices.

Kirchhoff gives the names of the following Italian manuscript-dealers and scribes whose scholarly activity during the latter half of the fifteenth century was especially important: Antonius Dazilas, Cæsar Strategus, Constantius Librarius, Andreas Vergetius, and Antonius Eparchus. The latter made various journeys to the East in search of manuscripts. The fact that the dealers in manuscripts very rarely placed their own names on the copies of the texts sent out from their work-shops has, in a large number of cases, prevented these names from being preserved for future record. The names that have come into record are in the main such as have been referred to in the correspondence of their scholarly friends and clients. I quote a few of these references from the lists given by Kirchhoff:

In Bologna the oldest *librarius* whose work is referred to is Viliaric, who was called an *antiquarius*, and whose shop was open in the beginning of the thirteenth century.   In a manuscript, previously referred to, containing a treatise of Paul Orosius, originally written in the seventh century, and from which this copy was transcribed early in the thirteenth, there is at the end an inscription, as follows:

Confectus codex in statione magistri Viliaric antiquarii,
Ora pro me scriptore, sic dominum habeas protectorem.[1]

[This codex was completed in the stall of Master Viliaric, the scribe; if you pray for (the soul of) me, the author, you will have (in heaven) a powerful patron.]

This codex seems to have been prepared, according to the usual university practice, for hire, as on the sixteenth page there is noted the memorandum, " this quaternio has five sheets."

In 1247, Nicolaus is recorded as being the *stationarius universitatis*, and in the same year a certain Johannes Cambii is recorded as a *stationarius librorum ;* and Minghinus as a *stationarius peciarum.*   Here we have in one year record of three classes of scribes being at work. They were all noted as being doctors of the law, and they all appear on the list of persons exempt from military service.

Later in the same century, a certain Cervotti, who had inherited from a deceased brother a collection of books, undertook to use these for profit by offering them for hire.   The list of the books, drawn up by the notary Noscimpax, has been preserved, and includes twenty different works.   Certain of these are collections of the university lectures in the Faculty of law, and the others have also, in the main, to do with the subject of jurisprudence.   The first book on the list is *Diversitates Dominorum*, and the

---

[1] Bandini, *Codd. Lat.*, ii., 727.

last *Margarita Gallacerti*, which latter does not appear properly to belong to the subject of jurisprudence.

In the year 1400, there is reference to a scribe named Moses and specified as a Jew, which, in view of the university regulations previously referred to prohibiting the sale of books by Jews or to Jews, is noteworthy.

The entry appears at the close of a manuscript of Bartholomæus Brixiensis:

Emi hunc librum anno domini MCCCC die XXI. Mensis novembris a Moysi Judeo pro viii. florenes.

Kirchhoff is of opinion that Moses must have been a travelling pedlar, as it is difficult to believe that a Jew could have at that time secured the post of a licensed university scribe.[1]

In Verona, there is reference to a certain Bonaventura, who is recorded as a *scriptor*, and who seems to have occasionally utilised for his manuscript work the hand of a woman. An inscription on one of the manuscripts by Bonaventura, quoted by Endlicher, reads as follows:

Dextra scriptoris careat gravitate doloris.
Detur pro penna scriptori pulchra puella.[2]

In Florence, the earliest *librarius* of note was probably Johannes Aretinus, whose work continued during the years between 1375–1417. Ambrosius Camaldulensis, who had so much to do with books and with literature, takes pains, in a letter written in 1391, to send a cordial greeting to the *librarius* Aretinus.[3] Bandini prints a letter of Petrarch's in which the latter refers to Aretinus as a friend for whom he has a high regard and as a man of exceptional knowledge and clearness of insight, and specifies, as works that he valued highly, nine manu-

[1] Pasini, *Rivantella et Berta*, pars ii., 77.
[2] Endlicher, *Catalogus Codd. MSS. Biblioth. Palat Vendo Bonensis*, tom. i., 89.
[3] Martene et Durand, tom. iii., 536.

scripts which had been written by the hand of Aretinus. These included Aristotle's treatise on Ethics, several Essays of Cicero, the Histories of Livy, Cicero's Orations, Barbari on Marriage, etc.

Kirchhoff gives a list of fourteen other Florentine *librarii*, whose work extended over the years between 1410 and 1480. The latter date is sixteen years later than the introduction of the printing-press into Italy.

The most noteworthy by far of these manuscript-dealers of Florence was Philippi Vespasiano, who has been previously referred to, and who is to be ranked not only as the most important publisher of the manuscript period, but as one of the great scholars of his time, and as a man whose friendship was cherished by not a few of the leaders of thought during the earlier period of the Renaissance. In one of the Florentine collections has been preserved a number of letters written to Vespasiano by his scholarly friends between the years 1446 and 1463, and these letters show how honoured a position he held in the generation of his time. He was, in fact, in character and in ambition, as well as in the nature of his work, a worthy predecessor of Aldus, and he lived long enough himself to have seen some of the productions of the Aldine Press.

In his earlier years, Vespasiano was for a time secretary to Cardinal Branda in Rome, and it is during this time that he devoted himself earnestly to classic studies. It was while he was in Rome that he began work upon a literary undertaking of his own, which comprised a series of Memoirs of the noteworthy men of his time with whom he had come into relations. The Medici, Duke Borso of Ferrara, and other of the scholarly nobles made large use of Vespasiano's collections of manuscripts and facilities for producing authentic transcripts.

He was one of the Italian dealers whose agents were actively at work in Greece and in Asia Minor in the collecting of manuscripts, and the clients to whom he supplied such manuscripts included correspondents in Paris, Basel, Vienna, and Oxford.

In the Bodleian Library in Oxford is a codex containing certain works of Cyprian, on the first sheet of which is inscribed :

Vespasianus librarius Florentinus hunc librum Florentiæ transcribendum curavit. (Vespasian, a Florentine *librarius*, had this book transcribed at Florence.)

Another manuscript in the same collection, containing a commentary on some comedies of Terence, is inscribed as follows :

Vespasianus librarius Florentinus fecit scribi Florentiæ. (Vespasian, a Florentine *librarius*, had this book written in Florence.)

Both codices are beautiful examples of the best manuscript work of the period.[1]

There are various references of the time showing that manuscripts which bore the stamp of Vespasiano were not only beautiful in their form, but possessed probably a higher authority than the work of any other manuscript-dealer of the age for completeness and for accuracy. He took contracts for the production of great libraries, and it is recorded that, in preparing for Cosimo de' Medici a collection of two hundred works, he employed forty-five scribes for a term of twenty-two months.[2] Vespasiano died in 1496, one year later than the establishment in Venice of the Aldine Press.

Agnolo da Sandro is described as a *bidellus*, a manuscript-dealer, in Florence as late as 1498, at which time the trade in manuscripts must already have begun very seriously to diminish. Niccolo di Giunta, who was active in the manuscript trade in Florence towards the end of the fifteenth century, is famous as having been the founder of the family of Giunta or Junta, which later took such an

---

[1] Coxe, *Coll. Lincoln*, tom. i., pp. 31 and 32.
[2] Kirchhoff, *Weitere Beiträge*, vii., 8.

important part in printing and publishing undertakings in Italy.

In Perugia, the first record of a manuscript-publisher bears date as late as 1430. The name is Bontempo, and his inscription appears on a parchment copy of an *Infortiatum*.

While there are various references to manuscript-dealers in Milan of an early date, the first inscription bears date as late as 1452. The name is Melchoir, who is described as a "dealer of note." Filelfo speaks of Melchoir as having copies of Cicero's *Letters* for sale at ten ducats each.[1]

Paolo Soardo, who was in business between 1470 and 1480, is described as an apothecary and also as a dealer in *delicatessen*, but he seems to have added to his employment that of a manifolder and seller of manuscripts.

Jacobus Antiquarius speaks of having purchased from Paolo in 1480 a Roman history for the sum of one *aureus*. In Padua, Jacob, a Jew, succeeded, notwithstanding the university regulations against dealing in manuscripts by Jews, in carrying on between 1455 and 1460 a business in the sale of manuscripts. His inscription appears on a number of classical codices of the time, and in a manuscript of Horace, dating from the twelfth century, the owner makes reference that he purchased the same in 1458 from Jacob, the Hebrew *librarius*.[2]

The records of Ferrara give the names of Carnerio, *bibliopola*, and of several others as doing business in manuscripts between 1440 and 1490.

In Rome the records of 1454 speak of Giovanni and Francisco as *cartolaji* and *librarii*, that is to say, dealers in paper and also in manuscripts. In that year these dealers had for sale among their things, *Letters of Cicero* (without which work no well regulated manuscript-dealer's collection appears to have been complete) and the works

[1] Filelfo, *Epistolæ*, x., 25.   [2] Bandini, *Codd. Lat.*, tom. ii., 145.

of Celsus. A copy of the latter was bought for Vespasiano for the sum of twenty ducats. There is record during the same year of a certain Spannocchia who also had Cicero's *Letters* for sale.

In Genoa there were at this time one or two manuscript-dealers, but, as before stated, the readers and scholars of Genoa appear for the most part to have supplied themselves from Florence.

The most important trade in manuscripts during the fourteenth and fifteenth centuries, as was the case during the fifteenth century with the trade in printed books, was carried on in Venice and Florence. As early as 1390 the inscription of Gabriel Ravenna, *librarius*, appears in a copy of Seneca's *Tragedies*.[1] Kirchhoff is of opinion that Gabriel conducted, during the last fifteen years of the fourteenth century, an important work-shop for the production of manuscripts.

A year or two later, occurs the name of Michael, a German *librarius*, but it is possible that Michael's work was more nearly that of a secretary than of a manuscript-dealer. As Kirchhoff points out, it is not always easy at this stage of the trade in manuscripts, to distinguish between the inscriptions of the manuscript-dealers certifying to the correctness of the copy sent out from their shops, and the inscriptions of the scribes or secretaries who, having completed for this or that employer specific copies of the works required, added their names as a record on the final sheet.

Reference has already been made to Johannes Aurispa, by far the most important of the manuscript-dealers of his time and possibly of the entire Middle Ages. Aurispa was born in 1369 in Sicily. The earlier years of his life were passed in Constantinople, where he appears to have held a position of some importance in connection with the Court. While in Constantinople, he began to make

---

[1] Bandini, *Codd. Lat.*, tom. ii., 251.

collections of manuscripts, and he organised there a staff of
skilled scribes.   In 1423, at the invitation of his friends,
Ambrosius Camaldulensis and Niccolo d' Niccoli, he came
to Florence, bringing with him an invaluable collection of
238 manuscripts.

To this store he afterwards added, while in Florence, a
further lot of codices which he had had sent from Constantinople to Messina.   At this time, his interest in the
collection of manuscripts appears to have been a matter
of scholarship merely and of sympathy with the efforts of
certain Florentine scholars whom he came to know, to
secure the material for their classical studies.

Later, however, in connection, doubtless, with the many
applications that came to him for transcripts of his codices,
he decided to organise a business as a bookseller and
publisher.   Before taking this course, he had, it appears,
sought a position as instructor, first in Florence and afterwards in Bologna and in Ferrara, but had not succeeded
in finding the kind of a post that suited him.

Part of the evidence of his change of mind comes to us
through letters from Filelfo, whose keen scholarly interest
brought him into close relations with men having to do
with literary production.   Filelfo writes to Aurispa, in
1440:

*Totus es in librorum mercatura, sed in lectura mallem.
Quid enim prodest libros quotidie, nunc emere, nunc vendere,
legere vere nunquam!* (You are completely absorbed in
the occupation of trading books, but I should choose that
of reading them.   For what does it profit you to buy and
sell books every day if you never have time for their
perusal.)

And again in 1441:

*Sed ex tua ista taberna libraria nullus unquam prodit
codex, nisi cum quæstu.*[1] (No book ever leaves your book-
shop, except at a profit to you.)

[1] Kirchhoff, p. 55.

The publishing undertakings of Aurispa were devoted almost entirely to works of classical literature. Among the authors whose names appear either in the lists of books offered by him or in the correspondence of his friends and clients, are as follows:

Philo Judæus, Strabo, Theophrastus, Demosthenes, Xenophon, Proculus, Homer, Aristarchus, Athenæus, Sophocles, Æschylus, Pindar, Oppian, Proclus, Eusebius, Gregory, Aristotle, Plutarch, Plotinus, Lucian, Dio Cassio, Diodorus, and other Greek authors. The Latin writers included Cicero (of necessity), Virgil, Pliny, Quintilian, Macrobius, Apicius, and Antonius.

Aurispa seems to have enjoyed the confidence and friendship of all the noted Italian scholars of his time, and the letters of his correspondents speak with very cordial appreciation as well of the importance of his services to literature, as of the extent of the accuracy of his own scholarship. The only correspondent with whom he appears to have had any trouble was Filelfi, but if Filelfi had not managed to have friction with Aurispa, the bookseller would have been an exception among the contemporaries of this irritable and self-sufficient scholar.

In 1450, being then well advanced in years, Aurispa gave up his business undertakings, took priestly orders, and lived thereafter as a *scriba apostolicus*, dividing his time between Ferrara and Rome. He declined tempting offers, made through his friend Panormita, to join the literary circle of King Alphonso which had been brought together about the Court in Naples.

After Aurispa's death, Filelfo gave to his son-in-law, Sabbatinus, a very cordial word of appreciation of the services and of the character of the publisher. A portion of the manuscripts belonging to Aurispa's collection was purchased in 1461 by Duke Borso of Ferrara for two hundred ducats.

A large collection of manuscripts was, however, in

Aurispa's possession at the time of his death, and these were taken charge of by Bartholomæus Facius, and, after various vicissitudes, many of them have since found place in existing collections of Florence, Venice, Vienna, Paris, and London.   A selection of the letters between Aurispa and his near friend Camaldulensis has also been preserved.

Books in Spain.—At the time when the great manuscript-dealers of Venice and Florence were carrying on business with the literary centres of France, Germany, and England, they had some dealings also with Spain; but their correspondence was practically limited to the University of Salamanca, which had been founded about 1220.   The literary activities of Spain during the fifteenth century were certainly much less important than those of either Italy or France.   They were of necessity seriously hampered by the long series of wars with the Moors, while the final overthrow in 1492 of the Moorish kingdom of Granada doubtless had, as one of many results, a decidedly unfavourable influence upon the intellectual development and the literary possibilities of the Peninsula.   For two centuries or more the scholars of the Moorish kingdom had busied themselves in making collections of Arabic literature, while of not a few of the more noteworthy works they caused to be prepared versions in Latin, by means of which the books were made available for the use of instructors and students in Salerno, Bologna, Padua, and Paris.   It was the case also that the first knowledge of certain Greek authors came to the scholars of Europe through the Latin translations which were produced in Cordova from the Arabic versions. The Moorish scholars thus became a connecting link for the transmission to the Western world of the philosophy and learning of the East.   Until its conquest and practical destruction by the Spaniards in 1236, Cordova had been not only the political capital but the centre of the intellectual life of the Moorish kingdom, so that it was spoken of as the Athens of the West. At the close of the tenth century it is said to have contained nearly one million inhabitants. In connection with the work of its university and of the great library, a large body of skilled scribes were busied with the manifolding of manuscripts, and there appears to have been a regular exchange of manuscripts between Cordova and Baghdad.

In the year 995, Thafar Al-baghdádé, the chief of the scribes of his time, came from Baghdad and settled in Cordova. The Khalif Al-hakem took him into his service and employed him in transcribing books. The Khalif surpassed every one of his predecessors in the love of literature and of the sciences, which he himself cultivated with success and fostered in his dominions. Through his influence, Andalusia became a great market to which the literary productions of every clime were immediately brought for sale. He employed merchants and agents to collect books for him in distant countries, remitting for the purpose large sums of money from the treasury, until, says the chronicler, " the number of books in Andalusia exceeded all calculation." The Khalif sent presents of money to celebrated authors in the East with a view to encourage the publication of works or to secure the first copies of these. Hearing, for instance, that Abú-l-faraj of Ispahán had written a book entitled *Kitdbu-l-aghani* (*The Book of Songs*), he sent him a thousand dinars of pure gold, in consideration of which he received a copy of the work before it had been published in Persia. He did the same thing with Abú Bekr Al-abhari, who had published a commentary on the *Mokhtassar*.

Al-hakem also collected and employed in his own palace the most skilful men of his time in the arts of transcribing, binding and illuminating books. The great library that he brought together remained in the palace of Cordova, until, during a siege of the city by the Berbers, Hájib Wadheh, a freedman of Al-mansúr, ordered portions of the books to be sold, the remainder being shortly afterwards plundered and destroyed on the taking of the city. The extent of the collection is indicated by the description of the catalogue. In the Tekmílah, Ibun-l-abbáns is quoted by Al-Makkari as saying that the catalogue comprised forty-four volumes, each volume containing twenty sheets. Makkari estimates that the library contained no less that four hundred thousand volumes. It is possible that this number was over-estimated, at least, if we are to believe the statement of Ibun-l-abbar that the Khalif Al-hakem had himself read every book in the collection, writing on the fly-leaf the dates of his perusal and details concerning the author.

Makkari gives a long list of famous authors who flourished in Andalusia during the reign of Al-hakem, their productions including works in law, medicine, history, topography, language, and poetry. One of the historians, Al-tári-khí, was a paper merchant, and was accordingly known by the name of Al-Warrak. I do not find record of the names of any dealers in books or any account of the means employed for their distribution.[1]

The Manuscript Trade in France.—While, in Italy, the more important part of the trade in manuscripts was carried on outside of the university circles, in France the university retained in the hands of its own authorities the control and supervision of the work of the manuscript-dealers; and the book-trade of the country, not only during the manuscript period, but for many years after the introduction of printing, was very directly associated with the university organisation. The record of the production and of the trade in books carried on by the *stationarii, librarii,* and the printer-publishers of the uni-

[1] *History of the Mohammedan Dynasties in Spain.* By Ahmed Ibu Mohammed Al-Makkari, translated by Pascual de Gayangos. 2 vols., quarto. London, 1843.

versity is presented in the chapter on the Making of
Books in the Universities.

During its earlier years, the trade in manuscripts was
limited practically to the city of Paris. The work of the
official university scribes in Paris was very similar to that
which has already been referred to for Bologna. It appears, however, that, in accordance with the Parisian
methods, there was less insistence upon the practice of
hiring manuscripts, either complete or in divisions, and
there was an earlier development of the practice of
making an absolute sale of the texts required.

Kirchhoff traces the beginning of the manuscript-trade
back to the second half of the eleventh century. He says
that it is not clear whether the earlier dealers were able
to devote themselves exclusively to the business of selling
books, or whether, as he thinks it more probable, they
associated this business with some other occupation.
Jean de Garland, who compiled a kind of technological
directory or list of industries carried on in Paris in 1060,
says : *Paravisus est locus ubi libri scholarium vendentur.*[1]
He is apparently referring to the Place near the Cathedral
Church, which later became the centre of the Parisian
book-trade. Peter of Blois, writing, in the middle of the
twelfth century, to an instructor in jurisprudence in Paris,
makes a more definite reference to the Parisian manuscript-dealers. He speaks of the great collections of
valuable books which the Parisian dealers have for sale,
and laments the narrowness of his purse which prevents
him from purchasing many things which have tempted
him.[2]

Bulæus, in his *History of the University of Paris*, published in 1665, maintains that as early as 1174, the
manuscript-dealers of Paris formed a part of the organisation of the university, and that their work had been

[1] Géraud, H., *Paris sous Philippe le-Bel*, Paris, 1837, iv., 608.
[2] Petit-Radel, 106.

brought fully under the regulation of the university authorities. The university statistics, before the thirteenth century, do not, however, appear fully to bear out this contention. The first statutes which give detailed regulations concerning the book-trade bear date as late as 1275. These statutes specify what texts and what number of copies of each text the licensed booksellers should keep in stock, and give a schedule, as was done in Bologna and Padua, of the prices at which the loans and sales should be made.

Kirchhoff is of opinion that, prior to the middle of the thirteenth century, the book-trade connected with the university, while it had already assumed considerable proportions, had not been brought thoroughly under university control. With this control came also as an effect, the privileges which attached to the dealers as members of the university body, and there is no evidence that the booksellers enjoyed these privileges before 1250. Depping takes the ground, that during the fifteenth century the sale of books in Paris was not sufficient to constitute a business in itself, and that all dealers in books had some other occupation or means of support, and interested themselves in the sale of manuscripts only as an additional occupation.[1]

It appears hardly likely, however, that manuscript-dealers should be able to secure immunity from the general tax, which fell upon nearly all other classes of dealers, on the ground of the importance of their trade for education, unless they were able to show that they were actively engaged in such trade. The regulation quoted by Depping specifies among the free citizens of the city of Paris who were not liable to the King's tax,— *libraires parcheminiers, enlumineurs, escriipveins.* It was evidently the intention of the framers of the law to include under the exemption all dealers upon whose

[1] Kirchhoff, 62.

trade the preparation and sale of manuscripts was directly
dependent. Under this heading were included, of necessity, the scribes, the illuminators (who added to the text
of the scribes the artistic decorations and initial letters),
and (most important of the three) the dealers in parchment.

The fact that the booksellers are named in this schedule
separately from the scribes is an indication of the existence of a bookselling trade of sufficient importance to
call for the work of capitalists employing in the preparation of their manuscripts the services of the scribes and
of the other workmen required. Work of this kind can
properly be classified as publishing.

The dealer was himself prohibited from making purchase of a manuscript left in his hands until this had
been offered for sale during the term of not less than one
month. Record was to be kept of the name of the
purchaser and of the price received.

The requirement that the price obtained for a manuscript
should be recorded, has secured the preservation, on a
number of manuscripts of the time, of a convenient record
of their market value.

In a collection of sermons dating from the latter part
of the fifteenth century, for instance, is the record, "This
book was sold for 20 Parisian sols." In a text of *Ovid*
of about the same time is noted simply the price,—6
sols, Parisian.[1]

Newly prepared transcripts could not be licensed for
renting until they had been examined and passed as correct by the officials, and until their renting prices had
been placed on record. No new work could be included
in the lists of the *stationarii* until license for the same
had been secured. At this date, the usual term of rental
of a manuscript was one week, and an additional charge

[1] *Catalogue Général des Manuscrits des Bibliothèques Publiques*, etc.,
Paris, 1849, tom. i., 172.

could be made if the manuscript was held in excess of
that time.   In case a member of the university had
transcribed an incorrect or incomplete manuscript, the
stationarius was liable to him for damages to cover his
wasted labour.   According to the general practice, the
hirer of a manuscript was obliged to deposit a pledge for
the same, which pledge could be disposed of by the
stationarius after the term of one year.

In the schedule presented by Chevillier of manuscripts
licensed in the early part of the thirteenth century, the
prices specified cover only the rates for renting.   Chevillier points out that there is in this schedule no indication
of the division of the manuscripts into *pecias*, the practice
which was, as we have seen, the usual routine in the
Italian universities.[1]

An appraisal of the books contained in the library of
the Sorbonne in the year 1292 gives a value of 3812 livres,
10 sous, 8 deniers.[2]

The regulations concerning the sale of works on commission were renewed in 1300, with provisions which must
have rendered this class of business not only unremunerative but peculiarly troublesome.   Such a sale could be
made only in the presence of two witnesses.   No other
bookseller was at liberty to purchase the book, excepting
with the permission and in the presence of the original
owner.   Before a sale was made to a bookseller, the manuscript must be allowed to remain exposed for sale not
less than four days in the library of the Dominican
monastery.

Exceptions to the above regulations were permitted
under the express authority of the Rector of the university
in case the original possessor of the manuscript might be in
immediate need of money, a condition which probably
obtained in a large number of cases.

[1] Chevillier, *L'Origine de l'Imprimerie de Paris*, 1694, iv., 346.
[2] Chevillier, 369.

The general purpose of these regulations appears to have been the prevention of any undue increase in the market price or selling value of manuscripts, or the " cornering of the market " on the part of the manuscript-dealers in connection with texts which might be in demand. Existing regulations of this kind tended, however, naturally to fall into desuetude.

In 1411, an ordinance of Charles VI. made fresh reference to the necessity of such supervision, mainly on the ground of the convenience of tracing stolen manuscripts or unlicensed manuscripts.

In 1342, the *librarii* were permitted to increase their selling commission from four deniers to six deniers in the case of manuscripts sold by them for clients who were not themselves members of the university. Kirchhoff points out, however, that this commission could by no means have represented the actual charges made. The University of Paris claimed the authority to license its *librarii*, and to carry on business not only in Paris but throughout France. *Librarii* from without were, however, strictly prohibited from carrying on business in Paris.

There were in Paris, in addition to the *stationarii* and *librarii*, a certain number of unlicensed dealers who were not members of the university, and who might be classed as book pedlars. While these book pedlars enjoyed no university privileges, their business was subjected to the supervision of the university authorities. It was the purpose of the regulations to prevent dealers of this kind from taking part in any higher grade book business. They were, for instance, forbidden to sell any volume for a higher price than ten sous, which, of necessity, limited their trade practically to chap-books, broadsides, etc. They were also forbidden to trade in any covered shops, their business being carried on in open booths. In case they were at any time found to be trenching upon the business of the licensed or certified book-dealers (*libraires jurés*), they forfeited promptly their permits as book pedlars.

In 1323, the Paris School was the most important in Europe for theological studies, as that of Bologna was the authority on jurisprudence, and that of Padua for medicine; and the trade of the Paris booksellers was, therefore, largely devoted to theological writings. It is partly on this ground that the records of the monasteries in which there was scholarly and literary activity make more frequent reference during this century to Paris as a book centre than to any one of the Italian cities. When, for instance, King Wenzell II. of Bohemia, at the time of the founding of the Cistercian abbey of Königsaal, presented two hundred marks of silver for the organisation of its library, the Abbot Conrad had, he reports, no other course to take than to travel to Paris in order to purchase the books. This was in the year 1327.[1] Johann Gerson, writing in 1395 to Petrus de Alliaco, speaks of the wealth of the literary stores available at this time in Paris. The list that he gives as an example of these treasures is devoted exclusively to theological works.

While it is difficult to understand from the evidence available what machinery may have been in existence during the thirteenth and fourteenth centuries for the distribution of the books, there are various references to indicate that such distribution took place promptly over a very considerable territory. The anonymous author of a polemical tract, written in order to point out the errors of some heretical production, says:

Is autem erroneus liber positus fuit publice ad exemplandum Parisius anno domini 1254. Unde certum est, quod jam publice predicaretur, nisi boni prelati et predicatores impedirent.[2]

(In Paris in the year of our Lord 1254, this heretical

---

[1] *Gesch. der Präger Univers. Bibliothek.*, Prague, 1851, viii., 8 and 9.

[2] Denis, part ii., p. 1262.

book was openly given to the scribes to be copied. Whence it is evident what manner of doctrine would now be set forth to the public had not good priests and preachers interfered.)

Kirchhoff is of the opinion that there began to be at this time in connection with the work of the contemporary authors a kind of publishing arrangement under which the author handed over to the *stationarii* or to the *librarii* his literary production for multiplication and for publication, either through renting, through sale, or in both methods. He finds in the manuscript of a tract by Gerson, which was given to the public in the year 1417, a notice to the effect that this was published in Paris under the instructions of the author and under the license of Magister Johannus, Cancellarius.[1]

The work of the manuscript-dealers was carried on in booths or shops in various open places, but as a rule in the immediate neighbourhood of the churches. Certain booths were to be found, however, on the bridges and by the courts of justice ; and a neighbourhood particularly resorted to by the booksellers was the Rue Neuve Notre Dame, where, in the year 1292, out of eight licensed booksellers, no less than three had their work-shops. On the bridge Neuf Notre Dame, there were at the time of its falling, in 1499, a number of booksellers, three of whom are recorded as having lost their stock through the accident. The places selected by the earlier dealers in manuscripts became later the centre of the Parisian trade in printed books.

As a result of their membership in the university, the dealers in manuscripts shared in the exemption from the taxation enjoyed by the university body. The royal tax collectors persisted, however, from time to time in ignoring this right of exemption, and it was therefore necessary at different periods to secure fresh enactments

[1] Denis, part ii., p. 1285, quoted by Kirchhoff, p. 71.

from the royal ordinances in order to confirm the privilege. An example of such an ordinance is that issued by Philip the Fair, in 1307. In the cases in which the university placed an impost upon its members for any special purpose, the manuscript dealers were, of course, obliged to assume their share of such impost. At the time of their acceptance as official or licensed dealers, they had to pay a fee, in the first place of four sous, but after 1467 of eight sous. For the privilege of keeping an open shop, the fee was twenty-four sous. A further fee of eight sous was payable for each apprentice, and a weekly payment of twelve deniers payable for each workman. These fees went into the treasury of the booksellers' corporation.

After 1456, under the enactment of the congregation of the university, each manuscript dealer and paper dealer was called upon to pay to the Rector of the university at the time of his acceptance and license a *scutum* of gold.

The four *taxatores*, the officials charged with the supervision of the fees for the booksellers' guild (usually the four senior or most important members of the guild), were also charged with the selection or approval of new members and with the supervision of the proper carrying out of the various regulations controlling the organisations of the guild. In the earlier period of the work, such censorship as was found necessary concerning the books to be published was exercised through these four taxators. They were also the official representative body of the university guild.

In case any member of the guild suffered injury from unauthorised competition, the guild had the power to suspend the business operation with the person charged with committing the injury, until the complaint could be passed upon. In case the rules of the corporation had been broken, the corporation appears to have had the power, at least up to the beginning of the fifteenth century, of withdrawing the trade privilege or license.

The taxators or *principales jurati*, as they were sometimes called, had power to proceed not only to supervise
the business undertaking of the members of the guild,
but were also authorised to take measures against the outside or unlicensed booksellers and to proceed, if necessary,
even to the point of seizure and confiscation of their
goods. In carrying out such measures, they were empowered to call upon the university bedels for co-operation.

These unlicensed dealers or book pedlars, as they increased in numbers, naturally attempted to withdraw
themselves from the jurisdiction and supervision of the
university authorities. An ordinance of Charles VI.,
dated June 20, 1411, confirms specifically the right of
control over the entire book-trade, and prohibits pedlars,
dealers, hucksters, etc., from taking part in the selling of
manuscripts, " of which business they could have no
understanding." The edict went on to specify that the
carrying on of the book business by ignorant and irresponsible dealers not only caused injury to the licensed
book-dealers, but was a wrong upon the public, in that
it furthered the circulation of incorrect, incomplete, and
fraudulent manuscripts. This ordinance was doubtless
issued at the instance of the book-dealers' guild, but it is
evident that it was not strictly carried out, as from year
to year there are renewed complaints of the competition
of these ignorant and irresponsible book pedlars.

It was considered important, in order to insure the
proper control by the university over the book-trade and
the interests of the scholars who depended upon the book-
dealers for their text-books, that the trade in the materials
used in the manifolding of books should also be strictly
supervised. The special purpose of the university authorities was to prevent any " cornering of the market " in
parchment, and to insure that the supply of this should
be regular and uniform in price.

Under the ordinance of 1291, the dealers in parchment

were forbidden to keep any secret stores of the same, but were obliged to keep on file with the managers of the book guild the record of the stock carried by them from month to month. The parchment-dealers licensed to do business in Paris were forbidden to sell parchment to dealers from outside of Paris. On the first day of the Trade Fair, when foreign dealers brought parchment to Paris for sale, the Parisian dealers were forbidden themselves to make purchases, this day being reserved for such purchases as the university officials might desire to make. In case, after the first day of the Fair, a foreign dealer in parchment had before him more applications for his stock than could be supplied, and among the applicants there should be one representing the university, the latter was to be served first. Outside of the time of the official Fair, the Paris dealers in parchment were allowed to make purchases of their material only in the monastery of S. Mathurin.

In case between the times of the Fair a foreign dealer or manufacturer of parchment came to Paris, he was obliged to place his stock in this same monastery and to give information concerning this deposit to the Rector of the university. The Rector sent a representative to examine and to schedule the parchment, and the stock was priced by four of the licensed parchment-dealers associated with the university. The university authorities had then for twenty-four hours the first privilege of purchase. This regulation was applied also to the parchment-trade carried on at the Fair of St. Germain.

It is evident from the many renewed edicts and ordinances referring to this trade that it was not easy to carry out such regulations effectively, and that much friction and dissatisfaction was produced by them. It seems probable also that, with the trade in parchment as in other trades, the attempt to secure uniformity of price, irrespective of the conditions of manufacture or of the

market, had the effect not infrequently of lessening the
supply and of causing sales to be made surreptitiously at
increased prices.

After the use of parchment had in large part been replaced by paper made of linen, the supplies of Paris came
principally from Lombardy.   Later, however, paper-mills
were erected in France, the first being at Troyes and
Esson.   These earlier paper manufacturers were, like the
book-dealers in Paris, made free from tax.   This exemption was contested from time to time by the farmers of
the taxes and had to be renewed by successive ordinances.   Later, the university associated with its body, in
the same manner as had been done with the parchment-
dealers, the manufacturers and dealers in paper, and confirmed them in the possession of the privileges previously
enjoyed by the *librarii* and *stationarii*.   The privileges
of the paper manufacturers extended, however, outside
of Paris, which was, of course, not the case with the
librarii.

While, in connection with the requirements of the university and the special privileges secured through university membership, the book-trade of Paris and the trades
associated with it secured a larger measure of importance
as compared with the trade of the provinces than was the
case in either Italy or Germany, there came into existence
as early as the middle of the fourteenth century a considerable trade in manuscripts in various provincial centres.

In Montpellier, the university was, as in Paris, a centre
for publishing undertakings, but in Angers, Rouen, Orleans, and Toulouse, in which there are various references
to book-dealers as early as the beginning of the fourteenth
century, the trade must have been supported by a public
largely outside of the university organisation.   The statutes of Orleans and of Toulouse, dating from 1341, regulate
the supervision of the trade in manuscripts.

In Montpellier, there appears to have been, during the

beginning of the fourteenth century, a business in the loaning of the manuscripts and of manuscript *hefts—pecias*, similar to that already described in Bologna. The university authorities, usually the bedels, supervised the correctness of the *pecias* and prescribed the prices at which they should be rented. The *stationarii* who carried on this business and also the *venditores librorum* were members of the university body. The sale of books on commission was also supervised under regulations similar to those obtaining in Bologna.

No *stationarius* was at liberty to dispose of a work placed in his hands for sale (unless it belonged to a foreigner) until it had been exposed in his shop for at least six days, and had at least been three times offered for sale publicly in the auditorium. This offering for sale was cared for by the *banquerii*, who were the assistants or tenants of the rectors. These *banquerii* were also authorised to carry on the business of the loaning of *pecias* under the same conditions as those that controlled the *stationarii*. They were also at liberty, after the close of the term lectures, to sell their own supplies of manuscripts (usually of course the copies of the official texts) at public auction in the auditorium.

It is difficult to understand how, with a trade, of necessity, limited in extent, and the possible profits of which were so closely restricted by regulations, there could have been a living profit sufficient to tempt educated dealers to take up the work of the *stationarii* or *librarii*.

It is probably the case, as Kirchhoff, Savigny, and others point out, that the actual results of the trade cannot be ascertained with certainty from the texts of the regulations, and that there were various ways in which, in spite of these regulations, larger returns could be secured for the work of the scholarly and enterprising *librarii*.

An ordinance issued in 1411 makes reference to booksellers buying and selling books both in French or in

Latin and gives privilege to licensed booksellers to do such buying and selling at their pleasure. This seems to have been an attempt to widen the range of the book-trade, while reference to books in the vernacular indicates an increasing demand for literature outside of the circles of instructors and students.

In the beginning of the fifteenth century, there was, among a number of the nobles of families in France, a certain increase in the interest of literature and in the taste for collecting elaborate, ornamented, and costly manuscripts.

The princely Houses of Burgundy and of Orleans are to be noted in this connection, and particularly in Burgundy, the influence of the ducal family was of wide importance in furthering the development of the trade in manuscripts and the production of literature.

A large number of the manuscripts placed in these ducal family libraries were evidently originally prepared by scribes having knowledge only of plain script, and the addition of the initial letters and of the illuminated head and tail pieces was made later by illuminators and designers attached to the ducal families. It was to these latter that fell the responsibility of placing upon the manuscripts the arms of the owners of the libraries. In case manuscripts which had been inscribed with family arms came to change hands, it became necessary to replace these arms with those of the later purchaser, and many of the illuminated manuscripts of the period give evidence of such changing of the decorations, decorations which took the place of the book-plate of to-day.

The taste for these elaborate illuminated manuscripts, each one of which, through the insertion of individual designs and of the family arms, became identified with the personality and taste of its owner, could not easily be set aside, after the middle of the fifteenth century, by the new art of printing. As a matter of fact, therefore, it not infrequently happened, towards the latter part of the fifteenth century, that these noble collectors caused elaborate transcripts to be made, by hand, of works which were already in print, rather than to place in their own collection books in the form in which ordinary buyers could secure them.

By the year 1448, the number of certified *librarii* in Paris had increased to twenty-four.[1] Kirchhoff is of opinion that a certain portion at least of these *librarii* carried on also other trades, but it is evident that there had come to be in these years, immediately preceding the introduction of the printing-press, a very considerable development in the demand for literature and in the book-trade of the capital.

In 1489, the list of book-dealers and of those connected with the manufacture of books who were exempt from taxation included twenty-four *librarii*, four dealers in parchment, four dealers in paper, seven paper manufacturers (having mills outside of Paris), two illuminators, two binders, and two licensed scribes.

In the following year, the list of *librarii* free from taxation was reduced to seventeen. It is probable that those *librarii* whose names had been taken off the exemption list undertook a general book business carried on outside of the university regulations, and were probably able to secure returns more than sufficient to offset the loss caused by the curtailing of their freedom from taxation and of their university privileges.

This reduction in the number of manuscript-dealers who remained members of the corporation was, however, very promptly made up by including in the corporation the newly introduced printers. As early as 1476, one of the four officials of the guild was the printer Pasquier Bonhomme.

The cessation of the work of the scribes and the transfer of the book-trade from their hands to those of the printers

[1] Chevillier, 336.

took place gradually after the year 1470, the printers being, as said, promptly included in the organisation of the guild. There must, however, have been, during the earlier years at least, not a little rivalry and bitterness between the two groups of dealers.

An instance of this rivalry is given in 1474, in which year a *librarius juratus*, named Herman von Stathoen (by birth a German), died. According to the university regulation, his estate, valued at 800 crowns of gold, (there being no heirs in the country) should have fallen to the university treasury. In addition to this property in Paris, Stathoen was part owner of a book establishment in Mayence, carried on by Schöffer & Henckis, and was unpopular with the Paris dealers generally on the ground of his foreign trade connections.

Contention was made on behalf of the Crown that the property in Paris should be confiscated to the royal treasury, and as Schöffer & Henckis were subjects of the Duke of Burgundy, whose relations with Louis XI. might be called strained, the influence of the Court was decidedly in favour of the appropriation of any business interest that they might have in their partner's property in Paris. In the contention between the university and the Crown, the latter proved the stronger, and the bookseller's 800 crowns were confiscated for the royal treasury, and at least got so far towards the treasury as the hands of the chancellor.

As a further result of the issue which had been raised, it was ordered on the part of the Crown that thereafter no foreigner should have a post as an official of the university or should be in a position to lay claim to the exemption and the privileges attaching to such post.

While in Paris the manuscript-dealers had been promptly driven from the field through the competition of the printers, in Rouen they held their own for a considerable term of years. The space which had been assigned to the *librarii* for their shops at the chief doorway of the cathedral, continued to be reserved for them as late as 1483, and the booksellers keeping on sale the printed books, were forbidden to have any shops at this end of the cathedral, but were permitted to put up, at their own cost, stalls at the north doorway.

The oldest Paris bookseller whose name has been placed on record is described as Herneis le Romanceur. He had his shop at the entrance to Notre Dame. His inscription appeared in a beautiful manuscript presenting a French translation of the Code of Justinian, a manuscript dating from the early part of the thirteenth century. It is possible that Guillaume Herneis, whose name appeared in the tax list of 1292 with a rate of ten livres, was the scribe and the publisher of the above manuscript, but if this were the case he must have been at the time of this tax rating well advanced in years.[1]   In 1274, the name of Hugichio le Lombard appears recorded on several manuscripts which have been preserved in existing collections. In the taxes of 1292, appears the name of Agnien, *Libraire*, in the Rue de la Boucherie, assessed for thirty-six sous. The tax is too large to make it probable that Agnien was a mere pedlar or did business from an open stall, and it is Géraud's opinion that he was charged probably as a university bookseller to whom the tax collector had refused the exemption belonging to university members.[2]

In the year 1303, the stock of books of a certain Antoine Zeno, *libraire juré*, was scheduled for taxation. Among the titles included in this schedule are the commentaries or lectures of Bruno on S. Matthew (57 pages, price one sol), the same on Mark, Luke, and John, the commentaries of Alexander on Matthew, the *Opera Fratris Richardi*, the *Legenda Sanctorum*, various texts of the

[1] Adrian, J. V., *Catalogus Codd. MSS. Biblioth. Acad. Gissensis*, 1840, iv., 276–278.

[2] Géraud, p. 175.

Decretals, commentaries of S. Bernard on the Decretals,
a treatise of a certain Thomas on metaphysics, on physics, on the heavens and the earth, and on the soul, and a
series of lectures on ethics, and on politics. The scheduled price ranged from one sol to eight sols, the latter
being the price of a manuscript of 136 pages. The books
were probably confined exclusively to texts used in the
university work.[1]

In 1313, appears in the tax list, assessed for twelve sous,
the name of Nicholas L'Anglois, bookseller and tavern-
keeper in Rue St. Jacques.

It is to be noted that the booksellers, and for that
matter the traders generally of the time, are frequently
distinguished by the names of their native countries. It
is probable that Nicholas failed to escape taxation as a
bookseller because he was also carrying on business (and
doubtless a more profitable business) in his tavern. The
list of 1313 includes in fact but three booksellers, and
each of these is described as having an additional trade.[2]

A document of the year 1332 describes a sale made by
a certain Geoffroy de Saint Léger, a *clerc libraire*, to
Gérard de Montagu, *avocat du roy au parlement*. Geoffroy acknowledges to have sold, ceded, assigned, and
delivered to the said Gérard a book entitled *Speculum Historiale in Consuetudines Parisienses*, comprised in four
volumes, and bound in red leather. He guarantees the
validity of this sale with his own body, *de son corps mesme*.
Gérard pays for the book the sum of forty Parisian livres,
with which sum Geoffroy declares himself to be content,
and paid in full.[3] It appears that the sale of a book in
the fourteenth century was a solemn transaction, calling
for documentary evidence as specific as in the case of the
transfer of real estate.

---

[1] Bulæus, iv., 62.

[2] *Chronique Métrique de Godefroy de Paris*, Buchon, Paris, 1827, viii., 167.

[3] De La Caille, *Histoire de l'Imprimerie*, Paris, 1689, iv., 5.

In the year 1376, Jean de Beauvais, a *librarius juratus*, is recorded as having sold various works, including the Decretals of Gregory IX., illustrated with miniatures, a copy of *Summa Hostiensis*, 423 parchment leaves, illustrated with miniatures, and a codex of Magister Thomas de Maalaa.[1]

In the year 1337, Guidomarus de Senis, master of arts and *librarius juratus*, renews his oath as a taxator. He seems to have put into his business as bookseller a certain amount of literary gaiety, if one may judge from the lines added at the end of a parchment codex sold by him, which codex contains the poems of Guillaume de Marchaut.

The lines are as follows:

> *Explicit au mois d'avril,*
> *Qui est gai, cointe et gentil,*
> *L'an mil trois cent soixante et onze.*
> *D'Avril la semaine seconde,*
> *Acheva à un vendredi,*
> *Guiot de Sens c'est livre si,*
> *Et le comansa de sa main,*
> *Et ne fina ne soir ne matin,*
> *Tant qu'il eut l'œuvre accomplie,*
> *Louée soit la vierge Marie.*[2]

Philip the Bold, Duke of Burgundy, was one of the more important book collectors of his time. In 1386, the Duke paid to Martin L'Huillier, dealer in manuscripts and bookbinder, sixteen francs for binding eight books, six of which were bound in grain leather.[3] The Duke of Orleans also appears as a buyer of books, and in 1394, he paid to Jehan de Marsan, master of arts and dealer in manuscripts, twenty francs in gold for the *Letters of S. Pol*, bound in figured silk, and illuminated with the arms of the Duke.

[1] Garnier, 275.　　[2] Bulæus, iv., 449.　　[3] Lalanne, 307.

Four years later, the Duke makes another purchase,
paying to Jehan one hundred *livres tournois* for a Con-
cordance to the Bible in Latin, an illuminated manuscript
bound in red leather, stamped.

The same Duke, in 1394, paid forty gold crowns to
Olivier, one of the four principal *librarii*, for a Latin text
of the Bible, bound in red leather, and in 1396, this persistent ducal collector pays sixty livres to a certain Jacques
Jehan, who is recorded as a grocer, but who apparently included books in his stock, for the *Book of the Treasury*, a
book of Julius Cæsar, a book of the King, *The Secret of
Secrets*, and a book of Estrille Fauveau, bound in one
volume, illuminated, and bearing the arms of the Duke
of Lancaster.   Another volume included in this purchase
was the *Romance of the Rose*, and the *Livres des Eschez*,
" moralised," and bound together in one volume, illuminated in gold and azure. [1]

In 1399, appears on the records the name of Dyne, or
Digne Rapond, a Lombard.   Kirchhoff speaks of Rapond's book business as being with him a side issue. Like
Atticus, the publisher of Cicero, Rapond's principal business interest was that of banking, in which the Lombards
were at that time pre-eminent throughout Europe.   In
connection with his banking, however, he accepted orders
from noble clients and particularly from the Duke of
Burgundy, for all classes of articles of luxury, among
which were included books.

In 1399, Rapond delivered to Philip of Burgundy, for
the price of five hundred livres, a *Livy* illuminated with
letters of gold and with images, and for six thousand
francs a work entitled *La Propriété de Choses*. A document, bearing date 1397, states that Charles, King of
France, is bound to Dyne Rapond, merchant of Paris,
for the sum of 190 francs of gold, for certain pieces of
tapestry, for certain shirts, and for four great volumes

[1] *Bibli. de l'École de Chartres*, v., 67.

containing the chronicles of France.   He is further bound
in the sum of ninety-two francs for some more shirts, for
a manuscript of Seneca, for the Chronicles of Charlemagne,
for the Chronicles of Pepin, for the Chronicles of Godefroy de Bouillon, the latter for his dear elder son Charles,
Dauphin.   The King further purchases certain hats,
handkerchiefs, and some more books, for which he in-
structs his treasurer in Paris to pay over to said Rapond
the sum of ninety francs in full settlement of his account;
the document is signed on behalf of the King by his
secretary at his château of Vincennes.[1]

Jacques Rapond, merchant and citizen of Paris, probably a brother of Dyne, also seems to have done a profitable business with Philip of Burgundy, as he received
from Philip, for a Bible in French, 9000 francs, and in the
same year (1400), for a copy of *The Golden Legend*, 7500
francs.

Nicholas Flamel, scribe and *librarius juratus*, flourished
at the beginning of the thirteenth century.   He was
shrewd enough, having made some little money at work
as a bookseller and as a school manager, to carry on some
successful speculations in house building, from which
speculations he made money so rapidly that he was ac-
cused of dealings with the Evil One.   One of the houses
built by him in Rue Montmorency was still standing in
1853, an evidence of what a clever publisher might accomplish even in the infancy of the book business.

The list of booksellers between the years 1486–1490
includes the name of Jean Bonhomme, the name which
has for many years been accepted as typical of the
French bourgeois.   This particular Bonhomme seems,
however, to have been rather a distinctive man of his
class.   He calls himself "bookseller to the university,"
and was a dealer both in manuscripts and in printed
books.   On a codex of a French translation of *The City*

[1] Kirchhoff, 100.

of God, by S. Augustine, is inscribed the record of the
sale of the manuscript by Jean Bonhomme, bookseller to
the University of Paris, who acknowledges having sold
to the honoured and wise citizen, Jehan Cueillette, treasurer of M. de Beaujeu, this book containing *The City
of God*, in two volumes, and Bonhomme guarantees to
Cueillette the possession of said work against all.   His
imprint as a bookseller appears upon various printed
books, including the *Constitutiones Clementinæ*, the *Decreta
Basiliensia*, and the *Manuale Confessorum* of Joh. Nider.

Among the cities of France outside of Paris in which
there is record of early manuscript-dealers, are Tours,
Angers, Lille, Troyes, Rouen, Toulouse, and Montpellier.
In Lille, in 1435, the principal bookseller was Jaquemart
Puls, who was also a goldsmith, the latter being probably
his principal business.   In Toulouse, a bookseller of the
name of S. Julien was in business as early as 1340.   In
Troyes, in the year 1500, Macé Panthoul was carrying on
business as a bookseller and as a manufacturer of paper.
In connection with his paper-trade, he came into rela-
tions with the book-dealers of Paris.

Manuscript Dealers in Germany.—The information
concerning the early book-dealers in Germany is more
scanty, and on the whole less interesting, than that which
is available for the history of bookselling in Italy or in
France.   There was less wealth among the German nobles during the fourteenth and fifteenth centuries, and
fewer among the nobles who had means were interested
in literary luxuries than was the case in either France,
Burgundy, or Italy.

As has been noted in the preceding division of this
chapter, the references to the more noteworthy of the
manuscript-dealers in France occur almost entirely in
connection with sales made by them to the members of
the Royal Family, to the Dukes of Burgundy, or to other
of the great nobles.   The beautifully illuminated manu-

script which carried the coat-of-arms or the crest of the
noble for whom it was made, included also, as a rule, the
inscription of the manuscript-dealer by whom the work
of its preparation had been carried on or supervised, and
through whom it had been sold to the noble purchaser.
Of the manuscripts of this class, the record in Germany
is very much smaller.   Germany also did not share the
advantages possessed by Italy, of close relations with the
literature and the manuscript stores of the East, relations
which proved such an important and continued source of
inspiration for the intellectual life of the Italian scholars.

The influence of the revival of the knowledge of Greek
literature came to Germany slowly through its relations
with Italy, but in the knowledge of Greek learning and
literature the German scholars were many years behind
their Italian contemporaries, while the possession of
Greek manuscripts in Germany was, before the middle of
the fifteenth century, very exceptional indeed.   The
scholarship of the earlier German universities appears
also to have been narrower in its range and more restricted in its cultivation than that which had been developed in Paris, in Bologna, or in Padua.   The membership
of the Universities of Prague and of Vienna, the two oldest
in the German list, was evidently restricted almost entirely to Germans, Bohemians, Hungarians, etc., that is
to say, to the races immediately controlled by the German Empire.

If a scholar of England were seeking, during the fourteenth and fifteenth centuries, special instruction or
special literary and scholarly advantages, his steps were
naturally directed towards Paris for theology, Bologna
for jurisprudence, and Padua for medicine, and but few
of these travelling English scholars appear to have taken
themselves to Prague, Vienna, or Heidelberg.

In like manner, if English book collectors were seeking
manuscripts, they betook themselves to the dealers in

Paris, in Florence, or in Venice, and it was not until after
the manuscript-trade had been replaced by the trade in
the productions of the printing-press that the German
cities can be said to have become centres for the distribution of literature.

Such literary interests as obtained in Germany during
the fourteenth century, outside of those of the monasteries already referred to, centred nevertheless about the
universities. The oldest of these universities was that of
Prague, which was founded in 1347, more than a century
later than the foundations of Paris and Bologna. The
regulations of the University recognised the existence of
scribes, illuminators, correctors, binders, dealers in parchment, etc., all of which trades were placed under the
direct control of the university authorities.

Hauslik speaks of the book-trade in the fourteenth
century as being associated with the work of the library
of the university, and refers to licensed scribes and illuminators, who were authorised to make transcripts, for
the use of the members of the university, of the texts
contained in the library.[1]

If we may understand from this reference that the university authorities had had prepared for the library authenticated copies of the texts of the works required in the
university courses, and that the transcribing of these texts
was carried on under the direct supervision of the librarians, Prague appears to have possessed a better system
for the preparation of its official texts than we have record
of in either Bologna or Paris. Hauslik goes on to say
that the entire book-trade of the city was placed under
the supervision of the library authorities, which authorities undertook to guarantee the completeness and the
correctness of all transcripts made from the texts in the
library. Kirchhoff presents in support of this theory
examples of one or two manuscripts, which contain, in

[1] *Gesch. der Prager Univ. Biblioth.*, Prague, 1851, p. 24.

addition to the inscription of the name of the scribe or dealer by whom it had been prepared, the record of the corrector appointed by the library to certify to the correctness of the text.[1]

The second German university in point of date was that of Vienna, founded in 1365, and, in connection with the work of this university the manuscript-trade in Germany took its most important development.   There is record in Vienna of the existence of *stationarii* who carried on, under the usual university supervision, the trade of hiring out *pecias*, but this was evidently a much less important function than in Bologna.

The buying and selling of books in Vienna was kept under very close university supervision, and without the authority of the rector or of the bedels appointed by him for the purpose, no book could be purchased from either a *magister* or a student, or could be accepted on pledge.

The books which had been left by deceased members of the university were considered to be the property of the university authorities, and could be sold only under their express directions.   The commission allowed by the authorities for the sale of books was limited to 2½ per cent., and before any books could be transferred at private sale, they must be offered at public sale in the auditorium. The purpose of this regulation was apparently here as in Paris not only to insure securing for the books sold the highest market prices, but also to give some protection against the possibility of books being sold by those to whom they did not belong.

The regulation of the details of the book business appears to have fallen gradually into the hands of the bedels of the Faculty, and the details of the supervision exercised approach more nearly to the Italian than to the Parisian model.

The third German university was that of Heidelberg,

[1] Kirch., p. 112.

founded in 1386. Here the regulations concerning the book-trade were substantially modelled upon those of Paris. The scribes and the dealers in manuscripts belonged to the privileged members of the university. The provisions in the foundation or charter of the university, which provided for the manuscript-trade, make express reference to the precedents of the University of Paris.

By the middle of the fifteenth century, there appears to have been a considerable trade in manuscripts in Heidelberg and in places dependent upon Heidelberg. In the library of the University of Erlangen, there exists to-day a considerable collection of manuscripts formerly belonging to the monastery of Heilsbronn, which manuscripts were prepared in Heidelberg between 1450 and 1460. The series includes a long list of classics, indicating a larger classical interest in Heidelberg than was to be noted at the time in either Prague or Vienna.[1]

The University of Cologne, founded a few years later, became the centre of theological scholarship in Germany, and the German manuscripts of the early part of the fifteenth century which have remained in existence and which have to do with theological subjects were very largely produced in Cologne. A number of examples of these have been preserved in the library of Erfurt.

One reason for the smaller importance in Germany of the *stationarius* was the practice that obtained on the part of the instructors of lecturing or of reading from texts for dictation, the transcripts being made by the students themselves. The authority or permission to read for dictation was made a matter of special university regulation. The regulation provided what works could be so utilised, and the guarantee as to the correctness of the texts to be used could either be given by a member of the faculty of the university itself or was accepted with the certified

[1] Kirch., p. 114.

signature of an instructor of a well known foreign university, such as Paris, Bologna, or Oxford.

By means of this system of dictation, the production of manuscripts was made much less costly than through the work of the *stationarii*, and the dictation system was probably an important reason why the manuscript-trade in the German university cities never became so important as in Paris or London.

It is contended by the German writers that, notwithstanding the inconsiderable trade in manuscripts, there was a general knowledge of the subject-matter of the literature pursued in the university, no less well founded or extended among the German cities than among those of France or Italy. This familiarity with the university literature is explained by the fact that the students had, through writing at dictation, so largely possessed themselves of the substance of the university lectures.

In the Faculty of Arts at Ingolstadt, it was ordered, in 1420, that there should be not less than one text-book (that is to say, one copy of the text-book) for every three scholars in baccalaureate. This regulation is an indication of the scarcity of text-books.

The fact that the industry in loaning manuscripts to students was not well developed in the German universities delayed somewhat the organisation of the book-trade in the university towns. Nevertheless, Richard de Bury names Germany among the countries where books could be purchased, and Gerhard Groote speaks of purchasing books in Frankfort. This city became, in fact, important in the trade of manuscripts for nearly a century before the beginning of German printing.[1]

Æneas Silvius says in the preface of his *Europa*, written in 1458, that a *librarius teutonicus* had written to him shortly before, asking him to prepare a continuation of

[1] Delprat, *Verhandlung over de Broederschop van G. Groote*, Amsterdam, 1858.

the book *Augustalis*."[1] This publishing suggestion was
made eight years after the perfection of Gutenberg's
printing-press, but probably without any knowledge on
the part of the *librarius* of the new method for the production of books.

In Germany there was, during the thirteenth and fourteenth centuries, outside of the ecclesiastics, very little
demand for reading matter. The women had their psalters, which had, as a rule, been written out in the monasteries. As there came to be a wider demand for books of
worship, this was provided for, at least in the regions
of the lower Rhine, by the scribes among the Brothers
of Common Life. The Brothers took care also of the
production of a large proportion of the school-books
required.

During the fourteenth century and the first half of the
fifteenth, the Brothers took an active part in the production and distribution of manuscripts. Their work was
distinct in various respects from that which was carried
on in monastery or in university towns, but particularly
in this that their books were, for the most part, produced
in the tongue of the common folk, and their service as
instructors and booksellers was probably one of the most
important influences in helping to educate the lower
classes of North Germany to read and to think for themselves. They thus prepared the way for the work of
Luther and Melanchthon.

As has been noted in another chapter, the activity of
the Brothers in the distribution of literature did not cease
when books in manuscripts were replaced by the productions of the printing-press. They made immediate use of
the invention of Gutenberg, and in many parts of Germany, the first printed books that were brought before the
people came from the printing-presses of the Brothers.

Some general system of public schools seems to have

[1] Wattenbach, 476.

taken shape in the larger cities at least of North Germany as early as the first half of the thirteenth century. The teachers in these schools themselves added to their work and to their earnings by transcribing text-books and sometimes works of worship. Later, there came to be some extended interest in certain classes of literature among a few of the princes and noblemen, but this appears to have been much less the case in Germany than in Italy or even than in France. In the castles or palaces where there was a chaplain, the chaplain took upon himself the work of a scribe, caring not only for the correspondence of his patron, but occasionally also preparing manuscripts for the library, so called, of the castle. There is also record of certain *stadtschreiber*, or public scribes, licensed as such in the cities of North Germany, and in some cases the post was held by the instructors of the schools.

Ulrich Friese, a citizen of Augsburg, writing in the latter half of the fourteenth century, speaks of attending the Nordlingen Fair with parchment and books. Nordlingen Church was, it appears, used for the purpose of this fair, and in Lübeck, in the Church of S. Mary, booths were opened in which, together with devotional books, school-books and writing materials were offered for sale.

In Hamburg also, the courts in the immediate neighbourhood of the churches were the places selected by the earlier booksellers and manuscript-dealers for their trade. In Metz, a book-shop stood immediately in front of the cathedral, and in Vienna, the first book-shop was placed in the court adjoining the cathedral of S. Stephen. Nicolaus, who was possibly the earliest bookseller in Erfurt, had his shop, in 1460, in the court of the Church of the Blessed Virgin.

From a school regulation of Bautzen, written in 1418, it appears that the children were instructed to purchase their school-books from the master at the prices fixed in

the official schedule.[1] A certain schoolmaster in Hagenau, whose work was carried on between 1443 and 1450,
has placed his signature upon a considerable series of
manuscripts, which he claims to have prepared with his
own hands, and which were described in Wilken's History
of the library in Heidelberg. His name was Diebold
Läber, or, as he sometimes wrote it, Lauber, and he describes himself as a writer, *schreiber*, in the town of Hagenau. This inscription appears in so many manuscripts
that have been preserved, that some doubt has been
raised as to whether they could be all the work of one
hand, or whether Lauber's name (imprint, so to speak)
may not have been utilised by other scribes possibly
working in association with him.[2]

Lauber speaks of having received from Duke Ruprecht
an order for seven books, and as having arranged to have
the manuscripts painted (decorated or illuminated) by
some other hand. Lauber is recorded as having been
first a school-teacher and an instructor in writing, later a
scribe, producing for sale copies of standard texts, and
finally a publisher, employing scribes, simply certifying
with his own signature to the correctness of the work of
his subordinates. There is every indication that he had
actually succeeded in organising in Hagenau, as early as
1443, an active business in the production and distribution of manuscripts. The books produced by him were
addressed more generally to the popular taste than was
the case with the productions of the monastery scribes.

In part, possibly, as a result of this early activity in the
production of books, one of the first printing-presses in
Germany, outside of that of Gutenberg in Mayence, was
instituted in Hagenau, and its work appears to have been
in direct succession to that of the public writer Lauber.

The relations between Hagenau and Heidelberg were

---

[1] Wattenbach, 478.
[2] Haupt, in *Der Zeitschrift f. Deutsches Alterthum*, iii., 191.

intimate, and the scholarly service of the members of the university was utilised by the Hagenau publishers. The book-trade of Hagenau also appears to have been increased in connection with the development of intellectual activity given by the Councils of Constance and Basel. In regard to the latter Council, Kirchhoff quotes Denis as having said:

Quod concilium, qui scholam librariorum dixerit haud errabit. [1]

Either as a cause or as an effect of the activity of the book production in Hagenau, the Hagenau schools for scribes during the first half of the fifteenth century became famous.[2] The work of producing manuscripts appears to have been divided, according to the manufacturing system; one scribe prepared the text, a second collated the same with the original, a third painted in the rubricated initials, and a fourth designed the painted headpieces to the pages, while a fifth prepared the ornamented covers. It occasionally happened, however, that one scribe was himself able to carry on each division of the work of the production of an illuminated manuscript.

Hagen quotes some lines of a Hagenau manuscript, as follows:

> *Dis buch vollenbracht vas,*
> *In der zit, also man schreip vnd las,*
> *Tusent vnd vyer hundert jar.*
> *Nach Christus gebort daz ist war,*
> *Dar nach jn dem eyn vnd siebentzigsten jar,*
> *Vff sant Pauly bekarung, daz ist ware,*
> *Von Hans Dirmsteyn, wist vor war,*
> *Der hait es geschreben vnd gemacht,*
> *Gemalt, gebunden, vnd gantz follenbracht.*[3]

Hagenau was one of the few places of book production

[1] Denis, ii., 2144. Cited by Kirchhoff, 131.
[2] Mone, *Zeitschrift f. Gesch. d. Oberrheins*, i., 312.
[3] *Litterar. Grundiss. zur Gesch. d. Deutsch. Poesie*, Berlin, 1812, 307.

(excepting the workshops of the Brothers of Common Life) in which, during the manuscript period, books were prepared to meet the requirements of the common folk. The literature proceeding from Hagenau included not only "good Latin books," that is to say, copies of the accepted classics as used in Heidelberg and elsewhere, but also copies of the famous Epics of the Middle Ages, the Sagas, Folk Songs, Chap-Books, copies of the Golden Bull, Bible stories, books of worship, books of popular music, books of prophecy, and books for the telling of fortunes, etc.[1]

Throughout both Germany and the Low Countries, it was the case that, during the manuscript period, the work of the school teachers was closely connected with the work of the producers and sellers of manuscripts, and the teachers not infrequently themselves built up a manuscript business. The school ordinance of the town of Bautzen, dating from the year 1418, prescribed, for example, the prices which the scholars were to pay to the *locatus* (who was the fifth teacher in rank in the institution) for the school-books, the responsibility for preparing which rested upon him.

A history of the Printers' Society of Dresden, printed in 1740, gives examples of some of these prices:

For one *A. B. C.* and a paternoster, each one groschen.

For a *Corde Benedicite*, one groschen.

For a good *Donat*, ten groschens.

For a *Regulam Moralem et Catonem*, eight groschens.

For a complete *Doctrinal*, a half mark.

For a *Primam Partem*, eight groschens.

In case no books are purchased from the *locatus*, there shall be paid to him by each scholar, if the scholar be rich, two groschens, if he be in moderate circumstances, one groschen, and if the scholar be poor, he shall be exempt from payment.[2]

[1] Kirchhoff, 119.   [2] Kirchhoff, 120.

A certain Hugo from Trimberg, who died about 1309, is referred to by Jaeck as having been a teacher for forty years, at the end of which term he gave up the work of teaching with the expectation of being able to make a living out of his collection of books. The collection comprised two hundred volumes, of which twelve are specified as being original works, presumably the production of Trimberg himself. Jaeck does not tell us whether or not the good schoolmaster was able to earn enough from the manifolding or from the sale of his books to secure a living in his last years.[1]

Kirchhoff refers to the importance of the fairs and annual markets for the manuscript trade. It is evident that, in the absence of any bookselling machinery, it was of first importance for the producers of copies of such texts as might be within their reach, to come into relations with each other in order to bring about the exchange of their surplus copies.

There is record of the sale and exchange of manuscripts, during the first half of the fifteenth century, at the Fairs of Salzburg, Ulm, Nordlingen, and Frankfort. It was in fact from its trade in manuscripts that Frankfort, by natural development, became and for many years remained the centre of the trade in printed books.[2] Ruland speaks of one of the most important items of the manuscript-trade at the Frankfort Fair between 1445 and 1450, being that of fortune-telling books and illustrated chap-books.

It appears also from the Fair records that in Germany, as in Italy, the dealers in parchment and paper were among the first to associate with their goods the sale of manuscripts. In 1470, occurs the earliest record of sales being made at the fair in Nordlingen of printed books.[3]

---

[1] *Gesch. d. Offentl. Bibliothek zu Bamberg*, Nurnberg, 1832, p. xvii.
[2] Kirch., 120.
[3] Kirch., 121.

The earliest date at which the sale of printed books at
the fair at Frankfort was chronicled was 1480. In 1485,
the printer Peter Schöffer was admitted as a citizen in
Frankfort.

While Kirchhoff maintains that the distribution of
books in manuscript was more extensive in Germany
than in either France or Italy, and emphasises particularly the fact that there was among circles throughout Germany a keener interest in literature than obtained
with either the French or the Italians, he admits that the
record of noteworthy booksellers in Germany, during the
manuscript period, is, as compared with that of France
and Italy, inconsiderable. In Cologne, he finds, as early
as 1389, through an inscription in a manuscript that has
been preserved, the name of Horstan de Ledderdam, who
called himself not a *librarius*, but a *libemarius*. The
manuscript that bears this record is a treatise by Por-
phyry on Aristotle.

In Nordlingen, the tax list of 1407 gives the name of
Joh. Minner, recorded as a *scriptor*. There is an entry
of a sale made by Minner to the Burgermeister Protzen
of a German translation of the *Decretals*. The tax list of
1415 gives the name of Conrad Horn, described as a
stadtschreiber. Horn seems to have carried on an extensive business in the production and the exchange of manuscripts. Kirchhoff quotes a contract entered into by him
in 1427 with a certain Prochsil of Eystet for the purchase
of a *buch*, the title of which is not given, for the sum of
forty-three Rhenish gulden.

The name of Diebold Lauber has already been mentioned. His inscription appears on a number of manuscripts that have been preserved principally through the
Heidelberg University. On the first sheet of a *Legend
of the Three Holy Kings* from this library, is written the
following notice, which can be considered as a general
advertisement:

Item welcher hande bücher man gerne hat, gross oder clein, geistlich oder weltlich, hübsch gemolt, die findet man alle by Diepold Lauber, schreiber in der burge zu hagenow.

Freely translated, this notice would read : " Any books that are desired, whether great or small, religious or profane, beautifully painted (adorned), all of these will one find by Diepold Lauber, scribe in the town of Hagenau." Among the manuscripts of Lauber, which have been preserved, is a beautiful copy of *Gesta Romanorum, mit den viguren gemolt*, a Bible in rhyme (*eine gerymete bibel, ein salter Latin und Tüstch*). Also a number of *gemolte losbücher* (illustrated fortune-telling books), etc.

In Heidelberg, the name of Wolff von Prunow, *bibliopola*, is recorded early in the fifteenth century, as associated with the university. In Bruges, in 1425, the list of manuscript-dealers is a more important one. It begins with Joorquin de Vüc, who is described as a cleric. He was bookseller to Duke Philip, and is spoken of by Labord as having had an extensive manuscript factory.[1] Colart Mansion has already been referred to. He is recorded in 1450 as an *escripvain*, but a few years later appears in the list of printers and is known as the friend and associate of Caxton. The books of Duke Philip of Burgundy include also the name of the bookseller Hocberque, in 1427, and that of Neste in 1423. In 1456, Morisses de Haat is recorded as an *escripvain de livres*, who rented out books. In order to do this, he must, as Kirchhoff points out, have carried some general stock. A certain Herr van Gruthuyse, a rich collector, of Bruges, bought a number of finely illuminated manuscripts from Jean Paradis, who was in 1470 made a member of the *librariers gild*.

Kirchhoff quotes a document dated 1346, the wording of which is in the form of a contract between Wou-

[1] Else, i., 242.

ters Vos and Jan Standard, described as manuscript-dealers, "parties of the first part," and a group of citizens, "parties of the second part." The contract has to do with the transfer of certain books as security for a loan. The list of the books includes copies of the Codex of Justinian, some essays on taxes, polities, and rhetoric, a work by Albertus, a treatise by Ægidius, the Physics of Aristotle, a commentary of Averrhoes, etc. These two dealers of Bruges seem to have had an important collection of literature for so early a period.

The manuscript-trade in the Netherlands was more important both in character and in extent than that carried on in Germany, and it had also a larger influence upon the general education of the people than the book-trade of the time in either France or Italy. In France and in Italy, the earlier book-trade was, as we have noted, connected principally with the work of the universities. In the Low Countries, on the other hand, particularly in such centres as Ghent, Antwerp, and Bruges, there came into existence, during the first half of the fifteenth century, an active and intelligently conducted business in the production of books both of a scholarly and of a popular character, the sale of which was made very largely among the citizens, outside of the university circles. One reason why the trade in books found a larger development in Belgium than in Germany, was the greater wealth of the trading class in the Low Countries. With the wealth, came cultivation and a taste for luxuries, and among luxuries soon came to be included art and literature.

As early as 1424, there was instituted a guild of publishers, *librariers gild*, in Ghent, and a year or two later one in Brussels. These guilds came into relations in 1450 with the St. Lucas Guild in Antwerp.

According to Kapp, the first evidences of an organised German trade in manuscripts are to be found at the beginning of the fifteenth century. He is, however, convinced that a very considerable exchange of literary material in manuscripts must have found place at a much earlier date. There came to be in the German towns and among the citzen class an earlier interest in literature than there is evidence of at this time in the same class of any other country of Europe. This demand for reading matter on the part of the citizen class brought into existence in Germany (at a time when in Italy, France, and England there were practically no books in other than the Latin language) a considerable mass of popular literature written in the vernacular, and copied out on cheap material in such way as to make possible a general circulation. This popular circulation of books written for the common folk was very much facilitated by the introduction into Germany, as early as the fourteenth century, of paper, which for the cheaper manuscripts took the place of the old-time parchment.

The Order of Brothers of Common Life carried on their literary work, so to speak, between the monasteries and the writers of the general lay community. They had for their first purpose the dissemination of sound doctrine, but as they were trying to give instruction direct to the common folk, they put their teachings into the dialect of the place, and they wrote out in their own monasteries the chap-books and instruction books which, at times distributed freely from the monastery centres, came to be very largely sold.

Their work lay between that of the monastery monks and that of the city scribes in another respect. As before indicated, the work of the scribes in the *scriptorium* was performed for no individual remuneration. If the manuscripts were sold or were exchanged for property of one kind or another, the benefit of the sale or exchange accrued to the monastery. On the other hand, the scribes of the cities, as they came to organise themselves into an accepted trade, arrived at a system of fixed charges for their work. The Brothers of Common Life, while living together in monkish centres, did not withdraw themselves from the life of the world, but made it their first duty, using their monastery homes simply as a starting-place or place of consultation or as centres of education, to go out into the highways and by-ways, teaching what they had to teach direct to the people whom they met; and as an important means of this instruction they used their facilities as scribes for manifolding the tracts and the scriptural classics with which they provided themselves. It was their recognition of the enormous service that could be secured in influencing a community through the distribution of books, that made them so prompt in their appreciation of the value of the printing-press and that caused them to take place among the first printers of Germany.

The term commonly given to the earlier German scribes was *clericus*, or *pfaffe*, and nearly every well-to-do nobleman or citizen had a *clericus*, or *pfaffe*, to take charge of his correspondence and his accounts.

While the general use of this term indicates the ecclesiastical origin of the scribes and confirms the previous records to the effect that the first scribes undoubtedly were monks trained in the monasteries, it is of course by no means to be accepted as evidence that the art of writing continued, at least after the fourteenth century, to be limited to ecclesiastics. As has before been indicated, the monastery schools accepted very many pupils who had no intention of entering the Church, but who secured from their monkish teachers a knowledge of reading and writing.

As early as 1403, mention is made of a certain Heilmannus, formerly a cleric of the diocese of Trier, licensed as a public scribe (*eyn offenbar schreiber*). At about the same time, Dr. Conrad Humery, of Mayence, is referred to in the chronicles as *pfaffe*, *jurist*, and *chancellor* of the city. Ulrich Zell, who later became the first printer in

Cologne, was accustomed to add to the imprint of his works the designation *clericus* from Hanau in the diocese of Mayence. Notwithstanding the term *clericus* and the reference to his diocese, Ulrich had never been an ecclesiastic.[1] The ecclesiastical divisions, parishes or dioceses, were utilised in those times, as political divisions are to-day, as the territorial designations that would be most readily understood.

The trade in books in manuscript was developed from two great sources. For a certain special and restricted class of work, the trade came into existence and continued, as we have seen, for some centuries, in the Italian universities, in the University of Paris, and in two or three of the older German universities. Some little time later, the scribes found place among the hand-workers and dealers of the larger cities. Their work was at first carried on most actively in connection with cathedrals and churches, and, later, associated itself with the annual markets and fairs.

In the trade centres, where the goldsmiths, designers, and illuminators found profitable occupation, the skilled writers (that is to say, those who were competent to prepare the elaborately ornamented manuscripts) soon found occupation, while the writers of common text came to be employed particularly, as mentioned, in the markets and fairs in connection with the records and correspondence required for business transactions.

Throughout the first half of the fifteenth century the production of manuscripts, which, from the beauty of their script and the artistic finish of their illustrations and ornamentations, could be classed as works of art, became an important industry, an industry of which the centres in Germany and the Low Countries were Bruges, Ghent, Antwerp, Aix-la-Chapelle, Cologne, Strasburg, Augsburg, Ulm, and Vienna.

[1] Kapp, 18.

As before indicated, the manuscripts produced in the Netherlands and in Burgundy far surpassed those of Germany and, for that matter, those of the rest of the world, in beauty and in the elaboration of their artistic finish and ornamentation. The Dukes of Burgundy took a large personal interest in this special industry of their dominions, and their patronage did much to make the art fashionable and to further its development.

When, after the introduction of printing, the printers and book-makers instituted their trade-unions or guilds in Ghent and in Bruges, they absorbed into their organisations the existing associations of fine writers, scribes, illuminators, etc.

In the library of S. Mark's, in Venice, there is a beautiful breviary known as that of Grimani, which was produced in 1478 by certain artists of Bruges, among whom is mentioned John Memmling, and which was purchased in 1489, for five hundred ducats, by the Cardinal Grimani. About the same time, that is to say, between 1468 and 1469, was produced the copy of Froissart's Chronicles which had been prepared in Bruges for the son of Duke Philip of Burgundy, and which is at present in the possession of the library of the University of Breslau.

The labour of the scribes of the fifteenth century was, however, by no means exclusively devoted to works of magnificence (*prachtwerke*). From the shops of the ordinary writers, were produced considerable masses of text-books, books of worship, cookery books, astrological treatises, almanacs, and even political tracts. Before the middle of the century, there are records of licensed scribes carrying on a general business for the public in Cologne, Frankfort, Augsburg, Vienna, and even in smaller towns, such as Nordlingen.

The scribes of the universities, who were included among the university officials, and who, in securing certain university privileges, subjected themselves also to a rather elaborate series of restrictions, were naturally not in a position to leave their university towns to do work in other centres. In fact, it was for a long time not permitted for them to take up any work outside of providing the copies required of the authorised university texts. The scribes who were not associated with any official bodies were, however, free to carry their work from place to place according as the varying demand of the seasons of the year, a demand dependent upon the markets, the fairs, and other special business conditions, might give opportunity for a profitable use of their labours. The shops of these town scribes were, as a rule, in the open places, more particularly in the market, in the neighbourhood of the town hall, or under the shadow of the cathedral or principal church. Frequently, where the business was not quite important enough to warrant a shop, it was carried on under the steps or in the porches of the church or the cathedral, and sometimes even within the church building, in one of the chapels.

It seems probable that the old-time ecclesiastical associations of the art (which was still known as " clerical ") may have caused the authorities having charge of the church buildings to look with special favour upon these later scribes, so that they were able to secure for their trade facilities and accommodations which would not have been afforded to workers or dealers in other occupations.

There is a reference, in 1408, in one of the Strasburg chronicles to a scribe named Peter von Haselo, who sells books on the steps of the cathedral of Our Lady.[1] In Cologne the manuscript-dealers took possession of various corners or angles of the cathedral for their shops or booths. In Münster the space immediately in front of the cathedral was allotted to them. In a number of the larger cities the scribes dealt not only in the productions of their own pens, but in such ancient manuscripts as they had been able to

[1] Kapp, 20.

collect, these coming for the most part from Italy. It was from this branch of their business that the booksellers came to be known quite frequently as *antiquarii*.

While there gradually grew up throughout Germany an active trade in manuscripts, the record shows an earlier development of this trade in Italy and France, and even in England. Reference has already been made to the activity as a book collector of Richard de Bury, who in the first half of the fourteenth century secured through travelling dealers manuscripts which had been brought from France and from Italy. De Bury speaks of these dealers as taking commissions for the delivery of the manuscripts at such interval of months as would be required for the long journeys from Oxford to Paris and back, or from Oxford to Florence or Venice.

It appears, however, that towards the middle of the fifteenth century, when the work of town scribes in Germany had once begun and the character of their productions came to be known to the common people, the circulation of books among the people was more extensive in amount and more wide-reaching in the territory and the classes of buyers concerned than was the case in any other state of Europe.

In 1439, some dealers from the Siebengebirge brought from Basel to Hermannstadt certain political controversies and tracts. Some of the latter treated of the work of the Council of Basel, and came, therefore, under the censorship of the Church, and their circulation in Hermannstadt was forbidden.[1]

Between 1440 and 1450, the records of the annual fairs of Nordlingen include repeated references to dealings in manuscripts.

After 1460, it is not always easy to determine whether the specifications of the prices paid for books refer to manuscripts or to printed copies. On the 27th of March,

[1] Kapp, 21.

1485, Rudolph Agricola, the librarian of the Elector of
the Palatinate, writes to his friend Adolph Rusch, a bookseller from Strasburg who was at that time in Frankfort,
ordering for his library copies of the following books:
Columella, *De Re Rustica*; Celsus, *De Medicina*; *Macrobii
Saturnalia, Statii, Opera,* and Silius Italicus.   It is certain,
says Kirchhoff, that these books had not yet been printed
in Germany, and he is, therefore, of opinion that Agricola
was expecting to secure manuscripts.   Kapp points out,
however, that certain of them had already been printed
in Italy; *Columella*, for instance, had been published in a
volume with *Cato* and *Varro*, in Venice in 1472, and in
Reggio in 1482.

Celsus appeared in Florence in 1478, and in Milan in
1481; *Macrobius*, in Venice in 1472 and 1483; *Statius* in
Rome in 1476, in Milan in 1483; *Silius* in Rome, in 1471,
in Milan in 1480, and in Parma in 1481.

It seems probable that, in connection with the correspondence between the scholars of Italy and the instruct-
tors in the University of Heidelberg, news might very
easily have come to the librarian of the Elector of these
important classical undertakings, and that he had naturally desired to secure copies of the books for the Elector's
library.   As far as I can understand from the reference
made by Kapp, there is no record of the result of
this order or inquiry, or of the prices at which Agricola
secured or hoped to secure the books in question.   It was
undoubtedly the case that, as the work of the printers,
both German and Italian, came to be known to the book
collectors, there was a steady decrease in the prices paid
for manuscripts, until the business of the manuscript-
dealers came to be limited to the sale as curiosities of old
codices, and the work of the scribes in the reproduction
of copies ceased altogether.

Reference has already been made to the prices paid
during the Middle Ages for more or less famous manu-

scripts. The difficulty with the prices of which we have record is that they vary so considerably for goods of apparently about the same description, a variation doubtless depending upon the special conditions of the sale, the wealth or eagerness of the purchaser, etc. In 1054, for instance, a *Book of the Mass* was sold by the monk named Ulrich (the sale being made with the consent of the Abbot) in exchange for a great vineyard covering the slope of a large hill, the exact dimensions of which are not given. In 1057, a nun named Diemude, of the convent of Wessobrunn, exchanged a Bible, which she had written with her own hand, for a farm on Peissenburg. Without, however, the exact description of any particular manuscript, a description which should specify the nature of the work put into it, the illuminations, the designs, the covers, etc., it is, of course, very difficult to compare one transaction with another.

Kapp speaks of a good copy of the *Corpus Juris* as being valued in 1350 at 1000 gold gulden.[1] He quotes a purchase made by a certain Prahel, in 1427, of a copy of *Livy* for 120 gold gulden, and the sale of a *Plutarch* in 1470 (twenty years after Gutenberg's press began to work) for no less than 800 gold gulden. Jan Van Enkhuisen, of Zwolle, received in 1460 for an illuminated Bible 500 gold gulden, and for a Bible with a plain text (*einfach geschrieben*) 100 crowns. In 1345, Etienne de Conty paid for a handsomely adorned copy of the *Commentaries* of Henry Bohic, 62 livres and 11 sous, a sum which Kapp calculates to be the equivalent of 825 francs in the money of the present day. For the production of this work, there were paid to the scribes 31 livres and 5 sous, for the parchment 18 livres and 18 sous, for six initials in gold, 1 livre and 10 sous, for other illuminations 3 livres and 6 sous, for the hire of the manuscript (paid to the university *bidellus*), 4 livres, and for binding the volume, 1 livre 12 sous.

[1] Kapp, 24.

The Countess of Anjou paid, in 1460, for a copy of the *Homilies* of Haimon, Bishop of Halberstadt, two hundred sheep, five measures of wheat, and five measures of barley.

In 1474, Louis XI. of France, pledged as security for the safe return of a manuscript containing a treatise by the Arabic physician Rhases, which he had borrowed from the medical Faculty of the University of Paris, his silver plate, while a nobleman also stood security for the King in the transaction.   In 1392, the Countess of Blois, wife of the Baron of Castellane, left in her will, as a bequest to her daughter, a manuscript on parchment of the *Corpus Juris*. It was made a condition of the bequest that the daughter should marry a jurist, in order that this valuable treasure could come into the right hands.

The National Library in Paris contains two manuscripts of the Bible in Latin and French text, written on parchment, which Firmin Didot appraised as having cost to produce not less than the equivalent of 82,000 francs. He excludes from this calculation of cost the price of the parchment, the hire of the scribes, and the cost of the binding. The principal item of the outlay for the more valuable of these manuscripts was incurred in the production of the 5,000 designs illuminated in gold and colour, the cost of preparing which Didot estimated at over 12,000 francs.

As before pointed out, the exceptional outlay incurred in the production of these illuminated manuscripts cannot be taken as in any way a guide for the average market price of manuscripts prepared for general circulation and sale. The text-books, chap-books, etc., which, during the fourteenth and fifteenth centuries, were prepared for the common folk, sold at prices that seem very low when one bears in mind the large amount of manual labour required for their production. The school ordinance of the town of Bautzen (in Saxony) of 1418 fixed the price of an

A B C book, containing also a *Paternoster*, at one groschen; of a *Doctrinal,* a half mark; and of a *Donatus,* ten groschens.

At this time, however, the market price in the same region for a hen was one pfennig, for a pound of beef two pfennigs, for a loaf of bread, containing rations for three men for one day, three pfennigs, for a pound of cheese one pfennig, for a measure of the best wine one kreutzer.

From this date on, however, there came to be, with the increase in the production of manuscript books in the common text, a very steady decrease in the selling price of such books.

At the end of the fourteeth century the average price in Italy for a well written copy of the *Corpus Juris* was 480 marks. In 1451, such a copy was sold in Florence for 14½ ducats, the equivalent of 90 marks.

In 1400, a manuscript containing writings of Justinian, Sallust, and Suetonius, written on 115 folio sheets of parchment, was sold in Florence for 16 ducats, the equivalent of 100 marks. In 1467, a copy of the comedies of Terence, written on 198 folio sheets (paper, however, instead of parchment), was bought in Heidelberg for three gulden. By this date, sixteen years, namely, after the printing of Gutenberg's first volume, the competition or the expectation of the competition of the printing-press, had already begun to affect the market prices of manuscripts. In 1499, there is record of the sale in Heidelberg for the price of two gulden, of a manuscript comprising 134 quarto sheets, containing the *Hecuba* of Euripides, and the *Idyls* of Theocritus.

In not a few of the monasteries, even of those which had an old-time repute for literary activity, the literary efforts came and went in waves, and sometimes for long periods, extending over a generation or more, there was an actual decrease in the extent of the attention given to the production of manuscripts and to the securing of additions to the library. In other instances the development of the libraries went on but slowly.

C. Schmidt refers to the record of the library of the Strasburg Cathedral, which in 1260 possessed a collection of fifty codices that had been for the most part presented by Bishop Wernher as far back as 1027. In the year 1372, the catalogue of the library shows that the number had increased to ninety-one, a gain of only forty-one manuscripts in a space of more than one century.

The renewed interest that came to the scholars of Italy in the works of classic writers with the revival of classical studies induced by the Renaissance caused manuscripts of these works to be searched for, not only in Italy and in the countries of the East that could most easily be reached by Italy, but throughout the monasteries of Europe. In 1517, there is record of instruction being given by Pope Leo X. to a certain cleric named Heytmer to visit the libraries of the Palatinate and of the adjoining districts and to search for classical manuscripts for purchase for the Papal collection. Heytmer was enjoined to make special inquiry for the missing books of Livy.

Another agent of Leo was fortunate enough to discover in the monastery of Corvey on the Weser the first five books of Tacitus. Being unable to induce the monastery to make sale of the manuscript, he succeeded in some way in appropriating it, and in getting it safely over the Alps. It was this manuscript that was used for the *editio princeps* of Tacitus, printed in Rome in 1515. The Pope sent to the library of the Corvey monastery a copy of this printed edition of the Tacitus as a restitution for the appropriated manuscript. The manuscript itself, in 1522, was taken (one does not know how) from Rome to Florence, where it is to-day chained in the Laurentian Library. I understand that this Corvey text constituted the only copy of the first five books of Tacitus which had been found when this author was first put into print.

The Manuscript Period in England.—During the thirteenth and fourteenth centuries, in England as in ancient Greece, and as also in mediæval Italy, Southern France and Germany, the people who were prepared to interest themselves in literary productions, received their literature, or at least their poetical literature, very largely by means of reciters or ministrels. In the prologue to his *Troilus and Cressida*, Chaucer tells us it was intended to be read *or elles sung*. George Ellis points out that this must relate to the chanting recitation of the minstrels. Ellis goes on to say: "A considerable part of our old poetry is simply addressed to an audience, without any mention of readers. That our English minstrels at any time united all the talents of the profession, and were at once poets and reciters and musicians, is extremely doubtful; but that they excited and directed the efforts of their contemporary poets to a particular species of composition, is as evident as that a body of actors must influence the exertions of theatrical writers. They were, at a time when reading and writing were rare accomplishments, the principal medium of communication between authors and the public; and their memory in some measure supplied the deficiency of manuscripts, and probably preserved much of our early literature until the invention of printing." [1]

Says Jusserand: "At a time when books were rare, and when the theatre, properly so-called, did not exist, poetry and music travelled with the minstrels and gleemen (*jongleurs*) along the highway, and such guests were always welcome." [2]

The connection of minstrelsy with the circulation of literature is referred to by Charles Knight as follows: "A popular literature was kept alive and preserved, however imperfectly, before the press came to make those

---

[1] *Early English Poetry*, Introduction, xi.
[2] *English Wayfaring Life*, 188.

who had learnt to read self-dependent in their intellectual gratifications; and what has come down to us of the old minstrelsy, with all its inaccuracy and occasional feebleness, shows us that the people of England, four or five centuries ago, had a common fund of high thought upon which a great literature might in time be reared. The very existence of a poet like Chaucer is the best proof of the vigour, and to a certain extent of the cultivation, of the national mind, even in an age when books were rarities." [1]

As early as the twelfth century, during such reigns as those of Henry I. (Beauclerc) and Henry II., there was in England a very considerable production of literature, under such various headings as chronicles, satires, sermons, works of science and of medicine, treatises on style, prose romances, and epics in verse. Jusserand points out that a large proportion of these compositions were written in Latin.[2] This would indicate a wider general understanding of Latin than prevailed three centuries later when Caxton's printing-press began its work; for, as will be noted in the chapter on Caxton, the proportion of Latin books issued by Caxton was very much smaller than was the case with the contemporary publishers in France and in Germany. Such an active and varied literary production as that described by Jusserand would also, of course, imply the existence of a considerable body of trained scribes in addition to those who were at work in the monastic *scriptoria* on the chronicles and books of devotion.

The very large measure of attention given to the production of legends and romances, and the great popularity of these among almost all classes of the people, was the distinctive feature of the literature of England during the three centuries preceding the introduction of printing. The scenes of many of these romances are laid in classic

[1] *The Old Printer*, p. 43.   [2] *Literary History*, i., 176.

times, and their characters bear classic names; but the stories are hardly constructed on classic lines, and very little attempt is made to preserve what the dramatic critic in *Nicholas Nickleby* calls "the oneness of the drama." Antiquity is presented in the garb of the Middle Ages. As Jusserand remarks: "Everything in these poems was really translated; not only the language of the ancients but their raiment, their civilisation, their ideas. Venus becomes a princess: the heroes are knights, and their costumes, pictured in the illuminations, are so much in the fashion of the day that they serve us to date the poems."

In addition to these classic romances, in which old-time heroes masquerade in mediæval garb and speak in mediæval language, there is a long series of tales which appear to have been of English origin. English readers and English writers of the time seem to have possessed a special penchant for story-telling. "Prose tales were written in astonishing quantities in the twelfth and thirteenth centuries by pious authors who under pretext of edifying and amusing their readers at the same time, began by amusing and frequently forgot to edify."[1] The Welshman, Walter Map, became famous at the Court of Henry II. for his satires and humorous stories. His work was done in Latin. His *De Nugis Curiatum* secured the most abiding repute. He might perhaps be considered as a twelfth-century Martial. That famous body of stories, the *Gesta Romanorum*, heretofore believed to be the result of German reshaping of legends originating with the monks of Italy, is now claimed to have been first compiled in England towards the end of the thirteenth century.[2] The *Gesta* was one of the most widely circulated books in Europe (outside of the accepted devotional

---

[1] *Literary History*, i., 182.
[2] Oesterly, *Die Literatur der Urkundensammlungen*, 2 vols., Berlin, 1885–86.

classics) both in the manuscript period, and during the first century of printing.

The stories of the time are of very varied origin and in many cases had evidently, in the rewriting, undergone material modifications or transformations. Whether the language used be Latin, French, or English, it is evident from the character of the tales that the writers were addressing themselves not to any limited group of scholars and clerics, but to what would to-day be described as a popular circle of readers and of hearers. Thomas Wright points out that even those tales which are presented in Latin give evidence from local references and from English quotations of having been written for Englishmen." [1]

The Canterbury Tales of Geoffrey Chaucer, chief among the story-tellers of England, if not of Europe, were written about 1390. After the long series of translations and adaptations, these tales of Chaucer mark a distinct epoch in the production of native romance, in which characters, incidents, and surroundings were alike English, although there are many evidences of continental influences. The circulation of the *Tales* in manuscript form was very extended, and Caxton showed his usual excellent judgment by including them in the first group of publications issued from his Westminster Press. This earliest printed edition was probably published in 1478. A second edition was issued by Caxton in 1484.

It seems probable, as well from the history of the *Canterbury Tales* as from that of the long series of romances which had preceded them, a history giving evidence of a wide-spread influence and repute, that there must have been, during the twelfth, thirteenth, and fourteenth centuries, a considerable book-production outside of the monastery *scriptoria*, and that there must also have been

[1] *Selection of Latin Stories from the MSS. of the Thirteenth and Fourteenth Centuries.* Percy Society, London, 1842.

a fairly effective machinery for the sale and distribution of the manuscript texts. The latter were doubtless supplied in great part by the travelling pedlars, who sold with their novelties in ribbons and trinkets the latest new tale, or the latest version of some very old tale.

Books in manuscript were included in the goods sold at certain of the great fairs, such as that of Stourbridge (near Cambridge),St. Giles (near Oxford), and St. Bartholomew, in London.[1] After the introduction of printing, such fairs did considerable business in the sale not only of the chap-books and almanacs, which were carried about in the pedlars' packs, but also of substantial and costly works. Professor Thorold Rogers explains that the rapid diffusion of books and pamphlets at a time when newspapers and advertisements were still unknown, can only be accounted for by the understanding that the book-dealers made large use of these fairs. He goes on to say that he finds entries of purchases for the libraries of the Oxford colleges, with the statement that the books were bought at St. Giles's Fair.[2] It will be remembered how two centuries or more after the period referred to by Thorold Rogers, Michael Johnson, the father of Samuel, made a practice of going on market days to Uttoxeter, taking there from his book-shop in Litchfield books to be offered for sale on a stall in the market-place. The market days had, in 1725, replaced in great measure the old-time fairs. In the chapter on Germany, I have referred to the early use made of the Fair at Nordlingen by the dealers in manuscripts, a practice which was later continued by the printers.

It does not appear that the manuscript-dealers were permitted to carry on their trade in the chapels or within the enclosures of the cathedrals, as was so largely done by their contemporaries in Germany and in France. The

[1] Harrison's *Description of England*. Ed. Furnivall. Part i., book ii., chap. xviii.

[2] Roger's *History of Agriculture and Prices in England*, iv., 155.

extensive multiplication of books by copyists is less easy to account for. I have not been able thus far to find record of any considerable production, in London or other commercial centres, of books in manuscript, and I can only infer such production from the wide-spread circulation and influence of the books themselves.

The literary activities of England during these centuries of the manuscript period were by no means limited to the production of fiction. The long series of contributions to local and national history made by the monkish chroniclers have been referred to in a previous chapter. In the twelfth century, Orderic Vital or Vitalis writes his *Angligenæ Historiæ Ecclesiasticæ*, Henry of Huntingdon, his *Historia Anglorum* (from A.C. 55 to A.D. 1154), and William of Malmesbury, his *Gesta Regum Anglorum*. The *Historia Anglorum* was printed in 1586, at the expense of Sir Henry Savile. William of Malmesbury was, like Richard de Bury, noted as a collector of books. His history was issued between 1112 and 1124. A few years later, in 1139, appears the great *Historia Regum Britanniæ*, of Geoffrey of Monmouth. Geoffrey begins his British history with the earliest times, and, thanks, as he explains, to certain special discoveries, or to a special revelation, he is able to write with as much certainty about the reign of King Arthur as concerning events of his own time. This chronicle must have been largely multiplied and widely distributed, as an exceptionally large number of copies have been preserved to the present time, the British Museum alone possessing no less than thirty-four.

In the thirteenth century the work of the historians is carried on by such writers as Roger of Wendover, and Matthew Paris, chief among English chroniclers. In the fourteenth century, the most noteworthy among a long series of historical writers is Ralph Higden, author of the *Polychronicon*, or "Universal History," which remained for centuries an accepted authority.

In the thirteenth century, Bartholomew or Glanville
compiles one of the oldest of the general cyclopædias.
Of this, many manuscripts have been preserved, eighteen
of which are in the National Library in Paris.[1]　John of
Gaddesden, court physician under Edward II. (1310–1312),
writes a medical cyclopædia, or compendium of prescrip-
tions, which not only secures a European reputation at
the time, but retains its prestige for nearly three centuries,
and is issued in print in Augsburg, in 1595, in two quarto
volumes.　As early as the reign of Henry II. (1154–1189)
an important group of law books had appeared, and the
law treatises of Henry of Bracton, issued early in the
thirteenth century, retained their value sufficiently to
appear two centuries later in a printed edition, abridged
from the original text.　These few typical writers are referred to simply as presenting some indication of the
variety and of the extent of the literary activities of England during the centuries preceding the beginning of
printing.　The popular interest in the works of such
writers, and the great influence exerted by them upon the
opinions of their own and of succeeding generations, is
evidence of a considerable multiplication of copies and of
an extended circulation, and this evidence is corroborated
by the fact that of many of the books of the period so
large a number of copies have been preserved to the
present time through the perils and vicissitudes of the
intervening centuries.

The most noteworthy example of the literary interests
of Britain during the manuscript period is afforded by
Richard Aungerville, better known as Richard de Bury,
Bishop Palatine of Durham, whose famous *Philobiblon*
was given to the world in 1345.　In his various travels,
and through his correspondents in England, France, and
Italy, he was able to get together a great collection of
books, which were later bequeathed to the University of

[1] Delisle, *Hist. Litt. de la France*, xxx., 334.

Oxford.   His eloquent tribute to his beloved books must,
I judge, be taken rather as expressing the enthusiasm of
an exceptionally devoted scholar than as fairly representing the literary spirit of the time :

" Thanks to books, the dead appear to me as though
they still lived. . . .   Everything decays and falls into
dust by the force of time : Saturn is never weary of de-
vouring his children, and the glory of the world would be
buried in oblivion, had not God as a remedy conferred on
mortal man the benefit of books. . . .   Books are the
masters that instruct us without rods or ferules, without
reprimands or anger, without the solemnity of the gown
or the expense of lessons.   Go to them, you will not find
them asleep : if you err, no scoldings on their part : if you
are ignorant, no mocking laughter." [1]

In 1344, (the year before his death) Richard writes as
follows :

" As it is necessary for a state to provide military arms,
and prepare plentiful stores of provisons for soldiers who
are about to fight, so it is evidently worth the labour of
the church militant to fortify itself against the attacks of
pagans and heretics with a multitude of sound books.
But because everything that is serviceable to mortals
suffers the waste of mortality through lapse of time, it is
necessary for volumes corroded by age to be restored by
renovated successors, that perpetuity, repugnant to the
nature of the individual, may be conceded to the species.
Hence it is that Ecclesiastes significantly says, in the
12th chapter. ' There is no end of making many books.'
For, as the bodies of books suffer continued detriment
from a combined mixture of contraries in their composition, so a remedy is found out by the prudence of clerks,
by which a holy book paying the debt of nature may obtain an hereditary substitute, and a seed may be raised
up like to the most holy deceased, and that saying of

[1] *Philobiblon*, Lond. 1888, chap. i., pp. 12. 13.

Ecclesiasticus, be verified, ' The father is dead and, as it were, not dead, for he hath left behind him a son like unto himself.' "

One of the earliest authorities concerning book publishing in England is Bishop Fell, who in his Memoir on the State of Printing in the University of Oxford, tells us that that university " possessed an exclusive right of transcribing and multiplying books by means of writing," a privilege which implies a species of copyright. The date referred to is about 1600.

In both Oxford and Cambridge, according to the statutes in force before the introduction of printing, the *stationarii* belonged to the class of *Servientes*, who were appointed by the chancellor or vice-chancellor of the university. The records of Oxford show many instances of the pawning of books by the undergraduates and occasionally by the instructors to the *stationarii*. In one codex, belonging to Mr. Thomas Paunter, there is an inscription showing that it was pawned to a *stationarius* in 1480, for the sum of thirty-eight shillings.[1] Books which had been so pledged, came frequently enough, after their forfeiture, into sale. An entry in the accounts of the library of S. John's College in Cambridge, dating from 1456, records a payment made, apparently from the treasury of the college, for the redemption of an *Avicenna* from the *stationarius* to whom a certain John Marshall had pledged the manuscript. The cost of the redemption was £1. 6s. 4d.[2]

The Oxford *stationarii* finally secured privileges as members of the university, but not before 1458, (as a result apparently of an arrangement between the university and the city authorities), did this agreement take the *stationarii* out of the jurisdiction of the city, and put

---

[1] Huber, *The English Universities*, London, 1840, p. 273.

[2] Hartshorne, C. A., *The Book Rarities of the University of Cambridge*, London, 1829, p. 338.

them into the same class with the dealers in parchment, the illuminators, and the scribes, who for many years had been subordinated to the university. The taxes on the *stationarii* were fixed by and collected by the chancellor, and the proportion due to the city treasury was paid over by him.

The term *stationarius*, which had, as we have seen, been in use for these university dealers throughout all Europe, secured in Great Britain a permanent association with the book-trade by its use as an appelation for the publishers' and booksellers' guild, which was chartered in 1403 as " The Stationers' Company." Its headquarters in London was entitled Stationers' Hall, and is still so known. The term in Great Britain, however, was made from a very early date to cover a larger variety of trade undertakings than that to which it was limited in the university towns in Italy, France, and Germany. The business of selling manuscripts on commission, which was, as we have seen, kept under very close supervision on the part of the university authorities of Paris and Bologna, appears to have been much less important in England, and the dealers seem for the most part to have been left free to make such terms either in buying or selling manuscripts as they saw fit, and as the necessities of their customers rendered practicable.

As early as the reign of Edward III. (1327–1377), there is record of a number of *stationarii* as carrying on business in Oxford. In an Oxford manuscript dating from this reign, there is an inscription of a certain Mr. William Reed, of Merton College, who tells us that he purchased this book from a *stationarius*.[1]

In London, there is record of an active trade in manuscripts being in existence as early as the middle of the fourteenth century. The trade in writing materials, such as parchment, paper, and ink, appears not to have been

[1] Coxe, *College of Merton*, p. 107.

organised as in Paris, but to have been carried on in large
part by the grocers and mercers. In the housekeeping
accounts of King John of France, covering the period of
his imprisonment in England, in the years 1359 and 1360,
occur entries such as the following ;

"To Peter, a grocer of Lincoln, for four quaires of paper,
two shillings and four pence."
"To John Huistasse, grocer, for a main of paper and a skin
of parchment, 10 pence."
"To Bartholomew Mine, grocer, for three quaires of paper,
27 pennies."[1]

The manuscript-trade in London concentrated itself in
Paternoster Row, the street which became afterwards the
centre of the trade in printed books.

The earliest English manuscript-dealer whose name
is on record is Richard Lynn, who, in the year 1358,
was *stationarius* in Oxford.[2] The name of John Browne
occurs in several Oxford manuscripts on about the
date of 1400. Nicholas de Frisia, an Oxford *librarius* of about 1425, was originally an undergraduate.
He did energetic work as a book scribe and, later,
appears to have carried on an important business in
manuscripts. His inscription is found first on a manuscript entitled *Petri Thomæ Quæstiones*, etc., which manuscript has been preserved in the library of Merton.

There is record, as early as 1359, of a manuscript-dealer
in the town of Lincoln who called himself Johannes
Librarius, and who sold, in 1360, several books to the
French King John. It is a little difficult to understand
how in a quiet country town like Lincoln with no
university connections, there should have been enough
business in the fourteenth century to support a *librarius*.

The earliest name on record in London is that of
Thomas Vycey, who was a *stationarius* in 1433. A few

---

[1] *Donnée des Comptes des Roys de France, au 14ᵉ Siècle.* Paris, 1852,
p. 227.   [2] Coxe, *History of New College*, p. 37.

years later we find on a parchment manuscript containing the wise sayings of a certain Lombardus, the inscription of Thomas Masoun, "*librarius of gilde hall.*"

Between the years 1461 and 1475, a certain Piers Bauduyn, dealer in manuscripts, and also a bookbinder, purchased a number of books for Edward IV. In the household accounts of Edward appears the following entry : " Paid to Piers Bauduyn, bookseller, for binding, gilding and dressing a copy of Titus Livius, 20 shillings; for binding, gilding and dressing a copy of the Holy Trinity, 16 shillings; for binding, gilding and dressing a work entitled ' The Bible ' 16 shillings."

William Praat, who was a mercer of London, between the years 1470 and 1480 busied himself also with the trade in manuscripts, and purchased, for William Caxton, various manuscripts from France and from Belgium.

Kirchhoff finds record of manuscript-dealers in Spain as early as the first decade of the fifteenth century. He prints the name, however, of but one, a certain Antonius Raymundi, a *librarius* of Barcelona, whose inscription, dated 1413, appears in a manuscript of Cassiodorus.

PART II.

THE EARLIER PRINTED BOOKS.

PART II.

THE EARLIER PRINTED BOOKS.

CHAPTER I.

THE RENAISSANCE AS THE FORERUNNER OF THE PRINTING-PRESS.

THE fragments of classic literature which had survived the destruction of the Western Empire, had, as we have seen, owed their preservation chiefly to the Benedictine monasteries. Upon the monasteries also rested, for some centuries after the overthrow of the Gothic Kingdom of Italy, the chief responsibility for maintaining such slender thread of continuity of intellectual activity, and of interest in literature as remained. By the beginning of the twelfth century, this responsibility was shared with, if not entirely transferred to, the older of the great universities of Europe, such as Bologna and Paris, which from that time took upon themselves, as has been indicated, the task of directing and of furthering, in connection with their educational work, the increasing literary activities of the scholarly world.

With the increase throughout Europe of schools and universities, there had come a corresponding development in literary interests and in literary productiveness or reproductiveness. The universities became publishing centres, and through the multiplication and exchange of manuscripts, the scholars of Europe began to come into closer relations with each other, and to constitute a kind of international scholarly community. The development of such world-wide relations between scholars was, of course, very much furthered by the fact that Latin was universally accepted as the language not only of scholarship but practically of all literature.

In Italy, by the beginning of the fourteenth century, intellectual interests and literary activities had expanded beyond the scholastic circles of the universities, and were beginning to influence larger divisions of society. The year 1300 witnessed the production in Florence of the *Divine Comedy* of Dante, and marked an epoch in the history of Italy and in the literature of the world. During the two centuries which followed, Florence remained the centre of a keener, richer, and more varied intellectual life than was known in any other city in Europe.

With the great intellectual movement known as the Renaissance, I am concerned, for the purposes of this study, only to indicate the influence it exerted in preparing Italy and Europe for the utilisation of the printing-press. The work of the Renaissance included, partly as a cause, and partly as an effect, the rediscovery for the Europe of the fourteenth and fifteenth centuries of the literature of classic Greece, as well as the reinterpretation of the literature of classic Rome.

The influence of the literary awakening and of the newly discovered masterpieces would of necessity have been restricted to a comparatively limited scholarly circle, if it had not been for the invention of Gutenberg and for the scholarly enterprise and devotion of such followers of Gutenberg as Aldus, Estienne, and Froben. It is, of course, equally true that if the intellectual world had not been quickened and inspired by the teachers of the

Renaissance, the presses of Aldus would have worked to little purpose, and their productions would have found few buyers. Aldus may, in fact, himself be considered as one of the most characteristic and valuable of the products of the movement.

The Renaissance has been described by various historians, and analysed by many commentators. The work which has, however, been accepted as the most comprehensive account of the movement and the best critical analysis of its nature and influence, and which presents also a vivid and artistic series of pictures of Italy and the Italians during the fourteenth, fifteenth, and sixteenth centuries, is Symonds' *Renaissance in Italy*. These volumes are so thoroughly imbued with the spirit of the period, and the author's characterisations are so full and so sympathetic, that it is difficult not to think of Symonds as having been himself a Florentine, rather than a native of the " barbarian realm of Britain."

I take the liberty of quoting the description given by Symonds of the peculiar conditions under which Italy of the fifteenth century, in abandoning the hope of securing a place among the nations of the world, absorbed itself in philosophic, literary, and artistic ideals. Freshly imbued with Greek thought and Greek inspiration, Italy took upon itself the rôle played centuries earlier by classic Greece, and, without political power or national influence, it assumed the leadership of the intellect and of the imagination of Europe.

" In proportion as Italy lost year by year the hope of becoming a united nation, in proportion as the military instincts died in her, and the political instincts were extinguished by despotism, in precisely the same ratio did she evermore acquire a deeper sense of her intellectual vocation. What was world-embracing in the spirit of the mediæval Church passed by transmutation into the humanism of the fifteenth century. As though aware of

the hopelessness of being Italians in the same sense as
the natives of Spain were Spaniards, or the natives of
France were Frenchmen, the giants of the Renaissance
did their utmost to efface their nationality, in order that
they might the more effectually restore the cosmopolitan
ideal of the human family.   To this end both artists and
scholars, the depositories of the real Italian greatness at
this epoch, laboured; the artists by creating an ideal of
beauty with a message and a meaning for all Europe; the
scholars by recovering for Europe the burghership of
Greek and Roman civilisation.   In spite of the invasions
and convulsions that ruined Italy between the years 1494
and 1527, the painters and the humanists proceeded with
their task as though the fate of Italy concerned them not,
as though the destinies of the modern world depended on
their activity.   After Venice had been desolated by the
armies of the League of Cambray, Aldus Manutius presented the peace-gift of Plato to the foes of his adopted
city, and when the Lutherans broke into Parmegiano's
workshop at Rome, even they were awed by the tranquil
majesty of the Virgin on his easel.   Stories like these
remind us that Renaissance Italy met her doom of servi-
tude and degradation in the spirit of ancient Hellas,
repeating as they do the tales told of Archimedes in his
study, and of Paulus Emilius face to face with the Zeus
of Phidias.[1]   . . .

"It is impossible to exaggerate the benefit conferred
upon Europe by the Italians at this epoch.   The culture
of the classics had to be reappropriated before the movement of the modern mind could begin, before the nations
could start upon a new career of progress; the chasm between the old and the new world had to be bridged over.
This task of reappropriation the Italians undertook alone,
and achieved at the sacrifice of their literary independence
and their political freedom.   The history of the Renais-

[1] *Renaissance in Italy—The Revival of Learning*, pp. 15, 16.

sance literature in Italy is the history of self-development into the channels of scholarship and antiquarian research. The language created by Dante as a thing of power, polished by Petrarch as a thing of beauty, trained by Boccaccio as the instrument of melodious prose, was abandoned even by the Tuscans in the fifteenth century for revived Latin and newly discovered Greek. Patient acquisition took the place of proud inventiveness; laborious imitation of classical authors suppressed originality of style. The force of mind which in the fourteenth century had produced a *Divine Comedy* and a *Decameron*, in the fifteenth century was expended upon the interpretation of codices, the settlement of texts, the translation of Greek books into Latin, the study of antiquities, the composition of commentaries, encyclopædias, dictionaries, ephemerides. While we regret this change from creative to acquisitive literature, we must bear in mind that these scholars, who ought to have been poets, accomplished nothing less than the civilisation, or, to use their own phrase, the humanisation, of the modern world. At the critical moment when the Eastern Empire was being shattered by the Turks, and when the other European nations were as yet unfit for culture, Italy saved the Arts and Sciences of Greece and Rome, and interpreted the spirit of the classics. Devoting herself to what appears the slavish work of compilation and collection, she transmitted an inestimable treasure to the human race; and though for a time the beautiful Italian tongue was superseded by a jargon of dead languages, yet the literature of the Renaissance yielded in the end the poetry of Ariosto, the political philosophy of Machiavelli, the histories of Guicciardini and Varchi. Meanwhile the whole of Europe had received the staple of its intellectual education."[1]

Symonds finds in the age of the Renaissance, or in what he calls the Humanistic movement, four principal

[1] *Renaissance in Italy—The Revival of Learning*, pp. 55-56.

periods: first, the age of inspiration and discovery, which
is initiated by Petrarch; second, the period of arrangement and translation.   During this period, the first great
libraries came into existence, the study of Greek began in
the principal universities, and the courts of Cosimo de'
Medici in Florence, Alfonso in Naples, and Nicholas in
Rome, became centres of literary activity; third, the age
of academies.   This period succeeded the introduction of
printing into Italy.   Scholars and men of letters are now
crystallising or organising themselves into cliques or
schools, under the influence of which a more critical and
exact standard of scholarship is arrived at, while there is
a marked development in literary form and taste.   Of the
academies which came into existence, the most important
were the Platonic in Florence, that of Pontanus in Naples,
that of Pomponius Lætus in Rome, and that of Aldus
Manutius in Venice.   This period covered, it is to be
noted, the introduction of printing into Italy (1464) and
its rapid development.   In the fourth period it may be
said that scholasticism to some extent took the place of
scholarship.   It was the age of the purists, of whom
Bembo was both the type and the dictator.   There is a
tendency to replace learning with an exaggerated attention to æsthetics and style.   It was about the Court of
Leo X. (1513–1522) that these æsthetic *literati* were
chiefly gathered.   "Erudition, properly so-called," says
Symonds, "was now upon the point of being transplanted
beyond the Alps."

The names of the scholars and writers who, following
Dante, gave fame to Florence and to Italy, are part of
the history of the world's literature.   It is necessary to
refer here only to those whose influence was most important in widening the range of scholarly interests and
in preparing Italy and Europe for the diffusion of literature, a preparation which, while emphasising the requirement for some means of multiplying books cheaply,

secured for the printing-press, as soon as its work began, an assured and sufficient support. The fact that a period of exceptional intellectual activity and literary productiveness immediately preceded the invention, or at least the introduction of printing, must have had an enormous influence in furthering the speedy development and diffusion of the new art. The press of Aldus Manutius seems, as before said, like a natural and necessary outgrowth of the Renaissance.

The typical feature of the revival of learning in Italy was, of course, the rediscovery of the literature of Greece. In the poetic simile of Symonds, " Florence borrowed her light from Athens, as the moon shines with rays reflected from the sun. The revival was the silver age of that old golden age of Greece." [1] The comparison of Florence with Athens has repeatedly been made. The golden ages of the two cities were separated by nearly two thousand years ; but history and human nature repeat themselves, and historians have found in the Tuscan capital of the fifteenth century a population which, with its keen intellectual nature, subtle and delicate wit, and restless political spirit, recalls closely the Athens of Pericles. The leadership which belonged to Italy in literature, art, scholarship, and philosophy, was, within Italy, conceded to Florence.

The first name in the list of Florentine scholars whose influence was important in this revival is that of Petrarch. He never himself mastered the Greek language, but he arrived at a realisation of the importance of Greek thought for the world, and he preached to others the value of the studies which were beyond his own grasp. It was at Petrarch's instance that Boccaccio undertook the translation into Latin of the *Iliad*. Among Latin authors, Petrarch's devotion was given particularly to Cicero and Virgil. The fact that during the first century of printing

[1] *Revival of Learning*, p. 43.

more editions of Cicero were produced than of any other classic author must have been largely due to the emphasis given by the followers of Petrarch to the beauty of Cicero's latinity and the permanent value of his writings.

Petrarch was a devoted collector of manuscripts, and spared neither labour nor expense to secure for his library codices of texts recommended as authoritative. Notwithstanding his lack of knowledge of Greek, he purchased for his collection all the Greek manuscripts which came within his reach and within his means. Fortunately for these expensive literary tastes, he appears to have possessed what we should call a satisfactory independence. Some of his manuscripts went to Boccaccio, while the rest were, at his death, given to the city of Florence and found place later in the Medicean Library.

Petrarch laid great stress on the importance, for the higher education of the people, of efficient public libraries, and his influence with wealthy nobles served largely to increase the resources of several of the existing libraries. In his scholarly appreciation of the value of such collections, he was helping to educate the community to support the booksellers, while in the collecting of manuscripts he was unwittingly doing valuable service for the coming printer. He died in 1374, ninety years before the first printing-press began its work in Italy. A century later his beautiful script served as a model for the italic or cursive type which was first made by Aldus.

Symonds thinks it very doubtful whether the Italians would have undertaken the labour of recovering the Greek classics if no Petrarch had preached the attractiveness of liberal studies, and if no school of disciples had been formed by him in Florence. Of these disciples, by far the most distinguished was Boccaccio. His actual work in furthering the study of Greek was more important than that of the friend to whom (although there was a difference of but nine years in their ages) he gave the title of " master." Boccaccio, taking up the study of Greek (at Petrarch's instance) in middle life, secured a sufficient mastery of the language to be able to render into Latin the *Iliad* and the *Odyssey*. This work, completed in 1362, was the first translation of Homer for modern readers. He had for his instructor and assistant an Italian named Leontius Pilatus, who had sojourned some years at Byzantium, but whose knowledge of classic Greek was said to have been very limited. Boccaccio secured for Pilatus an appointment as Greek professor in the University of Florence, the first professorship of Greek instituted in Europe.

The work by which Boccaccio is best known, the *Decameron* or the *Ten Nights' Entertainment*, was published in 1353, a few years before the completion by Chaucer of the *Canterbury Tales*. It is described as one of the purest specimens of Italian prose and as an inexhaustible repository of wit, beauty, and eloquence; and notwithstanding the fact that the stories are representative of the low standard of moral tone which characterised Italian society of the fourteenth century, the book is one which the world will not willingly let die. It is probably to-day in more continued demand than any book of its century, with the possible exception of the *Divine Comedy*. The earliest printed edition was that of Valdarfer, issued in Florence in 1471. This was three years before the beginning of Caxton's work as a printer in Bruges. The *Decameron* has since been published in innumerable editions and in every language of Europe.

A far larger contribution to Hellenic studies was given some years later by Manuel Chrysoloras, a Greek scholar of Byzantium, who, after visiting Italy as an ambassador from the Court of the Emperor Palæologus, was, in 1396, induced to accept the Chair of Greek in the University of Florence. "This engagement," says Symonds, " secured the future of Greek erudition in Europe." Symonds continues: "The scholars who assembled in the lecture-

rooms of Chrysoloras felt that the Greek texts, whereof
he alone supplied the key, contained those elements of
spiritual freedom and intellectual culture without which
the civilisation of the modern world would be impossible.
Nor were they mistaken in what was then a guess rather
than a certainty. The study of Greek implied the birth
of criticism, comparison, research. Systems based on
ignorance and superstition were destined to give way
before it. The study of Greek opened philosophical hori-
zons far beyond the dream world of the churchmen and
monks ; it stimulated the germs of science, suggested new
astronomical hypotheses, and indirectly led to the discovery of America. The study of Greek resuscitated a
sense of the beautiful in art and literature. It subjected
the creeds of Christianity, the language of the Gospels, the
doctrines of St. Paul, to analysis, and commenced a new
era of Biblical inquiry. If it be true, as a writer no less
sober in his philosophy than eloquent in his language has
lately asserted, that except the blind forces of nature,
nothing moves in this world which is not Greek in its
origin, we are justified in regarding the point of contact
between the Greek teacher Chrysoloras and his Florentine
pupils as one of the most momentous crises in the history
of civilisation. Indirectly the Italian intellect had hitherto
felt Hellenic influence through Latin literature. It was
now about to receive that influence immediately from
actual study of the masterpieces of the Attic writers. The
world was no longer to be kept in ignorance of those
'eternal consolations' of the human race. No longer
could the scribe omit Greek quotations from his Latin
text with the dogged snarl of obtuse self-satisfaction,
Græca sunt, ergo non legenda. The motto had rather to be
changed into a cry of warning for ecclesiastical authority
upon the verge of dissolution, *Græca sunt, ergo periculosa ;*
since the reawakening faith in human reason, the reawakening belief in the dignity of man, the desire for

beauty, the liberty, audacity, and passion of the Renaissance, received from Greek studies their strongest and most vital impulse."

Symonds might have added that the literary revival, which was so largely due to these Greek studies, made possible, a century later, the utilisation of the printing-press, the invention of which would otherwise have fallen upon comparatively barren ground; while the printing-press alone made possible the diffusion of the new knowledge, outside of the small circles of aristocratic scholars, to whole communities of impecunious students.

Florence had, as we have seen, done more than any other city of Italy, more than any city of Europe, to prepare Italy and Europe for the appreciation and utilisation of the art of printing, but the direct part taken by Florence in the earlier printing undertakings was, curiously enough, much less important than that of Venice, Rome, or Milan. By the year 1500, that is, thirty-six years after the beginning of printing in Italy, there had been printed in Florence 300 works, in Bologna 298, in Milan 629, in Rome 925, and in Venice 2835.

The list of the scholars and men of letters who, during the century following the work of Petrarch and Boccaccio, associated themselves with the brilliant society of Florence, and retained for the city its distinctive pre-eminence in the intellectual life of Europe, is a long one, and includes such names as those of Tommaso da Sarzana, Palla degli Strozzi, Giovanni da Ravenna, Niccolo de' Niccoli, Filelfo, Marsuppini, Rossi, Bruni, Guicciardini, Poggio, Galileo, Cellini, Plethon, and Machiavelli. It was to Strozzi that was due the beginning of Greek teaching in Florence under Manuel Chrysoloras, while he also devoted large sums of money to the purchase in Greece and in Constantinople of valuable manuscripts. He kept in his house skilled copyists, and was employing these in the work of preparing transcripts for a great public library, when, unfortunately for Florence, he incurred the enmity of Cosimo de' Medici, who procured his banishment. Strozzi went to Padua, where he continued his Greek studies.

Cosimo, having vanquished his rival in politics, himself continued the work of collecting manuscripts and of furthering the instruction given by the Greek scholars. The chief service rendered by Cosimo to learning and literature was in the organisation of great public libraries. During his exile (1433–1434), he built in Venice the Library of S. Giorgio Maggiore, and after his return to Florence, he completed the hall for the Library of S. Marco. He also formed several large collections of manuscripts. To the Library of S. Marco and to the Medicean Library were bequeathed later by Niccolo de' Niccoli 800 manuscripts, valued at 600 gold florins. Cosimo also provided a valuable collection of manuscripts for the convent of Fiesole. The oldest portion of the present Laurentian Library is composed of the collections from these two convents, together with a portion of the manuscripts preserved from the Medicean Library.

In 1438, Cosimo instituted the famous Platonic Academy of Florence, the special purpose of which was the interpretation of Greek philosophy. The gathering in Florence, in 1438, of the Greeks who came to the great Council, had a large influence in stimulating the interest of Florentines in Greek culture. Symonds (possibly somewhat biassed in favour of his beloved Florentines of the Renaissance) contends that the Byzantine ecclesiastics who came to the Council, and the long series of Greek travellers or refugees who found their way from Constantinople to Italy during the years that followed, included comparatively few real scholars whose classical learning could be trusted. These men supplied, says Symonds, "the beggarly elements of grammar, caligraphy, and bibliographical knowledge," but it was Ficino and Aldus, Strozzi and Cosimo de' Medici who opened the literature of Athens to the comprehension of the modern world.

The elevation to the papacy, in 1447, of Tommaso Parentucelli, who took the name of Nicholas V., had the effect of carrying to Rome some of the Florentine interest in literature and learning. Tommaso, who was a native of Pisa, had won repute in Bologna for his wide and thorough scholarship. He became, later, a protégé of Cosimo de' Medici, who employed him as a librarian of the Marcian Library. To Nicholas V. was due the foundation of the Vatican Library, for which he secured a collection of some five thousand works. Symonds says that during his pontificate, " Rome became a vast workshop of erudition, a factory of translations from Greek and Latin." The compensation paid to these translators from the funds provided by the Pope, was in many cases very liberal. In fact, as compared with the returns secured at this period for original work, the rewards paid to these translators of the Vatican seem decidedly disproportionate, especially when we remember that a large portion of their work was of poor quality, deficient both in exact scholarship and in literary form. To Lorenzo Valla was paid for his translation of Thucydides, 500 scudi, to Guarino for a version of Strabo, 1500 scudi, to Perotti for Polybius, 500 ducats. Manetti had a pension of 600 scudi a month to enable him to pursue his sacred studies. Poggio's version of the *Cyropædia* of Xenophon and Filelfo's rendering of the poems of Homer, were, from a literary point of view, more important productions. Some of the work in his series of translations was confided by the Pope to the resident Greek scholars. Trapezuntios undertook the *Metaphysics* of Aristotle and the *Republic* of Plato, and Tifernas the *Ethics* of Aristotle. Translations were also prepared of Theophrastus and of Ptolemy.

In addition to these paid translators, the Pope attracted to his Court from all parts of Italy, and particularly from

his old home, Florence, a number of scholars, of whom
Poggio Bracciolini (or Fiorentino) and Cardinal Bessarion
were the most important.   Bessarion took an active part
in encouraging Greek scholars to make their homes and to
do their work in Italy.   The great development of literary productiveness and literary interests in Rome during
the pontificate of Nicholas, is one of the noteworthy
examples of large results accruing to literature and to
literary workers through intelligently administered patronage.   It seems safe to say that before the introduction of
printing, it was only through the liberality of patrons that
any satisfactory compensation could be secured for literary productions.

During the reign of Alfonso of Aragon, who in 1435
added Sicily to his dominions, and under the direct incentive of the royal patronage, a good deal of literary activity
was developed in Naples.   Alfonso was described by
Vespasiano as being, next to Nicholas V., the most mu-
nificent patron of learning in Italy, and he attracted to his
Court scholars like Manetti, Beccadelli, Valla, and others.
The King paid to Bartolommeo Fazio a stipend of 500
ducats a year while he was engaged in writing his *Chronicles*, and when the work was completed, he added a
further payment of 1500 florins.   In 1459, the year of his
death, Alfonso distributed 20,000 ducats among the men
of letters gathered in Naples.   It is certain that in no
other city of Europe during that year were the earnings
or rewards of literature so great.   It does not appear,
however, that this lavish expenditure had the effect of
securing the production by Neapolitans of any works of
continued importance, or even of bringing into existence
in the city any lasting literary interests.   The tempera-
ment of the people and the general environment were
doubtless unfavourable as compared with the influences
affecting Florence or Rome.   It is probable also that the
selection of the recipients of the royal bounty was made

without any trustworthy principle and very much at hap-
hazard.

A production of Beccadelli's, perhaps the most brilliant
of Alfonso's literary protégés, is to be noted as having
been proscribed by the Pope, being one of the earliest
Italian publications to be so distinguished. Eugenius IV.
forbade, under penalty of excommunication, the reading
of Beccadelli's *Hermaphroditus*, which was declared to be
contra bonos mores. The book was denounced from many
pulpits, and copies were burned, together with portraits of
the poet, on the public squares of Bologna, Milan, and
Ferrara.[1] This opposition of the Church was the more
noteworthy, as the book contained nothing heretical or
subversive of ecclesiastical authority, but was simply
ribald and obscene.

Lorenzo Valla, another of the writers who received
special favours and emoluments at the hands of Alfonso,
likewise came under the ecclesiastical ban. But his writings contained more serious offences than obscenity or
ribaldry. He boldly questioned the authenticity of Constantine's *Donation* (a document which was later shown
to be a forgery), and of other documents and literature
held by the Church to be sacred, and the accuracy of his
scholarship and the brilliancy of his polemical style, gave
weight and force to his attacks. Denunciations came
upon Valla's head from many pulpits, and the matter
was taken up by the Inquisition. But Alfonso told the
monks that they must leave his secretary alone, and the
proceedings were abandoned.

When Nicholas V. came to the papacy, undeterred by
the charge of heresies, he appointed Valla to the post of
Apostolic writer, and gave him very liberal emoluments
for work on the series of Greek translations before referred to. Valla never retracted any of his utterances
against the Church, but he appears, after accepting the

[1] *Revival of Learning*, p. 256.

Pope's appointment, to have turned his polemical ardour
in other directions. He engaged in some bitter controversies with Poggio, Fazio, and other contemporaries,
controversies which seem to have aroused and excited the
literary circles of the time, but which turned upon matters
of no lasting importance. It is a cause of surprise to
later literary historians that men like Valla, possessed of
real learning and of unquestioned literary skill, should
have been willing to devote their time and their capacity
to the futilities which formed the pretexts for the greater
part of the personal controversies of the time. Professor
Adams says of Valla: "He had all the pride and insolence and hardly disguised pagan feeling and morals of
the typical humanist; but in spirit and methods of work
he was a genuine scholar, and his editions lie at the
foundation of all later editorial work in the case of more
than one classic author, and of the critical study of the
New Testament as well." [1]

During the two centuries preceding the invention of
printing, it was the case that more books (in the form of
manuscripts) were available for the use of students and
readers in Italy than in any other country, but even in
Italy manuscripts were scarce and costly. Even the collections in the so-called "libraries" of the cathedrals and
colleges were very meagre. These manuscripts were
nearly entirely the production of the cloisters, and as
parchment continued to be very dear, many of the works
sent out by the monks were in the form of palimpsests,
that is, were transcribed upon scrolls which contained
earlier writing. The fact that the original writing was in
many cases but imperfectly erased, has caused to be preserved fragments of a number of classics which might
otherwise have disappeared entirely. The service rendered by the monks in this way may be considered as at
least a partial offset to the injury done by them to the

[1] *Civilisation During the Middle Ages*, 378.

cause of literature in the destruction of so many ancient
writings. This matter has been referred to more fully in
the chapter on Monasteries and Manuscripts.

One of the Italian scholars of the fifteenth century who
interested himself particularly in the collection of manuscripts of the classics was Poggio Bracciolini. In 1414,
while he was, in his official capacity as Apostolic Secretary, in attendance at the Council of Constance, he ran-
sacked the libraries of St. Gall and of other monasteries
of Switzerland and Suabia, and secured a complete *Quintilian*, copies of *Lucretius*, *Frontinus*, *Probus*, *Vitruvius*,
nine of Cicero's *Orations*, and manuscripts of a number
of other valuable texts. Many of the libraries had been
sadly neglected, and the greater part of the manuscripts
were in dirty and tattered condition, but literature owes
much to the monks through whom these literary treasures had been kept in existence at all.

Poggio is to be noted as a free-thinker who managed
to keep in good relations with the Church. So long as
free-thinkers confined their audacity to such matters as
form the topic of Poggio's *Facetiæ*, Beccadelli's *Hermaphroditus*, or La Casa's *Capitolo del Forno*, the Roman
Curia looked on and smiled approvingly. The most
obscene books to be found in any literature escaped the
Papal censure, and a man like Aretino, notorious for his
ribaldry, could aspire with fair prospects of success to the
scarlet of a Cardinal.[1]

While there could be no popular distribution, in the
modern sense of the term, for necessarily costly books in
manuscript, in a community of which only a small proportion had any knowledge of reading and writing, it is evident from the chronicles of the time that there was an
active and prompt exchange of literary novelties between
the court circles and the literary groups of the different
cities, and also between the Faculties of the universities.

[1] *Revival of Learning*, 22.

A controversy between two scholars or men of letters
(and there were, as said, many such controversies, some
of them exceedingly bitter) appears to have excited a
larger measure of interest and attention in cultivated
circles throughout the country than could probably be
secured to-day for any purely literary or scholastic issues.
There must, therefore, have been in existence and in
circulation a very considerable mass of literature in manuscript form, and we know from various sources that
Florence particularly was the centre of an important
trade in manuscripts.   I have not thus far, however, been
able to find any instances of the writers of this period
receiving any compensation from the publishers, booksellers, or copyists, or any share in such profits as might
be derived from the sale of the manuscript copies of their
writings.   It seems probable that the authors gave to the
copyists the privilege (which it was in any case really impracticable to withhold) of manifolding and distributing
such copies of the books as might be called for by the
general public, while the cost of the complimentary copies
(often a considerable number) given to the large circle of
friends, seems as a rule to have been borne by the author.

As the author had to take his compensation in the
shape of fame (except in the cases of receipts from patrons), the wider the circulation secured for copies of his
productions (provided only they were not plagiarised),
the larger his fund of—satisfaction.   For substantial
compensation he could look only to the patron.   Fortunately for the impecunious writers of the day, it
became fashionable for not a few of the princes and
nobles of Italy to play the rôle of Mæcenas, and by
many of these the support and encouragement given to
literature was magnificent, if not always judicious.

During the reigns of the last Visconti and of the first
Sforza, or from about 1440 to 1474, literature became
fashionable at the Court of Milan.   Filippo Maria Vis-

conti is described as a superstitious and repulsive tyrant, and he could hardly by his own personality have attracted to Lombardy men of intellectual tastes. Visconti appears, however, to have considered that his Court would be incomplete without scholars, and to have been willing to pay liberally for their attendance. Piero Candido Decembrio was one of the most industrious of the writers who were supported by Visconti. According to his epitaph, he was responsible for no less than 127 books. Symonds speaks of his memoir of Visconti as a vivid and vigorous study of a tyrant. Gasparino da Barzizza was the Court letter-writer and rhetorician, and, as the official orator, filled an important place in what was considered the intellectual life of the city.

By far the most noteworthy, however, of the scholars who were attracted to Milan by the Ducal bounty was Francesco Filelfo. He could hardly be said to belong to Lombardy, as he was born in Ancona and educated at Padua, and had passed a number of years in Venice, Constantinople, Florence, Siena, and Bologna. The longest sojourn of his life, however, was made in Milan, where he arrived in 1440, and where he enjoyed for some years liberal emoluments from the Court.

Filelfo was evidently a man with great powers of acquisition and with exceptional versatility. He brought back with him from Constantinople (where he had remained for some years) a Greek bride from a noble family, an extensive collection of Greek manuscripts, and a working knowledge of the Greek language; and at a time when Greek ideas and Greek literature were attracting the enthusiastic attention not merely of the scholars but of the courtiers and men of fashion, these possessions of Filelfo were exceptionally serviceable, and enabled him to push his fortunes effectively. He seems to have possessed a self-confidence at least equal to his learning. He speaks of himself as having surpassed Virgil because he was an

orator, and Cicero because he was a poet.   Symonds says,
however, that, notwithstanding his arrogance, he is entitled to the rank of the most universal scholar of his age,
and his self-assertion doubtless aided not a little in
securing prompt recognition for his learning.   Venice
paid him, in 1427, a stipend of 500 sequins for a series of
lectures on Eloquence.   A year later he accepted the
post of lecturer in Bologna on Moral Philosophy and
Eloquence, with a stipend of 450 sequins.   Shortly afterwards, flattering offers tempted him to Florence, where
he lectured on the Greek and Latin classics and on Dante,
with a stipend first of 250 sequins, and later of 450 sequins.
He found time while there for the preparation of translations of the *Rhetoric* of Aristotle, and of a number of
other Greek works.

Filelfo's arrogance and bad temper, and his fondness
for invective and satire, soon brought him into trouble
with the literary circle of Florence, and finally with the
Medici, and he was compelled to withdraw to Siena,
where he remained four years with a stipend of 350
florins.   From there, after a brief visit to Bologna, he
removed to Milan, where his emoluments were much
larger than any heretofore received, and where, in the
absence of any other scholars of equal attainments or
assumptions, he had the satisfaction of being the accepted
literary leader of the capital.   In addition to his professional salary, he received large sums and presents for
addresses, orations, and commemorative poems, which he
was always ready to prepare.   Such a combination of
rhetoric and literature was peculiarly characteristic of the
Italy of the time, and may be said to constitute a distinct
phase in the history of compensation for intellectual productions.   Filelfo published, in two ponderous volumes,
his Satires, Odes, and other fugitive pieces, under the
title of *Convivia Mediolanensia.*
Notwithstanding the considerable sums which Filelfo

earned through his lectures and through his various rhetorical productions, he seems always to have been in need
of money. His tastes were expensive, while his three
wives had borne him no less than twenty-four children.
In his later years he gained the reputation of being very
greedy of gold and of making impudent demands which
bore very much the character of blackmail. Gregorio
Lollio, writing (in 1452) to the Cardinal of Pavia, describes
Filelfo in the following words: "He is calumnious, envious, vain, and so greedy of gold that he metes out
praise or blame according to the gifts he gets, both
despicable as proceeding from a tainted source."[1]

From Francesco Sforza, Duke of Milan, he received a
liberal stipend. Pope Nicholas V., after reading some
of his Satires (which Symonds characterises as "in-
famous") presented him with 500 ducats. Travelling
from Rome to Naples, Filelfo received more presents
from Alfonso, who dubbed him a knight. Continuing his
journey, he secured honours and rewards in Ferrara from
Duke Borso, in Mantua from Marchese Gonzaga, and in
Rimini from Gismondo Malatesta. After the death of
Sforza, he accepted, in 1475, from Pope Sixtus IV., a
professional Chair in Rome, with a salary of 600 florins.
He soon, however, quarrelled with the Pope, and withdrew to Florence, where Lorenzo de' Medici provided a
post for him as Professor of Greek Literature.

Filelfo died in Florence in his eighty-third year. He
had probably received larger emoluments for his work as
an instructor, as a rhetorician, and as a man of letters,
than any man of his generation, but he died without any
means, and was buried by the charity of the Florentines.
His career, in its activities, vicissitudes, controversies,
successes, and bitternesses, was very typical of the lives
of the Italian scholars of the period.

At the time of Filelfo's death, while in many other

[1] *Revival of Learning*, p. 284.

cities the influence of the Renaissance was bringing together collections of books and circles of scholars, and literary productiveness was increasing throughout Italy, Florence still remained the capital of learning and of refined culture. Lorenzo de' Medici had, in 1469, succeeded to Pietro, and of all the Medici it was Lorenzo whose influence was the most important in furthering the intellectual and artistic movements of the time. Symonds speaks of him as " a man of marvellous variety and range of mental power, in whom . . . the versatility of the Renaissance found its fullest incarnation."

Lorenzo attracted to his villa the greatest scholars and most brilliant men of the time, a circle which included Poliziano, Landino, Ficino, Pico della Mirandola, Alberti, Pulci, and Michael Angelo. The interests of this circle, as of all similar Italian circles of the time, were largely absorbed in the philosophy and literature of Greece, and special attention was devoted to the teachings of Plato. Plato's writings were translated into Latin by Ficino, and the translation was printed in 1482, at the cost of Filippo Valvio. Ficino was too poor himself to undertake the publication of his works, and this was the case with not a few of the distinguished authors of the age. The presentation of books to the public required at this time what might be called the endowment of literature, an endowment which was supplied by the liberality of wealthy patrons possessed of literary appreciation or public-spirited ambition, or of both. As Symonds expresses it, " Great literary undertakings involved in that century the substantial assistance of wealthy men, whose liberality was rewarded by a notice in the colophon or in the title-page." The formal dedication was an invention of a somewhat later date.

The Ficino edition of *Plotinus*, printed at the expense of Lorenzo de' Medici, and published a few weeks after his death, bears the inscription, *Magnifici sumptu Lau-*

rentii patriæ servatoris. The edition of *Homer* of Lorenzo Alopa, issued in 1488, was printed at the expense of either Bernardo Nerli or Giovanni Acciajuoli. These examples of printed publications belong, however, to a later chapter. Ficino followed up his translation of Plato's work with a *Life of Plato*, and an essay on the *Platonic Doctrine of Immortality.*

In 1484, appeared in the Florentine circle the beautiful and brilliant Pico della Mirandola, a man who through his exceptional gifts, his varied learning, and the charm of his personality, exercised a very wide influence over his generation, and who may possibly be accepted as at once the type and the flower of the Renaissance. Pico studied at Bologna, and later at Paris. He printed, in 1489, in defence of his philosophical theories, certain theses which were condemned as heretical by Innocent VIII. In 1493, the ban of heterodoxy was renewed by a brief of Alexander VI. Pico's enquiring mind and scholarly ardour covered a wide range of research, including the philosophy of the Platonists, the mysteries of the Cabbala, and the system and theories of Aquinas, Scotus, Albertus Magnus, and Averrhoes, and he proposed to devote his learning and his life to the task of reconciling classical traditions with the Christian creeds. Didot quotes the following characteristic sentence from a letter written by Pico, February 11, 1491, to Aldus Manutius: "*Philosophia veritatem quærit, theologia invenit, religio possidet.*" (Philosophy seeks truth, theology discovers it, religion possesses it.)

Pico died at the age of thirty-one, before the book had been written in which he proposed to demonstrate these positions. He was able, however, to render a great service to Italy and to Europe in securing for his friend Aldus the aid required for the establishment of the Aldine Press in Venice. The details of the relations of the two men are given in the chapter on Aldus.

Other noteworthy members of the literary circle which surrounded Lorenzo de' Medici, were Christoforo Landino, Leo Battista Alberti, and Angelo Poliziano. Landino edited *Horace* and *Virgil* and translated Pliny's *Natural History*, and in 1481 published an edition of *Dante*, and Battista Alberti, (whose comedy of *Philodoxius*, which passed for an antique, was published by the Aldi, in 1588, as the work of Lepidus Comicus), wrote three treatises on painting, and several volumes on architecture. Alberti was more distinguished as an artist, architect, and musician, than as an author. It was characteristic, however, of the men of this group to be universal in their genius.

Symonds speaks of Poliziano as emphatically the representative of the highest achievements of the age in scholarship, and as the first Italian to combine perfect mastery over Latin and a correct sense of Greek, with splendid genius for his native literature. His published works included annotated editions of *Ovid*, *Suetonius*, *Statius*, *Pliny*, and *Quintilian*, translations of *Epictetus*, *Galen*, and *Hippocrates*, a series of *Miscellanea*, and most important of all, the edition, printed from the famous Amalfi manuscript, of the *Pandects* of Justinian.

Among the smaller cities in which the Humanistic movement influenced literature and furthered the development of learning, may be mentioned Carpi, afterwards the home of Musurus and Aldus ; Mirandola, the birthplace of the brilliant Pico ; Pesaro, where Alessandro and Constanzo Sforza brought together a library rivalling that of the Medici ; Rimini, where Sigismondo Malatesta gathered about his fortress a circle of scholars; and Urbino, where the good Duke Frederick brought together one of the finest collections of manuscripts which Europe had known, a collection valued at over 30,000 ducats. Vespasiano, who served for some time as librarian, says that for fourteen years the Duke kept from thirty to forty copyists employed in transcribing Greek and Latin Manuscripts. The work of these copyists went on for some years after the introduction of printing into Italy, for Frederick, in common with not a few other of the scholarly nobles who were collectors of manuscripts, distrusted and looked down upon the new art, and had no interest in books which were merely mechanical reproductions.

Vespasiano da Bisticci, whose aid Frederick had secured in the preparation of his library, was noted as an author, as a scribe, and as a bookseller. Symonds speaks of the " rare merit " of the biographical work in Vespasiano's *Lives of Illustrious Men*, the memoirs of which Symonds utilised largely in the preparation of his *Renaissance*. Vespasiano's literary work must have been done " in the intervals of business," for his business undertakings were important. He was the largest dealer in manuscripts of his time. His purchasing agents and correspondents were armed with instructions to secure authenticated codices wherever these were obtainable, and the monasteries not only of Italy but of Switzerland, South Germany, Hungary, Transylvania, and the East were carefully searched for possible literary treasures. He employed a large force of skilled copyists in the production of copies of famous works, which copies were distributed through correspondents and customers in the different scholarly centres of Europe. Possessing himself a wide and exact scholarship, he gave his personal attention to the selection of his texts, the training of his copyists and the supervision of their work, so that a manuscript coming from Vespasiano carried with it the prestige of accuracy and completeness.

Vespasiano's scholarly knowledge and his special experience in palæography were utilised by such clients as Nicholas V., Cosimo de' Medici, Frederick of Urbino, and other lovers of literature, in the formation of and development of their libraries. Vespasiano united, therefore, the functions of a scholarly editor and commentator, a collector, a book-manufacturer, a publisher and a book-seller, a series of responsibilities which called for a wide range of learning, accomplishments, and executive ability. It is evident from his career and from the testimony of his friends and clients (terms in this case practically identical) that he was devoted to literature for its own sake. He accepted the rewards secured by his skill and enterprise, and promptly expended these in fresh efforts for the development and extension of liberal scholarship. Vespasiano may be called the last, as he was probably the greatest of the book-dealers of the manuscript period. Born in 1421 and living until 1498, he witnessed the introduction of printing into Italy, and may easily have had opportunities of handling the earlier productions of the Venetian printing-press. Vespasiano was a fitting successor of Atticus and a worthy precursor of Aldus, whose work in the distribution of scholarly literature was, in fact, a direct continuation of his own.

As before mentioned, the trade in the production of manuscript copies went on for a number of years after the introduction of printing. The noblemen and wealthy scholars who had inherited, or who had themselves brought together, collections of famous works in manuscript, were for some time, not unnaturally, unwilling to believe that ordinary people could, by means of the new invention, with a comparatively trifling expenditure secure perfect and beautiful copies of the same works. Before the death of Vespasiano, in 1498, however, the work of the printing-press had come to be understood and cordially appreciated by book-buyers and students of all classes, and the trade of the copyists and of the manuscript-deal-ers had, excepting for newly discovered texts, practically come to an end. The career of Vespasiano belongs strictly to the chapter on the publishers of manuscripts, of whom he was the most important. The man himself, however, through his character and services, belongs essentially to the movement of the Renaissance, of which movement he was at once a product and a leader.

During the reigns of Pope Innocent VIII., 1484–1492, and of Alexander VI. (Borgia), 1492–1503, little or nothing was done in Rome to further the development of literature. To the latter was in fact due the initiating of the system of the subjection of the press to ecclesiastical censorship, a system which for centuries to come was to exercise the most baneful influence over literature and intellectual activities and to interfere enormously with the establishment of any assured foundation for property in literature. Some account of the long contests carried on by the publishers of Venice against this claim for ecclesiastical control of the productions of their presses, is given in a later chapter.

Venice stood almost alone among the cities of Italy in resisting the censorship of the Church, and even in Venice, the Church in the end succeeded in the more important of its contentions. In Spain, the ecclesiastical control was hardly questioned. In France, it was, after a century of contest, practically merged in the censorship exercised by the Crown, a control which was in itself fully as much as the publishing trade could bear and continue to exist. In Austria and South Germany, after the crushing out of the various reformation movements, the Church and State worked in practical accord in keeping a close supervision of the printing-presses. In North Germany, on the other hand, ecclesiastical censorship never became important. The evils produced by it were, however, serious and long enduring throughout a large portion of the territory of Europe, and the papal Borgia, though by no means a considerable personage, is responsible for bringing into existence an evil which assumed enormous proportions in the intellectual history of Europe.

Towards the close of the fifteenth century begins in Italy the age of academies, associations of scholars and littérateurs for the furthering of scholarly pursuits and of literary undertakings. One of the earlier of these Academies was instituted in Rome, in 1468, by Julius Pomponius Lætus (a pupil of Valla), for the special purpose of promoting the study of Latin literature and Latin antiquities. Comedies of Plautus and of other Latin dramatists were revived, and the attempt was made to make Latin, at least for the scholarly circle, again a living language. The Academy was suspected by Pope Paul II. to have some political purpose, and it was for a time suppressed, but resumed its activities some years later under the papacy of Alexander VI.

The Academy of Naples was instituted in 1470, under the leadership of Beccadelli and Juvianus Pontanus, and with a membership comprising a number of the brilliant scholars whom Alphonso the Magnanimous had attracted to his Court. This society also devoted itself particularly to the revival of an interest in Latin literature, and not a few of the members became better known under the Latinised names there adopted by them than by their Italian cognomens. Pomponius had written little and hoped to be remembered through his pupils. Pontanus on the other hand, wrote on many subjects, using for the purpose Latin, of which he was a master. Symonds says that he chiefly deserves to be remembered for his ethical treatises, but he seems himself to have attached special importance to his amatory elegiacs and to a series of astronomical hexameters entitled *Urania*.

In Florence, the Platonic Academy continued to flourish under the auspices of the Rucellai family. It was suppressed in 1522, at the time of the conspiracy against Giulio de' Medici, but again revived in 1540. In 1572, was organised in Florence the famous academy called *Della Crusca*, which secured for itself a European reputation. In Bologna, in 1504, the society of the *Viridario* was instituted, with the purpose of studying printed texts and of furthering the art of printing. Bologna had a considerable number of other literary societies, for the study of jurisprudence, chivalry, and other subjects. Throughout Italy at this period academies multiplied, but the greater number exercised no continued influence.

It is probable, however, that they all proved of service in preparing the way for the printed literature which the Italian presses were, after 1490, beginning to distribute, and that in widening the range of popular interest in scholarship and in books generally, they did not a little to render possible the work of Aldus and other early Italian publishers. The academy founded by Aldus in Venice, for the prosecution of Greek studies, will be referred to in the chapter on Aldus.

" The fifteenth century rediscovered antiquity ; the sixteenth was absorbed in slowly deciphering it. In the fifteenth century ' educated Europe ' is but a synonym for Italy. What literature there was north of the Alps was in great part derived from, or was largely dependent upon, the Italian movement. The fact that the movement originated in the Latin peninsula, was decisive of the character of the first age of classical learning (1400–1550). It was a revival of Latin as opposed to Greek literature. It is now well understood that the fall of Constantinople, though an influential incident of the movement, ranks for little among the causes of the Renaissance. What was revived in Italy in the fifteenth century was the interest of the Schools of the early Empire—of the second and third century. . . . But in one decisive feature, the literary sentiment of the fifteenth century was a reproduction of that of the Empire. It was rhetorical, not scientific. Latin literature as a whole is rhetorical. . . . The divorce of the literature of knowledge and the literature of form which characterised the

epoch of decay under the early empire, characterised
equally the epoch of revival in the Italy of the Popes. . . .
The knowledge and wisdom buried in the Greek writers
presented a striking contrast to the barren sophistic which
formed the curriculum of the Latin schools. It became
the task of the scholars of the second period of the classical revival to disinter this knowledge. . . . Philology had
meant composition and verbal emendation; it now meant
the apprehension of the ideas and usages of the ancient
world. Scholars had exerted themselves to write, they
now bent all their effort to know. . . . There came now
into existence what has ever since been known as 'learning,' in the special sense of the term. The first period of
humanism in which the words of the ancient authors had
been studied, was thus the preparatory school for the
humanism of the second period, in which the matter
was the object of attention.

"As Italy had been the home of classical taste in the
first period, France became the home of classical learning
in the second. Single names can be mentioned, such as
Victorius or Sigonius in Italy, Mursius or Vulcanius in
the Low Countries, who were distinguished representatives of 'learning,' but in Bulæus, Turnebus, Lambrinus,
Scaliger, Casaubon, and Saumaise, France produced a
constellation of humanists whose fame justly eclipsed
that of all their contemporaries.

"If we ask why Italy did not continue to be the centre
of the humanist movement, which she had so brilliantly
inaugurated, the answer is that the intelligence was crushed
by the reviviscence of ecclesiastical ideas. Learning is
the result of research, and research must be free and
cannot coexist with the claim of the Catholic clergy to be
superior to enquiry. The French school, it will be observed, is wholly in fact or in intention Protestant. As
soon as it was decided (as it was before 1600) that France
was to be a Catholic country, and the University of Paris

a Catholic university, learning was extinguished in France. France saw without regret and without repentance the expatriation of her unrivalled scholars. With Scaliger and Saumaise, the seat of learning was transferred from France to Holland. The third period of classical learning thus coincides with the Dutch school. From 1593, the date of Scaliger's removal to Leyden, the supremacy in the republic of learning was possessed by the Dutch. In the course of the eighteenth century, the Dutch school was gradually supplanted by the North German, which from that time forward has taken, and still possesses, the lead in philological science." [1]

[1] Pattison's *Casaubon*, 453, 454.

CHAPTER II.

THE INVENTION OF PRINTING AND THE WORK OF THE FIRST PRINTERS OF HOLLAND AND GERMANY.

1440–1528.

"FOUR men, Gutenberg, Columbus, Luther, and Copernicus, stand at the dividing line of the Middle Ages, and serve as boundary stones marking the entrance of mankind into a higher and finer epoch of its development."[1]

It would be difficult to say which one of the four has made the largest contribution to this development or has done the most to lift up the spirit of mankind and to open for men the doors to the new realms that were in readiness. The Genoese seaman and discoverer opens new realms to our knowledge and imagination, leads Europe from the narrow restrictions of the Middle Ages out into the vast space of Western oceans, and in adding to the material realms controlled by civilisation, widens still more largely the range of its thought and fancy. The Reformer of Wittenberg, in breaking the bonds which had chained the spirits of his fellow-men and in securing for them again their rights as individual Christians, conquers for them a spiritual realm and brings them into renewed relations with their Creator. The great astronomer shatters, through his discoveries, the fixed and petty conceptions of the universe which had ruled the

---

[1] Kapp, *Geschichte*, etc., i.

minds of mankind, and in bringing to them fresh light on the nature and extent of created things, widens at the same time their whole understanding of themselves and of duty. The citizen of Mayence may claim to have unchained intelligence and given to it wings. He utilised lead no longer as a death-bringing ball, but in the form of life-quickening letters which were to bring before thousands of minds the teachings of the world's thinkers. Each one of the four had his part in bringing to the world light, knowledge, and development.

At the time when the art of printing finally took shape in the mind of Gutenberg, the direction of literary and intellectual interests of Germany rested, as we have seen, largely with Italy. The fact, however, that the new art had its birthplace, not in Florence, which was at that time the centre of the literary activities of Europe, but in Mayence, heretofore a town which had hardly been connected at all with literature, and the further fact that the printing-presses were carrying on their work in Germany for nearly fifteen years before two printers, themselves Germans, set up the first press in Italy, exercised, of necessity, an important influence in inciting literary activities throughout Germany and in the relations borne by Germany to the scholarship of the world.

The details of the life and early work of Gutenberg are at best but fragmentary, and have been a subject of much discussion. It is not necessary, for the purpose of this treatise, to give detailed consideration to the long series of controversies as to the respective claims of Gutenberg of Mayence, of Koster of Haarlem, or of other competitors, as to the measure of credit to be assigned to each in the original discovery or of the practical development of the the printing-press. It seems in any case evident that whatever minds elsewhere were at that time puzzling over the same problem, it was the good fortune of Gutenberg to make the first practical application of the printing-press to the production of impressions from movable type, while it was certainly from Mayence that the art spread throughout the cities, first of Germany, and later of Italy and France.

It is to be borne in mind (and I speak here for the non-technical reader) that, as indicated in the above reference, the distinction and important part of the invention of Gutenberg was, not the production of a press for the multiplication of impressions, but the use of movable type and the preparation of the form from which the impressions were struck off. The art of printing from blocks, since classified as xylographic printing, had been practised in certain quarters of Europe for fifty years or more before the time of Gutenberg, and if Europe had had communication with China, xylography might have been introduced four or five centuries earlier.

With the block-books, the essential thing was the illustrations, and what text or letterpress accompanied these was usually limited to a few explanatory or descriptive words engraved on the block, above, beneath or around the picture. Occasionally, however, as in the *Ars Moriendi*, there were entire pages of text engraved, like the designs, on the solid block. The earlier engraving was done on hard wood, but, later, copper was also employed. It is probable that the block-books originated in the Netherlands, and it is certain that in such towns as Bruges, Antwerp, and Amsterdam, the art was developed more rapidly than elsewhere, so that during the first half of the fifteenth century, the production of wood engravings and of books made up of engravings (printed only on one side, and accompanied by a few words of text), began to form an important article of trade. The subjects of these designs were for the most part Biblical, or at least religious. One of the earlier of the block-book publications and probably the most characteristic specimen of the class, is the volume known as the *Biblia Pauperum*.

This was a close imitation of a manuscript book that had
for five or six centuries been popular as a work of religious
instruction. It had been composed about 850, by S.
Ausgarius, a monk of Corbie, who afterwards became
Bishop of Hamburg. The *scriptorium* established by him
at Corbie was said to have been the means of preserving
from destruction a number of classics, including the *Annals* of Tacitus.[1] The use, five centuries later, as one of
the first productions of the printing-press, of the monk's
own composition, may be considered as a fitting acknow-
ledgement of the service thus rendered by him to the
world's literature. Examples of manuscript copies of the
Biblia Pauperum are in existence in the *Bibliothèque Na-
tionale* in Paris, in Munich, in the British Museum, and
elsewhere, and there is no difficulty in comparing these
with the printed copies produced in the Netherlands,
which are also represented in these collections.

It is probable that Laurence Koster of Haarlem, whose
name is, later, associated with printing from movable type,
was himself an engraver of block-books. Humphreys is,
in fact, inclined to believe that the first block-book edition
of the *Biblia Pauperum* was actually Koster's work, basing
this opinion on the similarity of the compositions and of
their arrangement to those of the *Speculum Humanæ Salvationis*, which was the first work printed from movable
type, and the production of which is now generally
credited to Koster.[2] The *Biblia Pauperum* was printed
from blocks in Germany as late as 1475, but before that
date an edition had been printed from movable type by
Pfister in Bamberg.

As has been pointed out by many of the writers on the
subject, the so-called invention of printing was not so
much the result of an individual inspiration, as the almost
inevitable consequence of a long series of experiments
and of partial processes which had been conducted in

[1] Humphreys, 38.   [2] Humphreys, 39.

various places where the community was interesting itself in the multiplication of literature.

If, as is probably the case, the first book printed from movable type is to be credited to Koster, it remains none the less the case that Gutenberg's process must have been worked out for itself, and that the German possessed, what the Hollander appears to have lacked, not merely the persistence and the practical understanding required to produce a single book, but the power to overcome obstacles and to instruct others, and was thus able to establish the new art on a lasting foundation.

The claims of the Hollanders under which Koster is to be regarded as the first printer, or at least (bearing in mind the Chinese precedents in the tenth century) the first European printer, from movable type, claims which Humphreys accepts as well founded, are in substance as follows : Laurence Koster was born, somewhere in Holland, about 1370, and died in Haarlem about 1440. He is believed to have made his first experiments with movable wooden types about 1426, and to have worked with metal types about ten years later. The principal of the earlier authorities concerning Koster's career is a certain Hadrian Junius, who completed, in 1569, a history of Holland, which was published in 1588. He speaks of Koster as being a man of an honourable family, in which the office of Sacristan (custos, Coster or Koster) was hereditary, and he describes in detail the development of the invention of type, from the cutting of pieces of beechbark into the form of letters, to the final production of the metal fonts. Junius goes on to relate the method under which Koster's first book (from type), *Speculum Humanæ Salvationis*, was printed, in 1430. This book, the origin of which is not known, had for many years been popular among the Benedictines, and few of their monasteries were without a copy. As a result of this popularity, many examples of the manuscript copies have been preserved, some of which are in the Arundel collection in the British Museum. Zani says that the *Speculum* was compiled for the assistance of poor preachers, and in support of this view he quotes certain lines, which may serve also as an example of Latinity and of the general style :

> *Predictum prohemium hujus libri de contentis compilavi*
> *Et propter pauperes predicatores hoc opponere curavi.*[1]

Koster appears to have produced, about 1428, an edition of a portion of the *Speculum* in which the entire pages (presenting on the upper half two designs, and on the lower two columns of text) are printed from solid wooden blocks. Humphreys gives examples of these pages. The cutting of the text, all the letters of which had, of course, to be cut in reverse, is a wonderful piece of work. About 1430, was completed the first issue printed from movable types. The arrangement of the pages is the same, the upper half is occupied with two designs (printed in brown ink, from wooden blocks), and the lower half is given to the text, printed in black ink, from the metal type. The first typographic edition contains a number of xylographic pages. In the type-pages, the block-illustration was printed first, and the sheet was then imposed again for the printing of the text. Both the designs and the text were modelled to follow very closely the character of the manuscripts of the period. The volume is undoubtedly the earliest European example of printing from type, and the evidence that it was the work of Koster, and that it was produced not later than 1430, or about twenty years earlier than the Bible of Gutenberg, is, I understand, now accepted by the best authorities as practically conclusive. Three editions of the book were printed by Koster before his death in 1440, the third being printed in Dutch (instead of Latin), and

---

[1] Cited by Humphreys, 59.

being entirely typographic. This is the edition seen and described (128 years later) by Junius. After specifying the method employed by Koster (according to his own views concerning movable type), Junius goes on to say, " It was by this method that he produced impressions of engraved plates, to which he added ' separate ' letters. I have seen a book of this kind, the first rude effort of his invention, printed by him on one side only ; this book was entitled the *Mirror of Our Salvation*." While this evidence of Junius comes first into record one hundred and twenty-eight years after the time assigned to the printing of Koster's first book, it is the conclusion of Humphreys, Blades, and other historians that, in consideration of the circumstances under which Junius wrote, and the nature of the information which was evidently at that time available for him, his testimony may safely be accepted as conclusive. Junius goes on to say that Koster, having perfected his system, and finding a rapidly increasing demand for his printed books, was unable to manage the work with the aid of the members of his own family. He took foreign workmen into his employ, which eventually led to the abstraction of his secret and caused the credit of his invention to be given to others.[1] Junius gives further details concerning the channels through which he secured the record of the work of Koster. He refers to a certain Nicholas Galius who had been his first preceptor, and who remembered having heard the facts connected with Koster's discovery from a certain Cornelius when the latter was over eighty years of age. Cornelius testified that he had himself been a binder in the establishment of Koster, and the Dutch historian, Meerman, has discovered in the records of the church of Haarlem a memorandum dated 1474, which is evidence that there was at that date a binder in the town called Cornelius.[2]

[1] Humphreys, 57.   [2] Meerman, cited by Humphreys, 58.

In claiming for Holland the prestige of inventing the several distinctive processes connected with the printing of books, Humphreys sums up as follows : It is beyond dispute that the Dutch were the first to produce block-books, and thus were virtually the first printers of books. It is also a matter of record that it was the printers of Holland who first devised the art of stereotyping, a process which was applied by John Miller of Amsterdam towards the close of the seventeenth century. There is, therefore, apart from the details above specified and from the evidence of tradition, a strong natural presumption in favour of the development in Holland of the intervening step of substituting movable types for carved pages of letters. Humphreys points out that there are other references to the production in the Netherlands of books from movable metal types, before the date at which Gutenberg's first volume was completed in Mayence. In a record of accounts of Jean Robert, Abbé of Cambrai, the manuscript of which has been preserved in the archives of the city of Lille, appears the entry : " Item, for a printed (*getté en molle*) *Doctrinal* that I sent for to Bruges by Macquart, who is a writer at Valenciennes, in the month of January, 1445, for Jacquet, twenty sous, Tournois. Little Alexander had one the same, that the church paid for." It is stated later in the record that one of these books proved to be so " full of faults " that it had to be replaced by a written copy.[1] The purport of the term *getté en molle* (which might possibly have been written *jetté* or *guetté*) was first elucidated by M. Besuard, who pointed out that it evidently stood for " cast in a mould," the reference being to the metallic types, which were so cast. In the letters of naturalisation accorded, in 1474, to the first printers with movable types established in Paris, the term used is *escritoire en molle*, or writing by means of moulds or moulded letters.

[1] Humphreys, 66.

Humphreys is inclined to give credit to the theory, which is presented by many of the advocates of Koster, that the first suggestion of the new art was brought to Gutenberg in Strasburg by a workman who had been employed by Koster in Haarlem, but he admits that this theory is supported by practically nothing that can be called evidence, and depends for its authority simply upon the sequence of events, and upon the surmises and probabilities suggested by Junius. It remains the case that after the death of Koster, which occurred either in 1440 or in 1439, the production of books from type came to an end in Holland, and that for instruction in the new art Europe was indebted not to Haarlem but to Mayence. We may accept as conclusive the evidence which gives to Koster the credit of producing the first book printed (outside of China) from movable type, without lessening the value of the service rendered by Gutenberg. The shores of our Western Continent were undoubtedly visited by Eric and his Northmen, but it was Columbus who gave to Europe the New World.

The production of printed books, which changed the whole condition of literary production and of literary ownership, is to be traced directly to the operations of Gutenberg and Fust. Kapp mentions that if it were not for the records of certain court processes of Strasburg and of Mayence, we should have hardly any trustworthy references whatsoever to the work or the relations of Gutenberg prior to 1450.

By means of these court records, however, it has proved possible to secure some data concerning various undertakings in which Gutenberg was engaged before he devoted himself to his printing-office. He belonged to a noble family of Mayence, the family name of which was originally Gensfleisch, a name Latinised by some writers of the time as Ansicarus. For more than a century, the Gensfleische stood at the head of the nobility of the city in the long series of contests carried on with the guilds and citizens.

Until the sacking of the city, after the outbreak of October, 1462, Mayence was the most important of the free cities and of the commercial centres of the middle Rhine district, and was an important competitor for the general trade of central Europe with Strasburg on the upper river and with Cologne in the region below. The citizens felt themselves strong enough, with the beginning of the fifteenth century, to make a sturdy fight against the old-time control claimed by the nobility, and as early as 1420, they had overcome the patricians in a contest which turned upon the reception of the newly chosen Elector, Conrad III. As one result of this struggle, a number of the Gensfleische found themselves among the exiles.

Gutenberg's father, whose name was Frilo, had held the office of Tax Receiver or General Accountant in the city, and was among those who were banished in 1420. Gutenberg himself was born either in 1397 or 1398. He appears to have passed a portion of his youth at the little village of Eltville, and from there went to Strasburg. In the year 1433, an entry in the tax record of Mayence speaks of Henne Gensfleisch, called Gutenberg, who was an uncle of the printer. About the year 1440, Gutenberg was engaged in Strasburg in the manufacture of looking-glasses, and is already referred to as a man of scientific attainments and learned in inventions.

One of the court records above referred to gives the details of a suit brought by the brothers Dritzehn against Gutenberg, in connection with this first manufacturing business. Another Dritzehn, a brother or a cousin of the above, had as early as 1437 applied to Gutenberg to be instructed (in consideration of the payment of an honorarium) in a " certain art " (*in etlicher kunst*). Shortly thereafter Gutenberg entered into an arrangement with a

certain Hans Riffe of Lichtenau, and instructed him in
the trade of manufacturing mirrors, Riffe making an investment in the business and sharing the profits.

Dritzehn made in all, three contracts with Gutenberg ;
under the first, he was instructed in the art of stone-
polishing, and took some interest in this branch of Gutenberg's business; under the second, he interested himself in
the manufacturing of mirrors ; while the third contract
refers to certain arts and undertakings (*kunste und afentur*)
in which Dritzehn also received instruction, and to the
carrying on of which he also contributed an investment.

It is the opinion of some of the students on the subject
that the researches of Gutenberg, which resulted in 1450
in the production of a working printing-press, had begun
at least ten years back, and that, in connection with these
researches, he had been obliged to borrow money or to
accept investments from Dritzehn and from other associates. The vague terms used in referring to the undertakings which were associated with or which followed the
mirror manufacturing business (" a certain art ") indicate
that these associates had been cautioned to give no information as to the precise nature of the work in which
Gutenberg was experimenting. Humphreys is of opinion
that the term " manufacture of looking-glasses " was used
partly as a blind and partly as a joke, and that Gutenberg
was actually engaged in the production (with the aid of
one of Koster's assistants) of copies of the *Speculum*
(Mirror). Against this view is the fact that Gutenberg
did not print the *Speculum* at all. If Gutenberg were
already working over the printing-press invention at the
time of his association with Dritzehn and with Riffe,
there may be some justice in the claim of Strasburg to be
the birthplace of the printing-press. The completed
press, however, was not produced until Gutenberg had
returned to the old home city of the family—Mayence.

After the close of the suit brought by Dritzehn against

Gutenberg, that is to say, after 1440, thère are no further references to Gutenberg's undertakings in Strasburg. It is not even known whether or not he continued business operations there, but it appears that he was dwelling there as late as 1444. In 1448, he is recorded as again a citizen of Mayence, and it was in Mayence that, in 1450, the completed invention became known to the world.

Gutenberg's name stands on no title-page and is connected with no colophon. The fact, however, that the full responsibility for the invention belongs to him is borne witness to by his contemporaries, Peter Schöffer, Ulrich Zell, the Abbot Trithemius, Jacob Wimpheling, and others. In a chronicle of the archbishop of Mayence, continued to the year 1555 and compiled by Count Wilhelm von Zimmern, it is recorded that the noble art of book-printing was discovered in Mayence by a worthy citizen named Gutenberg, who devoted to the invention all his time and resources until he had brought it to a successful completion.

In 1470, a letter was written by the scholar, Wilhelm Fichet, of Paris, to the historian, Robert Gaguin, which letter was later printed on the last sheet of a volume published in Paris and in Basel, entitled : *Gasparini Pergamensis Orthographiæ Liber*. This letter contains an enthusiastic description of the new art of book-printing discovered in Germany by Gutenberg. The writer says : " There has been discovered in Germany a wonderful new method for the production of books, and those who have mastered this method are taking their invention from Mayence out into the world somewhat as the old Grecian warriors took their weapons from the belly of the Trojan horse. The light of this wonderful discovery will spread from Germany to all parts of the earth. I have been told by three foreigners—Kranz, Freiburger, and Gering—that Gutenberg has succeeded in producing books by means of metal letters in place of using the handiwork of the scribes."

Fichet goes on to speak of Gutenberg as "bringing more blessings upon the world than were given by the goddess Ceres, for Ceres could bestow only material food, while through Gutenberg the productions of the thinkers could be brought within the reach of all people." This letter was written only two years after the death of Gutenberg, and as it came from Basel, one of the first cities to which the new art had been carried from Mayence, it constitutes very good contemporary evidence as to the immediate credit that was given to Gutenberg for the invention.[1]

The historical date now given for the completion of the invention is August 22, 1450. On this date Gutenberg entered into a contract with Johann Fust, a wealthy citizen and goldsmith of Mayence, under which contract Fust loaned to Gutenberg, with interest at 6 per cent. (a low rate for that period), the sum of 800 gulden in gold. This sum Gutenberg agreed to utilise in developing his invention, while the material of the workshop to be instituted was pledged to Fust as security for the repayment of the loan. The sum proved insufficient for establishing the necessary plant, and two years later Fust added a further sum of 800 gulden.

Gutenberg pledged himself, as afterwards stated in the lawsuit which arose between Fust and himself, to use this money for the printing of books,—"*das werk der bücher.*" At the time Gutenberg secured this loan, it seemed evident that, in experimenting with and in developing his invention, he had exhausted his own entire resources.

Gutenberg could, of course, lay no claim to being in any literal sense of the term the first printer. Printing in one form or another had been carried on in Germany and elsewhere for a number of years, and printing from movable blocks had, in fact, been done in China 400 years or more before the beginning of Gutenberg's work. As early as the twelfth century, says Kapp, there are numer-

[1] Kapp, 42.

ous references to cloth printers, stampers of letters, and printers of maps. The oldest wood-cut known to have been produced in Europe, is a representation of S. Christopher, and bears date 1423. At about this time, and probably, in fact, some years earlier, was begun in Holland, as previously stated, the work of printing from wooden blocks, the designs being principally devoted to holy subjects. In connection with such designs, there had been printing also from letterings cut out of solid wooden blocks, and these letterings had even in some cases been cut upon blocks sufficient to occupy an entire page.

The practical contribution made by Gutenberg, which developed from the easy processes of stamping designs and brief lines of lettering, a method by means of which whole books could be produced, was first, in the use of movable metal type, produced by casting, and second, in an improvement made in the mechanism of the hand presses by which larger sheets could be worked.

The first work produced with this movable metal type was a Latin version of the Bible. The description of this volume is first given in a chronicle of Cologne, dating from the year 1499, the statements in which rest upon the authority of Ulrich Zell, who was the first printer in Cologne.

Concerning the further operations of Gutenberg, we are mainly dependent upon the references in the records of the suit brought by Fust, in 1445, for the repayment of his loan, and upon a document of 1468 in which a certain Dr. Humery entered into an undertaking with the Archbishop of Mayence that the printing-office plant left by the deceased Johann Gutenberg shall not be permitted to be taken out of the city of Mayence. This later reference had to do with a second printing-press established by Gutenberg with the aid of the said Humery.

In the suit brought by Fust, Gutenberg contended that the second payment of 800 gulden agreed upon had never been given to him in full. He stated further that Fust had agreed to advance 300 gulden per year for use in the purchase of materials, paper, parchment, type-metal, and ink. The matter of the later accountings between Fust and Gutenberg is evidently a complicated one and need not be considered here in detail. Gutenberg's inability to repay the first and more important loan for the payment of which his first printing-press had been mortgaged, caused the ownership of this office to come into the control of Fust.

Fortunately, by the time his first venture had thus been closed, as far at least as he was concerned, he had been able to give sufficient evidence of the importance and of the commercial value of the undertaking to be in a position to interest others in his schemes.

His second printing-press was in like manner pledged to the associate who provided the capital,—Dr. Humery,— and the business of this office appears to have been continued without break until the time of Gutenberg's death in 1468. With these new resources at hand, Gutenberg was able to cast some new fonts of type, and to make various improvements in his working methods.

The first issues of the new press, the organisation of which appears to have been completed about 1457, were volumes containing the writings of Mätthaus de Cracovia and Thomas Aquinas. The third book was the famous first edition of the *Catholicon*, a grammatical compilation of the Dominican monk Balbus from Genoa. The *Catholicon* was a folio containing no less than 373 rather closely printed sheets. In the meantime, Fust had associated with him Schöffer or Schoiffher, who had been an assistant of Gutenberg, and the two were continuing work in the original printing-office.

The sacking of Mayence, in 1462, by Adolph of Nassau, put an end, for the time, to all business in the city, including the work of the new printing-presses. Gutenberg betook himself to the neighbouring town of Eltville, which, as early as 1420, had given shelter to his parents, and there he carried on his printing for a time under the protection of Archbishop Adolph.

Kapp points out that the printing art had its development, not in a university centre, but in a commercial town, and was from the outset carried on, not by scholars, but by workers of the people, and that this fact doubtless had an important influence in bringing the whole business of the production of books and the distribution of literature into closer relations with the mass of the German people than was the case in France.

In France, as will be noted later, the first printers were directly associated with the university, succeeding immediately to the official university scribes, and the production of books through the presses continued to be under direct control of the university, as had been the case from the beginning with the production of books in manuscript. The fact that the control of the first French presses rested with the university Faculty, undoubtedly exercised an important influence on the choice of the books to be printed, and the first issues of the French presses were, therefore, in the main restricted to editions of the classics or to works of jurisprudence and medicine belonging to the official lists of the university texts. The earlier issues of the German press, on the other hand, were books belonging in no way to the university *curriculum*, but were addressed directly to the interests of the people at large.

While the modifications introduced by Gutenberg into the methods of printing, under which the old engraved blocks were replaced by movable leaden type, seem slight in themselves, they constituted nevertheless a new art. The actual changes were but inconsiderable, but the practical result was a revolution in the possibilities of the press.

Gutenberg's work as a printer was, from a commercial point of view, never successful. During the eighteen years which elapsed between the time of his invention and the date of his death, he seems to have been always under the pressure of debt and money difficulties. He had in fact no time to make money. He had given up, in his devotion to his invention, previous business undertakings which were remunerative, and he had absorbed in the development of the printing-press all the resources that he could control. His interest, however, was evidently that of perfecting an art rather than of creating a business; and in spite of his various difficulties and his several lawsuits with his associates, it is in evidence as part of the testimony in these very suits, that he was recognised by all as a man of knowledge and character, and as a born leader, whose integrity of purpose and whose nobility of aim were acknowledged by all with whom he had to do. With all his misfortunes, he seems never for a moment to have lost confidence in the value to the world of his idea, and to this idea, with no thought of personal gain or advantage, he was willing to devote his means and his life.

The difference between the production each year of a few hundred copies of religious or classical works by the laborious toil of the monks or the university scribes, works which could at best benefit only the limited circle of readers who were within reach either of the monasteries or of the universities, and a world-wide distribution, as well of the great books of the earlier times which belonged to the world's literature as of the current thoughts of the contemporary generation, was a difference, not of degree, but of kind. It was a revolution in the history of human thought and in the influence of thought upon humanity.

If the invention of printing had not taken shape in the brain of Gutenberg, it would doubtless have come to the

world through some other worker, and, in fact, with no
very great delay, for other men were already busying
themselves with the same great need and were on the
track of the same means of supplying the need. As the
history stands, however, the credit for the revolution
must be given to the mirror-maker of Mayence. Other
sailors would certainly have found their way to the
Western Continent if the opportunity or the attempt of
Columbus had failed, but it is to Columbus that history
gives the laurel crown.

Gutenberg, and the printers who followed him, naturally
selected as the first models for their newly founded type
the script letters with which they were familiar in the
best manuscripts. The first font of type manufactured
by Gutenberg, which was used in his earliest publication,
The Folio Bible, was known as the "missal type," having
been copied from the script adopted by the monks for the
books of worship. This style of type was followed for a
long time for Bibles and for religious works generally.
One of the earlier objections against printed books was
that they were so much less beautiful in their appearance
than the work of the best scribes, and it was the finest
script that remained as the ideal to be attained by the
type-founders and the clear black impression of the best
oak-gall writing ink that was to be imitated by the impressions from the presses.

The scholarly lovers of fine books in Germany regarded
the new art at the outset with no little disapproval and
criticism. The collectors who had brought together, with
much labour and expenditure, stores of valuable manuscripts dreaded lest, through the multiplication of comparatively inexpensive copies of their texts, the value of
their collections should be taken away. When the messengers of Cardinal Bessarion were shown by the Greek
Laskaris (later the author of the first Greek grammar that
came into print), a specimen of one of the earlier printed

books, they spoke sneeringly of this so-called discovery which had been made by a barbarian from a German city.[1] The great manuscript-dealer, Vespasiano, writing in 1482 concerning the magnificent ducal library in Urbino, the volumes in which had been largely either collected or purchased by himself or under his own direction, says: " In this library all the volumes are of perfect beauty, all written, by skilled scribes, on parchment and many of them adorned with exquisite miniatures. The collection contains no single printed book. The Duke (Frederick) would be ashamed to have a printed book in his library."[2] By collectors like Frederick and manuscript-dealers like Vespasiano, the new art was considered to be merely a mechanical method of producing inartistic volumes, with which none but uncultivated people could be satisfied.

For a number of years, therefore, after the work of the first presses, there were still produced beautiful specimens of manuscripts, more particularly of Italian and French books of worship, and for this class of manuscripts the work of the hand illuminators and miniature painters continued to be utilised. In Germany there are various examples of books which had been printed, being again produced in written copy, as for instance, the *Chronicon Urspergense*, of Hroswitha.[3] It was also the case that for the production of large choir-books the work of the scribes continued to be useful.

Trithemius, Abbot of Sponheim, wrote to Gerlach, Abbot of Deutz, a letter which was printed in 1494 in Mayence, under the title, *De Laude Scriptorum Manualium*. In this he says:

" A work written on parchment could be preserved for a thousand years, while it is probable that no volume printed on paper will last for more than two centuries. Many important works have not been printed, and the copies required of these must be prepared by scribes.

[1] Kapp, 59. [2] Burckhardt, *Die Kultur der Renaissance*, i., 239. [3] Kapp, 60.

The scribe who ceases his work because of the invention of the printing-press can be no true lover of books, in that, regarding only the present, he gives no due thought to the intellectual cultivation of his successors. The printer has no care for the beauty and the artistic form of books, while with the scribe this is a labour of love." [1]

Notwithstanding such criticism on the part of a few scholarly churchmen, the influence of Rome and of the Church generally, during the earlier work of the printers, was very largely favourable and had not a little to do with the support given to the work which might easily otherwise have been given up for lack of adequate business return. The Church of Rome felt itself at this time sufficiently secure in its control of the minds of men to be prepared to utilise to full advantage all methods for distributing its doctrinal literature, and to have no dread as to these same means being used for the scattering of heretical teachings. The popes of the time, largely influenced by the spirit of the Renaissance, gave a cordial welcome to the revival of scholarly interests and to the printing-press as an important means for furthering the general education and the intellectual development of the community. Their interest was by no means limited to the distribution of doctrinal works, but in these earlier years of publishing they welcomed, and to a considerable extent co-operated in, the production of editions, for general circulation, of the works of the pagan classics.

Hegel says, in his *Philosophy of History*, that the renewed interest in the studying of the writings of the ancients found an important support in the service of the printing-press. He goes on to point out that the Church felt no anxiety concerning this renewed interest in pagan literature, and evidently did not imagine that this literature was introducing into the minds of men a new element of suggestion and of inquiry.

[1] Schneegans, p. 142.

It may be considered as one of the fortunate circumstances attending the introduction of the art of printing that the popes of the time were largely men of liberal education and of intellectual tastes, while one or two, such as Nicholas V., Julius II., and Leo X., had a very keen personal interest in literature and were collectors of books.

The fact that Leo X. was a luxury-loving, free-thinking prince rather than a devoted Christian leader or teacher, may very probably have been in the end a service for the enlightenment and development of his own generation and of the generations that were to come. An earnest and narrow-minded head of the Church could, during the first years of the sixteenth century, have retarded not a little the development of the work of producing books for the community at large.

It was a number of years before the dread of the use of the printing-press for the spread of heretical doctrines and of a consequent undermining of the authority of the Church assumed such proportions in the minds of the popes in Rome and with the bishops elsewhere, as to cause the influence of the Church to be placed against the interests of the world of literature. As a result of this early acceptance by the Church of the printing-press as a useful ally and servant, the first Italian presses were supported by bishops and cardinals in the work of producing classics for scholarly readers, while at the other extremity of the Church organisation, and at a distance of a thousand miles or more from Rome, the Brothers of Common Life were using the presses in their Brotherhood homes for the distribution of cheap books among the people.

Berthold von Henneberg, Elector of Mayence, speaks of " The Divine Art of Printing." [1] The Carthusian monk, Werner Rolewinck, writes, in his *Outline History of the World (Fasciculus Temporum)*: " The art of printing

[1] Kapp, 62.

which has been discovered in Mayence is the art of arts,
the science of sciences, by means of which it will be
possible to place in the hands of all men treasures of
literature and of knowledge which have heretofore been
out of their reach."

Joh. Rauchler, the first Rector of the Tübingen High
School (later the University of Tübingen), rejoices that
through the new art so many authors can now be brought
within the reach of students in Latin, Greek, and Hebrew,
authors who are witnesses for the Christian faith, and the
service of whose writings to the Church and to the world
is so great, that he can but consider "this art as a gift
directly from God himself."[1] Felix Fabri, Prior of the
Dominican monastery in Ulm, says, in his *Historia
Suevorum*, issued in the year 1459, that "no art that the
world has known can be considered so worthy, so useful,
so much to be esteemed, indeed, so divine as that which
has now, through the Grace of God, been discovered in
Mayence."

The first printing work done by the Brothers of Common Life dates from 1468. They appear to have promptly
utilised their scribes as compositors and their illuminators
as designers for the new form in which their books were
produced. Many of the Benedictine monasteries which
had for so many centuries led the way in the preservation
and the multiplication of literature at once associated
presses with their monasteries and had their monks trained
in the art of setting type and of printing sheets.

Among the monastery printing-presses were those of
the Carthusian monastery in Strasburg, the monastery of
S. Ulrich and Afra, in Augsburg, and the Benedictine
monasteries in Nuremberg and Rostock. As a rule, in
places where the work of scribes had been active, the
printing-press found a ready acceptance. It was not long,
however, before so great a development in the methods of

[1] Kapp, 62.

the printing business was brought about that it became difficult for the monasteries to carry on the work effectively, and by the middle of the sixteenth century the production of books in monasteries had practically ceased.

The favourable relations between the Church and the printers were checked by the Humanistic movement, which, a generation or more before the Reformation, began to bring into question the authority of the Church and the infallibility of papacy. The influence of the Humanistic teachers was so largely furthered by the co-operation of the printers that the jealousy and dread of the ecclesiastical authorities were promptly aroused, and they began to utter fulminations against the wicked and ignorant men who were using the art of printing for misleading the community and for the circulation of error. The ecclesiastics, who had at first favoured the widest possible circulation of the Scriptures, now contended that much of the heretical teaching was due to the misunderstanding of the Scriptures on the part of readers who were acting without the guidance of their spiritual advisers.

The authorities of the Church now began to take the ground that the reading of the Scriptures by individuals was not to be permitted, and that the Bible was to be given to the community only through the interpretation of the Church. At the same time, the authority of the Church was exerted to repress, or at least to restrict, the operations of the printing-press, and to bring printers and publishers under a close ecclesiastical supervision and censorship. It was now, however, too late to stand between the printing-press and the people. Large portions of the community had become accustomed to a wide circulation of books and to the selection without restriction of such reading-matter as might be placed within their reach, and this privilege they were no longer willing to forego.

It was nevertheless true that in certain countries, particularly in Italy and in France, the censorship of the

Church was strong enough seriously to hamper and interfere with publishing undertakings and to check the natural development of literary production. Even in Italy,
however, the critical spirit was found to be too strong to
be entirely crushed out, and from Venice, the most important of the Italian publishing centres, it proved possible to secure for the productions of the printing-press a
circulation that was practically independent of the censorship of Rome.

The Humanistic movement was, on other grounds, of
immediate service for the printers and publishers, in that
it brought about an active demand for the works of classical writers, a demand which it required the fullest resources
of the earlier printers to supply.

If the invention of Gutenberg had taken shape during
the period when there happened to be no such active
intellectual literary interests, the first printers might easily
have found it difficult to secure business for their presses
and the development of the business of book production
would have been seriously hampered. The long series
of controversies which were brought into being by the
Reformation, and the large mass of controversial literature
which was the result of the Reformation, constituted, a
generation later, another favourable influence in securing
an assured foundation for the business of the printers. If
it be the case that the work of the leaders of the Reformation could hardly have been carried on without the aid of
the printing-press, it is also true that at a time when the
business of the early printers was in a very critical and
unremunerative condition, the impetus given to the production of literature, and the increased eagerness on the
part of the common people for literature, formed an essential factor in making an assured foundation for the business of the printers and the publishers.

In 1462, on the 28th of October, Archbishop Adolph of
Nassau captured the city of Mayence and gave it over to

his soldiers for plunder. The typesetters and printers, with all other artisans whose work depended upon the commerce of the city, were driven to flight, and it appeared for the moment as if the newly instituted printing business had been crushed out. The result of the scattering of the printers, however, was the introduction of the new art into a number of other centres where the influences were favourable for its development.

The typesetters of Mayence, driven from their printing-offices by the heavy hand of the Church, journeyed throughout the world, carrying their new knowledge and training and they were able to give to many communities the means of education and enlightenment through which the great revolt against the Church was finally instituted. The work of the printers, checked for the time in Mayence, took shape promptly in Strasburg, and from there was taken down the Rhine to Cologne, and in a few years was also in active operation in Basel, Augsburg, Ulm, and Nuremberg. In 1464, as elsewhere described, German printers carried their invention into Italy and erected the first Italian printing-press in Subiaco. And in 1470, also through Germans, the work of the printers began in Paris.

The shrewd and enterprising merchant Fust, by means of whose capital Gutenberg had been able to begin his business operations, would hardly have pressed his suit against his associate, if he had not had confidence in the value of the invention. As soon as, through the decision of 1455, he came into possession of the presses, he at once put these again into operation. He found a practical superintendent or co-worker in Peter Schöffer. Schöffer was a German by birth, but had carried on work in Paris as a scribe or writer of higher class manuscripts, as illuminator, and as a manuscript-dealer. Returning to Mayence in 1454, he had entered the employ of Gutenberg as typesetter and proof-reader. Later, having married the

daughter of Fust, he was taken into partnership by his
father-in-law, and was able to make a satisfactory organisation and a wide development for the business of
the printing-office. The first publication issued by Fust
& Schöffer was a psalter printed (in Latin) on parchment,
with the great missal type.

The second work, undertaken, not at the risk of the
printers, but at the cost of two of the Mayence monasteries, was an edition of a great choir-book. This psalter,
or rather *psalterium*, is the first printed work in which the
name of the printer is given and the date of the publication. It apparently proved possible to secure for this
book even with the very inadequate distributing machinery that was available, a remunerative sale, as it was
printed again in 1490, in 1502, in 1515, and in 1516.

Among the earlier publications of Fust & Schöffer are
the *Rationale Divinorum Officiorum* of the Dominican
monk Durandus, which was issued in 1459, the *Codex
Constitutionum* of Pope Clement, issued in 1460, and
the *Bull* of Emperor Frederic III. against Diether
von Isenburg, printed in 1461. The most beautiful and
most important production of their press was, however,
the great Latin Bible issued in 1462, in two folio volumes,
and which is known as the " 48 line Bible."

The work of the printing-office was, as previously stated,
stopped by the sacking of the city, and the two partners
appear to have migrated for the time to Frankfort. In
1464, they were again in Mayence, and in that year they
published the sixth book of the *Decretals* of Pope Boniface VIII., and the *De Officiis* of Cicero. The latter
was the first of the German editions of the classics, and
remained a favourite book with the German printers, being
repeatedly reprinted.

In 1453, Fust made a journey to Paris in order to find
sale there for his big Bible. This was four years before
the first Paris printing-press began its work, and it was in

connection with this big Bible that the gossip arose of Fust being able, through compact with the Devil, to produce an indefinite number of copies of a book. It could not be understood how in any other way these copies could be offered so cheaply. The University of Paris was at that date the most important in Europe, and the influence of the University upon the cultivation of the city and its close relations with the old book-trade in manuscripts, had made Paris the most important European centre for literary production and the place where scholars were in the habit of looking for their material. It was in Paris, if anywhere, that it should prove possible to find sale for the Latin Bible, and Fust's efforts appear to have met with a prompt success. The first Bible bearing a date was completed in 1462, and is known as the Mayence Bible. At the time it was in readiness (in October) nothing could be done in getting it into the market, as Mayence was being besieged by Adolph of Nassau. In 1466, Fust is again in Paris with copies of the second edition of his *De Officiis*, and with other of his publications.

There is still preserved in the city library of Geneva a copy of this edition of Cicero, which contains the record that it was bought by Louis de la Vernada, in Paris, in July, 1466, from Fust.[1]

Fust & Schöffer may claim to have been the first printers who acted also as publishers and booksellers. Notwithstanding the many difficulties with which they had had to contend, they were able to offer their books at prices which, to the old dealers in manuscripts, seemed astounding and which gave some pretext for the charge of magic. Madden says that a copy of the " 48 line Bible " printed on parchment, could be bought in Paris, in 1470, for 2000 francs, and that the cost of the same text a few years earlier in manuscript form would have been five times as great. Bishop John of Aleria, writing in 1467 to Pope

---

[1] Wetter, J., *Gesch. der Erfindung der Buchdruckerkunst*, 483.

Paul II., says that it is now possible to purchase in Rome for 20 gulden, gold, works which a few years earlier would have cost not less than 100 gulden, and that other books now selling as low as 4 gulden would previously have cost not less than 20 gulden. The first results of the printing-press appear, therefore, to have been a reduction of about four fifths in the price of work of a scholarly character.

Fust is entitled to the description, not only of the second printer and of the first publisher, but of the first pirate in printed books. In 1465, Mentel printed in Strasburg under the title of *De Arte Prædicatoria*, the fourth book of S. Augustine's *De Doctrina Christiana*. The editor states that he had, for the purpose of this edition, collected manuscript texts in the libraries of Heidelberg, Speyer, Worms, and Strasburg, and that he had induced Joh. Mentel, a "master of the art of print-ing," to put the volume into a form available for the general use of clerics.

Fust reprinted this volume in 1466, following the text with precision, and simply replacing Mentel's name with his own. This is the first instance of literary appropria-tion of which there is any record, after the beginning of printing.[1]

After the death of Fust, which occurred early in 1467, Schöffer continued the business with Fust's sons, and established branches in Paris and in Angers. His name appears for the first time alone on the title-page of the *Thomas Aquinas*, published in a folio of 516 pages in March, 1467. He prints it in full as Petrus Schoiffher de Gernsheim. In a receipt for 15 gold crowns, paid by the College of Autun for a copy of this, Schoiffher styles himself *Impressor Librorum*. He appears to have made sale in Paris not only of his own publications, but of the books issued by other German printers.

In a copy of the work of Johannus Scotus, printed by

---

[1] Schmidt, C., *Gesch. der ältesten Bibliothek in Strasburg*, 1881, p. 92.

Koberger in 1474, now contained in the library of the Paris Arsenal, appears the entry, " I, Peter Schöffer, printer from Mayence, acknowledge that I have received from the worthy Magistrate, Johannus Henrici, of Pisa, three *scuta* as the price of this book." [1] Schöffer seems to have acted in some measure also as purchasing agent for the University of Paris, through an associate, Guimier, who was a licensed member of the Paris guild.   The Paris branch of the business was given up a few years later, and Schöffer devoted his energies to extending his trade in Germany.   In 1479, his name appears in the list of the citizens of Frankfort, and the removal to Frankfort of his publishing headquarters constituted the first step towards the selection of that city as the centre of the publishing and bookselling trade of Germany, a position that it retained for more than a century.   Schöffer continued, however, to do the work of his printing in Mayence.

Some light is thrown upon the extent of the publishing undertakings carried on at the time by Schöffer with his associate Hancquis, by the record of a suit brought by the two partners in 1480 against a certain Bernhard Inkus, of Frankfort.   They charged Inkus with having begun the publication of a considerable series of books, the property right in which (*Eigentumsrecht*) vested in themselves and in Conrad Henki (who was a son of Fust).   It does not appear from the record of this trial on what grounds Schöffer and his associates claimed the right to control these books, or whether the unauthorised issues of which they complained had been printed by the defendant Inkus or were simply being offered for sale by him on behalf of other printers.

The case appears to have been referred or possibly appealed to a court in Basel, and by this court was issued some preliminary injunction against the continued sale of the books complained of.   The record giving the final

[1] Kapp, 71.

decision of the case is, however, missing. The lack of
full details of the suit is the more to be regretted as it
appears to have been the first case after the invention of
printing involving, if not copyright ownership, at least a
certain control by contract.

In the same year we find the Magistracy of the City of
Frankfort applying to the Magistracy of the City of
Lübeck for the protection of Schöffer against some ille-
gitimate infringement of Schöffer's business rights on the
part of the Lübeck citizen Hans Bitz. Here also is there
no record as to the result of the application. The firm
also had dealings with Ulm, as appears from a claim
made, in 1481, for the collection of the moneys due from
certain citizens in Ulm—Harscher, Ruwinger, and Ofener,
for books delivered. They sent to Ulm, with a protection certificate given by Elector Diether of Mayence, a
representative who was empowered to collect the money.
There was at the outset some delay in connection with
an alleged informality in his authorisation, but the Magistracy of Ulm sent back word that as soon as the
requisite authorisation was secured, the collection of the
money would be enforced in due course.

These cases are evidence of a certain organisation of
machinery for the distribution of books and for the management of a publishing business, within a comparatively
brief period after the beginning of the work of the printing-presses, and they indicate also that the second firm
which entered into the business of printing had succeeded
in establishing such business on fairly assured foundations,
and in carrying on successfully large undertakings. It is
to be noted further that Fust & Schöffer, and other of
the earlier German printers, did their work without the
assistance of any patronage, and without even the advantage of a university connection. The early printers of
Italy would have found it impracticable to carry on their
operations without the assistance of certain wealthy and

enterprising noblemen who were prepared to interest themselves in the new art either from curiosity or from philanthropy, and as late even as 1495, that is to say nearly half a century after the beginning of printing, the organisation of the business of Aldus was dependent upon the favour and services of certain of his noble friends. In Paris the first printers were helped, and in part supported, by the money of patrons or of the Crown, and by the co-operation and influence of the University. In England also the influence of Oxford was of material importance in securing for the first printers some assured foundation and support, while the work of Caxton and his immediate successors in London was also largely furthered by, if not actually dependent upon, the work or help of noble and wealthy friends.

In Germany, however, the printing work began, as we have seen, through the enterprise and ingenuity of a citizen manufacturer who was supported by the middle class of the community, and who made his first connections directly with the townspeople. The help of the universities appears to have been of comparatively smaller importance. It probably counted for more in Cologne than in any other of the university cities in which the earlier printers did their work.

In the course of the thirty-six years of his independent business activity, that is from the death of Fust in 1466 to the time of his own death, Schöffer printed in all fifty-nine works which bear date and which have been identified as his. His firm took rank for this period as by far the most important printing and publishing concern in existence.

With hardly an exception, the books issued from his press were folios. They were printed with fifty to sixty lines on the page, and contained an average of about 300 pages or 150 sheets.

Among the works included in the list are the *Constitu-*

tiones of Clement V., the *Institutions* of Justinian, the *Expositio Sententiarum* of Thomas Aquinas, the *Epistolæ* of S. Jerome, the sixth book of the *Decretals* of Boniface VIII., the *Decretals* of Gregory IX., the *Codex* of Justinian, and the *Expositio Psalterii* of Joh. Torquemada. The last named volume had already been printed in Subiaco and again in Rome under the direct supervision of the author, who was supplying the funds for carrying on the first printing-office established in Italy.

After Schöffer's death in 1502, his son printed an edition of the *Mercurius Trimegistus.*

I do not find record of the arrangement entered into by Schöffer for the editing of the texts of the works printed by him. The collection of manuscripts for use as " copy " for printers, and the collection of different manuscripts in order to secure the most complete and accurate texts, must have called for a considerable measure of scholarly and of general literary knowledge.

It does not appear that Schöffer had enjoyed opportunities for making himself a scholarly authority, or that he ever made claim to any special scholarly attainments. There is no record of editorial work done by himself in the books issued from his press, as was the case to so exceptional a degree a few years later with the books printed by Aldus; nor has Schöffer preserved in connection with his editions the names of the editors who supervised their publication, as came to be the practice later with the issues of the Aldine press, of Froben in Basel, and of Koberger in Nuremberg. As far as I can ascertain, however, the Schöffer texts compared favourably for accuracy and for authority with other of the earlier printed books, and it is to be assumed, therefore, that he had been able to organise an adequate critical staff or to secure from time to time, as required, the services of competent scholars.

The business founded by Gutenberg, taken possession

of under mortgage by Fust, and carried on first by Fust
& Schöffer, and later by Schöffer and other associates,
lasted nearly one hundred years. The first publication
was, as noted, the big *Psalterium*, printed in 1457, and
the last, an edition of the German version of the books of
Livy, printed by Ivo Schöffer in 1557.

It seems evident that while the credit for the great
invention fairly belongs to Gutenberg, and the original
planning and initiative of the business were his, a large
measure of business capacity must have belonged to his
partner Fust, who had also, to be sure, the advantage of
being a capitalist to begin with, a factor as important in
the earliest time of publishing as in the present day.

One of the most definite pieces of testimony in regard
to the connection of Gutenberg with the invention of
printing, testimony which possesses special value as coming from a person possessing first-hand knowledge of the
facts, is contained in an Epilogue written in verse by John
Schöffer (son of Peter), and printed at the end of the *Livy*
published by him in 1505. It is addressed to the Emperor
Maximilian, and reads as follows:

" May your Majesty deign to accept this book which
was printed at Mayence, the town in which the admirable
art of typography was invented, in the year 1450, by John
Gutenberg, and afterwards brought to perfection at the
expense, and by the labour, of John Fust and Peter
Schöffer."

It would not belong to the plan of this historical sketch
to give in detail a record of the successive concerns which
carried on throughout Germany, with increasing rapidity
and with undertakings of ever widening importance,
the business of printing and publishing. I propose merely
to present the records of a few of the earlier concerns, and
to make such reference to typical firms of later generations as may give an impression of the gradual development of the book-trade, and as may serve also as

examples from which to judge of the development of
the idea of the literary property in Germany, and the
varying positions taken under the enactments and other
governmental measures in regard to such property.

The books printed during the first half-century were, as
we shall note, almost exclusively reissues of ecclesiastical
or pagan classics, and apart from such original work as
may have been put into introductions or notes, did not
call for the labour of contemporary authors.   Among the
earlier of original German publications is to be classed a
German grammar entitled *Die Leyenschul*, printed by Peter
Jordan in Mayence in 1531.   This grammar, which remained for a considerable time an authority on its subject, does not bear the name of the author or editor.

Another of the earlier original works for the sale of
which the author may have secured some compensation
was the *Astronomie* of Joh. Stöffler, which was printed in
Ottenheim in 1513.

One of the more important of the earlier publishing
concerns of Mayence was that of Franz Behem, who
printed in the ten years succeeding 1539 an important
series of theological works.   With the close of Behem's
business in 1552, Mayence appears to have lost its relative
importance in connection with the work of printing and
publishing.

In Strasburg, which had contested with Mayence the
prestige of being the actual birthplace of the printing-
press, important publishing undertakings were carried on
from a very early date, and for a number of years the
city of Basel alone could compete with Strasburg in the
number and importance of the books issued from its
presses.   The two publishing concerns whose individual
enterprises and whose rivalry with each other did so much
to bring Strasburg into importance as a factor in the German book-trade, were those of Johann Mentel and of
Heinrich Eggestein.   Mentel's first publications were a

Latin Bible in two folio volumes, which was the first
Bible printed in the smaller Gothic type; an edition of
De Doctrina Christiana of S. Augustine; an edition of
the *Summa* of Thomas Aquinas; an edition of the
Bible in German, which appeared in 1466; the *Speculum Historiale* of Vincentius Bellovacensis, etc. Madden
finds record of twenty-one publications which can certainly be identified as Mentel's, and which comprise in
all forty-one volumes, of which thirty-seven are in large
folio. During the time of his business activity, (1465–1478)
he appears to have published about two volumes a year.[1]

Humphreys points out that Mentel was in advance of
the other German printers of the day in first using, in
place of the confused old Gothic black letter, the clear
Roman letter which was in use in Italy. Mentel's most
important publication, the collection of the *Specula* of S.
Vincent of Beauvais, issued in 1473, in eight volumes
folio, was printed in type of the Roman letter.[2] M.
Bernard, in his *Origines de l'Imprimerie*, is of opinion that it was in printing these theological works which
were in accord with the taste of the reading public of his
day, that Mentel realised a fortune, while many of his
competitors ruined themselves in reproducing the Latin
classics, the taste for which before the close of the fifteenth
century was not sufficiently developed to ensure a remunerative sale. He was also the first of the German printers
to print descriptive catalogues of his books. At the head
of the catalogue was a notice to the following effect:
" Those who wish to possess any of these books have
only to address themselves to the sign of ———."
Here a blank was left, in order that each retail bookseller to whom the catalogue was sent might fill in his
own name and sign. Such a detail (which is, I may mention, quite in accord with modern publishing methods)
indicates that there was as early as 1470, a well developed
bookselling machinery in western and central Germany.

---

[1] Madden, iv., 40.   [2] Humphreys, 99.

Mentel's principal rival in Strasburg was Heinrich Eggestein. Eggestein appears to have been a man of scholarly training, and had received from some university the degree "Magister." To him belongs the credit of the issue, in 1466, of the first Bible printed in German. Important as was this work, the printer was not interested in associating with it his imprint, and the volumes are identified as the work of his press only by circumstantial evidence.[1] The first work which was edited and which bears his imprint was an edition of the *Decretum Gratiani*, printed in a gigantic folio in 1471. Before this date, he had issued three Bibles in Latin text. The *Decretum* was again printed by Eggestein in 1472, although the original issue of 1471 had been promptly pirated by the enterprising Schöffer. It is evident that it proved possible to secure for the book an immediate and presumably remunerative sale.

Another of Eggestein's publications in 1472 was an edition of *Clementinæ*. In this he gives his imprint and gives notice also that he has already issued a long series of books treating of "divine and human law." The last book bearing a date, issued by Eggestein is the *Decretals* of Innocent IV., printed in 1478.

The third Strasburg printer was George Huszner, who was originally a goldsmith. He married the daughter of another goldsmith, Nikolaus of Hanau, who later worked with his son-in-law as *aurifaber et pressor librorum*.[2] The *Speculum Judiciale* of Bishop Wilhelm Duranti, printed by Huszner in 1473, is described by Kapp as a masterpiece of typography. This bears the name as editor of Joh. Beckenhub, who calls himself a cleric. Martin Flach of Strasburg, whose business activity covered the years 1475 to 1500 published something over seventy works, which were, with hardly an exception, devoted to theology and dogma.

In 1480, was printed a magnificent edition of the Latin

[1] Linde, p. 65.   [2] Schmidt, C., 160.

Bible in four volumes, known as *Biblia Latina cum glossa ordinaria Walafridi Strabonis et interlineari Anselmi Laudunensis*. This was issued by Anton Koberger of Nuremberg and it has only recently been discovered that it was printed for him by Adolph Rusch of Strasburg. While it was by far the most noteworthy typographical undertaking that had been completed up to that date, the printer had not thought it important to associate his name with the volumes. Rusch was a publisher as well as a printer, and was also a large dealer in paper, supplying this to printers in Strasburg, Nuremberg, Basel, and elsewhere. He further carried on a miscellaneous business as a bookseller and in purchasing from other publishers for his miscellaneous trade supplies of other publications, and he was accustomed to make payment for the same in paper. He seems altogether to have been a man of very wide activities, whose influence must have been of considerable importance in connection with the early organisation of the German book-trade. He had married a daughter of the Strasburg printer, Mentel, and through his wife, inherited an interest in Mentel's business. Rusch purchased from the printer Amerbach, in exchange for paper stock, a portion of the edition of S. Augustine's *De Civitate Dei*, which appears to have shared with certain essays of Cicero the honour of being one of the most frequently printed books in the early lists.

One of the earlier of the Strasburg printers who gave particular attention to works in German was Johann Reinhart, also known (from his birthplace) as Johann Grüninger, whose list comprised German editions of works in theology and religion, and in poetic literature, together with a series of folk-songs and stories for the people. While his fellow publishers were at that time, with hardly an exception, limiting their undertakings to works planned for scholars, such as reprints of the classics and theological works printed in Latin, Reinhart addressed himself at once to a popular audience, and while in so doing he was undoubtedly of service in furthering the education of his generation, he appears also to have secured for himself satisfactory business results. He gave particular attention to illustrated books, securing the service of a number of noteworthy designers and engravers, and ornamenting his books, not only with full-page illustrations, but with elaborate initial letters and head- and tail-pieces. He is chronicled as being the only publisher in Strasburg who, after the Reformation was in full development, continued to print Catholic tracts and pamphlets. As an instance of the large distribution that it was possible to secure at the beginning of the sixteenth century for certain classes of books, is to be noted the sale made by Reinhart in 1502 to Schönsperger, of 1000 copies of a volume of *The Lives of the Saints*. Reinhart was one of the printers whose presses were utilised by the great publisher Koberger of Nuremberg. In 1525, he printed for Koberger the translation by Pirckheimer of the great Geography of Ptolemy. In this work the translator appears himself to have retained an interest.

There have been preserved a number of the letters which passed between Pirckheimer, Koberger, and Reinhart, while this work was going through the press. It appears that, notwithstanding Reinhart's personal supervision of the undertaking and his interest in securing for the pages satisfactory ornamentations, Pirckheimer had found frequent occasion for dissatisfaction and criticisms, and in his letters there are many expressions which might have been written by authors of to-day who were not satisfied that the printers were following "copy" correctly. At one point, Pirckheimer says that if he could have foreseen all the difficulties that he was to experience in securing a correct printing for his volume, he would have burned the manuscript rather than have put it to press.

Reinhart points out, on his part, however, that, in the first place, the manuscript had not been prepared in such manner that the compositors could follow it correctly, and that, secondly, he had given no little of his own personal attention to re-arranging and re-shaping the "copy" in order that the text might be as correct as possible.

Pirckheimer was also unhappy in connection with certain of the designs with which the printer had ornamented his text, and expresses the wish that in place of using Italian designers, the printer had given the work to good Germans.[1]

From the middle of the eleventh century, Cologne had competed with Mayence for the distinction of being the most important trade centre of Germany. Its favourable position made it a natural point of exchange for business operations between the dealers of the North Sea and those of the Mediterranean. To Cologne came from the south by way of the passes of the Alps, the wares, not only of Italy, but those which had been brought from the East by the vessels of Venice and of Genoa, while from the great Russian mart of Novgorod and the enterprising Hanseatic city Lübeck, were brought the goods of Russia and of the far North. In Cologne were also warehouses under the charge of trading guilds of their several nations, whither were brought the goods of England, France, and the Low Countries.

It was not only in mercantile undertakings, however, that the city had secured for itself prestige. The University, founded in the early part of the fourteenth century on the model of that of Paris, was considered to have surpassed in the importance of its scholarly work the older institutions of Heidelberg, Prague, and Vienna; and it remained for many years at the head of the scholarship of Germany and a particular exponent of the doctrinal theology of the Catholic Church. Cologne was, therefore,

[1] Kapp, 91.

recognised by the early printers as an exceptionally favourable centre for the prosperous development of their work, and the printing and publishing undertakings of the city assumed at an early date very considerable importance.

The existing library of the city contains over 400 works, principally theological, but including also volumes in jurisprudence and in higher class instruction, which were produced by Cologne printers before the close of the fifteenth century. At this time the University contained no less than 4000 students, and the requirements of these students for text-books and of their instructors for works of reference, must have given a very decided impetus to the work of the earlier publishers, while the trade connections possessed by Cologne with the cities of the North and East furnished channels through which the publishers were able to extend the demand for their books. The first introduction of the printing-press into Cologne was due to the sacking of the City of Mayence in 1462, when Ulrich Zell, of Hanau, who like Peter Schöffer, called himself a *clericus moguntinensis*, and who had been an apprentice of Gutenberg, having been driven from Mayence, brought to Cologne the invention of his master. While it is possible that his printing undertakings began earlier, the first dated work issued from his press was published in 1466, and was an edition of the *Liber Johannes Chrysostomi super Psalmo Quinquagesimo*. This was promptly followed by a volume containing the *De Officiis* of Cicero. No publishing list of the period appears to have progressed very far without including one or more of the essays of Cicero. The latest book published by Zell was a commentary by Girard Hardervicus on the new Logic of Albertus Magnus. The list of books known to have been produced by Zell includes no less than 120 titles, but a large number of these were pamphlets of moderate compass, and only eighteen were in the folio form which was the standard of the time.

A printer whose work was in part contemporary with that of Zell, was Johann Koelhoff, who included in his list eighty publications, of which seven were in the German tongue. These last are spoken of by Kapp as possessing distinctive interest for theologians, because they included some of the earliest printed examples of the Low-German dialect. Bartholomäus Unkel, whose list included in all twenty works, printed, in 1480, in the Low-German dialect an edition of the *Sachsenspiegel*, a work which found place during the following century in the lists of very many of the German publishers.

As before mentioned, the influence of the University was given strongly to the support of Orthodox doctrines of the Catholic Church, and doctrinal books which did not conform to the university standard of orthodoxy were not printed in Cologne. It is probable that in the beginning of the publishing operations, no direct censorship was attempted on the part of the theologians of the University, but it seems evident that they were able notwithstanding, to discourage publications the opinions of which they might consider pernicious.

The name of Franz Birckmann, whose printing operations began in 1507, occupies an important place in the list of the publishers of Cologne, and his business relations with Paris and his connections with the book-dealers of London have brought his name into reference in much of the correspondence of his time. Birckmann appears, at the outset at least, not to have himself been a printer. His first book, the *Missale Coloniense*, was printed for him in Paris. Kirchhoff speaks of Birckmann as possessing a fine business capacity and exceptional enterprise and creative genius, and refers to him as carrying on his undertakings now in London and Canterbury, then in Bruges, Liége, or Frankfort ; again in Cologne, Antwerp, Tübingen, and Basel. The list of the places visited by this enterprising publisher of the time serves to give an indication as to the centres where literary activities were the most important.[1] Erasmus, writing on the 21st of December, 1520, from Canterbury, to his friend Andreas Ammonius in Rotterdam, speaks of Birckmann as being ready himself to undertake the introduction into England of any books that might be called for. Birckmann appears finally to have established in London a permanent business office, for the volume, *Graduale ad Usum Sarum*, which was printed for him in Paris in 1528, bears as an imprint, Franz Birckmann of St. Paul's Church Yard.[2]

This early connection of the publishers of Cologne with London is of special interest in connection with the record of William Caxton, the first English printer, who was said to have learned his art in Cologne and to have brought it thence (by way of Bruges) to London.   In the same series of letters to Ammonius, Erasmus speaks of giving to Birckmann the manuscript of his *Proverbia*, of his *Plutarch*, and the *Lucian*, in order that he might arrange to have the books printed in Paris, by Jodocus Badius. For some reason, not stated, Birckmann decided not to place these works in the hands of Badius, but took them to Froben, in Basel, which was the means of bringing Erasmus into connection with that publisher, with whom he had satisfactory intimate relations for so large a portion of his life.

As has been stated in another chapter, the theologians of the Faculty of the Sorbonne had taken a strong stand against the writings of Erasmus, and it is very possible that Badius was unable to secure a permit or a privilege for these volumes.

Birckmann seems, at about this time, to have secured some interest, if not in the general business of Froben, at least in a certain number of his publishing undertakings. In 1526, Birckmann came into trouble with the authorities

---

[1] Kirchhoff, A., *Gesch. des Deutsch. Buchhandels*, Leipzig, 1851, i., 41.
[2] Erasmi, *Opera*, London, 1703, iii., 105.

of Antwerp on account of his having sold there an edition of the translation of S. Chrysostom, which had been made by Ökolampadius, and which had come under the ban of the Antwerp censorship. The publisher succeeded in freeing himself from the penalties imposed by the Antwerp magistracy only after a long contest and a considerable expenditure of money.[1] It is a little difficult to understand the precise grounds of the opposition raised by the Antwerp censors, and I have not been able to get at the details of the case. It is of interest as one of the earliest examples of censorship upon the press which occured in Northern Europe. Kapp is of opinion that the censorship exercised by the Church authorities in Cologne was more rigorous than that instituted by the authorities in Bavaria. It seems certain that the Catholic University of the Rhine was able to exercise no little influence in shaping the direction of the earlier literary undertakings of North Germany.

Caxton's sojourn in Cologne must have been some time between the years 1471 and 1474. Further details concerning his work in Bruges and his later publishing undertakings in London will be given in the chapter on printing in England. During the latter part of the fifteenth century and the earlier years of the sixteenth, Cologne printers secured for themselves an unenviable reputation as unauthorised reprinters of works which were the result of the scholarly labours and investment of publishers elsewhere. They issued editions as nearly in *fac-simile* as might be of a number of the classics published in Venice by Aldus, and they followed these, later, with the imitations of the scholarly texts published by Plantin in Antwerp and by the Elzevirs in Leyden.

While it was the case that these texts, with rare exceptions, were the work of authors dead centuries before, and that in the works themselves the original publishers

[1] Kirch., i., 103.

could rightfully claim no control, it is to be borne in mind
that the production of the earlier editions of such classics
had nevertheless called for a very considerable expenditure
of capital and of labour, as well in the securing of the
codices used as "copy" by the type-setters as in the
revision and editing of these codices by the scholarly
commentators employed, and also in the preparation of
notes, introductions, and elucidations for the volumes.
The risk and investment incurred by Aldus in the production of his edition of *Aristotle*, and the exceptional
character of the original labour invested by the publisher
in such a work are grounds for considering that his contention for the control of the text which came from his
printing-office, at least for a certain term of years, was as
well founded as might be a contention of to-day for a
book which was in its entirety the work of a contemporary writer.

The city whose publishing operations are next to be
considered in the chronological record is Basel. For a
number of years after the invention of printing, Basel remained one of the most important publishing centres, not
only of the German Empire (to which at this time the
city belonged), but of Europe. Its position on a direct
line of communication between Italy and Germany had
given it an importance in connection with the general
trade of Europe, and the facilities which furthered this
general trade became of value also in connection with the
production of books. The University of Basel, founded
in 1460, speedily brought to the city men devoted to
scholarly pursuits, many of whom took an early interest
in the work of the printing-press, and were ready to give
their co-operation to publishers like Froben, not only in
editing manuscripts for the press, but even in the routine
work of the printing-offices in the proof-reading and correcting. In 1501, at the time Basel broke away from the
imperial control, the city had already secured for itself a

cosmopolitan character, and had become a kind of meeting place for the exchange of thought as well as for the goods of representatives of all nations. At this time there were in the city no less than twenty-six important publishing and printing concerns. The earliest book bearing a date and an imprint which was issued from a Basel printing-press was an edition of the *Gregorii Magni Moralia in Jobum*, which appeared in 1468. But one or two copies exist, of which the one that is in the best preservation is contained in the National Library of Paris.

Printing was introduced into Basel by Berthold Ruppel, who, in 1455, had been an apprentice with Fust. The first work which is identified as Berthold's, but which does not bear a date, is the *Repertorium Vocabulorum Exquisitorum* of Conrad de Mure. The difficulties which have attended all organisations of labour appear to have begun at an early date in Basel, as there is record of a strike of the compositors occurring as early as 1471. This strike lasted for a number of months and was finally adjusted by the arbitration of the authorities of the town, certain concessions being made on the part of both the master and the employees. The magistrate issued a decision or mandate to the effect that on a certain date the workmen must return to their shops and accept the authority of their masters, and this order appears to have been accepted. It does not appear what course could have been taken to force the men to their work in case they might still have been recalcitrant. The fact that a difference between the printers and their men should have been a matter of such general importance indicates that already within twenty years of the beginning of printing in Germany, the business in Basel had assumed large proportions.

In 1474, there was printed in Basel an edition of the *Sachsenspiegel*, a work of popular character, which can share with the Bible and with different essays of Cicero, the honour of being the most frequently published book in Germany during the first quarter century of printing.

Between 1478 and 1514, Johann Amerbach, one of the most scholarly of the early editors, printers, and publishers of Germany, made Basel his headquarters. His work was, however, by no means limited to Basel, as he co-operated with Koberger in Nuremberg and with other of his contemporaries in editorial and publishing responsibilities in other cities.

His most important publication in Basel was a series of the works of the Church Fathers. In carrying these books through the press, he was able to secure the co-operation of a number of the well known scholars of the time, including Beatus Rhenanus, Dodo, Conon, Wyler, Pellikan, and, above all, his old instructor, Heynlin.

Before beginning business in his own name in Basel, Amerbach had co-operated with Koberger in the production of the great Bible with the commentaries of Hugo, and he was also in active relations with Rusch of Strasburg. The last book which was printed with his own name is an edition of the *Decretum Gratiani*, which appeared in 1512. His edition of the works of S. Jerome, left unfinished at the time of his death, was completed by his pupil and successor, Johann Froben.

Froben, who was like his master, not only a printer but a scholar of wide attainments, did more, possibly, than any printer of his time, except Aldus of Venice, to further through his publishing undertakings the development of scholarship and of literature. He appears to have had a thorough knowledge, not only of Latin, which was common to all the scholars of his time, but of Greek and Hebrew, which were rarities even in university centres. It was the case with Froben, as with Aldus, that he himself assumed the task of preparing for the press the texts of a number of works issued by him, a task which included a comparison of manuscripts, in order to secure the most

correct readings, and such thorough knowledge of the
text as would make possible the correction of errors, not
only of typography, but of statement. Froben's work
and character have been commemorated by the loving
words of Erasmus, who during the last twenty years of
Froben's life held with him the closest relations of friendship as well as of business.

It was through Froben that the larger publishing undertakings of Erasmus were carried on, undertakings which
were later in part shared with Aldus of Venice. Froben's
work was done exclusively for scholarly readers. His imprint appears upon no book printed in German, while the
list of books issued by him during the thirty-six years of
his business activity includes no less than 257 works,
nearly all of which were of large compass and distinctive
importance. Erasmus himself, ranking at that time possibly as the greatest scholar of Europe, was ready to give
to Froben his assistance in supervising texts for the
compositors and in the corrections of the proofs. The
details of the business arrangements entered into by publishers like Froben with their scholarly assistants have unfortunately not been preserved, but it would appear as if
in many cases these scholars had given their services as a
labour of love, and solely with a view to furthering the
development of scholarship and literature. Erasmus was
for a number of years an inmate of Froben's house, and it
is probable that he received a certain annual stipend for
his editorial services, in addition to the returns paid to
him from the sale of his books. The most important of
the issues from the Froben press in the matter of popular
sale and of business success were, as indicated, the writings of Erasmus. Erasmus, in fact, was possibly the first
author who was able, after the invention of printing to
secure from the sale of his books any substantial returns.
It is evident from the various references made by Erasmus
that those returns were sufficient to make him substan-

tially independent, notwithstanding the fact that piracy
editions of his books were printed in Paris, in Cologne,
and elsewhere.

Further information concerning the publishing undertakings of Erasmus will be found in the chapter devoted
to him.

Pamphilus Gengenbach, described as the first dramatist
of the sixteenth century, and who was also a poet, undertook between the years 1509 and 1522, the business of
a printer. We do not learn with what success. A more
noteworthy printer of Basel of the same period, noteworthy at least from the point of view of commercial success, was Langendorf. He built up his business by the
publication of piracy editions of the writings of Luther,
out of which he is reported to have made large profits.[1]

The first German printer who appears to have received
honours from royalty was a certain Heinrich Petri, who was
carrying on business between 1520 and 1579, and who in
1556, in recognition of his services to the community, was
knighted by Charles V.

As before indicated, the work of the printers and publishers of Basel was very much furthered by the presence
and by the intelligent co-operation of the members of its
University Faculty. The University was of service not
only in making a certain important market for editions of
scholarly books, but, as a more important consideration,
in giving to the publishers the aid of scholarly advisers,
editors, and proof-correctors. By the close of the fifteenth
century, Basel had secured so great a prestige for the production of accurate editions of important texts, and for
the beauty and costliness of its typography, that commissions came to its printers from all parts of Europe.

In 1510, Sir Thomas More, desiring, as he writes, to
secure a European circulation for his books, causes the
same to be printed in Basel, while during the years be-

[1] Kapp, 121.

tween 1490 and 1520, the popes send to Basel printing-offices the orders for their commercial printing.

The next city in chronological order to be considered as a publishing centre is Zurich, in which printing began in 1504.

The first of the Zurich printers whose name has been preserved is Christ Froschauer, who is known principally through his association with Zwingli.   Froschauer, who devoted himself earnestly to the cause of the Calvinists, had a religious as well as a business interest in securing a wide circulation for the works of Zwingli and his associates, and together with these works, he printed editions of the Bible, not only in German, but in French, Italian, Flemish, and English.   Froschauer's editions were the first Bibles printed on the Continent in the English language.   For these Bibles, which were distributed at what to-day would be called popular prices, very considerable sales were secured, and the presses of Froschauer were thus made an important adjunct to the work of the Reformation.

In Augsburg, the printing business of which began to assume importance in 1468, the interests of the publishers were, on the other hand, largely associated with the cause of the Roman Church.   The first book with an Augsburg imprint and date was issued by Zainer, and was an edition of the *Meditationes Vitae Domini Nostri Jesu Christi*.   In 1470, was published by Schüssler a Latin edition of *Josephus*, and in 1477, Sorg, who was one of the most active of the Augsburg publishers, issued the book of the Council of Constance, which contained no less than 1200 wood-cuts, presenting the 1156 coats-of-arms which were represented at the Council.

The most famous of the printer-publishers of Augsburg was, according to Kapp, Ratdolt, whose list comprised principally mathematical works and books of religious music.   His edition of *Euclid*, issued in 1482, constituted the first European edition of the Syracusan mathematician. The sales of the orthodox theological books, which constituted a special interest of the Augsburg publishers, were largely checked by the Reformation. George Willer, an enterprising Augsburg bookseller, who sold not only his own publications but those of other German publishers, is to be credited with the printing of the first classified catalogue known to Germany.

Among the earlier publications of Ulm, the most important was the geography of Ptolemy, issued by Holl in 1484, with important maps.

The eminence of the city of Nuremberg in the work of publishing is principally due to the scholarly enterprise of one family, that of the Kobergers, whose work began about 1470. Antonius Koberger, the first of the line, is grouped with Froben of Basel and with Aldus of Venice for the commercial importance of his undertakings, and above all for the scholarly ideal of his business operations. His active business work covered the years 1470–1503. Among his earlier important publications was an edition of *Thomas Aquinas*, issued in 1474, and of the *Consolations of Philosophy* of Boëthius, printed in 1475. The latter was the first printed edition of a book which had been for nearly a thousand years famous among books in manuscript, and which possibly shares with S. Augustine's *City of God* the reputation of being the work most frequently found in the old monastery libraries. By the year 1500, Koberger was utilising no less than twenty-four presses, and undoubtedly was sending out annually more books than any other publisher of his time. He had branches or agencies in Frankfort, Paris, and Lyons, a business correspondence in the Netherlands, Italy, Austria, Hungary, Poland, and England, as well as, of course, throughout Germany. In respect to the bulk of the business done by him and of the commercial success secured, he was a greater publisher than either Aldus or

Froben, his two most famous contemporaries. The work of Aldus, which is considered in detail in another chapter, was, however, distinctive on the ground of the special difficulties to be overcome and of his enterprise and scholarly ambition in the production of Greek literature. The interest of the work of Froben centres partly in his close friendship and long association with Erasmus, and in the fact that, as the publisher for Erasmus, he secured the first important copyright returns for a contemporary author which had been known in the record of publishing.

Koberger gave special attention to the production of Bibles and of works in orthodox theology. The latter division of his list was largely interfered with by the increasing influence of the Lutherans.

Koberger took the initiative in the production of books containing expensive and elaborate illustrations, and his illustrated editions will compare more favourably with those of Plantin and with the other publishers of the Low Countries, than is the case with the issues of any other German publisher. Nuremberg had always been the centre of art interests, and there appear to have been in the town many designers whose services could be secured for the production of wood-cuts.

The great German Bible, published by Koberger in 1483, filled with artistic illustrations engraved on wood, compares not unfavourably with the illustrated Bible issued by Plantin fifty years later.

The *Schedelsche Chronik*, published in 1493, contained no less than 2000 wood-cuts prepared by the Nuremberg artists, Wohlgemut and Pleydenwurf. After the work of the Reformers became active, the presses of Nuremberg were occupied for some years in issuing controversial tracts and pamphlets upholding the orthodox views of the Church ; while, under an edict of the magistrates issued in 1520, the printers of Nuremberg were forbidden to print and the dealers were forbidden to sell

the writings of Luther, Calvin, Zwingli, and their associates. Notwithstanding this prohibition, however, there
was enough sympathy with the Reformation among many
of the Nuremberg printers to keep them interested in the
surreptitious production (under risk of fine, confiscation,
and imprisonment) of very many of the Protestant tracts
of the times. While the Catholic tracts were, however,
catalogued in due course and openly sold, the Protestant
pamphlets had to be smuggled in and out of the city and
disposed of under various covers and precautions.

In giving chronological consideration to certain of the
distinctive publishing centres and printer-publishers of
Germany, it is necessary at this time to refer to the important undertakings of the Brothers of Common Life,
whose work in the manuscript period has already been
described.

As in the earlier manuscript publishing, the Brothers
had interested themselves particularly in reaching with
their books the common people, and had for this purpose produced their versions in the folk dialects. When,
therefore, they had replaced the *scriptoria* of their Houses
with well organised printing-offices, they devoted their
presses mainly to the production of devotional books, and
of books of general instruction planned for the service
and information of the middle and lower classes, and
printed in the vernacular.

While I have not found record of the business results
secured through these printing-offices established by the
Brothers, it seems probable, in view of the excellent
distributing machinery they possessed for their output,
and from the fact that they were almost the first among
printers to prepare publications expressly for the use
of the lower and middle classes, that they secured from
the sales of their books satisfactory business returns,
so that the profits produced by their presses may easily
have formed an important part of the resources and

the income of the Order.   Their first printing-presses
were established in Marienthal in 1468, in Brussels and in
Rostock in 1476, and in Nuremberg in 1479.   In 1490,
there were no less than sixty different printing establishments carried on under the supervision of the Brothers.
I am not sufficiently familiar with the various phases of
the complex history of the Reformation to be able to
speak definitely concerning the influence exercised upon
the controversies and the contest of the time by the publications of the Brothers.   It is my impression that these
publications remained on the whole orthodox, but that
they represented the more liberal wing of Catholic Orthodoxy.

The city of Leipzig, which a century after the invention
of printing became the centre of the book-trade of Germany, and the most important book-producing city in the
world, began its printing somewhat later than the other
German cities whose work has already been referred to.

The earliest printing-press set up in Leipzig was that of
an anonymous printer who issued, in 1481, an edition of
the essay of the Dominican Annius von Viterbo, entitled
Glosa Super Apocalipsim.   The second Leipzig publication, also issued without imprint, was an edition of the
fifteen astrological propositions of Martin Polich.   The
first Leipzig publisher whose name is recorded is Markus
Brandis, who issued, in 1484, a volume entitled *Regimen
Sanitatis,* which was the work of Archbishop Albicius of
Prague, who had died in 1427.   It is not easy to decide
on what basis these first three publications of the future
publishing mart were selected, and it is difficult to understand how a remunerative sale could have been depended
upon for any one of the three.

By the year 1513, the production of Breviaries had become an important interest with the Leipzig presses.   A
printer named Lotter secured a reputation in the earlier
years of the sixteenth century for the excellence of his

typography, and was employed by the Archbishop of Heller in printing the Breviaries and the Missals of the Dioceses of Brandenburg. In 1492, a certain Gregor Werman printed *Sacrarum Historiarum Opus*. The name of the author does not appear in connection with the work. In 1497, Bötticher issued an edition of Virgil's *Bucolics*, the first classic which bears a Leipzig imprint.

By the year 1495, the book-trade of Leipzig had assumed very considerable proportions, not only in connection with printing and publishing, but in the organisation of machinery for collecting and distributing the publications of other cities. In this branch of the book business, Leipzig was already beginning to rival Frankfort. The booksellers' association, organised in 1525, is, at the present time, 370 years later, the most effective and intelligently managed trade organisation that the world has known. Leipzig publishers gave from an early period special attention to the printing of the controversial literature of the Reformation, and, as was natural from their close relations with Wittenberg, the sympathies of the larger proportion of the printers were in accord with the Lutherans.

Under the trade restrictions established by Duke George of Saxony, who was a Catholic, and whose reign covered the period between 1524 and 1533, the work of the Protestant printers was very seriously hampered, and the whole book-trade of Leipzig was affected. The writings of the Reformers were repressed as far as practicable by rigorous censorship, while those of the Romanists found few buyers. Lotter, the son of the first printer of that name, removed his printing-office to Wittenberg, where he continued, though still under the difficulties of a rigorous supervision, to distribute the writings of the Reformers. The magistracy of Leipzig, appreciating the importance of the book-trade, attempted in the first place to secure for its operations the necessary protection.

Later, however, it was compelled, under pressure from the Duke, to put into effect the ducal regulations for supervision and censorship, and two ecclesiastical censors, appointed under the ducal authority, secured the aid of the city officials in making examination of the books printed, and in confiscating or cancelling all heretical works found in the book-shops of either Leipzig or Dresden.

Under the edict issued in 1528, all books printed by Vogel, Goltz, and Schramm of Wittenberg, were forbidden to be offered for sale in Leipzig or Dresden, and were forbidden transportation to the Frankfort Fair. The immediate result of these anti-reform operations of the Church and of the Duke was the practical destruction for the time being of the book-trade of Leipzig.

In 1539, a printer of Leipzig, named Michel Wohlrabe, secured for himself notoriety through the extent of his piracy publications. He issued editions of the Lutheran Bible and of other writings of the Reformers, in the face, not only of the claims of these writers to control their own publications, but of the prohibition of Duke George against the production of any Lutheran literature whatever. After the death of George, however, there came a change in regard to the influence of the ducal government, and at the request of the Elector John Frederic, an edict was issued forbidding the further printing in Leipzig of any anti-Lutheran literature. This removed one difficulty in the way of Wohlrabe's operations, and Luther and his friends found that they were helpless, in the conditions which then obtained in the law and in the book-trade, to prevent the circulation of these unauthorised editions.

Luther's complaints, referred to further on, were principally directed, as it must be remembered, not against the loss of profits to himself, but to the injury to the community and the grievance to the writers in having books circulated in an unrevised and incorrect text.

CHAPTER III.

THE PRINTER-PUBLISHERS OF ITALY, 1464–1600.

THE reproduction and distribution of the works of classical writers to such an extent as not only to influence the scholarly thought of the time, but to widen enormously the circles of society reached and affected by intellectual influences, became possible only through the new art of printing which had been brought across the Alps by German workmen ; while the prompt utilisation of printing for the service of scholarship called for the devoted labour of printers who were themselves scholars and who were prepared to subordinate and even to sacrifice, in the cause of a literary ideal, their immediate business advantage. It was to the high scholarly ideals and courageous and unselfish labours of Aldus Manutius and his immediate successors no less than to the imagination, ingenuity, and persistency of Gutenberg and Fust, that the Europe of 1495 was indebted for the great gift of the poetry and the philosophy of Greece. Mayence and Venice joined hands to place at the service of the scholarly world the literary heritage of Athens.

The close of the fifteenth century witnessed a great expansion in more than one direction of European thought. In the West, Columbus had opened up a new world, and his discovery, while giving manifold incentives to the men of action, must also have served as a powerful stimulus to the imagination of the thinkers of the time, in its suggestions concerning the possibilities of the future.

In the East, the printers of Venice were making use of scholars from Constantinople to rediscover for Europe the vast realm of Greek thought, and to bring Homer, Plato, and Aristotle to the knowledge of the students of Bologna, Paris, and Oxford. Perhaps in no other epoch of the world's history has there been so great an expansion of the possibilities of thought and of action, so suggestive a widening of range of the imagination, as in the decade succeeding 1492.

The introduction into Italy of the art of printing was due to Juan Turrecremata, who was Abbot of the monastery of Subiaco, and who later became Cardinal. He was a native of Valladolid in Spain, and his family name was Torquemada, of which name Turrecremata is the Latinised form. The Cardinal has been confused by Frommann[1] with the Torquemada who was Inquisitor-General of the Inquisition during the period of its most pitiless activity. The latter probably belonged to the same family, but his Christian name was Tomas, and he was not born till 1420, thirty years later than the Cardinal. Juan Torquemada had, however, been one of the confessors of Queen Isabella, and was said to have made to her the first suggestion of the necessity of establishing the Inquisition, in order to check the rising spirit of heresy. He did not realise what a Trojan horse, full of heretical possibilities, he was introducing into Italy in bringing in the Germans and their printing-press.

The monastery of Subiaco was some sixty miles from Rome. Among its monks were, in 1464, a number of Germans, some of whom had, before leaving Germany, seen or heard enough of the work done by the printers in Mayence or Frankfort to be able to give to the Abbot an idea of its character. The Abbot was keenly interested in the possibilities presented by the new art, and with the aid of these German monks he arranged to bring to

[1] *Aufsätze der Buchhandlung*, p. 6.

Subiaco two printers, Conrad Schweinheim, of Mayence, and Arnold Pannartz, of Prague, who were instructed to organise a printing-office in the monastery. They began their operations early in 1464, their first work being given to the printing in sheet form of the manuals of worship or liturgies used in the monastery.

In 1465, they published the first volume printed in Italy, an edition of a Latin syntax for boys, edited by Lactantius. This was followed in the latter part of the same year by an edition of Cicero's *De Oratore,* and in 1467, by the *De Civitate* of Augustine.

It was only the enthusiasm of the Abbot that rendered it possible, even for a short period, to overcome the many obstacles in the way of carrying on a printing-office in an out of the way village like Subiaco. But the difficulties soon became too great, and in 1467, the two German printers found their way, under the invitation of the brothers Massimi, to Rome, where they set up their presses in the Massimi palace. There they carried on operations for five years, during which time they produced a stately series of editions of the Latin classics, including the works of Cicero, Apuleius, Gellius, Cæsar, Virgil, Livy, Strabo, Lucan, Pliny, Suetonius, Quintilian, Ovid, together with editions of certain of the Church Fathers, such as Augustine, Jerome, and Cyprian. They also published a Latin Bible, and the Bible commentaries of Nicholas de Lyra, in five volumes.

With the production of the last work, the resources which had been placed at their disposal by their friends the Massimis and by another patron, Bussi, Bishop of Aleria, were exhausted. The Bishop addressed an appeal to the Pope on their behalf, setting forth the importance of their work for the " service of literature and of the Church." Sixtus IV., who had just succeeded to the papacy, while apparently not affected by the dread which influenced future popes concerning the pernicious influence of the printing-press, evidently did not share in the enthusiasm of the Bishop as to its present value for the Church. He was also somewhat avaricious and preferred to use his money to provide for a large circle of relatives rather than to support a publishing business. The printers were, therefore, unable to secure any aid from the papal treasury, and, in 1472, they brought their business to a close. Schweinheim transferred his activities to the work of engraving on copper, while concerning the further undertakings of Pannartz there is no record.

During the seven years of their operations in Subiaco and in Rome, these two printers, who constituted the first firm of publishers in Italy, had printed twenty-nine separate works, comprised in thirty-six volumes. The editions averaged 275 copies of each volume, the total output aggregating about 12,500 volumes. There is no record of any attempt being made to secure for this first list of publications the protection of privileges, and there could in fact have been at the time no competition to fear.

Shortly after the cessation of Schweinheim's business, Turrecremata became a cardinal, and he immediately invited another German printer, Ulrich Hahn, from Ingolstadt, to settle in Rome. Hahn's first publications were the *Meditationes* of the Cardinal himself, and these were followed by a number of editions of the Latin classics. The learned Campanus, Bishop of Teramo, was one of Hahn's patrons and gave also valuable service as a press-corrector, working so diligently that at one time he reserved for himself only three hours' sleep. The Bishop writes with great enthusiasm to a friend concerning the art of printing, "by means of which material which required a year for its writing could be printed off ready for the reader in one day."

Other German printers followed Hahn, and before the close of the century more than twenty had carried on work in Rome with varying success. The influence of

the Church was at this time decidedly favourable to the
new art, and nearly all the Roman printers of the earlier
group were working at the instance of ecclesiastics, and
often with the direct support of ecclesiastical funds. It
is to the Church of Rome, therefore, that belongs the
responsibility for the introduction into Italy of the printing-press, the work of which was later to give to the
Church so much trouble. The little town of Subiaco
can, as the record shows, claim the credit of the first
printing, while it was in Rome that the first publications
of importance were produced.

The leading place, however, in the production of books
was almost from the outset taken by the printers of
Venice, and as well for the excellence of their typography
as by reason of the scholarly importance of the publications themselves, the Venetian printers maintained for
many years a pre-eminence not only in Italy but in
Europe. The distinctive prestige secured by Venice came
through the printing of Greek texts, the beginnings of
which, under the direction of Aldus Manutius, will be
referred to later.

Venice.—The first book printed in Venice was the
famous *Decor Puellarum*, a treatise of instruction for
young girls as to the ruling of their lives. Its date has
been claimed by Venetians to be 1461, but it appears
from the judgment of the best authorities that this date
must have been erroneous and that the volume really
appeared in 1471. The printer of the *Decor Puellarum*
was Jenson, a Frenchman, and the contest for priority in
Italian publishing has rested between him and the two
Germans of Subiaco.

Another printer whose first Italian volume, *Epistolæ
Familiares*, appeared in Venice in 1470, was also a German, John of Speyer. A fourth volume in this earlier
group of publications bore the title *Miracoli della Glo-
riosa Verzine*. This was the only one of the four which

was printed by an Italian, Lavagna of Milan, while it was also the only early printed book in the Italian language.

In the year 1493, the earliest official document relating to the printing-press in Venice was published by the Abbate Jacopo Morelli, prefect of the Marcian Library. That document is an order of the *Collegio* or cabinet of Venice, dated September 18, 1469. The order was proposed by the Doge's councillors, and grants to John of Speyer, for a period of five years, the monopoly of printing in Venice and in the territory controlled by Venice. John did not long enjoy the advantages of this monopoly, having died in 1470, but the business was continued by his brother Windelin, to whom, apparently, was conceded the continuance of the monopoly.

John of Speyer was one of the few of the earlier printers who left information concerning the size of their editions. If he had also thought it important to specify the price at which the books were sold, we should have had data for calculations concerning the relative profit from the different works.

Of the *Epistolæ Familiares*, the first edition comprised but one hundred copies, but the demand must have been greater than had been calculated for, as four months later the printing of a second edition of six hundred copies was begun, which was completed (in two impressions) within the term of three months.

The printer, Nicolas Jenson, was born in the province of Champagne about 1420, and was brought up in the Paris Mint. He was sent to Mayence in 1458 by Charles VII. to learn the secrets of the new art of printing. He returned to France in 1461, shortly after the accession of Louis XI. It is not clear whether the new king was less interested than had been his predecessor in the development of French printing, or whether Jenson was afforded any opportunity for excercising his art in Paris. In 1465, however, he is heard of in Venice, and he began there, in

1470, a printing and publishing business which soon became the most important in Italy.

There were many reasons to influence Jenson in his choice of Venice as the scene of his operations. In the first place, the tide of printers was flowing steadily towards Italy. Apprentices who had acquired the new art in Germany set out to seek their fortunes by the exercise of their skill. It was natural that they should turn to Italy, where the nobles were rich, where learning had its home, where there were already many manuscripts available for the printers, and where there was a public, both lay and ecclesiastic, ready to pay for the reproductions. The Venetian Republic offered special attractions in the security afforded by its government, and in the protection and liberty she promised to all who settled in her dominions. Venice was, moreover, the best mart for the distribution of goods, and the trade in paper was facilitated by the ease and cheapness of sea-carriage.

The first rag paper was made about the year 1300, and the trade of paper-making soon became an important one in Italy. In 1373, the Venetian Senate forbade the exportation of rags from the dominions of the Republic, an act which recalls the edict of Ptolemy Philadelphus in 290 B.C., forbidding the exportation of papyrus from Alexandria.

The position of Venice secured for it exceptional facilities for becoming a literary and a publishing centre, facilities in some respects similar to those which eighteen hundred years earlier had given to Alexandria the control of the book production of its time. The Venetian Contarini, writing in 1591, speaks of "the wonderful situation of the city, which possesses so many advantages that one might think the site had been selected not by men but by the gods themselves. The city lies in a quiet inlet of the Adriatic Sea. On the side towards the sea, the waters of the lagoons are spread out like a series of lakes, while

far in the distance the bow-shaped peninsula of the Lido
serves as a protection against the storms from the south.
On the side towards the main land, the city is, in like
manner, surrounded and protected by the waters of its
lagoons.   Various canals serve as roadways between the
different islands, and in the midst of the lakes and of these
watery ways arise in stately groups the palaces and the
towers of the city."

It was by the thoroughness of the protection secured
for Venice through its watery defences, no less than by
its isolated position outside of, although in immediate
connection with, the Italian territory, that the Republic
was enabled to keep free from a large proportion of the
contests petty and great that troubled or devastated
Italian territory during the sixteenth century.

When it was drawn into a conflict, its fighting was done
very largely by means of its fleets, operating at a distance,
or with the aid of foreign troops hired for the purpose, and
but rarely were the actual operations of war brought within
touch of Venetian territory.   Its control of the approaches
by sea prevented also the connections with the outer world
from being interfered with.   The city could neither be
blockaded nor surrounded, and in whatever warlike operations it might be engaged, its commercial undertakings
went on practically undisturbed.   It was under very similar conditions that Alexandria secured, in literary production and in publishing operations during the fourth and
the third centuries B. C., pre-eminence over Pergamus and
the other Greek cities of Asia Minor.   The fact that
manuscripts and printing-presses could be fairly protected
against the risks of war, and that the road to the markets
of the world for the productions of the presses could not
easily be blocked, had an important influence during the
century succeeding 1490, in attracting printers to Venice
rather than to Bologna, Milan, or Florence.   The Venetian
government was also prompt to recognise the value of the

new industry and the service and the prestige that were
being conferred upon the city by the work of the printer-
publishers and their scholarly editors. The Republic
gave, from the outset, more care to the furthering of this
work by privileges and concessions and by honourable
recognition of the guild of the printers than was given in
any other Italian state. To these advantages should be
added the valuable relations possessed by Venice with
the scholars of the Greek world, through its old-time
connections with Constantinople and Asia Minor. It was
through these connections that the printers of Venice
secured what might be called the first pick of the manuscripts of a large number of the Greek texts that became
known to Europe during the half-century succeeding
1490.

These texts were brought in part from the monasteries,
which had been spared by the Turkish conquerors in the
Byzantine territory and in Asia Minor, while in other
cases, they came to light in various corners of Italy, where
the scholars, flying from Constantinople after the great
disaster of 1453, had found refuge. As it became known
that in Venice there was demand for Greek manuscripts,
and that Venetian printers were offering compensation to
scholars for editing Greek texts for the press, scholars
speedily found their way to the City of the Lagoons. To
many of these scholars, who had been driven impoverished
from their homes in the East, the opportunity of securing
a livelihood through the sale and through the editing of
their manuscripts must have opened up new and important
possibilities.

In 1479, Jenson sold to Andrea Torresano of Asola,
later the father-in-law of Aldus Manutius, a set of the
matrices punched by his punches. These matrices were
probably the beginning of the plant of the later business
of Aldus. In 1479, Pope Sixtus IV. conferred upon
Jenson the honourary title of Count Palatine. He was

the first nobleman in the guild of publishers, and he has had but few successors. He died in 1480.

John of Windelin, John of Speyer, and Nicolas Jenson, the three earliest Venetian printers, employed three kinds of characters in their type—Roman, Gothic, and Greek. The Gothic character secured, as compared with the others, a considerable economy of space, and its use became, therefore, more general in connection with the increased demand from the reading public for less expensive editions. Before the Greek fonts had been made, it was customary to leave blanks in the text where the Greek passages occurred and to fill these in by hand.

It was the practice of the later printer-publishers to place in their books the date, place of publication, and their own names, and considering how much the editing, printing, and publication of a book involved, it was natural that those who were responsible for it should be interested in securing the full credit for its production It is nevertheless the case that quite a number of books, of no little importance, were issued by the earlier printers without any imprint or mark of origin, an omission which, as Brown remarks, is certainly surprising in view of the high esteem in which printers were held and of the large claims made by them upon the gratitude of their own age and of future generations.

The larger proportion of the outlay required for these early books was not the expense of the manufacturing, heavy as this was, but the payments required for the purchase of manuscripts, and for their revision, collation, correction, and preparation for the type-setters.

The printer-publisher needed to possess a fair measure of scholarly knowledge in order to be able to judge rightly of the nature of the editorial work that was required before the work of the type-setters could begin. If, as in the case of Aldus, this scholarly knowledge was sufficient to enable the printer himself to act as editor, to revise the

manuscripts for the press, and to write the introduction
and the critical annotations, he had of course a very great
advantage in the conduct of his business.

As an example of the cost of printing in Venice at this
period, Brown cites an agreement entered into in 1478
between a certain Leonardus, printer, and Nicolaus, who
took the risk of the undertaking, acting, therefore, as a
publisher. An edition of 930 copies of the complete Bible
was to be printed by Leonardus for the price of 430
ducats, the paper being furnished by Nicolaus. Twenty
of the copies were to be retained by Leonardus, and the
cost to Nicolaus of the 910 copies received by him would
have been, exclusive of the paper, about $2150, or per
copy about $2.50. The cost of the paper would have
brought the amount up to about $3. The selling price of
Bibles in 1492 appears to have varied from 6 ducats to 12
ducats, or from $30 to $60, but it is probable that these
prices covered various styles of bindings.

The years between 1470 and 1515 witnessed a greater
increase in the number of printers at work in Venice, a
considerable proportion of the newcomers being Germans.
With the rapid growth in the production of books, there
came a material deterioration in the quality of the typography. The original models for the type-founders had
been the letters of the manuscripts, and it was the boast
of the earlier founders that their type was so perfect that
it could not be distinguished from script. The copyists
realised that their art was in danger, and, in 1474, they
went so far in their opposition in Genoa as to petition the
Senate for the expulsion of the printers. The application
was, however, disregarded ; the new art met at once with
a cordial reception, and from the beginning secured the
active support of the government.

The trade of the printers could, however, not rest upon
a secure foundation until the taste for reading had become
popularised. The wealthy classes were not sufficiently

numerous to keep the printing-presses busy, while it was also the case that for a number of years after the invention of printing, a considerable proportion of the wealthier collectors of literature continued to give their preference to manuscripts as being more aristocratic and exclusive. The earlier books issued from the presses were planned to meet the requirements of these higher class collectors, whose taste had been formed from beautiful manuscripts. With the second generation of printers, however, a new market arose calling for a different class of supplies. The revival of learning brought into existence a reading public which was eager for knowledge and which was no longer fastidious as to the beauty of the form in which its literature was presented. By 1490, a demand had arisen for cheap books for popular reading, and in changing their methods to meet this demand, the printers permitted the standard of excellence of their work to suffer a material decline.

Brown gives an abstract from the day-book of a Venetian bookseller of 1484–1485, the original of which is contained in the Marcian Library. Even at that early date, we find represented in the stock of the bookseller, classics, Bibles, missals, breviaries, works on canon law, school-books, romances, and poetry.

The record shows that the purchases of the bookseller from the publisher were usually made for cash, and that for the most part he received cash from his customers. In some cases, however, these latter made their payment in kind. Thus a chronicle was exchanged for oil; Cicero's *Orations* for wine ; and a general assortment of books for flour ; while different binders' bills were settled, the one with the *Life and Miracles of the Madonna*, and the other with the series of the *Hundred Novels*. The proof-reader was paid for certain services with copies of a Mamotrictus, a Legendary, and a Bible, and an account from an illuminator was adjusted with an Abacus, (a multiplication table, or a condensed arithmetic).

The prices of books ruled lower than might have been expected, the cheapest being volumes of poetry and romance. For instance, Poggio's *Facetiæ* sells for nine soldi, and the *Inamoramento d' Orlando* for one lira, while Dante's *Inferno* with a commentary, brings one ducat, and Plutarch's *Lives*, two ducats. A small volume of Martial brought fifteen soldi. The editions of certain printers realised higher prices than those of the same books by other printers whose imprint did not carry with it so much prestige.

It was during the last ten years of the fifteenth century that the business of printing and publishing in Venice reached its highest importance as compared with that done elsewhere. It was this decade that witnessed the founding of the Greek press by Aldus, Vlastos, and Caliergi, the first printing in Arabic and in the other Eastern languages, and the beginning of the publication of romances and *novelieri*.

The part taken in these new undertakings by Aldus Manutius was of distinctive importance, not only for Venice and Italy, but for the civilised world. He was a skilled printer, and an enterprising, public-spirited publisher, and he was, further, a judicious and painstaking critic and editor, and a scholar of exceptional attainments. To him more than to any other one man is due the introduction into Europe of the literature of Greece, which was in a measure rediscovered at the time, when, by the use of the printing-press, it could be placed within the reach of wide circles of impecunious students to whom the purchase of costly manuscripts would have been impossible.

In his interest in Greek literature, as well as in his scholarship and public-spirited liberality, Aldus was a worthy successor to the Roman publisher of the first century who had earned the appellation of Atticus on account of the attention given by him to the reproduction for the reading public of Italy of the great classics of

Greece. Atticus was, however, a man of large means, gained chiefly through his business as a banker and a farmer of taxes, and it appears to have been to him a matter of indifference whether or not his publishing undertakings returned any profits on the moneys invested in them. Aldus began business without capital and died a poor man. Not many of his books secured for the publisher profits as well as prestige. He lived modestly and laboured continuously, but he expended in fresh scholarly publishing undertakings all the receipts that came to him from such of his ventures as proved remunerative.

As before pointed out, the payments made by Aldus for the work of editing his series of classical publications, payments which were probably the first ever made in Italy for literary work in connection with printing, were not only of material service to many of the impecunious Greek scholars, but must have served as precedents for fixing, for Italy at least, a market value for literary service. The payments to the Greek refugees included in a number of cases compensation for the use of the manuscripts they had brought with them, manuscripts which not infrequently constituted practically everything in the shape of property that they had been able to save from the grasp of the Turks. For a number of the more scholarly of these refugees, places were made in the universities, or as we should now say, Chairs were endowed, for instruction in the language and literature of Greece. Aldus himself took the initiative in inducing the Venetian Senate to institute such a professorship in Padua for his friend Musurus.

For a number of years, a larger proportion of the scholars and the manuscripts was absorbed by Venice than by any other of the Italian cities. The production of books progressed more rapidly in Venice than elsewhere, and the art of bookmaking reached a higher perfection there during the first decade of the sixteenth

century than in any city in Europe. As before noted,
however, Subiaco had preceded Venice in the printing of
books, while the use of Greek type, in which Venice
so rapidly attained pre-eminence, occurred first in Milan.
The introduction of illustrations into book-printing probably originated in Rome.

Aldus Manutius.—It seems to me in order, for the
purpose of my narrative, to present in some detail the
record of the life and work of Aldus. The history of any
representative printer-publisher whose career belonged to
the earlier stages of the business of making and selling
books, would have value in throwing light on the extent
of the difficulties and obstacles to be overcome and on
the nature of the methods adopted ; the career of Aldus
possesses, however, not merely such typical value but a
distinctive and individual interest, as well because of the
personality of the man as on the ground of the exceptional importance, for his own community and for future
generations, of the service rendered by him.

Aldus Manutius was born at Bassiano in the Romagna,
in 1450, the year in which Gutenberg completed his
printing-press. He studied in Rome and in Ferrara, and
after having mastered Latin, he devoted himself, under
the tutorship of Guarini of Verona, to the study of Greek.
Later, he delivered lectures on the Latin and Greek
classics. One of his fellow students in Ferrara was the
precocious young scholar Pico della Mirandola, whose
friendship was afterwards of material service. In 1482,
when Ferrara was being besieged by the Venetians and
scholarly pursuits were interrupted, Aldus was the guest
of Pico at Mirandola, where he met Emanuel Adramyttenos, one of the many Greek scholars who, when driven
out of Constantinople, had found refuge in the Courts of
Italian princes. Aldus spent two years at Mirandola, and
under the influence and guidance of Adramyttenos, he
largely increased his knowledge of the language and

literature of Greece. His friend had brought from the East a number of manuscripts, many of which found their way into the library of Pico.

In 1482, Aldus took charge of the education of the sons of the Princess of Carpi, a sister of Pico, and the zeal and scholarly capacity which he devoted to his task won for him the life-long friendship of both mother and sons. It was in Carpi that Aldus developed the scheme of utilising his scholarly knowledge and connections for the printing of Latin and Greek classics. The plan was a bold one for a young scholar without capital. Printing and publishing constituted a practically untried field of business, not merely for Aldus but for Italy. Everything had to be created or developed; knowledge of the art of printing and of all the technicalities of book-manufacturing; fonts of type, Roman and Greek; a force of type-setters and pressmen and a staff of skilled revisers and proof-readers; a collection of trustworthy texts to serve as "copy" for the compositors; and last, but by no means least, a book-buying public and a book-selling machinery by which such public could be reached.

It was the aim of Aldus, as he himself expressed it, to rescue from oblivion the words of the classic writers, the monuments of human intellect. He writes in 1490: "I have resolved to devote my life to the cause of scholarship. I have chosen in place of a life of ease and freedom, an anxious and toilsome career. A man has higher responsibilities than the seeking of his own enjoyment; he should devote himself to honourable labour. Living that is a mere existence can be left to men who are content to be animals. Cato compared human existence to iron. When nothing is done with it, it rusts; it is only through constant activity that polish or brilliancy is secured." The world has probably never produced a publisher who united with these high ideals and exceptional scholarly attainments, so much practical business ability and persistent pluck.

The funds required for the undertaking were furnished by the Princess of Carpi and her sons, probably with some co-operation from Pico, and in 1494, Aldus organised his printing-office in Venice. His first publication, issued in 1495, was the Greek and Latin Grammar of Laskaris, a suitable forerunner for his great classical series. The second issue from his Press was an edition of the Works of Aristotle, the first volume of which was also completed in 1495. This was followed in 1496 by the Greek Grammar of Gaza, and in 1497 by a Greek-Latin Dictionary compiled by Aldus himself.

The business cares of these first years of his printing business were not allowed to prevent him from going on with his personal studies. In 1502, he published, in a handsome quarto volume, a comprehensive grammar under the title of *Rudimenta Grammatices Linguæ Latinæ, etc. cum Introductione ad Hebraicam Linguam*, to the preparation of which he had devoted years of arduous labour. Piratical editions were promptly issued in Florence, Lyons, and Paris. He also wrote the *Grammaticæ Institutiones Grœcæ* (a labour of some years), which was not published until 1515, after the death of the author.

It will be noted that nearly all the undertakings to which he gave, both as editor and as publisher, his earliest attention, were the necessary first steps in the great scheme of the reproduction of the complete series of the Greek classics. Before editors or proof-readers could go on with the work of preparing the Greek texts for the press, dictionaries and grammars had to be created. Laskaris, whose Grammar initiated the series, was a refugee from the East, and at the time of the publication of his work, was an instructor in Messina. No record has been preserved of the arrangement made with him by his

Venetian publisher, a deficiency that is the more to be regretted as his Grammar was probably the very first work by a living author, printed in Italy. Gaza was a native of Greece, and was for a time associated with the Aldine Press as a Greek editor.

In 1500, Aldus married the daughter of the printer Andrea Torresano of Asola, previously referred to as the successor of the Frenchman Jenson and the purchaser of Jenson's matrices. In 1507, the two printing concerns were united, and the savings of Torresano were utilised to strengthen the resources of Aldus, which had become impaired, probably through his too great optimism and publishing enterprise.

During the disastrous years of 1509–1511, in which Venice was harassed by the wars resulting from the League of Cambray, the business came to a stand-still, partly because the channels of distribution for the books were practically blocked, but partly also on account of the exhaustion of the available funds. Friends again brought to the publisher the aid to which, on the ground of his public-spirited undertakings, he was so well entitled, and he was enabled, after the peace of 1511, to proceed with the completion of his Greek classics. Before his death in 1515, Aldus had issued in this series the works of Aristotle, Plato, Homer, Pindar, Euripides, Sophocles, Aristophanes, Demosthenes, Lysias, Æschines, Herodotus, Thucydides, Xenophon, Plutarch, and others, in addition to a companion series of the works of the chief Latin writers. The list of publications included in all some 100 different works, comprised (in their several editions) in about 250 volumes. Considering the special difficulties of the times and the exceptional character of the original and creative labour that was required to secure the texts, to prepare them for the press, to print them correctly, and to bring them to the attention of possible buyers, this list of undertakings is, in my judgment, by far the greatest and the most honourable in the whole history of publishing.

It was a disadvantage for carrying on scholarly publishing undertakings in Venice, that the city possessed no university, a disadvantage that was only partly offset by the proximity of Padua, which early in the fifteenth century had come under Venetian rule. A university would of course have been of service to a publisher like Aldus, not only in supplying a home market for his books, but in placing at his disposal scholarly assistants whose services could be utilised in editing the texts and in supervising their type-setting. The correspondence of members of a university with the scholars of other centres of learning, could be made valuable also in securing information as to available manuscripts and concerning scholarly undertakings generally. In the absence of a university circle, Aldus was obliged to depend upon his personal efforts to bring him into relations, through correspondence, with men of learning throughout Europe, and to gather about the Aldine Press a group of scholarly associates and collaborators.

The chief corrector or proof-reader for Greek work of the Press was John Gregoropoulos, of Candia. Some editorial service was rendered by Theodore Gaza, of Athens, who took part, for instance, in the work on the set of *Aristotle*. The most important, however, of the Greek associates of Aldus was Marcus Musurus, of Crete, whose name appears as the editor of the *Aristophanes, Athenæus, Plato*, and a number of other of the Greek authors in the Aldine series, and also of the important collection of *Epistolæ Græcarum*.

Musurus was an early friend of Pico, and later of his nephew, Alberto Pio, and it was at Carpi that he had first met Aldus, with whom he ever afterwards maintained a close intimacy. In 1502, probably at the instance of Aldus, Musurus was called by the Venetian Senate to occupy the Chair of belles-lettres at Padua, and he appears to have given his lectures not only in the University, but also in Venice. Aldus writes: " Scholars hasten to Venice, the Athens of our day, to listen to the teachings of Musurus, the greatest scholar of the age."

In 1503, the Senate charged Musurus with the task of exercising a censorship over all Greek books printed in Venice, with reference particularly to the suppression of anything inimical to the Roman Church. This seems to have been the earliest attempt in Italy to supervise the work of the printing-press. It is natural enough that the ecclesiastics should have dreaded the influence of the introduction of the doctrines of the Greek Church, while it is certainly probable that many of the refugees from Constantinople brought with them no very cordial feeling towards Rome. The belief was very general that if the Papacy had not felt a greater enmity against the Greek Church than against the Turk, the Catholic states of Europe would have saved Constantinople. The sacking of Constantinople by the Christian armies of the Fourth Crusade was still remembered by the Christians of the East as a crime of the Western Church. There were, therefore, reasons enough why the authorities of Rome should think it necessary to keep a close watch over the new literature coming in from the East, and should do what was practicable to exclude all doctrinal writings, and the censorship instituted in 1502 was the beginning of a long series of rigorous enactments which proved, however, much less practicable to carry out in Venice than elsewhere in Italy.

Other literary advisers and associates of Aldus were Hieronymus Alexander (later Cardinal), Pietro Bembo, Scipio Carteromachus, Demetrius Doucas, Johann Reuchlin, and, above all, Erasmus of Rotterdam, whose learning rivalled that of Musurus, and who, outside of Italy, was far more widely known than the Greek scholar.

It was in the year 1500 that the scheme took shape in the mind of Aldus of an academy which should take the place in Venice that in Florence was occupied by the academy instituted by the Medici. The special aim of the Aldine Academy, to which Aldus gave the name *Ne-accademia Nostra*, was the furthering of the interest in, and knowledge of, the literature of classic Greece. Aldus himself was the first president of the Academy, and while the majority of the members were residents either of Venice or of Padua, the original list included scholars of Rome, of Bologna, and of Lucca, Greeks of Candia, Erasmus of Rotterdam, and others from distant places.

Aldus applied to the Emperor Maximilian for a diploma giving imperial sanction to the organisation of his Academy, but the Emperor, although, as is shown in other correspondence, friendly in his disposition to the printer, was from some cause unwilling to give an official recognition to the Academy. The constitution of the Academy was printed in Greek, and certain days were fixed on which the members gave their personal consideration to the examination of Greek texts, the publication of which was judged likely to be of service to scholarship.

With the editorial aid of certain members of the Academy, Aldus arranged to print each month, in an edition of one thousand copies, some work selected by the Council. This Council, therefore, took upon itself in the matter of the selection of Greek classics for presentation, a function similar to that exercised 300 B.C. by the scholars appointed for the purpose in the Academy of Ptolemy Philadelphus, while some of its functions might be paralleled by those exercised to-day by the Delegates of the Clarendon Press of Oxford. It was the hope of Aldus that this Venetian Academy would take upon itself larger responsibilities in connection not only with Greek literature but with arts and sciences generally. When, how-

ever, with the death of its president, the Academy lost
the service of his energetic initiative, its work soon came
to a close.

For the sale of his publications, Aldus was in the main
dependent upon direct correspondence with scholars. In
Italy prior to 1550, bookselling hardly existed as an
organised trade, and while in Germany there was a larger
number of dealers in books, and the book-trade had by
1510 already organised its Fair at Frankfort, the communications between Italy and Germany were still too
difficult to enable a publisher in Venice to keep in regular relations with the dealers north of the Alps. Paris
was probably easier to reach than Frankfort, but the sales
in Paris were not a little interfered with by the Lyons
piracy editions before referred to, and even by piracies of
the Paris publishers themselves. Aldus succeeded, however, before his death in securing agents who were prepared to take orders for the Aldine classics, not only in
Paris, but in Vienna, Basel, Augsburg, and Nuremberg.
With Frankfort he appears to have had no direct dealings, as his name does not appear in the list of contribu-
tors to the recently instituted Book-Fair.

As an example of a business letter of the time, the
following lines from a bookseller in Treviso, who wanted
to buy books on credit, are worth quoting:

Alde, libros quos venales bene credere possis
Hic pollet multa bibliopola fide.
Fortunis pollet quantum illa negotia possunt ;
Hoc me, Manuti, credere teste potes !
Ignoras qui sim, nec adhuc sine pignore credis ;
Te meus erga ingens sit tibi pignus amor.

(You have books for sale, Aldus, which you are able to
entrust to me, if as a dealer, you have sufficient faith. This
confidence would secure for you as much business advantage
as is possible in such transactions. You can accept in this

matter my personal word.   You do not know who I am, and
do not make a practice of giving credit.   My great regard for
you should, however, serve as a sufficient pledge.)[1]

The business of the time was done very largely by personal correspondence, and as the knowledge of his editions of the Greek classics came to be spread abroad,
Aldus found himself overburdened with enquiries calling
for personal replies.   In order to save time in replying to
such enquiries, Aldus printed on a folio sheet the descriptive titles of his publications with the prices at which
they were offered.   This sheet, printed in 1498, was the
first priced catalogue ever issued by a publisher.

The orders that came to Aldus for his books differed
in one important respect from those received by a publisher or bookseller to-day.   The buyers did not write as
a matter of ordinary business routine, or as if they were
conferring any favour upon the publisher in taking his
goods, but with a very cordial sense of the personal obligation that the publisher was, through his undertakings,
conferring upon them and upon all scholarly persons.   As
an example of many such letters, I will quote from one
written in 1505, from a Cistercian monastery in the Thur-
ingian Forest, by a scholarly monk named Urbanus:

" May the blessing of the Lord rest upon thee, thou
illustrious man.   The high reward in which you are held
by our Brotherhood will be realised by you when you
learn that we have ordered (through the house of Függer
in Augsburg) a group of your valuable publications, and
that it is our chief desire to be able to purchase all the
others.   We pray to God each day that He will in His
mercy, long preserve you for the cause of good learning.
Our neighbour, Mutianus Rufus, the learned Canonicus
of Gotha, calls you 'the light of our age,' and is never
weary of relating your great services to scholarship.   He

[1] Frommann, p. 30.

sends you a cordial greeting, as does also Magister Spala-
tinus, a man of great learning.   We are sending you with
this four gold ducats, and will ask you to send us (through
Függer) an *Etymologicum Magnum* and a *Julius Pollux*,
and also (if there be money sufficient) the writings of
Bessarion, of Xenophon, and of Hierocles, and the Letters
of Merula." [1]

Troublesome as Aldus found his correspondence, letters
of this kind must have been peculiarly gratifying as evidence that his labours were not in vain.

He had similar correspondence with the well-known
scholar, Reuchlin, an appreciative friend and a grateful
customer, who in 1501, at the time of the first letters,
was resident in Heidelberg, and also with Longinus
and the poet Conrad Celtes in Vienna.   The latter was
later of service to Aldus in securing for his Press valuable manuscripts from Bohemia, and from certain monasteries in Transylvania.   The name of Celtes is further
of note in the literary history of Germany because to him
was issued the earliest German privilege of which there
is record.   It bears date 1501, and protected the publication of an edition by Celtes of the writings of the
Benedictine nun Hroswitha (Helena von Rossow), who
had been dead for 600 years.

The most famous of the transalpine scholars with
whom Aldus came into relations was, however, Deside-
rius Erasmus, of Rotterdam, or to speak with more precision, of Europe.   Erasmus has many titles to fame, but
for the purposes of this treatise his career is noteworthy
more particularly because he was one of the first authors
who was able to secure his living, or the more important
portion of this, from the proceeds of his writings.   The
career of Erasmus belongs properly to the chapter on
Germany, as it was in Basel, at that time a city of the
Empire, that he made his longest sojourn, in close asso-

---

[1] *Sagittarii Historia Gothana*, Jena, 1701, quoted by Frommann, 43.

ciation with his life-long friend Froben, the scholarly publisher whom Erasmus called the "Aldus of Germany."

In 1506, Erasmus, who had been in England for a second visit, came to Italy, where he lectured in the Universities of Bologna and Padua, and from Padua he was induced by Aldus to transfer himself to Venice. There he remained during the year 1508, making his home with the publisher, and rendering important service as a literary adviser and in editorial work. There is no record of any formal or continued business arrangement between the scholar and the publisher, and it is very possible that no such arrangement took shape.

Erasmus took charge of the preparation for the press, among other works, of the Aldine editions of *Terence*, *Seneca*, Plutarch's *Morals*, and *Plautus*. For his work on the *Plautus* he tells us that he received twenty pieces of gold (*i. e.*, ducats). Later, however, he denied with some indignation, in writing to Scaliger, that he had worked as a "corrector" or proof-reader for Aldus. It should be borne in mind that in connection with the many difficulties in securing from more or less doubtful manuscripts trustworthy texts, and in educating compositors to put such texts correctly into type, the work of reviser, press-corrector, or proof-reader, in the earlier days of printing, demanded a very high standard of scholarship and a wide range of knowledge. There was, therefore, no reason why Erasmus should have been ashamed to admit that he had done work of this kind. Some years later he gave to his friend Froben, the great publisher of Basel, similar service and co-operation. The intimate relations of Erasmus with Aldus and Froben, by far the greatest publishers of the time, had no little influence in furthering the world-wide circulation secured for his works.

While in Venice, Erasmus also supervised the printing of a revised edition of his *Adagia* (Proverbs) which ap-

peared in 1508. For this work, Aldus obtained a privilege
both in Venice and in Rome, and there were printed in
Venice alone eight editions. When, however, in 1520,
Paul Manutius undertook again to reprint the *Adagia*,
he found that he had to contend with an increasing
hostility on the part of the Church against anything
bearing the name of Erasmus. The book was finally
issued anonymously, and it was described in the catalogue
as the work of " *Batavus quidam homo* " (a certain Hollander).

In 1512, Aldus printed, under the instructions of Erasmus, (who was, however, at that time no longer in Italy)
the *Colloquies* and the *Praise of Folly*. There is unfortunately no record of the publishing arrangement arrived
at for these, but as Erasmus complained bitterly of the
loss and injury caused to the author through the wide
sale of the piracy issues, it is fair to assume that he had
reserved an interest in the authorised editions. In the
introduction to his *Adagia*, Erasmus writes as follows:
" Formerly there was devoted to the correctness of a
literary manuscript as much care and attention as to the
writing of a notarial instrument. Such care and precision
were held to be a sacred duty. Later, the copying of
manuscripts was entrusted to ignorant monks and even
to women. But how much more serious is the evil that
can be brought about by a careless printer, and yet to this
matter the law gives no heed. A dealer who sells English
stuffs under the guise of Venetian is punished, but the
printer who in place of correct texts, misleads and abuses
the reader with pages the contents of which are an actual
trial and torment, escapes unharmed. It is for this reason
that Germany is plagued with so many books that are
deformed (*i. e.*, untrustworthy). The authorities will
supervise with arbitrary regulations the proper methods for
the baking of bread, but concern themselves not at all as
to the correctness of the work of the printers, although

the influence of bad typography is far more injurious than
that of bad bread."

The relations of Aldus with Johann Reuchlin were
longer and more intimate than with Erasmus. It was
natural enough that the scholar who may properly be
called the founder of Greek studies in Germany, should
have come into close relations with the publisher who had
undertaken to produce Greek texts for Europe and who
had founded a Greek academy in Venice. In 1498, Aldus
printed the Latin oration which Reuchlin had addressed
to Pope Alexander VI., in behalf of the Prince Palatine
Philip, and from that date the two men remained in
regular correspondence with each other. In 1502, Aldus,
writing to Reuchlin (who was at that time in Pforzheim),
gives, as to a trusted friend upon whose sympathy and
intelligent interest he could depend, the details of his
publishing undertakings and of his plans and hopes for
the future, and asks for counsel on various points. A few
months later, in another letter, Aldus writes:

"I am hardly able to express my gratification at your
friendly words concerning the importance and the value
of my publishing undertakings. It is no light thing to
secure the commendation of one of the greatest scholars
of his time. If my life is spared to me, I hope more
fully to deserve the praise that you give to me for service
rendered to the scholarship and enlightenment of the
age."

Reuchlin was not only a friendly counsellor of the
Venetian publisher, but a valuable customer also for his
books. In addition to purchasing for his own library a
full series of the Aldine editions, Reuchlin appears to
have interested himself keenly in commending these to
his scholarly acquaintances, not only, as he states, in
order to encourage a great undertaking, but for the purpose of doing service to German students. In 1509,
Reuchlin was appointed by the Duke of Bavaria, Professor

of Greek and Hebrew in the University of Ingolstadt,
the first professorship of Greek instituted in Germany.
Reuchlin said more than once that the work of his Chair
had been made possible only through the service rendered
by Aldus in providing the Greek texts.

The influence of Aldus not only on the publishing
standards but on the scholarly and literary conditions of
Germany, was in fact widespread and important. Kapp,
the historian of the German book-trade, speaks of it as
more important than that of all the German publishers of
his generation. This influence was due not only to the
publishing undertakings of the Aldine Press, but to the
intimate relations maintained by its founder with many
of the German scholars, relations which helped to establish a community of interests between the literary centres
of Italy and Germany and to direct German scholarship
into new paths. The separation of political boundaries
had no significance for a man with the humanitarian ideals
of Aldus, while the fact that Latin was the universal language of scholarship and of literature, helped not a little
to bring about that community of feeling among scholars
which was the special aim of the Venetian publisher. In
1502, Aldus writes to John Taberio, in Brescia:

" I am delighted to learn that so many men of distinction in the great city of Brescia are, under your guidance,
devoting themselves with ardour to Greek studies. The
expectations with which I undertook the publication of
Greek texts are being more than realised. I am, in fact,
not a little astonished to find that even in these sad times
of war in which my undertakings have been begun, so
many are found ready to give the same ardour to scholarly pursuits that they are giving to fighting against the
infidel and to civil strife. Thus it happens that even
from the midst of war arises literature, which has for so
many years lain buried. And it is not only in Italy, but
also in Germany, in France, in Pannonia, in Spain, and in

England, and wherever the Latin language is known, that young and old are devoting themselves to the study of Greek. The joy that this brings to me causes me to forget my fatigues, and redoubles my zeal to do what is in my power for the service of scholarship, and particularly for the students who are growing up in this time of the renaissance of letters."

During the first years of the sixteenth century, the difficulties in the transmission either of merchandise or of money were many. The packages of books which Aldus had occasion to send to Reuchlin in Stuttgart, for instance, came forward sometimes by way of Milan, Vienna, or Basel, and later through Augsburg. The Augsburg banking-house of Függer, founded about 1450, possessed in 1500 (and for half a century thereafter) connections which enabled them to take charge not only of what we should call mercantile bills and banking credits, but also of the forwarding and delivery of the goods against which the bills were drawn. They carried on what to-day would be called an express business, and in a majority of instances the instructions were evidently to make collections on delivery. During the first half of the sixteenth century, the Függers, with their branch houses in Florence, Venice, and Genoa, supplied the most valuable machinery for the transaction of business between Italy and Germany. These communications, however, were of necessity very frequently interrupted by the troubles of the times.

In 1510, Mutianus Rufus writes to Urban that " in connection with the conflicts between the French and the Venetian soldiers, the passes of the Alps have been blocked, so that literature from Venice can no longer find its way into Germany. I had hoped with the next Frankfort Fair, to be able to place in the hands of my students the beautiful Aldine editions. But my hopes were in vain. When the Fair was opened, there was not a single

volume from Italy. We shall be able this spring to do
nothing in our classical schools. Oh, the stupidities of
war ! "

In 1514, the Elector Frederic the Wise of Saxony
applied to the several powers interested for a safe conduct for his librarian, Spalatin, whom he desired to send
to Venice to purchase directly from Aldus the Aldine
classics for the library of Wittenberg. Some difficulties
intervened, however, as Spalatin appears never to have
reached Venice. It was doubtless due to the long-con-
tinued wars between the Emperor and the States of
Italy, that Aldus was unable, during his own lifetime, to
establish direct agencies in Germany for his publications.
We find record of such agencies in Frankfort, Basel,
Augsburg, and Nuremberg, first in the time of his son,
agencies which were extended by the grandson.

The active work of Aldus extended over a period of
twenty years, from 1495 to 1515. This time included the
wars of 1500, 1506, 1510, and 1511, in which Venice was
directly engaged, wars which had of necessity much to do
with the interference with his business, and with the difficulties, of which he makes continual complaint, in securing returns for his sales. " For seven years," writes Aldus
in 1510, "books have had to contend against arms."
There appears to have been no single year of the twenty
in which he was free from pressing financial cares, while
from time to time the work of the presses and in the
composing room came to an actual standstill for want of
funds. During these twenty years he printed not less
than 126 works which previously existed only in manuscript form, and the manuscript copies of which had to
be secured and carefully edited.

It is probable that Aldus, in his own enthusiasm concerning the value and importance of the re-discovered
classics, had overestimated the extent of the interest that
could be depended upon for these classics throughout

the world. It is evident, however, that there were enough scholars in Italy, Germany, France, and the Low Countries, to assure a widespread demand for the Aldine editions, and that the larger part of the publisher's difficulties consisted in the lack of convenient machinery for making known to these scholars the fact that such books had been prepared, for the delivery of such copies as might be ordered, and for the collection of the payments due.

Another serious difficulty with which Aldus had to contend was the competition of the piratical copies of his editions which promptly appeared in Cologne, Tübingen, Lyons, and even so close at home as Florence. The most serious interference with his undertakings appears to have come from the printers of Lyons, who in their enterprising appropriations from Paris on the one hand and from Nuremberg, Basel, and Venice on the other, speedily won for their city notoriety as the centre of piratical publishing. The Lyons printers printed editions of the Aldine Latin classics, making a very close imitation of the cursive or italic type, and issued the volumes without imprint, date, or place of publication.

The privileges secured from the government of Venice had effect, of course, only in Venetian territory. Privileges were given by the Pope for a number of the Aldine publications, and these covered, in form, at least, not only the States of the Church but the territory of all States recognising the papal authority, while the penalties for infringing such papal privileges were not infrequently made to include excommunication. There was, however, no machinery by means of which the papal authority could be brought to bear upon Catholics infringing or disregarding the privileges, and as a fact the papal privileges proved of very little service in protecting the literary property either of Aldus or of later literary workers. A further word concerning the privileges issued in Venice and in the other States of Italy will be given in a later division of this narrative.

Apart from this important work in the scholarly and editorial divisions of publishing, Aldus made several distinctive contributions to the art of book-making. He was, as before stated, the first printer who founded complete and perfect fonts of Greek type, fonts which for many years served as models for the printers of Europe. He invented the type which was first called cursive, and which is known to-day as italic, a type having the advantage of presenting the text in a very compact form. (The cursive font was said to have been modelled on the script of Petrarch.) And finally, he was the first publisher who ventured upon the experiment of replacing the costly and cumbersome folios and quartos, in which form alone all important works had heretofore been issued, with convenient crown octavo volumes, the moderate price of which brought them within the reach of scholars of all classes and helped to popularise the knowledge and the influence of classic literature. This constituted a practical revolution in publishing methods.

Aldus had possibly read the remark of Callimachus, the librarian of the Alexandrian library in 290 B.C., that " A big book is a big nuisance." These Aldine classics, while printed in octavo (*i. e.*, upon a sheet folded in eights), were of a size corresponding more nearly to what would to-day be known as a sixteenmo, the size of the sheet of paper being smaller than that used to-day. Aldus had no presses which would print sheets large enough to fold in sixteen or even in twelve. The price of these small octavos averaged three *marcelli* or two francs, say forty cents. Making allowance for the difference in the purchasing power of money between the year 1500 and the year 1895, I judge that this may represent about $2.00 of our currency.

For centuries the Aldine editions served as the authoritative texts for the authors presented, and even to-day they stand as a wonderful monument of the imagination, the learning, the courage, and the persistency of their publisher. Good Italian though he were, Aldus was by some of his countrymen charged with want of patriotism on the ground that if he helped to make the study of the classics easy for the Barbarians of the outer world, they would no longer need to come for their learning to Italy, heretofore the centre and source of all scholarly enlightenment. To this effect writes Beatus Rhenanus in his introduction to the Works of Erasmus :

Quidam Venetiis olim Aldo Manutio commentarios Græcos in Euripidem et Sophoclem edere paranti dixit : Cave, cave hoc facias, ne barbari istis adjuti domi maneant et pauciores in Italiam ventilent.

Kapp is of opinion that the dread was well founded and that the distribution throughout Germany and France of popular editions of the classics, did have the result of keeping at home many students who would otherwise have crossed the Alps. That they were now able to secure, at moderate cost and in their own homes, learning for which heretofore they had been obliged to make long and costly journeys, was due to the unselfish and public-spirited labours of Aldus. It was, therefore, with good reason that he was held in high regard by the Humanists of Germany. They sought his friendship and nearly overwhelmed him with correspondence. In 1498, Conrad Celtes and Vincenzo Longinus commemorated his service in verse. Aldus thanked them for their courtesy, and in sending them as an acknowledgment copies of his *Horace* and *Virgil*, he asked them to bring him into communication with any scholarly Germans who were interested in the classics. Aldus did not, however, consider it wise to print the ode of eulogy that Celtes had written upon the Emperor Maximilian, because he was afraid of causing offence to the Bohemians and Hungarians through

whose scholars he had secured not a few rare manuscripts.

Throughout Germany the productions of the Aldine
presses were received with enthusiasm. Mutianus Rufus
speaks of himself as weeping with joy when there came
to him from a friend the precious gift of the editions of
Cicero, Lucretius, and other classics. He and his friends
Urban and Spalatin deprived themselves almost of the
necessaries of life, in order to save moneys with which to
bring across the Alps the other volumes of the series.
Pirckheimer and Reuchlin were among the first of the
German buyers of the Aldine classics. Hummelsburger
writes in 1512 to Anselm in Tübingen, "I shall buy my
Hebrew books in Italy, where Aldus has printed them in
beautiful texts. . . . Germany no less than Latium owes
a great debt to Aldus."

The political status of Italy and its division into a
number of states or principalities which carried on independent policies and which were frequently in active war-
fare with each other, entailed serious difficulties upon the
new business of publishing, difficulties which, while
troublesome enough for Aldus in Venice, were still more
serious for his competitors in Florence and Milan. A
privilege secured for Venice was not binding even in times
of peace outside of Venetian territory, while in the frequently recurring times of war, any privileges which a
Venetian or a Milanese publisher had been fortunate
enough to secure in the Italian States were abrogated
in fact if not in form. In this respect, the early publishers of Paris, whose privileges covered (nominally at
least) the territory of the kingdom, had a decided advantage over their rivals in the much divided territory
of Italy or of Germany.

Aldus had the feeling, for which in his case there
appears to have been sufficient ground, that his business
undertakings, with which were connected far-reaching

plans for furthering scholarly knowledge, were absolutely dependent upon his own continued and persistent personal attention. While he had succeeded in securing the services of scholarly associates to share with himself the editorial responsibilities of his work, he does not appear to have been able, with the material at his command, to train up any assistants competent to take any important share in the business management. One of his many complaints concerning the repeated interruptions which interfere with his important daily labours, might have been uttered by many a publisher of later times. He writes in 1514 (the year before his death) to his friend Navagerus:

"I am hampered in my work by a thousand interruptions. . . . Nearly every hour comes a letter from some scholar, and if I undertook to reply to them all, I should be obliged to devote day and night to scribbling. Then, through the day come calls from all kinds of visitors. Some desire merely to give a word of greeting, others want to know what there is new, while the greater number come to my office because they happen to have nothing else to do. 'Let us look in upon Aldus,' they say to each other. Then they loaf in and sit and chatter to no purpose. Even these people with no business are not so bad as those who have a poem to offer or something in prose (usually very prosy indeed) which they wish to see printed with the name of Aldus. These interruptions are now becoming too serious for me, and I must take steps to lessen them. Many letters I simply leave unanswered, while to others I send very brief replies; and as I do this not from pride or from discourtesy, but simply in order to be able to go on with my task of printing good books, it must not be taken hardly. . . . As a warning to the heedless visitors who use up my office hours to no purpose, I have now put up a big notice on the door of my office to the following effect:

' Whoever thou art, thou art earnestly requested by Aldus, to state thy business briefly and to take thy departure promptly.   In this way thou mayst be of service even as was Hercules to the weary Atlas.   For this is a place of work for all who may enter.' "

Aldus Manutius died January 25, 1515, (Venetian style, corresponding to February 6, 1515, modern style) aged sixty-five years.   Until 1529, the business was carried on for the heirs by his father-in-law, Torresano, and in that year was taken over by Paul Manutius, the son of Aldus. In 1540, Paul took into partnership his son, Aldus the younger, and the firm took the title of *Aldi Filii*.   With the death of Aldus the grandson, in 1597, the family, in its main line, became extinct, and the work of the Aldine Press, which had continued for a little more than a century, came to a close.   To his children, Aldus was able to bequeath little besides his fame and the value of his name.   The moneys that had been earned during his work of twenty-five years from the successful undertakings had been for the most part absorbed in other ventures which were either unremunerative, or from which the returns came but slowly.   The carrying out of such great publishing plans required, in fact, business connections and methods which did not yet exist, and was dependent also upon the continuance of peace in Europe for a quarter of a century, an impossible condition for the beginning of the sixteenth century.

In entering upon business ventures under such difficult circumstances, Aldus was doubtless, from a business point of view, unwisely optimistic; but it is difficult not to admire the public spirit and the pluck with which, in the face of all difficulties, he persisted till the day of his death in the great schemes he had marked out for himself.

While his work had brought no wealth, his life had been rich in the accomplishment of great things and in the appreciation given to his labours.   It was also his fortune to

gather about him and to come into relations with many
noteworthy men, who as friends and co-workers shared his
enthusiasm, and who gave with him unselfish labour for a
scholarly ideal.   Partly because the editors and the publishers were working for results other than profits, partly
because the books published were (with a few noteworthy
exceptions, like the writings of Erasmus) not original works,
but editions of old classics, and partly because the whole
business of publishing was still in its infancy, the history
of the Aldine Press does not present any important precedents as to the compensation earned by authors for
their productions, or as to the protection of the author's
property rights in these productions.   The relations of
Aldus with all the authors, editors, and scholars with
whom he had to do were however more than satisfactory ;
they were cordial, resting in a number of cases on a close
personal friendship.   The scholars regarded the publisher
as one of themselves, and, in fact, accepted him as a leader.

It is evident that Erasmus, whose writings formed an
important property, was satisfied with the returns secured
for him by Aldus.   He speaks with cordial appreciation
of the services rendered by his " authorised publishers,"
Aldus of Venice, and Froben of Basel, and speaks further
of the losses caused to himself by the competition of the
piracy reprints of Lyons and Paris.   It appears, therefore,
that he retained a continued interest in the sale of his
authorised editions, but unfortunately no details of his
publishing arrangements have been preserved.

The history of the publishing work of Aldus, while not
presenting precedents for royalty or copyright arrangements, constitutes nevertheless a very important chapter
in the history of property in literature.   Aldus was able,
by combining skilled editorial labour with selected classics,
to create a great literary property, which needed only distributing machinery and a peaceable Europe to become
commercially valuable.   He set the example also, for

Italy at least, of securing privileges in each of the Italian States possessing any literary centres, and although he was not always able to prevent piratical reprinting on the part of his competitors in Florence, or even always to keep out of other cities in Italy the piracy editions from Lyons, he accomplished something towards the ideal of a copyright that should hold good for Italian territory. He even had hopes of securing, through the authority of the Pope, a system of copyright that should prove effective in all Catholic States, and it was not until long after Aldus's death that the attempts to establish a Catholic copyright system were given up by publishers as practically futile.

His latest biographer, Didot, himself both a fine scholar and a great publisher, contends that Aldus accomplished more than the greatest scholars of his time for the spread of learning and the development of literature; and the testimony of the three great scholars who were contemporaries and near personal friends of the Venetian publisher, Musurus, Reuchlin, and Erasmus, fully bears out M. Didot's opinion. It was the exceptional combination of a creative imagination and scholarly knowledge with practical business ability and unfailing pluck and persistency, that enabled the young tutor to create the Aldine Press, the work of which will cause to be held in continued honour, in the history alike of scholarship and of publishing, the memory of Aldus Manutius.

The Successors of Aldus.—Paul Manutius, the son of Aldus, continued for some years the business of the Aldine Press, giving special attention to editions of the writings of Cicero. In 1561, he accepted an invitation from Pope Pius IV. to come to Rome and to take charge there of the publication of the writings of the Fathers of the Church, and of such other works as might be selected. The amount required for the organisation of an adequate printing-office was to be supplied from the papal treasury.

Paul was to receive an annual stipend of 500 ducats, together with one half of the net profits realised from the sales of the works published, and the contract was to continue for twelve years.

An interesting series of letters has been preserved, written by Paul to his brother Manutius in Asola, and to his son, Aldus the younger, in Venice. These letters, which are quoted by Renouard, Frommann, and Didot, contain a number of details and references which throw light not only upon the personal relations of the writers, but upon the business conditions of the time. We learn that Paul was a good deal of an invalid throughout his working years, and we gather the impression that his feeble health was an important ground for the apparent lack of ambition which made him willing to give up his work as an independent publisher in Venice and to accept the position of Pope's printer in Rome.

We also learn that his son Aldus, while bright-witted, was lacking in persistency and in industry. The youngster never, in fact, accomplished anything of importance. Paul had himself inherited the scholarly tastes of his father, and had received a good classical education, but he does not appear to have possessed very good business faculty, and he made no distinctive mark as a publisher. The Pope had, however, asked for his aid rather as a scholarly editor than as an experienced man of business.

Pius appears to have been impressed with the belief that the printing-press, under scholarly management, could be made of service to the cause of the Church in withstanding the pernicious influence of the increasing mass of the publications of the German heretics. These Protestant pamphlets and books were not merely undermining the authority of the Church in Germany, Switzerland, and France, but were even making their way into Italy itself. The first issues of the Aldine Press in Rome were the *Decrees* of the Council of Trent, in a variety of editions, the writings of Cyprian, and the letters of S. Jerome.

Pius V., who in 1565 succeeded Pius IV., was equally favourable to the undertakings of the printing-office, and gave to Paul the necessary support. The work was carried on in a building which was the property of the municipality, and some issues arose with the magistrates concerning its continued use as a printing-office. From a letter dated September 27, 1567, it appears that the magistrates had required that Paul should pay taxes or license-fees on his printing business, which they classed as a trade. He took the ground that printing was not a trade but an art, and that it was so defined in the invitation given to him to come to Rome, and in the agreement executed with him by the Pope. He contended, further, that, as the Pope's printer, whose work was devoted to the Church, he was in any case entitled to exemption from the municipal taxes imposed on traders. The Pope does not appear to have fully backed up his printer in this contention, and a compromise was finally arrived at under which a portion of the proceeds of the business was paid to the magistracy. The precise terms of the arrangement are not clearly stated, but it seems probable that the half share of the profits previously payable to the papal treasury was divided into two portions, one of which went to the municipality.

The profitable part of the business was in the printing of the official editions of the Catechisms and Breviaries. Paul complains, in fact, that the presses are so occupied with the work of the Breviaries, that he is not able to make progress with the printing of his own *Commentaries on the Letters of Cicero*. In June, 1568, Paul writes to his son Aldus, who was now of age, expressing his regret that the young man was not interested in devoting himself to carrying on the printing-office in Venice. Aldus had, it seems, expressed a preference for the study of law.

The business in Venice was finally turned over to Basa, who paid, for a term of five years, twenty *scudi* gold a month for the use of the existing material and for the good-will.

In July, 1569, difficulties began to accumulate about the printing-office in Rome. The Pope was less interested and the magistrates were troubling the office with what Paul calls unintelligent interference. There were, in fact, too many parties interested in the management of the business to enable its control to be easily or consistently exercised. Paul's health was also failing seriously and he was longing for rest and for leisure to carry on his scholarly undertakings. In 1570, the ownership of the receipts of the printing-office was somewhat simplified, the change being probably due, in part at least, to the representations of Paul that the many-headed control was unworkable.

In May, 1570, Paul writes rather pathetically to Aldus : " In my case, scholarship and industry have never brought rest or fortune. . . . I pray God that you may be better favoured. . . . I must beseech you, however, to put away childish things. It is full time that you recalled to yourself the honourable traditions of our family. . . . My own active work must be nearly over."

In June, of the same year, he again counsels Aldus, who had for some time been betrothed, to make a speedy marriage, and then to concentrate himself upon the work of the printing-office in Venice. He advises against a a plan that the young man had in view, of opening a retail book-shop. He emphasises, however, that there is no chance of success for a printer-publisher without the most persistent and arduous labour.

In 1571, Paul's failing strength compelled him to leave Rome, resigning (as he hoped, for a time only) the income of the papal printing-office. He devoted the winter months to the completion of his *Commentaries on the Ora-*

tions of Cicero. The work was published in 1578-9 (after the author's death) by his son Aldus in Venice, and, under arrangement, by Plantin in Antwerp. The negotiations with Plantin had been completed by Paul. He had specified the form and style of the Antwerp edition, and had arranged to take his share of the profits in the shape of a royalty on the sales.

In 1572, Paul being yet in Milan, one of his hopes was fulfilled in the marriage of his son Aldus. "Now," he wrote, "I can pass my days in peace. I feel hopeful for your future and rejoice that our line is to be continued." Later in the year, with no little difficulty (partly on the ground of his feeble health, and partly because of the floods and wretched roads) he made his way to Venice for a brief visit. He wanted to see his son's wife, and he desired also to give personal instructions for the printing of his *Commentaries.* "I feel very hopeful," he writes, " concerning the sale of my *Cicero,* and hopeful also that it will not be reprinted (in piracy editions) during my lifetime."

Paul was obliged to leave Venice before the printing of his work was begun, and the letter written after the receipt of the first sheets expresses his bitter disappointment at the manner in which this all-important commission had been attended to. "If you had had in your hands some utterly contemptible scribble," he writes, " you could hardly have printed it in a more tasteless and slovenly style . . . and you knew I had this undertaking so much at heart ! . . . I have instructed Basa to burn all the sheets that have been printed, and to print these signatures again, with a proper selection of type and on decent paper."

Aldus the younger seems never to have had his heart fairly in his business, and under his management (or lack of management), the prestige of the Aldine Press in Venice fell off sadly. He appears to have been extravagant, or at least uncalculating, in his expenditures, and was also spending moneys which he could ill afford, not like his grandfather for manuscripts and type, but for clothes and artistic curiosities.

Paul had accepted the pressing invitation of the new Pope, Gregory XII., to resume his place as manager of the printing-office in Rome, but with less exacting duties, and with a fixed salary. A plan was even talked over between the Pope and Paul for the establishment of another printing-office, which should be devoted entirely to the publication of classical works and of " expurgated " editions of works, portions of which had been condemned in the Index. Paul was to act as editor and supervisor of the series, because his name was already recognised as that of a scholarly authority. The scheme never, however, took shape. Paul's strength failed rapidly, and he died in the spring of 1574.

While he had devoted many years to his business as a printer-publisher, and had maintained the reputation of his name for a high standard as well of typography as of scholarly writing, his own preference had been for a scholarly rather than a business career. He went on with the work of his Press very largely because he felt that it was a duty he owed to his father's name and memory. His own memory is, however, chiefly to be honoured for his scholarly edition of *Cicero*, with its comprehensive and analytical commentaries, an edition which long remained the accepted authority for Europe.

A few years after the death of Paul, his son Aldus gave up the attempt to carry on the Press in Venice, a work for which he had never been really fitted, and accepted a position in the University of Bologna, as professor of archæology. The printing business was sold, and the Aldine Press, after a century of work, came to an end.

Milan.—During the fifteenth century, Italy presents a curiously complex and varied series of pictures and conditions. We find, together with constantly recurring civil strife, successive wars of invasion from the North and from the East, and in the train of the frequent armies, those inevitable camp followers, pestilence, famine, and misery. To the contests against the French and German invaders and the strifes between states and cities, were added schism and discord in the Church itself, and there were long periods during which pope was contending against anti-pope for the right to rule the world as the infallible head of an infallible church. Yet these years, when the land was troubled by schism and devastated by strife and pestilence, were years during which the cities of Italy were becoming rich with an active and prosperous trade; while it was also at this time that the art of Italy brought forth its greatest production and that the development of its literature made most important advances. The vitality of the people was so exuberant, its productive force so enormous, that notwithstanding the frightful waste caused by war and pestilence, its energies were still sufficient for some of the greatest of artistic creations, for active and scholarly work in the new learning and literature, and for a sharp competition for the leadership of the world's commerce and industries. A typical example of the life and strife of the time is afforded by Milan, the capital of Lombardy. Its position as the northernmost of the great cities and in the centre of the open territory of the plains, exposed it to the first attacks of invaders from across the Alps, while the ambition of the rulers and of the people kept it in frequent strife with its Italian rivals. Its trade seems to have continued active, however, (except when armies were actually at its gates) and while in art more important work was done in Florence, the first steps in the new literature, that is, in the literature connected with printing, were taken in Lombardy.

The first printing in Milan was done in 1469 by Philip

of Lavagna, who was followed in 1470 by Antonio Zarotus.   In the printing of books Milan holds precedence,
therefore, over all the towns of Italy except Subiaco and
Rome, antedating Venice by about a year.   The publishing undertakings of the Lombardy capital never, however, rivalled in importance those of Venice.   In 1476,
Paravisinus, printed an edition of the Greek Grammar of
Laskaris, the first volume printed in Europe in Greek
characters.   In the previous volumes containing Greek
text, this had been printed in Latin characters.   The editor of the Grammar was Demetrius, a refugee from Crete.
He was also the editor of the first edition in Greek of
Homer.   The first Missal was printed by Zarotus in 1475.

While in Rome the work of printing was begun by a
German and in Venice by a Frenchman, the first printers
in Milan were native Italians.   Among the earlier of the
Lombard printer-publishers, we find the name of Alexander Minutianus, a learned professor, who devoted himself to the editing of a valuable series of Latin classics,
and whose publishing activities extended over a term of
twenty years.   Minutianus published in 1498–99, in four
folio volumes, the first complete edition of *Cicero*.   The
relations of Milan with the cities north of the Alps were
more intimate at this time than those of any other Italian
city, and it was natural, therefore, that as the printing
business in Lombardy increased in importance, German printers should begin to seek employment there.
The first whose name is recorded was Waldorfer (or Valdarfer) from Regensburg, whose work began in 1474, and
who brought with him fonts of Gothic type.   Waldorfer
printed an edition of *Pliny's Letters* and a selection of the
Orations of Cicero.   These were followed by the *Commentary* of Servius on *Virgil*, and by the first issue in print of
the famous *Decameron* of Boccaccio.   The *Decameron* had
been written in 1353, and had, therefore, waited 120
years for a publisher.   In 1493, Henricus Germanus and

Sebastian Pontremulo printed the first Greek edition of
Isocrates.   In Milan, however, work in law, science, and
medicine constituted a more important proportion of the
earlier publications than in Venice or in Rome.   The De
Honate Brothers were printing as early as 1472, works in
jurisprudence, and Frommann is of opinion that before
1480 several firms were devoting their presses exclusively
to the departments of law and science.   In 1472, a
company was formed for the printing and publishing of
books, probably the first publishing association in existence.
There were at first five members or associates, as follows :

Antonio Zarotus, a printer from Parma; Gabriel degli
Orsoni, a priest; Colla Montana, an instructor in the
High School (he was concerned some years later in
the murder of the Duke Galeazzo Maria); Pavero de'
Fontana, a professor of Latin, afterwards editor of *Hor-
ace ;* and Pedro Antonio de' Burgo, of Castiglione, a
lawyer.   Subsequently a sixth associate was added,
Nicolao, a physician and a brother of the last named.

The Association was organised for a term of three
years and its purpose was stated to be the instituting of
a printing-office, with not less than four presses, and the
carrying on of a book-manufacturing and publishing
business.   The capital was to be contributed in equal
shares by four of the associates, the printer, Zarotus,
investing no money, but contributing his knowledge of
the business and undertaking its general management.
The printer was to receive one third of the net proceeds,
and the remaining two thirds were to be divided equally
among his four associates.   From the printer's share were
to be repaid the first expenditures contributed by the
other four.   The subsequent expenditures were to be
met by the sales of the books.   The person acting as
corrector for the press, usually one of the scholarly associates, secured as his compensation one or two copies of
the work corrected.

The selection of the books to be printed was to be
made by the unanimous decision of the whole board, and
the selling price was also to be fixed by the board. The
organisation was to remain secret, and all employees
were to take an oath of secrecy and obedience. Each
member bound himself to give no council or aid to any
other publishing concern and to print no work with
another printer except under the permission of his associates. At the termination of the agreement, the printer
was to have a right to purchase at a valuation the presses
and the manuscripts.

The capitalist of the concern was the lawyer Antonio
de' Burgo, and he found the funds (100 ducats) with
which the first operations were initiated. Under a sup-
plementary agreement, the lawyer Burgo and his brother
the physician assumed for their individual account one
half of the rent of the premises and purchased three
additional presses. These presses were kept at work
exclusively in the production of a series of works in the
departments of law and medicine. The printer Zarotus
took charge of the manufacture of these books for the
brothers Burgo, in addition to those printed for the
Association. The editorial work in selecting the material and in preparing them for the press was cared for by
the Burgos, who also appear to have attended to the
publishing details.

The brothers paid over to the treasury of the Association twenty-five ducats for the use of the plant (type,
etc.) outside of the presses, and were to pay also one
fourth of the proceeds of the sales of their series. Each
associate was also to receive a copy of each book printed.

The brothers agreed to print no books excepting in the
departments of canon and civil law and of medicine, and
the Association was to include in its list no works in these
departments. The penalty for infringing this provision
was fixed at 200 ducats.

The brothers were not at liberty to dispose of their portion of the printing-office to any other parties. At the end of three years, the presses and publications belonging to the two Burgos were transferred, on an appraisal, to Zarotus.

No records have been preserved of the results of their undertakings, or of those of the Association as a whole. The fact, however, that as early as 1472, only eight years after the introduction of printing into Italy, there should have been sufficient business, or even expectation of business, to warrant the organisation of such a publishing company, is certainly noteworthy, if only as evidence of the intellectual activity and business enterprise of the Italy of the fifteenth century. It is curious also that special provision should have been made for legal and medical publications, as the literary interests of the period of the Renaissance, which had so much influence in furthering the activities of the earlier Italian printers, were so largely classical.

It was necessary for the first publishers to be both printers and scholars, and this necessary condition of early publishing undertakings, the association of adequate scholarship with technical knowledge required for the making of books, was fully provided for in the Milan company, which included, as we have seen, two classical professors, one theologian, one jurist, and one physician.

More than a century later, in 1589, was organised the Guild of the Printers, Publishers, and Booksellers of Milan. During the hundred years that had passed since the printing-press began its work in Lombardy, the city had known various rulers, and had, for a brief term, enjoyed independence. By far the larger portion of the century had been for Lombardy periods of turmoil, and the years of uninterrupted peace had been few. It was, therefore, not surprising that the business of the production of books had developed more rapidly and more prosperously in

Venice, Rome, and Bologna, which were from their position better protected against the mischances of war.

In 1589, Lombardy was a portion of the great Spanish Empire, and (as it contained few heretics) it was enjoying under the rule of Philip II., a period of peace and of comparative prosperity. The charter of the Guild or Corporation of the Printers and Publishers was confirmed by King Philip himself. The Stationers' Company of England had received its charter from Queen Mary in 1556, or thirty-three years earlier. The Guild of the Venetian Printers dated from 1548, and was the earliest association of the kind in Europe. The affairs of the Guild of Milan were managed by a board of directors, comprising a Prior, a Bursar, and two Councillors. The Board had charge of the property of the corporation, and was responsible also for the protection of its privileges under the charter, and for the defence of any of its members whose rights might be assailed. It rested also with the Board to see that the regulations of the Corporation were properly carried out, and in the event of any assessment being laid upon the organised Printers and Publishers, it was the duty of the Bursar to apportion the payments equitably among the members of the Guild.

To the Board was also given authority to adjudicate disputes not only between members of the Guild, but between the members and outsiders, and its jurisdiction extended over the entire duchy. From the decisions of the Board there was, as a rule, no appeal. In case, however, the issue involved any complicated questions of law, so that it became necessary for the Board to call in the counsel of a jurist, an appeal could be made from the decision arrived at to a special court of arbitration, which was also, however, to be made up of members of the Guild. The roster of the Guild was in the special control of the Prior, and this record was of special importance, because no one whose name was not on this roster

as a member in good standing was permitted to print or
to sell books in Milan, under a penalty for each offence of
fifty gold *scudi*.

No one was eligible for membership who had not served
an apprenticeship of eight years to a printer or book-
dealer in Milan. The fee for admission was, for one born
in Milan, thirty lire, for others one hundred lire.

One purpose of the organisation of the Guild was to
prevent the competition of foreign printers and booksellers
from breaking down the trade of the Milanese. A more
legitimate object was to keep the business of printing,
publishing, and selling books in the hands of trained men
of high character, good education, and technical training,
who should conduct their work in a manner worthy of the
repute of Milan. It had been the complaint that many
unworthy and unskilled men had crowded into the business of making and selling books, lowering the standard
of the trade and diminishing the profits. It was complained also that the paper-manufacturers or paper-dealers
had undertaken to sell books, notwithstanding a specific
statute prohibiting them from so doing. The royal com-
missioner, whose sanction was required to validate on
behalf of the King the regulations of the new Guild,
stipulated, however, in confirming the renewal of this
prohibition, that the paper-makers should still be permitted to sell certain special books which had for some
years been in their hands, but that no other publications
must be sold by any paper-dealer who had not secured
membership in the Guild as a properly qualified bookseller.

It is not easy, after an interval of three centuries, to
decide whether this undertaking for the closer organisation of the book-trade was really prompted, as was contended, by the desire to keep on the highest possible
plane the business of making and selling books, or
whether it was the result of a selfish desire on the part

of the older Milanese dealers to increase their profits and to keep out competitors. It is probable there was a mixture of motives, but it is certain that in Milan, as in other book centres, the formation of the Guild gave an important incentive to printing and publishing, improved the quality of the work done, and tended to keep the business in the hands of a good class of men, and it is evident also that such results must have brought advantages also to the general public.

The more important of the regulations of the Guild can be summarised as follows :

1. No member of the Guild shall reprint or shall sell any book issued by another member, provided such book has not before been printed in Milan, and provided also that the edition claiming protection shall itself have been printed in Milan. A book printed outside of the duchy cannot secure the protection of a Milanese privilege. The penalty for infringement is the forfeiture of the copies printed and the payment of ten gold *scudi*.

2. Each publication shall bear the imprint of its printer or publisher (usually, of course, the same person).

3. Apprentices and assistants must be registered on the records of the Guild.

4. The sale of books in any places other than the registered shops or places of business is forbidden ; and the purchase of books from apprentices or from any not known to be duly authorised dealers is also made a misdemeanour.

5. The sale of books on Sundays or holidays, either in the shops or in the dwellings, is forbidden.

6. No printer or dealer must use for his sign a token identical with or closely similar to that already in use with an authorised printer or dealer.

These regulations appear to have had the desired effect of repressing if not of entirely exterminating the business of the unauthorised printers and traders. In 1614, however probably for the purpose of impressing a fresh generation of unauthorised traders, the Guild secured a fresh royal edict, which again confirmed the authority of the Guild and enjoined, under heavy penalties, the strictest obedience to its regulations.

Frommann points out that in the application for this new decree, the Guild no longer lays stress upon the necessity of upholding the dignity and honourable standard of the book-trade, but emphasises the risk to the Church and to the community of believers if uneducated and irresponsible persons, not familiar with the lists of forbidden works, should be permitted to print or to sell books. Experience had evidently made clear to the publishers that with a government like that of Spain (which might be described as despotism tempered by the Inquisition) this class of considerations would be much more influential than any thought of upholding the dignity of the business of making and selling books.

The petitioners make reference to the decree accompanying the latest *Index Expurgatorius*, which forbids any one from carrying on business as a printer, publisher, or bookseller, who has not taken oath before the ecclesiastical superiors or the Inquisitor of his district to conduct his business in full loyalty to the holy Catholic Church, and to give explicit obedience to all the decrees and enactments of the Church and of the Inquisitor for the regulation and supervision of the press.

The petitioners go on to state that this edict of the Church has largely fallen into disregard because ordinary traders, *merzeranii*, uneducated and irresponsible men, not trained to the book-business and having no knowledge of or no respect for the *Index Expurgatorius*, have been allowed to print and to sell books, to the detriment not only of the legitimate book-trade, but of the Church and of the community. The King (Philip III.) appears to have agreed with the Guild that this interference with an organised book-trade (which from the very fact of its organisation could be and was effectively supervised by the Church) constituted a very dangerous abuse.

The new edict, with its severe penalties, and with the effective co-operation of the local inquisitors and other ecclesiastics, appears to have had the effect desired. We hear no more from the publishers of Milan about irresponsible competition, and the business prospered as far as was practicable within the rather narrow limits fixed by the censorship of the Church. The most noteworthy productions of the Milanese presses between the years 1500 and 1700, were, as stated, in the departments of jurisprudence and medicine. The greater activity of publishing in these two departments may very possibly have been in part due to the fact that they were less affected by the ecclesiastical censorship.

Lucca and Foligno.—The little city of Lucca is entitled to mention in connection with the introduction of printing into Italy, if only because it was the only city in Italy (and possibly the only one in Europe), in which the new art secured the direct support and co-operation of the government in the form, first of a municipal decree in favour of the printing-press, and secondly of a direct subvention from the municipal treasury in encouragement of the first printer. The printer was Clemente, a native of Padua, who was engaged in business in Lucca as a scribe and illuminator. It was made a condition of the appropriation (the amount of which is not stated) that the printer, who was to be classed as a public functionary, was to hold himself in readiness to teach the art to all who might desire to learn. Clemente established his press in Lucca in 1477, and printed there in that year, an edition of the *Triumphs of Petrarch*. He had previously printed in Venice a work by John Mesne, of Damascus, on universal medicine, a large folio of 400 pages.

A still smaller city than Lucca, Foligno in Umbria,

enjoys the distinction of having received as its first printer, Johann Numeister, who had been a pupil and assistant of Gutenberg himself. After the death of his master, Numeister came to Italy with the intention of setting up a press in Rome. He was induced to settle at Foligno at the instance of Orfinis, a wealthy citizen, who supplied the funds necessary for the undertaking. The first publication of the Foligno Press was *Leonardi Aretini Bruni de Bello Italico adversus Gothos*, which bears date 1470.

The imprint states that the book was "printed by Numeister in the house of Emilianus de Orfinis." The second work selected was an edition of the *Divina Commedia* of Dante, the manuscript copy of which had been collated and corrected for the press by Orfinis. Orfinis died in 1472, just before the printing of the *Commedia* was completed. Numeister paid a tribute to his patron in the last line of the rhyming imprint:

> *Nel milla quatro cente septe e due*
> *Nel quarto mese; a di cinque et sei,*
> *Questa opera gentile impresso fue,*
> *Io maestro Johanni Numeister opera dei*
> *Alla dicta impressione, et meco fue,*
> *El Elfuginato, Evangelista mei.*

—Humphreys interprets the words "Evangelist mine" as standing for "the one who made me known to the world."[1] "Artifice new" refers, of course, to the "new art" (of printing). The last volume bearing the name of Numeister was an edition of Torquemada's *Contemplations*. With his death in 1479, the brief record of the press of Foligno comes to a close.

Florence.—Florence, which for a century or more had been the centre of the intellectual life of Italy, and which presented in its great collection of manuscripts, its central

[1] Humphreys, 117.

position, and its important trade connections, distinctive advantages for the work of book-publishing, was comparatively late in giving attention to the new art, and the issues from the Florentine presses before the close of the fifteenth century, were much less important than those of Venice and of Milan.

The first book printed in Florence, a commentary on Virgil, by Servius, bears date 1471. It was issued by Bernardo Cennino, and appears to have been his sole publication.

Cennino was by trade a goldsmith, and had been associated with Ghiberti in the work on the famous gates of the Baptistery.[1] An enthusiast about the artistic pre-eminence of Florence and of Italy, he was said to have been jealous of the glory that had come to Germany through the invention of printing, and he determined to master the art without German aid.[2] In the colophon to his work, he describes the labour of the creation of his press, a labour which included the engraving of the steel punches and the casting of the type. His publishing venture was costly and probably unprofitable, and he appears to have printed no second book. He continued, however, in connection with his trade as a goldsmith, the work of engraving punches for type.

The German printers speedily found their way to Florence as they had already done to Rome, Venice, and Milan. In 1472, a certain Peter, describing himself as "de Moguntia," (of Mayence) printed an edition of the *Philocolo* of Boccaccio, and in the same year, he issued the *Triumphs of Petrarch*.

The subscription reads: " Master Peter, son of John of Mayence, wrote (*scripsit*) this work in Florence, the 12th day of November, 1472."

---

[1] Humphreys, 121.

[2] Lorck, C. B., *Handbuch der Gesch. der Buchdrücker-Kunst*, 13, Leipzig, 1882.

Humphreys points out that this imprint is an example
of the habit of the early printers of considering their art
as a kind of magical *writing* rather than as a mechanical
contrivance.

The most important of the early printer-publishers of
Florence was Nicholas of Breslau. In 1477, he published
Bettini's *Monte Sancto di Dio*, which, according to
Humphreys, presents the first example of illustrations by
means of engraved plates. In 1478, Nicholas published
an edition of Dante, the most elaborate that had yet
appeared. Dante had evidently already taken possession
of the intellectual interest of Italy, and as early as 1472,
no less than three editions had appeared. The fact that
the poetry of Dante was given to the public in Italian,
secured for it a much wider range of popular appreciation
than was within reach of works written in Latin. The
same was true of the works of Boccaccio and of Petrarch,
which, with the aid of the printing-press, promptly came
into the hands of large circles of readers. *Petrarch* was
first printed in 1470, and *Boccaccio* in 1471, and thereafter
editions of both authors followed rapidly.

In 1474, a press was set up in the monastery of San
Jacopo di Ripili, near Florence, by two monks of the
Brotherhood of S. Dominic. The greater part of the
books printed by them were distributed among the monasteries as gifts or in exchange, but as the reputation of
their publications increased, they found it necessary to
accept orders from booksellers and from the outside
public. Later, they added a type-foundry to their plant.

Genoa.—The first printing-office in Genoa was established in 1471 by a German from Olmutz, named Moravus,
who associated with himself, in 1474, an Italian named
Michael da Monaco. The scribes, or *manuscriptists*, as
they called themselves, made a vigorous protest against
the new art. They addressed, in 1471, a petition to the
magistracy in which they prayed to be protected from

the competition of these newly arrived printers, at least
as far as the production of Breviaries, Donati, and Psalters
was concerned, as upon the multiplication of these they
depended for their livelihood. Humphreys states that the
original of this petition is still in existence.[1] The record
of the reply given by the magistrates has not been preserved.

The printers were evidently not forbidden to print these
books of service, as editions were speedily produced. The
influence of the scribes appears, however, in the end, to have
been sufficient to establish a kind of cabal against the printers, and in the course of a year or two the German gave up
the attempt and removed his press to Naples. There
was doubtless in all the Italian cities a large measure of
jealousy and opposition on the part of the old *librarii*,
stationarii, and *scriptores*, but Genoa appears to have been
the only city where they were strong enough actually to
drive out the printers, at least for a time.

The first Hebrew Bible printed in Europe was issued in
Soncino in 1488, from the press of Abraham Colonto. It
is described as a very fine piece of typography and as noteworthy for the artistic chapter-headings and for the
elaborate decorations of the marginal borders of the
pages.

[1] Humphreys, 124.

END OF VOLUME I.

DATE DUE

OCT 23 '67			
GAYLORD			PRINTED IN U.S A.